JUSTICE AND

JUSTICE AND TRUTH

PATRICK VICTORY

SINCLAIR-STEVENSON
LONDON

First published in the United Kingdom in 2001
by Christopher Sinclair-Stevenson
3 South Terrace, London SW7 2TB

ISBN 0 9540476 7 2

Typeset by Rowland Phototypesetting Ltd., Bury St Edmunds, Suffolk.
Printed and bound in the United Kingdom by
St Edmundsbury Press, Bury St Edmunds, Suffolk.

CONTENTS

ACKNOWLEDGEMENTS

I am much indebted to many people for their help in preparing this book. In order of involvement they were: Robert Kee, author of *Trial and Error*, for many papers and for his advice and encouragement in the planning and later stages: Alastair Logan, who played a central part in both the Guildford Four and Maguire Seven cases from the trials onwards, was convinced of their innocence from the outset, and generously made available much documentation and his encyclopaedic knowledge of the cases: Gareth Peirce, for her significant contributions, in particular relating to the case of Gerard Conlon; Grant Mckee and Ros Franey, for their book *Time Bomb*, their powerful T.V. programmes and other documentation; Nikki Evans, who laid out and typed the first six chapters: Anne-Marie Traynor, who, for a year, was a most effective researcher, so reducing the time required for completion of the text: James Parker, who amongst his many other duties, found time to read and then reproduce the whole text and disc for presentation to the printers; and to Christopher Sinclair-Stevenson, who as my agent and publisher, edited the book and gave me much valuable advice and guidance in a field which was new to me.

Photographs of Lord Devlin, Lord Scarman, Lord Jenkins of Hillhead and Lord Merlyn-Rees are by Universal Pictorial Press and Agency.

ACKNOWLEDGMENTS

PREFACE

THE CONVICTIONS of the Guildford Four and the Maguire Seven were as great a miscarriage of justice as any known to have occurred in the twentieth century in the United Kingdom. Many people were concerned at the time of the trials in 1975 and 1976 that the wrong people had been convicted.

Following the quashing by the Court of Appeal of the convictions of the Guildford Four in 1989, and of the Maguire Seven in 1991, even more misgivings concerning how convictions had come about arose from some of the accounts of events given in the Final Report in 1994 of the May Inquiry which had been set up after the quashing of the convictions.

This book records developments in the cases from the trials in 1975/76 onwards to 1994. It sets out the relevant facts. I find it is a fascinating account. It illustrates some of the many ways in which criminal investigations can come to the wrong conclusions. The vindication of the Guildford Four and the Maguire Seven now achieved is consistent with, and a contribution to, the high quality to which British justice has always aspired.

Justice and Truth will be of tremendous importance not merely to those concerned with criminal law but to all who live and work in the United Kingdom. The Guildford Four and Maguire Seven cases will come to be seen as milestones in the history of British criminal justice.

Scarman

CHRONOLOGY

1974

July 20	Body of murdered British ex-soldier Brian Shaw discovered, Belfast.
Early August	Brendan Dowd and Joseph O'Connell arrive London to set up IRA London Active Service Unit (ASU).
August 3	Gerard Conlon arrives England from Belfast.
23	Paul Hill arrives England with girlfriend Gina Clarke who later went to Southampton.
September 20	Paul Hill and Gerard Conlon move to Conway House, Irish Hostel in Kilburn.
29	Police search Patrick Armstrong and Carole Richardson's squat for drugs.
October 5	'Phase One' of main IRA bombing campaign begins. Five members London ASU plant time bombs in two Guildford pubs, the Horse and Groom and the Seven Stars: five people killed and 42 injured.
6	150 detectives drafted into Guildford Police Station, Surrey. Bomb Squad formed.
10	Harry Duggan and Edward Butler join London ASU.
11	London ASU bombs Victory Club and Army and Navy Club.
19	Gerard Conlon leaves Conway House hostel and returns to Belfast. Paul Hill also leaves hostel and moves in with his aunt and uncle, Anne and Frank Keenan in Kentish Town.
20	Patrick Armstrong and Carole Richardson leave for hitch-hiking trip round England and Wales.
22	London ASU bombs Brooks's club.
24	London ASU plants time bomb at Harrow School. Armstrong and Richardson call police in Folkestone after Richardson assaulted by a drunk.
25	DCS Walter Simmons of Surrey Police on ITV programme *Police Five* issues descriptions of 'courting

	couple' sought by police as being the only people not accounted for in the Horse and Groom bombing.
30	Armstrong and Richardson return to London.
November 6	London ASU has dummy run to bomb King's Arms, Woolwich.
7	Four members of London ASU throw bomb at King's Arms, Woolwich. Two killed and 26 injured.
15	Armstrong leaves London to stay with sister in Hertfordshire.
21	IRA bombs Mulberry Bush and Tavern in the Town, pubs in Birmingham. 21 killed and 171 injured.
26	London ASU bombs three London pillar-boxes.
27	Home Secretary Roy Jenkins introduces Prevention of Terrorism Bill.
28	Hill arrested in Southampton. Taken to Guildford.
29	Prevention of Terrorism Act becomes law. Hill begins to give details on involvement in Brian Shaw murder and Guildford bombing.
30	Conlon arrested in Belfast. Also many arrests in London and the Home Counties including Anne and Frank Keenan (Hill's aunt and uncle), Hugh Maguire (brother of Paddy Maguire and Conlon's uncle), Brian Anderson, Paul Colman and John McGuinness.
Early December	Hugh Doherty joins London ASU.
December 1	Squatters living with Armstrong, now at Algernon Road, Kilburn, raid chemist's shop for drugs. Armstrong and Richardson start three-day drug taking bout.
2	Patrick Joseph ('Giuseppe') Conlon (Gerard Conlon's father) travels overnight from Belfast to London to meet his son's lawyer. Gerard Conlon begins to make admissions on Guildford.
3	Arrests made at 43 Third Avenue, Harlesden – Anne and Paddy Maguire, two of their children, (Vincent and Patrick) Sean Smyth (lodger and brother of Anne Maguire), and two visitors, Giuseppe Conlon, Patrick O'Neill. (The Maguire Seven) Armstrong and Richardson also arrested.
4	Gerard Conlon sees solicitor and is charged with murder at Guildford. Armstrong makes first admissions on Guildford.
5	Richardson makes first incriminating statement.

7	Armstrong, Richardson, Anne Maguire, Brian Anderson, Paul Colman and John McGuinness charged with murder.
11	Armstrong and Richardson see solicitors for first time.

1975

January 27	After placing many bombs around London and Home Counties during preceding weeks, London ASU now plants seven time bombs in London. This marks end of 'Phase One' of its campaign.
February 3	Charges of murder dropped against Brian Anderson, Paul Colman and John McGuinness.
8	Provisional IRA announces cease-fire.
24	Murder charge against Anne Maguire dropped, so leaving only the Guildford Four charged with murder – Armstrong, Conlon (Gerard), Hill and Richardson. Anne Maguire and her two sons (Vincent and Patrick) now charged with unlawful possession of nitroglycerine.
March 17	Committal opens, Guildford Four, Guildford.
20	Committal opens, Maguire Seven, Guildford.
April 15	Hill charged with Shaw murder, Belfast.
June 23	Hill convicted of murdering Shaw, Belfast.
July 10	Brendan Dowd and members of the Northern ASU arrested, Manchester.
August 27	Beginning of London ASU's 'Phase Two' bombings – time bomb at the Caterham Arms, Caterham, Surrey.
September 16	Guildford trial opens at Old Bailey.
October 17	The 'Confait' case. Court of Appeal quashes convictions of three youths sentenced (largely on confession evidence) for murdering Maxwell Confait.
22	Armstrong, Conlon, Hill and Richardson convicted only on confession evidence of murder, Guildford and Woolwich.
December 6	The Balcombe Street gang (London ASU) – Joseph O'Connell, Harry Duggan, Hugh Doherty and Edward Butler – hold occupants of a flat in Balcombe Street, London NW1 hostage for six days.
13	Balcombe Street siege ends. London ASU members arrested.

1976

January 27 Maguire Seven trial opens, Old Bailey.
March 4 Maguire Seven found guilty of possession of nitroglycerine.
May 11 Brendan Dowd and members of the Northern ASU convicted.
October/November Alastair Logan and James Still interview Balcombe Street gang and Dowd in prison.

1977

January 24 Trial of Balcombe Street gang (London ASU) opens at the Old Bailey.
February 7 Balcombe Street gang convicted.
July 20 Maguires' appeal opens, Old Bailey.
29 Maguires' appeal rejected.
October 10 Guildford appeal opens, Old Bailey.
28 Guildford appeal rejected.

1978

Late December Cardinal Hume visits Giuseppe Conlon (father of Gerard Conlon) in Wormwood Scrubs Prison.

1979

March 26 Cardinal Hume writes to the Home Secretary, Merlyn Rees, about Giuseppe Conlon. (This was to be the first of 19 letters to Home Secretaries, and two to the Prime Minister, about him and, later, about the whole Maguire Seven case, extending to 1988).

1980

January 23 Giuseppe Conlon dies.
Mid February BBC TV Northern Ireland screens *Spotlight* programme featuring the case of Giuseppe Conlon. Questions quality and credibility of scientific evidence.
August 4 Giuseppe Conlon case debated in House of Commons – a need to reassess the scientific evidence. No progress.

1983

December 20 Home Office rejects submission by Christopher Price and independent forensic scientist Dr Brian Caddy on the latter's misgivings about the scientific evidence at the Maguire Seven trial and the conduct of the TLC test.

1984

March 6 *Aunt Annie's Bomb Factory* screened by ITV (*First Tuesday* series). Dr Caddy makes his most damning analysis yet of conduct and use of TLC test.

1985

February 22 Anne Maguire, the last of the Maguire Seven to be set free, released from prison.

April 20 Anne and Paddy Maguire interview by Robert Kee on *Seven Days* (Channel 4) reveals extreme improbability they had carried out what they were alleged to have done.

27 David Frost interview of the Maguires on *Good Morning Britain* (TV AM) gives rise to same conclusion.

May 17 Maguire case debated in House of Lords – suggestion is that independent scientific advisers be appointed to advise Home Secretary. Not accepted.

1986

January Early Day Motion in House of Commons, supported by 200 signatories, to review the Maguire Seven case. No movement.

April 30 Home Office agrees recommendation by Director of the Prison Medical Service that Carole Richardson be examined by two independent doctors – Dr J. MacKeith, consultant psychiatrist, and Dr G. Gudjonsson, consultant clinical psychologist.

July 1 *The Guildford Time Bomb* screened by ITV (*First Tuesday* series). Opens by baldly asking, 'Did the police get the wrong people – were they guilty as charged?' Lord Fitt and Merlyn Rees take part.

2 Home Secretary announces internal Home Office review of Guildford Four case.

October 13 *Trial and Error* by Robert Kee published. First book on both cases. Exceedingly well researched. Aroused wide public interest and concern.

Lord Scarman, Cardinal Hume and Lord Devlin write to *The Times*.

November 4 *Beyond Reasonable Doubt* screened by Channel 4 TV. Programme discusses doubts arising in the

	Guildford Four, Maguire Seven and Birmingham Six cases.
1987	
January 7	All party delegation of MPs and Peers press Home Secretary to review Guildford, Maguire and Birmingham cases.
15	Cardinal Hume writes to Prime Minister saying he, Lord Scarman and Roy Jenkins concerned at press reports action might be taken only on the Birmingham Six case.
20	Douglas Hurd announces in Parliament he would be referring only the Birmingham Six case to Court of Appeal. Has placed in library two Home Office memoranda amplifying decisions not to refer the Guildford and Maguire cases.
Late January	Sees final coming together with Cardinal Hume of two of probably the greatest Law Lords of the twentieth century, Lord Devlin and Lord Scarman, and two distinguished former Home Secretaries, Roy Jenkins and Merlyn Rees, to form what came to be known as the 'Deputation'. They fear there has been serious miscarriage of justice.
February 3	Three members of Deputation (Cardinal Hume, Lord Scarman, Roy Jenkins) hold preliminary meeting prior to full discussions by whole Deputation.
March 3	*A Case That Won't Go Away* screened by ITV (*First Tuesday* series). Reference made to new witnesses in the Guildford Four case. Cardinal Hume and Lord Devlin take part.
4	Home Secretary agrees to examine new evidence in Guildford case.
April/May/June	Deputation assesses position of Guildford Four and Maguire Seven cases in the light of the Home Office memoranda and prepares 'submission' for presentation to the Home Secretary.
July 23	Cardinal Hume and all other members of the Deputation present submission to the Home Secretary, Douglas Hurd. Basis is reiteration of certain facts, new facts and evidence, and a point of law.
August 14	Home Secretary announces investigation into Guildford Four case by Avon and Somerset Police

	under James Sharples, Deputy Chief Constable.
October 29	'Relatives Action Group' hands in to Home Office 55,000 signature petition for re-trial of Guildford Four.
November 12	Cardinal Hume sees James Sharples, accompanied by his deputy, Superintendent Coates, for first time.
December 17	Douglas Hurd writes to Cardinal Hume concerning some difficulties being encountered by police in interviewing witnesses. This would result in some delays in the report.
1988	
January 13	Cardinal Hume sees Sharples and Coates for second time. Sharples assures him all problems now resolved. Sharples hopes to report to Home Secretary within two months.
January 14	Cardinal Hume writes to Home Secretary regarding meeting with Sharples and enquires if Deputation can see his report before decisions are made. Home Secretary responds on 27 January saying this would not be possible.
January 28	Birmingham Six appeal is dismissed.
March 16	Following meeting on 10 March, comprehensive, self-contained Deputation letter sent to Home Secretary re-iterating their views and incorporating comments on some of his responses to Cardinal Hume.
March 29	Home Secretary assures Cardinal Hume letter of 16 March would be considered very carefully but declines to reply in detail to points made.
April 8	Avon and Somerset police report on Deputation's submission received by Home Secretary.
June 22	Birnberg & Co letter giving comprehensive, detailed review of Gerard Conlon's case sent to C3 at Home Office. Eight witnesses now available. Letter became generally known as 'The Birnberg letter.'
July 12	Interview by Ludovic Kennedy of Sir Peter Imbert, Commissioner of Metropolitan Police, published in *The Times*. Latter has 'no doubt about the convictions' but ends saying 'we policemen are far too ready to assume a suspect's guilt in the early stages when we should be presuming his innocence.'
July	*Time Bomb* by Grant McKee and Ros Franey

	becomes available. (This followed *First Tuesday* TV programmes *Aunt Annie's Bomb Factory*, *The Guildford Time Bomb* and *A Case that Won't Go Away*.) Book carried forward convincing analysis of cases in Robert Kee's *Trial and Error*.
September 8	Home Secretary visits Cardinal Hume, has received police report, looked at the evidence, has decided not to refer the Guildford Four case. Gives his reasons which Cardinal Hume refutes there and then. Home Secretary adds finality has not yet been reached.
September 16	Gareth Peirce (Birnbergs) hands over to C3, Home Office, statements of eight unnamed witnesses in the 'Birnberg letter' (see June 22), and medical evidence Conlon ill at time of confession; also still looking for a Charles Burke who might be able to make statement about Conlon.
September 22	Cardinal Hume sends powerful Deputation letter to Home Secretary – strongly rebutting his reasons for non-referral, re-iterating many important facts he had not referred to, emphasising key considerations including Deputation will not rest until justice can be seen to have been done.
November 16	Deputation deeply concerned at delays on decision in both cases. Cardinal Hume sends strong letter to Home Secretary covering three key considerations. Released to the press but so worded Deputation not departing from self-imposed restriction of confidentiality. Some newspapers publish the three considerations in full.
November 30	Major joint paper by Lord Devlin and Lord Scarman 'Justice and the Guildford Four' published on the 'Op-Ed' page of *The Times* which had to be cleared to accommodate it.
December 28	*The Independent* reports Home Secretary received from Barry Irving of Police Foundation statements and affidavits (commissioned by Alastair Logan, solicitor for Carole Richardson) on treatment of witnesses Frank Johnson and Lisa Astin and will consider them.

1989

January 16	Home Secretary informs Cardinal Hume he will be publishing a Written Reply to a Parliamentary Question that day – he has decided to refer the Guildford Four case to the Court of Appeal. Deputation regards this as 'the end of the beginning.'
January 17	Deputation decides to remain in being, but lie dormant, until appeal heard. Arrangements made to keep them informed.
Early May	Gareth Peirce of Birnbergs finds statement by Charles Burke (whom she had been seeking) dated 18 January 1975. The 'Burke alibi.' If true would have constituted alibi for Conlon at Guildford. Existence of statement not known of by the defence since it was made in January 1975. (See 16 September, 1988)
Early June	Gareth Peirce discovers Avon and Somerset police had traced Charles Burke in June 1988 and he had confirmed his statement of 18 January 1975. Also unknown to the defence. (See 16 September 1988).
July 26	At directions hearing Lord Chief Justice confirms Guildford appeal will be heard on 15 January 1990.
October 17	CPS announces 'would be wrong to seek to sustain convictions.' Expedited hearing by Court of Appeal to be on 19 October.
October 19	Court of Appeal sits. Defence had two days to prepare full case. In the event not presented. Convictions quashed same day on evidence not wholly disclosed to the defence. Home Secretary announces in Parliament Inquiry to be set up under Sir John May. Purpose included '. . . to establish as far as possible the details of what had occurred.' This phrase not included in formal terms of reference issued later.
October 20	Deputation notes DPP set up criminal investigation concerning Surrey police evidence at Guildford trial. Deputation notes Home Secretary and Attorney General recognise May Inquiry might have to 'adjust and adjourn' its work in light of criminal investigation.
November 22	Deputation discusses relationships and cooperation

	with May Inquiry, and its terms of reference. Notes it is not a statutory inquiry – no powers to call for documents, require attendance of witnesses, or take evidence on oath. Not clear what it is designed to achieve.
November 30	Cardinal Hume writes to Home Secretary (now David Waddington), welcomes inclusion of Maguire Seven in May Inquiry; in view of delays in Guildford case hopes Inquiry makes early interim report on Maguires.
1990	
January 22	Deputation meets for first time Sir John May, at his request, to discuss Maguire and Guildford cases. May Inquiry plans to produce interim report on scientific evidence at Maguire Seven trial – requests further briefing on whole case.
March 13	May Inquiry holds preliminary meeting on scientific evidence in Maguire Seven case. Later appoints, as scientific advisor, Professor Thorburn Burns, independent, expert, analytical chemist.
March 27	Cardinal Hume sends substantial submission on the Maguires to Sir John May – drafted by Lord Scarman, agreed by whole Deputation.
April 11	*The Guardian* publishes what comes to be known as the 'Imbert Tapes' – interview regarding Guildford bombings by DCS Imbert with Gerard Conlon in prison on day after he was sentenced on 22 October 1975.
May 21/ June 18	Public hearings by May Inquiry on Maguire Seven case – scientific evidence only. Government Laboratory(RARDE) decline to attend.
July 12	May Inquiry publishes 'Interim Report on Maguire Seven.' Heavily criticises work of RARDE scientists, and DPP/Prosecution on disclosure of evidence. Home Secretary refers case to Court of Appeal same day.
September/ October	May Inquiry holds further public hearings on scientific evidence in Maguire case. Sets up independent scientific committee under Professor T. S. West. RARDE seeks representation at hearings.
November 12	DPP institutes proceedings against the three Surrey police officers who interviewed Armstrong in Guildford case.

December — BBC screens Panorama programme *Guildford – The Untold Story*. Highlights serious issues May Inquiry expected to address.

1991

March 14 — Court of Appeal quashes convictions of Birmingham Six.
Home Secretary Kenneth Baker announces setting up of Royal Commission on Criminal Justice.

June 26 — Court of Appeal quashes convictions of Maguire Seven.

July 11 — Magistrate discharges Surrey police officers on grounds of abuse of process.

September/October — May Inquiry holds public hearings on circumstances in which Attorney General's fiat applied for, and role of Home Office in view of repeated representations on scientific evidence.

November 7 — Cardinal Hume sends Deputation submission to Lord Runciman, chairman of the Royal Commission on Criminal Justice.

1992

January 24 — High Court reverses decision and case against three Surrey police officers reinstated.

March 27 — Surrey police officers committed for trial – delay granted – one leading counsel engaged in another major case.

June 2 — Court agrees defence request for trial of Surrey police officers to be not before April 1993.

July 31 — Home Office announces Sir John May's decision to end all public hearings in Guildford case because prosecution of Surrey police officers still outstanding ; also enables him to report as a member to the Royal Commission, due to report July 1993.
Sir John May announces Guildford report to be prepared from papers available to him and by private hearings.

August 6 — Deputation much concerned at abandonment of public hearings. Cardinal Hume places matter in public domain in letter to *The Times*. He calls for clarification of the 'difficulties.'

August 8 — DPP (Mrs Barbara Mills) responds in *The Times* and in explanatory letter to Cardinal Hume referring again to 'difficulties.'

(NOTE: This marked the beginning of what, to the Deputation, was an unsatisfactory exchange of letters between Cardinal Hume and the DPP culminating on 22 September 1993, but towards the end of which there was a letter to the DPP on 27 July 1993 signed by *all* members of the Deputation.)

August 18	Lord Scarman writes to *The Times*, deprecating abandonment of public hearings, emphasising need to investigate role of senior police officers, concluding 'very much in the public interests that full facts relating to this serious miscarriage of justice should be made known, even if we have to wait for it.'
September 30	Whole Deputation gives oral evidence to all members of the Royal Commission on Criminal Justice.
December 3	May Inquiry publishes 'Second Report on the Maguire Case.' Concludes Home Office should have sought scrutiny by independent scientists of evidence by RARDE.
1993	
May 19	Three Surrey police officers found not guilty.
May 20	Many in the press experience bewilderment at the conduct and outcome of the case. Direct criticisms and adverse reports appear in *The Independent, The Times, The Daily Telegraph, The Guardian* and, on 23 May, in *The Sunday Times*.
Late May	Word reaches Deputation publication of the Final Report of the May Inquiry (originally expected autumn 1993) may be delayed by discussions at private hearings between the Inquiry, prosecution team for the Guildford case, and certain police officers on the 'Burke alibi' and other matters.
June 2	In consultation with Lord Scarman, Cardinal Hume sends substantial letter to Home Secretary (now Michael Howard) (copy to Sir John May) reviewing all aspects of Guildford Four case, listing 'eight questions' which May Inquiry, as last institution left, must answer fully if 'whole truth' to be established.
July	Report of Royal Commission on Criminal Justice published.
September 3	Cardinal Hume and Lord Scarman, at their request,

have special discussions with Sir John May. Importance of 'whole truth' about the 'eight questions' being established emphasised if justice to be seen to have been done.

September 16 Cardinal Hume sends to Sir John May lengthy letter in forthright terms confirming view of whole Deputation on need for Inquiry to give full and clear answers to the 'eight questions.'

1994

February 2 Crucial letter to May Inquiry by Birnbergs concerned at assertions and assumptions they had heard were being made by others at private hearings of Inquiry, and making startling revelation that, amongst papers released for Court of Appeal in Belfast 1994 (Hill appeal on Shaw murder), were statements taken by Avon and Somerset police since 1990 affecting Guildford case not revealed to defence.

May 24 Cardinal Hume sends to Home Secretary Deputation's response to Home Office Discussion Paper 'Criminal Appeals and the establishment of a Criminal Cases Review Authority.'

June 30 Final Report of May Inquiry published (Guildford Four case). Some aspects not well received – press critical.

July 6 Deputation registers disappointment with Final Report by all signing letter to *The Times*:

> '. . . A penetrating and more robust examination . . . was required. The weakness of the report is that it does not go far enough in exploring and attributing the extent of responsibility and blame for the miscarriage of justice which Sir John recognises did occur.'

1995

January 18 Deputation (less Lord Devlin who died 1992) see Home Secretary at meeting sought by Deputation after publication of Final Report of May Inquiry to discuss failings of the criminal justice system revealed in the Report, also proposals for Criminal Cases Review Authority.

1997

January 1 Newly titled 'Criminal Cases Review Commission' established. Final organisation does not wholly reflect views of Deputation on conduct of investigations.

1

OVERVIEW

AT 8.50 pm on Saturday 5 October, 1974 a time bomb exploded in Guildford at the Horse and Groom public house which was frequented by soldiers from barracks in the Guildford and Aldershot areas. Shortly after, a second time bomb exploded in the Seven Stars pub some two hundred yards away. Five people were killed and 42 were injured, some of them very seriously, and mostly in the Horse and Groom.

On the night of 7 November, 1974, at 10.17 pm, a bomb was thrown into the King's Arms public house in Woolwich which was the nearest pub to the large Royal Artillery barracks. Two men, a soldier and a barman, were killed, and 26 other people, including three servicemen and two WRACs, were injured.

Those two appalling events led to tragedy which extended beyond the many wholly innocent people who were killed and wounded, and their families who were left to grieve and to suffer the consequences. There was to be another tragedy – the failure of the British criminal justice system. That failure resulted in a miscarriage of justice for eleven people – the Guildford Four and the Maguire Seven. They were all arrested, charged and convicted of being responsible for the bombings, or possessing explosives, and had to remain in prison for many years before their convictions were finally quashed.

The Guildford bomb left the country in a state of shock. The Surrey Constabulary were quick off the mark and by the next day had assembled a 'bomb squad' of some 150 detectives of all ranks from all over the county, centred on Guildford police station. Their immediate task was to trace everyone who had been in the Horse and Groom and Seven Stars on the evening of 5 October.

By the end of October, over three weeks later, the only people unaccounted for who had been in the pubs at the time of the bombings were a man and a woman who were together in the Horse and Groom, and two men and one woman who were in the Seven Stars. This was a significant achievement by the police. The two people in the Horse and Groom emerged in some of the great number of police statements as a 'courting couple'. It was assumed that they had almost certainly planted the bomb in the Horse and Groom. The many and varied descriptions of those unaccounted for were conflicting and confusing. Photofit pictures were prepared, and some were shown on television and published in the national press. Somewhat embarrassingly, two photofit pictures of women turned out to be of two of the victims. One of the photofit pictures was of a woman with long hair. This led to a tip-off to the police from an intelligence officer in Northern Ireland which resulted in the arrest of Paul Hill, one of the Guildford Four, who also had long hair at that time and had had connections with the IRA in the past. Apart from this, the photofit pictures bore no resemblance to any of the Guildford Four who were finally arrested and convicted of the bombings.

Meanwhile, the IRA continued with their bombing campaign. Before 7 November, when a throw bomb was used at the King's Arms in Woolwich, there had been other throw bombs during October at the Victory Services Club, the Army and Navy Club, Brooks's Club, and at Harrow School. Hundreds of people had been interviewed but by the time of the Woolwich bomb no arrests had yet been made. During the first three weeks of November there was still little progress being made by the Surrey Police. They knew very little about the type of people used by the IRA for their various activities in 1974 and, even at that time, Scotland Yard Special Branch still had much to learn about their organisation and methods. But pressure for results was building up on the Surrey Police.

During the week beginning 21 November there were four more small bombs in London pillar-boxes. But on the evening of 21 November there was an event of far greater significance, and brutality, in Birmingham – large bombs exploded in the Mulberry Bush and the Tavern in the Town, two public houses crowded mainly with young people. 21 people were killed and some 171 injured. This was a savage act of terrorism and there were immediate reverberations within the Government and throughout the country. The same night, 21 November, the West Midlands police arrested six Irishmen who were charged four days later with murder and were remanded in custody by the court. Within a week the Prevention of Terrorism Act (PTA) was piloted through Parliament by the Home Secretary, Roy Jenkins. The pressures on the Scotland Yard Bomb Squad and the whole of the Surrey Constabulary mounted still further.

The Prevention of Terrorism Act (PTA) became law on 29 November, 1974. After the arrest and interrogation of Paul Hill, and the passing of the PTA, there was a frenzy of arrests within a few days in London and the Home Counties. Over 50 people were taken into custody. Many were released within days or even hours. It was clear at the time that these arrests could only have been undertaken with close planning and cooperation at the highest level between the Metropolitan Police and the Surrey Constabulary.

Amongst those arrested with Paul Hill, who was then aged 21, were the remaining three of the Guildford Four – Gerard Conlon, also aged 21, Patrick Armstrong, aged 24, and Carole Richardson, an English girl who was only 17. By 7 December all four had been charged with murder for the bombings at Guildford, based solely on their uncorroborated confessions. They had implicated each other during interrogations within a few days of arrest. They said the confessions had been obtained by threats and violence. The confessions were inconsistent and, in many places, contradictory. There were some 150 discrepancies between the confessions of each of the four relating to those who took part, how the bombing had been carried out, where the bombs came from, and many other details. There was no other evidence whatsoever against them. During some of the interrogations there was talk of 'bombers', which they were accused of being, and of 'bomb makers' in 'bomb factories'.

Meanwhile there had been activity on the evening of 3 December at the home of Anne and Paddy Maguire at 43 Third Avenue, Harlesden. Nearly all who were in the house that evening, including their children and visitors, were detained and subsequently charged. They were:

Anne Maguire, aged 40
Patrick ('Paddy') Maguire, aged 43
Vincent Maguire, aged 16
Patrick Maguire, aged 13
Sean Smyth, aged 38
Visitors { Patrick Joseph ('Giuseppe') Conlon, aged 52
Patrick O'Neill, aged 35 }

Somewhat remarkably, the middle son John Maguire, who was 15 at the time and had been in the house when the explosives were alleged to have been handled, was swabbed but tested clean and was not charged at all. Giuseppe Conlon had arrived from Northern Ireland at the Maguires' house only on the afternoon of the arrests. He was a very sick man, suffering from tuberculosis, emphysema and bronchitis, and he had made the journey to obtain legal aid for his son, Gerard Conlon, who had been arrested. Although they were solicited, there were no confessions by anyone in the Maguire household. All the Maguire Seven were charged with being in possession of nitroglycerine. Initially Anne Maguire was also charged with murder, as were the Guildford Four. After an inordinate length of time this charge was finally dropped, on 24 February 1975, through lack of evidence that she had ever been at Guildford. Anne Maguire, and all in the household, protested their innocence from the moment they were arrested. They continued to do so throughout their time in prison, which in Anne Maguire's case was some 10 years, and after their release from prison. Giuseppe Conlon maintained his innocence, even on his deathbed in 1980, while still serving his sentence.

No bulk or even trace of explosive or bomb making equipment was found in the Maguire home. All those charged, except Anne Maguire, were charged solely on forensic evidence based on swabs taken from their hands. In Anne Maguire's case, her hands were found to be clean; the evidence against her was based on swabs taken from her kitchen gloves, which were collected from her house the day after the arrests.

In the event, the arrests and charging of the Guildford Four and the Maguire Seven by early December 1974 did not bring to a halt the wave of bombings in London which had occurred during October and November. This was to continue until early in 1975. The end of January 1975 marked, as was subsequently established, the conclusion of Phase One of the bombing activities of the IRA Active Service Unit (ASU) operating in London and the Home Counties. The IRA announced a cease-fire on 9 February, 1975. There were no further explosions until a time bomb went off at the Caterham Arms in Caterham, Surrey on 27 August, 1975. The Guildford Four had been in custody since December 1974. The implications of all this did not appear to have been fully appreciated at the time by some of those who could have been expected to realise their significance.

The first to go to trial were the Guildford Four – on 16 September, 1975 at the Old Bailey. The trial ended on 22 October. Ironically, during the trial there were further explosions in London. All four were charged with murder at the Horse and Groom in Guildford on 5 October, 1974 and, additionally, Paul Hill and Patrick Armstrong were charged with murder at the King's Arms at Woolwich on 7 November, 1974. In the end the Crown case rested solely on the confessions. There was no fingerprint evidence, forensic evidence or any identity evidence. Carole Richardson had not been identified as one of the 'courting couple.'

The basis of the defence case rested on the confessions having been obtained by threats and violence, and on alibis, that for Carole Richardson being particularly strong. 'The Guildford Four were by their own account a pitiable lot.' So wrote Lord Devlin later in a joint paper with Lord Scarman. It went on . . . 'they were all of the sort that lives from hand to mouth, that does not look beyond the hour and that tells a lie as easily as the truth. Their answers under interrogation were contradictory and confused.' They were part of a set that lived mainly in squats, took drugs and drink, and generally drifted. Certainly, they did not have trained or disciplined minds, nor were they familiar with court procedures as were of course the many police officers called as witnesses by the Crown.

The jury had to decide whether or not the confessions, all four of which had been retracted, were false and had been obtained by threats and violence. They found the Guildford Four guilty. Paul Hill was sentenced to life, which the judge said would mean life, Patrick Armstrong life with a minimum of 35 years, and Gerard Conlon life with a minimum of 30 years. Carole Richardson was to be detained for life at Her Majesty's pleasure for murder because she was under 18 at the time of the bombing.

The trial of the Maguire Seven was also held at the Old Bailey. It started on 27 January, 1976, some three months after the Guildford Four trial, and lasted for six weeks. The family and their visitors simply could not understand how they found themselves in such a position. Paddy and Anne Maguire had been living in England for 19 years. After he had left the British Army they had settled in North London where they brought up a family of three sons and a daughter. They were respected in their neighbourhood and had no record whatsoever of association with criminals, let alone terrorists.

The sole evidence against the Maguire Seven was forensic. There were lengthy, complex, scientific arguments and counter-arguments by the Crown and the defence as to the efficiency and specificity of the Thin Layer Chromatography (TLC) Test which had been applied to the swabs and nail scrapings, particularly in view of some of the anomalies which had been thrown up. These arguments overshadowed an exploration of whether or not Anne Maguire's gloves and the hands of one of the other defendants could have had nitroglycerine on them at the time of their arrest. After all, no bulk or even trace of explosive had been found anywhere in the house or the neighbourhood. The searches were conducted by experienced explosives police officers from the bomb squad, and by dogs specially trained to sniff out explosives, and included the swabbing of all internal surfaces. Moreover, the sniffer device had found nothing on Anne Maguire's gloves at the time of the arrests.

Although there were no confessions by any members of the household, some spoke of maltreatment and even brutality by the police. The police denied these allegations. At one stage the jury was told – 'You have seen the officers. Are they the sort of officers that you think would behave in this fashion? Are they the sort of officers that you think would lie about it? You have got to make up your minds about that . . . if they did it, they did, but did they do it? Is it that he merely has some feeling against the police in general or is he attempting in a rather stupid, muddled sort of way to discredit the police . . . ?'

The Maguire Seven were found guilty by the jury. Anne and Paddy Maguire were sentenced to 14 years' imprisonment, Giuseppe Conlon, Sean Smyth and Pat O'Neill to 12 years' imprisonment, Vincent Maguire to 5 years' imprisonment, and the youngest, Patrick, to 4 years in youth custody. As she was dragged from the dock, Anne Maguire screamed 'I am innocent, you bastards. No, no, no.' She had protested her innocence on arrest. She continued to do so until, and after, her release from prison 11 years later. All seven of the Maguire household were devastated by the verdict.

The trials of the Guildford Four and the Maguire Seven need to be seen in the context of the culture and tradition of courts in the 1970s, accepted by most juries and judges but, even then, not by all judges. That was still an era in which, whatever might have been the nature and effectiveness of cross-examinations, evidence by police officers, prison officers and expert witnesses such as Government forensic scientists was very likely to be accepted completely, or at least sufficiently so as to weaken gravely the defence case. This is graphically illustrated by Lord Denning's judgement in January 1980 concerning a civil action brought by the Birmingham Six in November 1979 to sue the police for injuries they said had been inflicted on them in police custody:

> If the six men win, it will mean that the police were guilty of perjury, that they were guilty of violence and threats, that the confessions were involuntary and were improperly admitted in evidence, and that the convictions were erroneous. That would mean the Home Secretary would either have to recommend they be pardoned or he would have to remit the case to the Court of Appeal. This is such an appalling vista that every sensible person in the land would say: it cannot be right that these actions should go any further.

In due time an application for leave to appeal was subsequently set in motion by the Maguire Seven. The hearing at the Court of Appeal, which was presided over by Lord Roskill, opened on 20 July, 1977. On 27 July Lord Roskill delivered the Court's judgement. The application to appeal was rejected. As the months went by, amongst defence solicitors and experienced observers of trials, anxieties about certain aspects of the case, and the final outcome, continued to grow. By the early '80s they had extended to several members of both Houses of Parliament and to a growing list of distinguished individuals.

Meanwhile, on 7 December, 1975, some five weeks before the trial of the Maguire Seven trial opened, there was a remarkable event in Balcombe Street NW1 which, ultimately, was to have a far-reaching effect on the overall bombing situation. Four Irishmen were caught red-handed firing shots and, after a police chase, they took over a flat in Balcombe Street where they held the occupants hostage for six days. Detective Chief Superintendent Imbert, as he then was, of the Metropolitan Police Bomb Squad, who had previously questioned Paul Hill and Gerard Conlon, talked the Balcombe Street gang into surrender. They freely admitted to him they were part of an IRA Active Service Unit operating in London and the Home Counties, and that two of them had taken part in the Guildford bombing, and three at Woolwich.

The Balcombe Street gang were Joseph O'Connell, Edward Butler, Harry Duggan, and Hugh Doherty. Brendan Dowd, who had originally set up the IRA London ASU, had moved earlier in 1975 to Manchester to set up an IRA Northern ASU. He had surrendered to the police in a shoot-out and, together with the Northern ASU, was tried and convicted in May 1976. When O'Connell and Butler were arrested by Chief Superintendent Imbert in December 1975, they told him and Commander Nevill of their respective involvement in Guildford and Woolwich and said that the four people who had been convicted had nothing to do with either operation.

In mid 1976, the solicitor Alastair Logan, who at the time was representing two of the Guildford Four, Patrick Armstrong and Gerard Conlon, heard from an anonymous source that it could be helpful to his clients if he were able to see the Balcombe Street gang, all of whom were in prison pending trial. During October and November 1976 he arranged to interview Dowd and each of the four Balcombe Street gang in the presence of their solicitors, and wisely took with him, as principal interviewer, James Still, who was a former Chief Superintendent of the Metropolitan Police. They were accompanied by an official court shorthand reporter.

In summary, from all these interviews it emerged that Dowd had led the operation at Guildford, accompanied by O'Connell, another man and two girls whom the Balcombe Street ASU would not identify because they had not yet been arrested; O'Connell, Dowd, Butler and Duggan were all at Woolwich; O'Connell and Butler confirmed what they had told Detective Chief Superintendent Imbert and Commander Nevill; neither Butler nor Duggan had arrived in England until after the Guildford bombing; Doherty was involved in neither operation; the descriptions of the arrangements for both operations were dramatically accurate and tallied although they had all been interviewed separately. They said that the Guildford Four were not known to any of them and were not present at either operation; the IRA had high standards for Active Service Units and would not recruit or use people who were based in squats or who took drugs or drink.

This information could have been of considerable importance if satisfactory explanations to many aspects of it had been forthcoming. Not least of these was to what extent the police and the Director of Public Prosecutions had followed up the effects it might or could have had on the fortunes of the Guildford Four, and even on the Maguire Seven, who had by then all been convicted. Much interest, however, was now to be focused on the forthcoming trial of the Balcombe Street ASU.

The bombing campaign in London and the Home Counties had come to an end on their capture one year before the trial which took place over the period 27 January to 7 February, 1977. It was a significant occasion – most revealing, surprising in places, and embarrassing to some. The Balcombe Street ASU had admitted some 144 offences to the police. At the trial they proclaimed their membership of the IRA and made no effort whatsoever to defend themselves. The verdict was predictable. However, the jury sprang a few surprises in the light of some of the revelations.

One of these concerned the indictments which the Crown had understandably reduced to 100, but unfortunately this was partially achieved by eliminating bombings which had taken place before the arrest of the Guildford Four in early December 1974. These included Guildford and Woolwich to which some of the Balcombe Street ASU had emphatically and freely confessed. During the trial it came as a great surprise to many to hear Commander Nevill confirm it was at the direction of the Director of Public Prosecutions that he had instructed an officer to tell the forensic science experts to make alterations to their statements. This was to be done by deleting Guildford and Woolwich. The statements had shown forensic idiosyncrasies in any comparison between these two bombings and other offences for which the Balcombe Street ASU were responsible and the Guildford Four could not have been.

The Balcombe Street ASU refused to plead to any of the charges because Guildford and Woolwich had not been included. The jury sprang the final surprise, somewhat to the embarrassment of the police and the Director of Public Prosecutions, by acquitting the ASU on five of the charges which appeared to be linked forensically to the Guildford explosions. At the end of the trial Joseph O'Connell made a dramatic speech from the dock which left many with much to think about and to which reference will be made later.

The Guildford Four based their grounds for leave to appeal on the claims made in the affidavits secured by Alastair Logan from the Balcombe Street ASU, which were confirmed during their trial. The hearing was presided over by Lord Roskill and lasted from 10 to 28 October, 1977. The application for leave to appeal was rejected. The

Court accepted that O'Connell and Dowd might have taken part in Guildford but refused to believe that the Guildford Four were not involved as well. They described the conflicting confessions of the Guildford Four as 'the partially true intermingled with the deliberately false.' Lord Devlin and Lord Scarman, in their joint paper some years later, were to observe, 'They did not seem to appreciate that this damaging criticism was being made of the only evidence of guilt that the Crown had produced.' It was in the same paper, 'Justice and the Guildford Four', that they expressed grave doubts about the handling of the appeal by the Court.

On rejection of the appeal, the Guildford Four were left in a despondent state. As the years went by, they and the Maguire Seven continued to proclaim their innocence. Individuals and groups became sympathetic to their causes, as did growing numbers of Members of Parliament and journalists. Anne Maguire was the last of the Maguire Seven to complete her sentence. Following her release on 22 February, 1985, activities in support of the causes of the Maguire Seven and the Guildford Four rapidly gained momentum.

The first of a series of television programmes called *Aunt Annie's Bomb Factory* had already appeared on 6 March, 1984 in the *First Tuesday* series by Yorkshire Television. The following year, on 1 July, 1986, saw the screening in the same series of the powerful and revealing documentary *The Guildford Time Bomb*. It was in this programme that Merlyn Rees, the first former Home Secretary to do so, aired his uneasiness and doubts about the Guildford Four case.

In early October 1986 Robert Kee, knowing that Cardinal Basil Hume had been concerned about the cases for many years, presented him with a copy of his book *Trial and Error*. This was an impressive and thoroughly researched account of the cases. It articulated the serious anxieties shared by many about possible miscarriages of justice and served as a catalyst in the minds of those with an interest in justice. In discussions with Robert Kee, Cardinal Hume made the point that, in parallel with the current grass roots campaigns such as 'Free the Guildford Four', there was now a need for action at a different level. It must not smack of the raucous, but rather should be carefully thought out, be extremely well co-ordinated, and must also be both sophisticated and penetrating. The question was – how was this to be brought about? It so happened that a sequence of events which would facilitate all this was about to unfold.

On 7 October, 1986 Lord Scarman had written to *The Times* saying, amongst other things, that the trial and appeal process had shown itself 'an uncertain instrument' in uncovering irregularities. This was followed by letters from Cardinal Hume and Lord Devlin. On 20 January, 1987 the Home Secretary, Douglas Hurd, announced that he would be referring the Birmingham Six case to the Court of Appeal, but not the Guildford Four or the Maguire cases. By May 1987 Cardinal Hume, Lord Devlin, Lord Scarman, Roy Jenkins and Merlyn Rees had all came together, each of their own volition and for their own reasons, in the common belief that there had been a miscarriage of justice in both the Guildford Four and Maguire Seven cases. Their aim was to secure from the Home Secretary a reference back to the Court of Appeal of, initially anyway, the Guildford Four case. They were to encounter constant problems and difficulties and, in pursuit of their aim, they came to be generally known as the 'Deputation'.

The 'Deputation' had many concerns and among them were lurking doubts about the uncorroborated and conflicting confessions of the Guildford Four. They regarded Carole Richardson as the weakest part of the case. The improbability of the professional IRA using a 17 year old English girl living in squats, and given to shoplifting and drugs, was a cogent factor. The accuracy and precision of the evidence by the Balcombe Street ASU on how they had bombed Guildford and Woolwich were compelling. Finally, in the case of the Maguire Seven, given that there were no confessions, and no bomb making equipment or even trace of explosives had been found in the house, it had to seem improbable that the nitroglycerine on the swabs came from their hands.

Armed with additional evidence on alibis from Alastair Logan, the whole Deputation presented to the Home Secretary on 23 July, 1987 a major submission incorporating matters of fact and a point of law. Following this Douglas Hurd set up an investigation by the Avon and Somerset Police and it was anticipated they would report to him in April/May 1988. The report was not to be made public. July 1988 saw the publication by Grant McKee and Ros Franey of *Time Bomb* – a very well researched book which expanded on earlier information and widened considerably the circle of those with knowledge about the cases.

On 8 September, 1988, Douglas Hurd visited Cardinal Hume to say he would not be referring the Guildford Four case to the Court of Appeal. He gave his reasons and added that he would be making an announcement before the end of the month. Cardinal Hume refuted the reasons there and then, and followed up the meeting by writing, on behalf of the Deputation, a powerful seven-page letter with attachments. An early paragraph reflected the determination of the Deputation:

> Having looked again at the points you raised, to which I refer below, I have to say at the outset I am now even more convinced than ever that the convictions in these cases cannot be regarded as safe and

> satisfactory. This view is shared by the whole of our Deputation. Unless a reference is made now to the Court of Appeal, or to a Tribunal set up under the 1921 Act, the country will have to face up to the fact that, not only will the Deputation continue what it regards as the pursuit of justice, but your successor, and probably mine, will be left to continue grappling with the problem.

Further letters from the Deputation to the Home Secretary followed during the autumn. Alastair Logan, and Gareth Peirce who by now was representing Gerard Conlon, also each submitted additional evidence. On 16 January, 1989 the Home Secretary announced that the Guildford Four case would be referred to the Court of Appeal.

A special session of the Court of Appeal was suddenly and unexpectedly arranged for 19 October, 1989. The Crown Prosecution Service had announced on 17 October that 'Circumstances have recently come to the notice of the Director of Public Prosecutions which have caused him to conclude that it would be wrong for the Crown to sustain the convictions.' At the hearing Roy Amlot QC, for the Crown, spoke at length about how police interviews had been conducted, records of statements prepared, the existence of undisclosed papers relating to police evidence and other matters.

The Court gave judgement immediately – the convictions were quashed. The entire hearing took about two hours. The ramifications of all this, and the substantial evidence the defence was ready to produce if the need should have arisen, are reviewed later.[1] Of particular interest to the defence was the question of what became known as 'the Burke alibi.' Gerard Conlon had been arrested on 30 November, 1974 in Belfast. On 18 January, 1975 Charles Burke made a statement to the police which constituted an alibi for Gerard Conlon. That statement was not disclosed to the defence at the trial or the first appeal. Its existence was not even known to them until it was finally served on them in May 1989. Although those representing Gerard Conlon had known of Charles Burke, they had searched in vain for him in England and Northern Ireland. Consequently, they were unable to present him as a witness at the trial of the Guildford Four which started on 16 September, 1975 – some eight months after he had made his statement to the police.

Immediately after the quashing of the convictions of the Guildford Four, the Home Secretary set up an inquiry into the Guildford Four and Maguire Seven cases under Sir John May, a former High Court judge. The Deputation gave substantial evidence to the May Inquiry.

[1]See Chapter Seven

This inquiry led to the quashing of the convictions of the Maguire Seven by the Court of Appeal.

Unfortunately, the inquiry was unduly extended because of delays by the Director of Public Prosecutions in bringing three Surrey police officers to trial. Cardinal Hume was to have a not wholly satisfactory exchange of correspondence with the Director of Public Prosecutions on this matter. In his judgement on the Guildford Four case, Lord Lane, who had presided, in referring to the police who had been responsible for the malpractices reported by Roy Amlot, had said – 'May we express the hope that nothing will be allowed to stand in the way of the speedy progress of those proceedings.'

The Guildford Four case appeared to have set the pace in terms of exposing failings in the system. After a second reference back to the Court of Appeal of the Birmingham Six case, the convictions were finally quashed on 14 March, 1991. Following this the Government set up a Royal Commission on Criminal Justice to which the Deputation also gave evidence. This Commission led, amongst many other things, to the establishment of the Criminal Cases Review Commission, on the operation of which the whole Deputation had meetings with the Home Secretary in the planning stages. The setting up of such a body had been advocated by the Deputation from its early days. The long journey undertaken by the Deputation was nearing completion.

It so happened that, as retirement work, I became an Assistant for Public Affairs to Cardinal Hume, in June 1986, on a voluntary and part-time basis. Almost immediately I became involved in problems concerning miscarriages of justice which were building up with increasing momentum at that time.

As an Assistant to the Cardinal, it fell to me to co-ordinate the work of the Deputation and to give them all the assistance they would require for their task. Robert Kee was in attendance at all meetings of the Deputation from the outset.

This book sets out to record the part played by the Deputation in the struggle to secure justice for the Guildford Four and the Maguire Seven and, also, to record their contributions to the May Inquiry and the Royal Commission on Criminal Justice. It is fervently to be hoped that the individual deficiencies and failings which came to light during this period within all parts of the criminal justice system will help to safeguard against possible future miscarriages of justice.

The activities of the Deputation extended over a period of some seven years from late 1986 to beyond publication of the Final Report of the May Inquiry in June 1994. As each year went by additional information and reports became available to them. In this account of their work, and of developments over the period in the two cases, care has been taken in subsequent chapters to use only such information as was available to the Deputation at the time they were engaged in the activities related in each of the chapters.

2

THE EARLY DAYS

. . . Well, Father, first of all I want to tell you right away that I am completely innocent of the charge that they framed me with. I have never been in trouble in my life and the Chief Constable of Surrey got in touch with the Police back home and he could not find out anything to connect me with the IRA or any other organisation and he told the Court this . . .

SO WROTE Patrick Joseph ('Giuseppe') Conlon, father of Gerard Conlon, to Cardinal Hume from his cell in Wormwood Scrubs on 30 November, 1978.

Cardinal Hume had heard during the summer of 1978 about Patrick 'Giuseppe' Conlon (so named because of his Italian godfather), from his wife, Mrs Sarah Conlon in Belfast, and from the prison chaplain and others – about his forceful protestations of his innocence, and his poor state of health. He had already arranged to see him on one of his visits to Wormwood Scrubs in December 1978, just before Christmas.

It was during that visit that some professed IRA prisoners cornered the Cardinal, pointed to Gerard Conlon who was also in Wormwood Scrubs at the time, and said that he and the other three of the Guildford Four convicted with him were innocent. Before seeing Giuseppe Conlon the Cardinal knew that he was suffering from pulmonary tuberculosis and a crippling form of emphysema. This was all too obvious as he tried to relate to the Cardinal how he had struggled over to England on 3 December, 1974 to arrange legal representation for his son Gerard who had been arrested for the Guildford bombings; how he went to the home of his brother-in-law Paddy Maguire and the latter's wife Anne; was arrested that evening with the whole of the Maguire household, and had been in custody and prison ever since. He said he had protested his innocence at the time he was arrested, had continued to do so ever since, and would continue to do so until the truth was established.

This long meeting with Giuseppe Conlon had a profound effect on

Cardinal Hume. He was very concerned about the state of the man's health, but also he became deeply aware of the strong likelihood that this man was innocent and that there could well have been a miscarriage of justice. As regards the safety of the conviction, the Cardinal knew that he was unable at that time to produce any evidence other than his own judgement. Consequently, he decided to pursue a parallel course of acquiring more background knowledge about Giuseppe Conlon, while at the same time exploring the possibility of obtaining his release on compassionate grounds.

At that time Monsignor George Leonard was Personal Assistant to the Cardinal for Non-Diocesan Affairs. He set about securing additional information about the Maguire case in general and Giuseppe Conlon in particular. Over a period of time some interesting facts emerged.

The day after the arrest of his son Gerard, Giuseppe Conlon had set off for London to arrange legal defence for him. He was only 53 years of age but by then his health was very poor indeed and he had not been able to work since 1963 because of his medical condition. It was his first visit to England for 17 years. His doctor had advised him not to make the journey but, after talking to his solicitor and his wife Sarah, who would have lost her job if she had accompanied him, he was left with no option but to go alone. He informed the Springfield Road RUC police barracks of his journey, why he was going and where he was staying. He travelled on the overnight boat from Belfast. He arrived at the Maguire home at lunchtime on 3 December, 1974, and by evening he and the whole Maguire household had been arrested. This came as an immense shock to a man who was a semi-invalid, who had been known locally at home as a peace-loving, kindly man who abhorred violence, and who was not a member of any paramilitary organisation. He rarely strayed from the shelter of his home.

Against this background, and in pursuance of his two-pronged approach, Cardinal Hume wrote to the Home Secretary, Merlyn Rees, on 26 March, 1979:

> . . . My anxiety arises from the fact that there are strong indications that this man is not guilty of the crime for which he was convicted . . .
>
> . . . I have met Mr Conlon in person myself and would have little doubt in my own mind that he is innocent.
>
> I recognise, of course, that it would not be at this stage a question of putting into motion a judicial process to reconsider the verdict which was passed on him.

> . . . he is a very sick man and I am very gravely concerned about the state of his health. This anxiety is shared by many other persons who are concerned with his case. He will certainly not live long enough to complete his sentence. So I am asking you quite frankly for an act of clemency towards him and that he should be released on compassionate grounds.

Shortly after that letter, Airey Neave M.P. met his terrible and tragic death at the hands of the IRA. In no way whatsoever could it ever be said that this influenced the outcome of the Giuseppe Conlon case. On the other hand that event can only have made even more difficult the task of those who were concerned about the safety of his conviction.

In his reply on 24 April 1979 Merlyn Rees said:

> I have considered Mr Conlon's case very carefully in the light of your letter. There is certainly no doubt that he is a very sick man. But he could be released from prison for this reason only by the exercise of the Royal Prerogative of Mercy, and successive Home Secretaries have taken the view that this interference with the decisions of the judiciary should be recommended only in exceptional circumstances . . .
>
> . . . I have however arranged for his case to be kept under continuous review so that if there should be any significant deterioration in his medical condition further consideration can be given immediately to the question of his early release . . .
>
> . . . I am grateful to you for having written to me about this case and am sorry to have to send you a disappointing reply.

In May there was a change of Government and on 15 May William Whitelaw became Home Secretary. In a letter to Cardinal Hume Mrs Sarah Conlon had described how her husband's condition continued to deteriorate rapidly, and she said his weight was now down to just over seven stone. Cardinal Hume arranged to see the new Home Secretary on 4 July. At the meeting Whitelaw had a phalanx of civil servants on either side of him. The Cardinal presented a similar case for compassionate release to that which he had put to Merlyn Rees, but with increased emphasis on the now rapidly worsening medical condition. On 31 December Giuseppe Conlon was admitted to Hammersmith Hospital. On 11 January, 1980, because of an erroneous rumour that he might be 'sprung', he was bundled into a wheelchair and, surrounded by police and prison staff, was taken back to Wormwood Scrubs. On 18 January he was returned to Hammersmith Hospital. He died on 23 January still protesting his innocence.

On 24 January the Home Secretary wrote to Cardinal Hume IN

CONFIDENCE, recalled his visit to him at the Home Office the previous July, and went on to say:

> As you will no doubt have seen from Press reports, Mr Conlon unfortunately died in Hammersmith Hospital last night. I had been keeping a close watch on his condition, and although it will be of no comfort to his family I thought you should know in confidence that I had in fact already come to the conclusion that should Mr Conlon recover sufficiently to be discharged from hospital it would not be right to return him to prison.

Cardinal Hume replied to the Home Secretary on 31 January. He made the point that, as the intention not to return Mr Conlon to prison should he recover enough to leave hospital had been published in at least two national newspapers shortly after he had received the Home Secretary's letter, he presumed the confidentiality of the letter no longer bound him. He went on to say –

> You will no doubt have noticed that Patrick Conlon was not given an IRA funeral, and that he was buried by the priest who had refused to bury the man involved in the bomb explosion on the Belfast train. Furthermore, Patrick Conlon was never claimed by the IRA as a member . . .
>
> It was always my personal conviction that Patrick Conlon was not a member of the IRA and that he was almost certainly innocent of the crime of which he was accused. There was no new evidence to support my view and so my plea to you was on the grounds of ill-health; I asked for a gesture of clemency.

In a fairly lengthy response on 3 March the main points made by the Home Secretary were:

> . . . On the question of Mr Conlon's possible innocence, I do not think I can usefully add anything to what I told you when we met . . .
>
> I can intervene in a criminal case by recommending the exercise of the Royal Prerogative of Mercy to set aside a conviction, and it is possible to do this even after a convicted person has died. But the Prerogative is not a means of reviewing decisions of the courts or of duplicating the ordinary machinery of appeal. I cannot reconsider cases on the basis of facts already considered by the courts, but only where some relevant new evidence or consideration of substance has come to light.

Although it was not known at the time, the phrase 'new evidence or consideration of substance' was to be used – some would say over-used – by the Home Office for many years to come.

After the trial of the Maguire Seven Sir Peter Matthews, the Chief Constable of Surrey, said 'We are delighted with the verdicts. These are the people we were after . . . We have cut off a major pipeline to the terrorists. We are only sorry we did not find the bombs.' In his autobiography *Bomb Squad*, Commander Huntley, formerly head of the squad, in referring to the arrests of the Maguire household, including Giuseppe Conlon, was to write, 'A bonus . . . was the cutting of a major supply line of explosives to the IRA in Britain.' If, as it would appear, both the Surrey Constabulary and the Metropolitan Police believed they had uncovered a major bomb-making unit of the IRA of considerable importance, many people reflected it was strange, even astonishing, that apparently the forensic tests on some of the swabs from the surfaces in the Maguire household and Anne Maguire's gloves should have been allegedly assigned initially to an 18-year old junior assistant scientist with two months service at the Royal Arsenal Research and Development Establishment (RARDE) – the Government's forensic laboratory in Woolwich.

Cardinal Hume's involvement in the case of Giuseppe Conlon had a deep and disturbing effect on him. He was, by now, wholly convinced that he had been an innocent man. This was a view shared by the MP for West Belfast Gerry (now Lord) Fitt and Sir John Biggs-Davison, both of whom had visited Giuseppe Conlon in Wormwood Scrubs in his dying days, and had heard his constant protestations of innocence. Cardinal Hume reasoned that, if he was proved to be innocent, where did that leave the convictions of the rest of the Maguire household? And, if they were proved to be innocent, the convictions of the Guildford Four would be brought into question. He was fearful there was a danger that there might have been a major miscarriage of justice in both cases. It was at that point he resolved to delve into matters further. The first step was to acquire more information about the remaining six of the Maguire Seven and this was done by Archbishop's House.

At the time no member of the legal profession, or of any other for that matter, knew more about the Maguire Seven than their solicitor, Alastair Logan. He had done more to assist them in their struggle for justice than any other person in the criminal justice system. His encyclopaedic knowledge of the case, and the clarity and soundness of his legal arguments, were to be of considerable assistance to the growing number of people, including some Members of Parliament, who were becoming uneasy about the case. Some of the facts that emerged were compelling.

Paddy Maguire, and his wife Anne, were both born in Belfast and moved to North London the day after their wedding in 1957, some nineteen years before their trial and conviction on 4 March, 1976. Prior to moving to London Paddy Maguire had spent three years in the British Army. They had four children and two of the older ones, their sons Vincent then aged 16 and Patrick aged 13, were convicted with them. Paddy Maguire worked for the Gas Board for many years and then became a school caretaker. He was a member of the Paddington Conservative Club. Anne Maguire had two cleaning jobs.

The whole family was well known and respected in the area of 43, Third Avenue, London N10 where they were living at the time of their arrest. Two other men, Sean Smyth and Patrick O'Neill, were also arrested the same evening, together with Giuseppe Conlon. Smyth, who was Anne's brother, had been living with the family for some months while working in London. On the day of the arrests he returned to the house at 6.30pm. Pat O'Neill had three small daughters under the age of six. His wife, Helen, a friend of Anne Maguire, was expecting her fourth child and was in hospital for observations, but hoped to return home that evening. O'Neill telephoned Anne Maguire at about 6.00pm asking if she could look after the three little girls for a few days as he had now heard from the hospital that his wife would not be returning home that evening. Anne agreed and he brought the little children along at about 6.45pm, close to the time Sean Smyth had arrived.

The Metropolitan Police started observing the house at the latest from about 7.00pm at the request of the Surrey Police. They had been interrogating Paul Hill and Gerard Conlon, who was Anne Maguire's nephew by marriage. Giuseppe Conlon had arrived at about 1.30pm and, shortly afterwards, he and Paddy Maguire had gone to the Grey Horse pub in Kilburn Lane. They remained there until the afternoon closing time, then returned to 43, Third Avenue and slept off their lunchtime drinking session. At about 6.00pm Paddy Maguire went to Harrow Road police station to enquire about his brother Hugh whom he had not been able to raise on the telephone all day. After that Paddy Maguire, Giuseppe Conlon, Sean Smyth and Pat O'Neill, who was by then on his way home, went for a drink in the Royal Lancer pub while Anne Maguire was cooking supper.

A salient point which emerged from these timings was that Sean Smyth and Pat O'Neill, and also Giuseppe Conlon for that matter, would have had little time in which to handle nitroglycerine, had they in fact been doing so. The police entered the house at about 8.30pm. In arresting those present in the house, including the two sons Vincent Maguire aged 16 and Patrick Maguire aged 13, they did not detain the middle son, John Maguire, who was 15. He had been in the house at the time when explosives were alleged to have been handled.

Up until the time they were arrested, not one of the seven people in the Maguire house on 3 December, 1974 had ever been under suspicion for terrorist activities. The IRA had never claimed or even recognised any of them either prior to their trial or thereafter. The only reason the police went to Third Avenue was because Gerard Conlon, who on that day at Guildford Police Station was under an interrogation leading to his 'confessions', subsequently retracted, had said that his aunt Anne Maguire made bombs, had taught him and others how to do it, and had taken part in the Guildford bombings. Anne Maguire was also named by Paul Hill during his interrogations at Guildford Police Station.

The sole charge against the Maguire Seven was:

> That between the first and fourth days of December 1974 they knowingly, had, in his or her – as the case may be – possession or under his or her control an explosive substance, namely nitroglycerine, under such circumstances as to give rise to a reasonable suspicion that he or she – as the case may be – did not have in his or her possession or under his or her control for a lawful object.

They were all found guilty and given the following sentences, ages at the time in brackets:

Anne Maguire (40)	14 years
Patrick Maguire (43)	14 years
Vincent Maguire (16)	5 years
Patrick Maguire (13)	4 years
Giuseppe Conlon (52)	12 years
Sean Smyth (38)	12 years
Patrick O'Neill (35)	12 years (later reduced to 8 years)

They were convicted on 4 March, 1976. They applied for leave to appeal and the hearing opened on 20 July, 1977. Their application was rejected by the Court of Appeal on 29 July, 1977.

It is to be noted that in the charge there was no reference to 'handling' as such, to any specific act of terrorism, or to any explosive other than nitroglycerine.

Cardinal Hume continued to be even more concerned about the case of Giuseppe Conlon. His widow maintained contact with the Cardinal and the latter also received many letters from members of the public, particularly in Northern Ireland. They all expressed distress and misgivings about the outcome of the Conlon case and the circumstances of his death after nearly four years in prison.

Given their background, it was highly improbable that any of the convicted were members of any terrorist organisation or had had anything to do with terrorist activities. Their continual protestations of innocence would point to this – but there was more. They had all resolutely refused to make any form of confession despite considerable pressure, not to say provocation, from the police. In addition, there was no documentary evidence whatsoever against them, no identity evidence and no fingerprints. The sole evidence against them, and on which alone they were convicted, was the forensic findings on the swabs and the one glove of Anne Maguire as presented at the trial by scientists from RARDE.

Both Sir Peter Matthews of the Surrey Constabulary and Commander Huntley of the Metropolitan Police had described the Maguire household as important 'bomb-makers'. And even Sir Michael Havers, prosecuting counsel in the Guildford Four trial, which was concluded four months before the Maguire Seven trial began, spoke of 'Aunt Annie's bomb factory.' He was also to prosecute in the Maguire trial when he claimed there was no connection between the two trials. It was surely extraordinary that such competent 'bomb-makers', who had cleaned, so efficiently and so meticulously, every single surface in the house in Third Avenue of any trace of nitroglycerine, should have apparently overlooked the need to clean their own hands.

Questions were beginning to arise about the forensic evidence – in essence was it proved without doubt that nitroglycerine was on the convicted people's hands at the time the swabs were taken? In February 1980 BBC TV Northern Ireland screened a programme called Spotlight which featured the case of Giuseppe Conlon. It tackled head on the quality and credibility of the evidence on which he had been convicted. In the circumstances at the time this was a courageous undertaking. Although it was not networked in England, the programme was widely viewed in Northern Ireland. It raised doubts and anxieties in many people's minds, some of whom were to write to Cardinal Hume. It was no doubt because of his recent death that concern about the Maguire case still centred at the time on Giuseppe Conlon. Indeed, this was to be so for some time to come.

Alastair Logan had always been concerned about the finality of the forensic evidence in the Maguire case. He had wished to arrange for an independent assessment of the scientific evidence presented at the trial, by both the prosecution and defence, and also of the Thin Layer Chromatography (TLC) procedure from which the evidence had been deduced. This might have led to 'new evidence or consideration of substance'. Unfortunately he had no funds available with which to support such a project. It was not generally known at the time that, without any remuneration whatsoever, he had continued to represent the Maguire Seven and three of the Guildford Four since their respective appeals in 1977. Such was the depth of his belief in the need to continue the pursuit of justice on their behalf.

A number of people in public life were becoming increasingly concerned about the case including, in particular, three Members of Parliament – Sir John Biggs-Davison, Gerry Fitt and Christopher Price. In a debate in Parliament on 4 August, 1980 Biggs-Davison raised the case of Giuseppe Conlon. He proposed that there was a need for a reassessment of the scientific evidence. He was supported by Christopher Price who called for a reinterpretation of the scientific evidence. This did not attract a positive response from the Government Front Bench. Things were to move slowly but none of the three MPs was prepared to let the matter rest. Indeed their pursuit of justice strengthened as time went by. Archbishop's House continued to monitor the media, both press and television, and the proceedings in Parliament for references to the case.

The scientific evidence against the Maguire Seven was given by RARDE. During their trial the whole argument on the scientific evidence between prosecution and defence had depended on whether or not the TLC procedure could give a specific and unique test for nitroglycerine. This was the only explosive named in the charges against the Maguire Seven. The prosecution maintained that it did – the defence that it did not. At that time scientific expertise in explosives was very largely centred only in Government forensic laboratories such as RARDE. This limited the field open to the defence for presentation of expert scientific evidence at trials. For the trial of the Maguire Seven, and for their appeal hearing 20 to 29 July, 1977, the defence had secured the services of John Yallop. By then retired, he had been a Principal Scientific Officer at RARDE, had invented the TLC procedure, and had no less than 34 years' experience of working with explosives.

There were two main thrusts in Yallop's evidence. He explained that the TLC procedure had originally been designed as a screening test to identify traces of an explosive where an explosion had already occurred, but he had never contemplated its use as the sole evidence in a case. He specifically stated in court that he no longer thought a single TLC test was a satisfactory basis on which to form a firm conclusion that nitroglycerine had been present. He maintained that a confirmatory test was necessary. His second, and main, thrust was that he believed that, on a single TLC test using toluene as the element, some other substance was capable of giving the same reading as nitroglycerine.

At the end of the trial, on the last day, as Mr Justice Donaldson was to begin his summing up, John Yallop found a report to him in June 1974 (after he had retired from RARDE) from a Principal Scientific Officer at the Woolwich laboratory, Walter Elliott, who gave evidence at the trial. This report demonstrated that another explosive, Pentaerythritol Tetranitrate (PETN), a substance chemically completely dissimilar to nitroglycerine, gave during the TLC test in toluene an identical and indistinguishable result. This showed that the identification of nitroglycerine in the TLC test was not, after all, unique, as had been claimed by the prosecution. The scientists from RARDE who gave evidence at the trial of the Maguire Seven knew this before the trial. Some anxieties were expressed over the years about how the matter had been handled during the trial and at the appeal hearing. The essence of the matter was that the question of whether or not the swabs and nail scrapings contained nitroglycerine had been allowed to become synonymous with the question of whether or not the Maguire Seven had had nitroglycerine on their hands. This was not fully explored at the trial or the appeal hearing.

In advancing the cause of Giuseppe Conlon, Christopher Price MP was to succeed, where, because of unavailability of funds Alastair Logan had not, in that he was able to set up an independent scientific investigation. Christopher Price secured the cooperation of an independent forensic scientist, Dr Brian Caddy of Strathclyde University, to re-run the tests in toluene. Alastair Logan made available to Christopher Price, for use by Dr Caddy, substantial documentation from the trial and appeal hearing of the Maguire Seven, and also from other sources. During 1982/83 reports prepared by Dr Caddy reflecting misgivings about the TLC test and other matters were sent to, and discussed with, the Home Office by Christopher Price. Details of the presentation, which was rejected by David Mellor MP, then Minister of State, on 20 December 1983, were not known publicly at the time. Nor was it known who the Home Office had asked to examine the Caddy report, who had decided it should be rejected, and for what reasons.

Concern about what had happened to Giuseppe Conlon was now extending quite rapidly into other circles – grass roots campaign groups in London and Northern Ireland, more Members of Parliament, press and television journalists, and television producers. As was inevitable by this stage, the Giuseppe Conlon case was merging into that of the entire Maguire Seven which now became the focus of concern.

On 6 March 1984, in their *First Tuesday* series, Yorkshire TV screened *Aunt Annie's Bomb Factory*. It majored in the first part on the special case of Giuseppe Conlon: the short time he was in the house in Third Avenue; his extreme ill-health which would have prohibited him from assisting in speedy action to dispose of the alleged nitroglycerine in the house; his constant assertions of innocence; his death-bed request to Lord Fitt 'to do everything you can to prove I did not do this.' It related how he had even informed the RUC of his visit to London and why it was taking place following the arrest of his son Gerard. It had been suggested in court that this was a cover up, but the programme showed a letter from the RUC confirming what Giuseppe Conlon had said. That letter was never seen by the jury.

Dr Caddy made a damning analysis in the programme of the way in which the TLC test had been conducted and used to convict the Maguire household. He said the RARDE analysis was deficient in not applying enough safety standards, and added that it was essential to confirm results by an additional test. Alastair Logan asserted that the test on the swabs had been carried out in such a way that it could not be repeated. He also emphasised the unlikelihood of anyone in the Maguire household, because of their demeanour and background, being involved in any form of terrorism. The programme emphasised that none of the Maguire Seven had made any confessions and the IRA had disowned them all. There had been no para-military trappings at the funeral of Giuseppe Conlon.

Christopher Price again expressed his uneasiness about the forensic evidence. He had previously raised it in a debate in Parliament in August 1980 when he had called for a reinterpretation of the scientific evidence. In addition, in 1982 – 83, he had presented to Ministers in the Home Office the report by Dr Caddy, which he had commissioned, and which was highly critical of the procedures adopted by RARDE when analysing the evidence against the Maguire Seven. Many who heard Caddy's damning observations in the programme on how the TLC test had been conducted by RARDE must have concluded at the time that this alone constituted a 'consideration of substance'. The Home Office did not see it in the same way.

A telling point was made by Alastair Logan. He said it was common knowledge that when nitroglycerine is handled it is rapidly absorbed through the skin and this results in a near-instantaneous blinding headache – known as an NG headache. There were no reports by the police that any of the seven arrested were suffering from such headaches. This knowledge would not have sat well with the jury at the trial when they heard Sir Michael Havers, prosecuting counsel, speaking of a state of panic in the household on hearing of the arrest of Gerry Conlon and, in his phrase, it had been 'all hands to the pump' to move the nitroglycerine.

The programme said that the TLC test which was at the heart of the Giuseppe Conlon case had been used controversially in other IRA trials. Sir John Biggs-Davison, who had a special interest in Northern Ireland affairs, said – 'our defence of the rule of law against terrorism must be seen to be just that' . . . 'let justice be done though the heavens fall.' The programme concluded with Gerry Fitt saying to camera:

> I know that there is an official mind in connection with this case. I know many members of the police in London, and, indeed, throughout Britain. I know many of the Ministers in the Home Office. I have no doubt that at the back of their mind there is the feeling that Giuseppe Conlon and the others may be innocent of this crime for which they have been convicted. But if we find them not guilty then it will open up the floodgates to other people who have been sentenced on very much the same evidence.

On 16 July, 1984 Cardinal Hume wrote to the Prime Minister:

> For a number of years now I have experienced grave disquiet over the case of Patrick Conlon who died, you will recall, on 23 January 1980 in Hammersmith Hospital, while still serving a sentence of 12 years for his alleged involvement in the alleged manufacture of explosives in the house of the Maguire family in 1974.
>
> I discussed my misgivings with you soon after you first arrived at Downing Street. I must confess that I have not been at all satisfied with the official answers that have so far been offered. I know that my anxiety over Patrick Conlon's innocence and how he and those accused with him were convicted is shared by some public figures including Lord Fitt and Sir John Biggs-Davison, surely no friends of terrorists or the IRA. His protestations of innocence until his death and his funeral in Belfast – with no hint of paramilitary presence – must surely give rise to the most grave anxiety about the likelihood of a major miscarriage of justice. Whatever the forensic evidence may seem to prove, every other indication would argue for the intrinsic improbability of the charges levelled against the Maguire family in general and Patrick Conlon in particular.
>
> I am disturbed too by the evidence produced by Yorkshire Television's programme on this case screened on March 6 1984. I would hope that the relevant authorities have called for a transcript of that programme and have weighed the serious doubts and questions it raised.
>
> I am well aware that it is normal practice to produce fresh evidence to justify the re-examination of a judicial sentence. As events subsequent to the trial have cast doubt on the justice of its conclusion, I would suggest that an examination of the evidence actually presented in Court needs to be conducted.
>
> I am understandably reluctant, as you will well appreciate, to cause fresh controversy in the present state of Anglo-Irish relations. That, however, can never be the only consideration. Justice remains an absolute priority. I am sure I speak for others when I say we would be reassured only if we could be convinced that every aspect

of this case has been objectively and fairly reviewed after the death of Mr. Conlon, and every reasonable anxiety allayed, not only about his case, but of the people convicted with him, one of whom, Mrs. Annie Maguire, is still in prison.

I would ask you to ensure that the Home Secretary looks carefully at this whole case and its consequences. There are so many indications which cast doubt on the justice of the Court's verdict.

The Prime Minister replied on 3 August, 1984:

Thank you for your letter of 16 July about the late Patrick Conlon who, together with members of the Maguire family and others, was convicted, in March 1976, of unlawfully possessing an explosive substance.

I do indeed recall your raising this case with me, and I believe that shortly after you saw me you had a meeting with the then Home Secretary, Willie Whitelaw.

I understand that the case for the Crown rested largely upon expert scientific evidence based on the results of thin layer chromatography tests used in detecting nitroglycerine. The validity of the test, the possibility of other substances giving similar test results and the way the technique was used in this particular case were thoroughly gone into during the examination and cross-examination of expert witnesses both for the prosecution and the defence. Later, the scientific evidence was central among the issues considered in great detail by the Court of Appeal at a hearing lasting ten days, at the end of which they found no grounds for disturbing the convictions.

You will know that neither I nor any Minister has power to re-assess a case on the basis of evidence that has already been before the courts. Nor can we act as a further Court of Appeal when the normal avenues have been exhausted. As you say, the Home Secretary is empowered under section 17 of the Criminal Appeal Act 1968 to refer a case to the Court of Appeal (Criminal Division). But it would not be right for him to do so unless significant new facts or considerations of substance had come to light which threw doubt on the rightness of the conviction and which had not previously been before the courts. In Mr Conlon's case there have also been requests that the Home Secretary recommend the exercise of the Royal Prerogative of Mercy to grant a posthumous Free Pardon. But again it would only be proper for him to do so in exceptional circumstances where he was satisfied that the defendant had no intention of committing an offence and had not, in fact, committed one.

The whole case has been examined very closely on a number of

> previous occasions but each time the Home Secretary has concluded that there are insufficient grounds to justify intervening in either of the ways I have described. The points raised in the television programme to which you refer were indeed taken into account. Most of them had, in fact, been advanced and considered before. Account was taken also of the reports by Dr Brian Caddy of Strathclyde University, an independent forensic scientist commissioned by Mr Christopher Price and others who have been active campaigners on Mr Conlon's behalf.
>
> I am sorry to say that in the circumstances there is no action I can properly take in relation to this case. But if you would like to discuss your concerns once more with the Home Secretary, I know that Leon Brittan would be ready to meet you.

The Prime Minister adhered to the Home Office position in saying there could be no movement 'unless significant new facts or considerations of substance had come to light which threw doubts on the rightness of the conviction and which had not previously been before the courts.'

By now even more people were wondering why Dr Caddy's reports were not considered to be a 'consideration of substance.' The fact that the Home Office had apparently offered no convincing reasons to support this view only served to increase the ever-widening unease amongst people with an interest in justice. It was strange that the Home Office appeared to be unable to appreciate this state of affairs and where it might lead. In May 1985 Gerry Fitt (by now a Life Peer) introduced a debate on the Maguire case in the House of Lords and was supported by several Peers. Knowing that the Northern Ireland Forensic Science laboratory had abandoned TLC tests for explosives in 1973 as being too unreliable, he asked the specific question as to whether it was true that a case like the Maguire Seven would not now be brought on forensic tests alone, that it would not reach court without evidence of the existence of a bulk of explosives, and that a parallel case against a Palestinian terrorist had been dropped for lack of such evidence even though the TLC test had proved positive.

His question was never properly answered. In the same debate Lord Mishcon had asked for independent scientific advisers to be appointed to examine the evidence that was given at trial so as to advise the Home Secretary whether there were grounds to refer the case to the Court of Appeal. This proposal was subsequently rejected but, again, with no reasons given. It would, of course, have been very awkward if such independent scientific advisers had supported Dr Caddy's views.

Meanwhile, Anne Maguire, who was the last member of the household to be released, left prison on 22 February, 1985. She had never confessed to any crime and when she eventually applied for parole during her imprisonment she adamantly refused to express the desired remorse for a crime which she did not commit.

At the time of their trial the Maguire Seven had been subjected to an adverse press, particularly Anne Maguire who was described as 'Evil Aunt Annie' and 'senior armourer to the IRA.' It needs to be recalled that the public had been outraged by the Guildford bombings. At the time of the trials, anti-Irish emotion ran high and people were looking for retribution. However, by 1985, when Anne Maguire was finally released, the climate had changed somewhat. Both she, and her husband Paddy, did much to help that change during two television interviews.

They were first interviewed on 20 April, 1985 by Robert Kee in his *Seven Days* programme on Channel 4. They came over exactly as they were – good, straightforward, sincere and typical North Londoners. They were not embittered but did feel they had been badly let down by the British criminal justice system. 'Some mistake must have been made,' said Anne Maguire. The second interview by David Frost was a week later on 28 April, 1985 on the TV AM programme *Good Morning Britain*. Again there was no bitterness and they were clearly the least likely people the IRA would use as 'bomb makers.' They were too well known and too well settled in their neighbourhood for that. The viewing public could not fail to have been impressed by these two interviews.

Cardinal Hume wrote again to the Home Secretary, by now Douglas Hurd, on 19 November, 1985 about the Maguire case. He said: 'It has been a matter of considerable worry to me that there could be innocent people in our prisons while guilty men were at large.' In his reply of 11 February, 1986 the Home Secretary said – '. . . further consideration of representations about the forensic evidence presented at their trial has been completed. Although doubts have been expressed about the nature of this evidence, I have had to conclude that they are not such as to offer grounds for referral to the Court of Appeal.' No reasons were offered.

Meanwhile, in January 1986, an Early Day Motion was put down in the House of Commons in the names of John Wheeler, constituency MP for the Maguires, and Sir John Biggs-Davison who had started campaigning on their behalf before the death of Giuseppe Conlon. By June the motion had attracted over 200 signatories from all parties. The motion was:

> That this House notes the widespread concern felt in Parliament, by eminent scientists, by other responsible observers and by members of the public . . .' that the Maguire Seven '. . . sentenced

> in 1976 to long terms of imprisonment since served, now appear, despite confirmation of their convictions at the time by the Court of Appeal, to have been entirely innocent of the crime with which they were charged; further notes at the conclusion of a debate in the other place on 17 May 1985, the recognition by the Parliamentary Under Secretary at the Home Office [Lord Glenarthur] of the strength of feeling on this matter in that House and his pledge to draw the attention of the Secretary of State for the Home Department to what had been said; and therefore earnestly urges the Secretary of State for the Home Department in the interests of the highest standards of British justice of which this country needs to feel rightly proud, to move without delay for a review of these convictions, either under the provisions of section 17 of the Criminal Appeal Act 1968, or by such other public process of review as he may deem appropriate to this disturbing case.

There was no movement by the Home Office following this Motion as was evident from the following extract from a letter from the Home Secretary in response to an MP who had signed the Motion

> These representations have largely rested on the continued expression of doubts about the forensic evidence and the nature of the test techniques used. The views of Dr Brian Caddy of the University of Strathclyde, and Dr Peter Boyle, of Trinity College, Dublin, have been presented to me, but I have had to conclude that they do not offer evidence of a kind which would justify me in referring the case to the Court of Appeal.

There were, no doubt, reasons why the views of Dr Caddy and Dr Boyle, whose report had been sent to the Home Office by Alastair Logan, were not accepted but, again, none was offered. By now, March 1986, criticisms of and anxieties about the forensic evidence presented at the trial of the Maguire Seven had been represented to the Home Office for some four years. Many held the view that they constituted at the very least a 'consideration of substance', if not 'new evidence.' On 31 January, 1986, in replying to a letter written by Lord Fitt in October 1985 asking for action to be taken, the Under Secretary at the Home Office, David Mellor, said in a lengthy reply

> Whatever action the accused may have taken in respect of the explosives they were found guilty of possessing, it remains the case that the jury was satisfied that there was evidence to show that explosives had been handled.

In spite of the repeated representations, the Home Office was clearly not prepared to re-examine the scientific evidence presented to the jury and on which they had found the Maguire Seven guilty.

Taking into account the seeming impasse over the previous six years in the cases of Giuseppe Conlon and the rest of the Maguire Seven, it came as a surprise to some that in 1986 the Home Office agreed that Carole Richardson, of the Guildford Four, could be examined by two independent doctors. The lengthy interview, over some five hours, took place on 30 April. It was conducted by Dr James MacKeith, a consultant forensic psychiatrist, and Dr Gisli Gudjonsson, a consultant clinical psychologist, who worked together at the Royal Bethlem and Maudsley Hospitals in South London. They had developed methods of testing the suggestibility of witnesses and to what extent their evidence was reliable. They were leaders in research in the field of false confessions. Although the examination was originally at the instigation of the defence, the full background as to how it finally came about was not known to Cardinal Hume's Deputation until publication in July 1988 of the excellent and convincing book *Time Bomb* by Grant McKee and Ros Franey.

Apparently the idea of an examination had been sparked off some two years earlier by an unexpected phone call, on 30 March, 1984, from a doctor in the Prison Medical Service at Styal prison to the clerk to Carole Richardson's solicitor at that time. The doctor said he believed that Carole Richardson was innocent and that something must be done about it. Shortly afterwards Alastair Logan, who was now representing her and had been pressing for such an examination by the two doctors to take place, discussed the matter with Dr MacKeith. Eventually, at the request of Styal's senior medical officer, and with the approval of the Director of the Prison Medical Service, the interviews took place. By then two valuable years from the point of view of the defence had been lost. In December 1986 Dr MacKeith obtained permission from the Home Office to send the reports to Alastair Logan. In a covering letter Dr MacKeith stated, 'I have profound doubts about whether the statements given by Carole Richardson to the police were voluntary and whether the self-incriminating contents were reliable.'

The combined reports by the two doctors were a model in thoroughness. Before conducting the interview substantial documentation was made available to them by Alastair Logan. This included evidence offered in court at the trial, pre-trial statements and police reports. Amongst the areas covered in the two reports by the doctors were developments in assessing retracted statements, Carole Richardson's personal background, her medical and psychiatric history, pre-trial medical reports, accounts of her arrest and interrogation, opinions and conclusions on her state at the time of arrest, and comments for use by the Prison Medical Service.

She was 17 when she was arrested on 3 December, 1974. In the background section of his report Dr MacKeith recorded:

> She had at least 14 short-term jobs between August 1972 and her arrest. She was almost continually in employment. By the age of 13 years, she had become involved in petty theft and sometimes stole money from home. She was arrested for shoplifting and put on probation for two years following a conviction for burglary at age 15 years. From age 13 years she drank alcohol and began abusing drugs. She smoked cannabis regularly, was for years prescribed amphetamines by her general practitioner, took LSD, sometimes by injection, and cocaine on two occasions. For months prior to her arrest, she was taking barbiturates in quantity, as much as 20 capsules a day.

She had been arrested in London at 7.00pm and was driven down to Guildford. Her interrogation by the police started the next morning, which was between 15 and 20 hours after she said she last took tuinal. She was apparently told that 'others had accused her of participating in preparations to cause bomb explosions.' She was also 'confronted by a claim by police that Mr Armstrong, her boyfriend, had said she was in Guildford.' She went on to allege that she was struck once by one officer and then twice by another. Dr MacKeith reported that, by the afternoon of 4 December, she said that further threats were made and that she had become 'very distressed, tremulous and frightened of further violence.' She apparently became hysterical and this led to an interview with a police surgeon, Dr Makos, who saw her at 8.15pm on that day. He prepared a report.

Dr MacKeith was somewhat critical of the statement by Dr Makos:

> There is no indication that Dr Makos undertook a psychiatric assessment, determined her understanding or perception of her circumstances or generally enquired into matters relevant to the reliability of subsequent statements that she might make . . . He states that she last took barbiturates on 2 December, although Miss Richardson made the unchallenged claim that she took capsules on 3 December. He mentions her 'admitting to be addicted' to LSD and Tuinal. True dependence on LSD does not occur. . . . He refers for some reason to Miss Richardson's apparently self-incriminating remarks.

Dr MacKeith went on to say:

> Given Dr Makos' description of her condition, it is, in my opinion, most unlikely that a doctor with appropriate awareness and knowledge would have regarded her as fit for further interrogation and giving of reliable statements without making and recording a careful psychiatric assessment. If one accepts the police evidence about the absence of ill-treatment, as the court did, it is still quite possible that Miss Richardson had the firm understanding that she was unsafe in police custody and so been prone to try to engineer her release from stress by making admissions.

In his separate report, after reviewing the psychological test results, Dr Gudjonsson said:

> . . . in spite of her good memory and intelligence Miss Richardson is very suggestible. That is, she yields very readily to subtly leading questions and her answers can be easily altered by pressure. Related to this is her marked tendency towards compliance and eagerness to avoid conflict and confrontation with people in authority.
>
> Bearing in mind the circumstances of the lengthy interrogations and the likelihood that she was exceptionally vulnerable at the time (e.g. low self-esteem, drug withdrawal, highly suggestible) the validity of the confessions made in 1974 must be seriously questioned.

In moving to his opinion and conclusion in his report Dr MacKeith stated:

> In my opinion, at the time of her arrest, Miss Richardson had a vulnerable personality with low self-esteem, poor self-confidence and an undue reliance on the good opinion of others. She was abusing drugs heavily and usually under the influence of them as well as psychologically and possibly physically dependent. Her own account, confirmed to a considerable degree in Dr Makos' statement, indicates that she was in an abnormal state of mind, probably suffering from an acute anxiety state and, by her own account, very distressed, frightened and desperate to be relieved of the stress of further interrogation.
>
> **I conclude that the statements that resulted in her conviction on the several charges were very probably unreliable.** (Dr MacKeith's emphasis). This opinion does *not* have to rely on accepting Miss Richardson's allegations of police threats, violence or other gross improprieties. It does rely on her specific vulnerable qualities and also her state of mind at the time.

If the reports by Drs MacKeith and Gudjonsson had been available and known to the jury at the trial of the Guildford Four in 1974, it is more than possible that they would not have found Carole Richardson guilty. She was English and only 17 when arrested in a squat. Her background, lifestyle, history of drug taking and shoplifting made her a most unlikely candidate to be recruited and trained by the IRA, and entrusted with an important bombing mission. If her conviction could have been shown not to be safe and satisfactory, this would have brought into question the convictions of the rest of the Guildford Four – Paul Hill, Gerard Conlon and Patrick Armstrong. The sole evidence against all four of them was their 'confessions', which they later retracted, and in which they had implicated each other.

Grant McKee and Ros Franey of Yorkshire Television made *The Guildford Time Bomb* which was shown, and networked, in their *First Tuesday* series on 1 July, 1986. The programme opened by baldly asking, 'Did the police get the wrong people – were they guilty as charged?' It was acknowledged the matter was 'delicate and contentious' as it 'called into question the verdicts.' Time bombs had been placed in the Horse and Groom and Seven Stars public houses in Guildford on 5 October, 1974. There were five killed and 42 injured in both pubs.

The programme went on to say that on 7 November a bomb was thrown into the King's Arms pub in Woolwich leaving two killed and 26 injured. All four of the Guildford Four had been convicted of the Guildford bombings, and Paul Hill and Patrick Armstrong had also been convicted of the Woolwich bombing. They were all sentenced to the longest terms of imprisonment ever awarded by a British judge. Having covered this background, the programme said what made the case remarkable was that in 1986, twelve years after the trial, all four of those convicted, and their solicitor, continually protested their innocence.

Early in the programme Lord Fitt said:

> I have now serious doubts that, allied with other cases, the convictions have been wrongly made and I believe it would be in the interests of the Home Office, and the British Government, whether Conservative or Labour, to look into the validity of those convictions.

He was followed by Merlyn Rees who had been Secretary of State for Northern Ireland at the time of the trial in 1975 and was Home Secretary from 1976 to 1979:

> Looking at this case afresh, years afterwards, it raises doubts in my mind at the way confessions were made. It raises doubts, particularly

in one case, that the wrong person has been sentenced. And because of that I think we must find a way of looking again. Were we clouded by the emotion at the time – quite understandable emotion?

After reviewing the lifestyle of the Guildford Four through the eyes of various people, the programme concluded that none of them had any of the essential attributes the IRA would require of members of its Active Service Units (ASU), including even Paul Hill who had been in trouble in Northern Ireland before coming to England in the summer of 1974. The programme then focused on several key aspects of the evidence presented in court on which the convictions hinged, the first five of which related to Carole Richardson:

The police had accounted for everyone who had been in the Horse and Groom except for a 'courting couple' who were sitting where the bomb had been planted. Sir Michael Havers, prosecuting counsel, said two soldiers would identify Patrick Armstrong and Carole Richardson as the 'courting couple.' This did not happen. Even after an identity parade before eight people whom the Surrey police knew had been in the pub at the time, Carole Richardson was not picked out by any of them. After that Patrick Armstrong had not been put on any identity parades.

Some 15 days after the bombings, and before their arrest, Patrick Armstrong and Carole Richardson hitchhiked to Folkstone where she was assaulted by a drunk. They both went straight to the police and gave their correct names and address. Alastair Logan posed the question – would someone who had taken part in the Guildford bombing voluntarily get in touch with the police in this way?

Lisa Astin, a friend of Carole Richardson, said she had been with her all day Saturday 5 October 1974, including the pop concert at the South Bank Polytechnic in the evening. Lisa Astin maintained she could not have been at Guildford. It was easily established Carole Richardson had been at the concert because there was a photograph of her with the band 'Jack the Lad', a Newcastle group. Moreover the doorman remembered them arriving barefoot, with back stage passes, at 7.45pm. For Carole Richardson to be guilty she had to get from the Horse and Groom to the concert in 52 minutes. Lisa Astin's statement had been unshakeable throughout the trial.

The defence had maintained that such a complicated journey of 29 miles would have taken at least 64 minutes. The prosecution said a police car had done the journey in exactly 52 minutes. This was just enough time for her to have arrived at the concert at 7.45pm. The jury had accepted the possibility Carole Richardson could have planted the bomb and got to the concert by 7.45pm.

Frank Johnson, a second alibi for Carole Richardson, was interviewed on the programme. When he heard she had been arrested he went to the police in Newcastle and made a statement about how he had met Carole and Lisa for drinks and went to the concert with them. His statement wrecked the case against Carole Richardson. Frank Johnson was arrested under the Prevention of Terrorism Act and at Guildford Police station he was subjected to interrogation for three days without a solicitor. In his own words he said to camera –

> By that time I was quite confused and did not know what was happening. I was willing to sign anything – write down whatever you want – I'll admit doing the whole thing on my own if you want – you just write it down – give it to me and I'll put my name at the end – you don't have to read it to me or anything.'

He then retracted his alibi statement and agreed it was a concoction. In court he reverted to his original account but the jury rejected his alibi. The programme might well have also asked why the IRA would organise an alibi for the one member of the group who was not Irish and not organise alibis for the others, and why, if the desperate dash through Saturday evening traffic congestion was done to provide her with an alibi, she was unaware of it when she was questioned by the police.

The programme went on to examine in some detail the question of confessions, the discrepancies, the impact of the Balcombe Street ASU affair, and the appeal. The only evidence against all of the Guildford Four was their own confessions and it was on these alone that they were convicted. All four had pleaded not guilty in court, claimed they had made false confessions due to physical and psychological abuse by the police, but had now retracted them. Carole Richardson and Patrick Armstrong had been on drugs when arrested.

Barry Irving, Director of the Police Foundation, was interviewed. He had undertaken much of the research on police evidence for the Royal Commission on Criminal Procedure – Police Interrogation, which overhauled the law on confessions and was published in 1986. He had followed through the case of Patrick Armstrong prior to publication of the report and had been asked by Alastair Logan to examine the evidence against him. He said there were three key aspects – the effects of drugs on persons being interrogated; adequacy of rest between periods of interrogation allowing time for meals and normal sleeping hours; access to a solicitor. He went on to say the Police and Criminal Evidence Act 1984 had, for him, dealt with these matters but they had not been dealt with in 1974 when the arrests took place. He added that some confessions without corroboration could be entering a dangerous area.

Professor Lionel Haward of Surrey University was then interviewed. He was a forensic psychologist and an expert in the field of confession and testimony of witnesses. He had interviewed Patrick Armstrong in 1977 at the request of Alastair Logan and summarised his findings:

> Armstrong was maintaining all along that the confession was false and that most of the things he had been saying to the police had been to alleviate his anxiety and escape from what he regarded as an intolerable situation. And under hypnosis he had presented a very consistent picture of this rather inadequate passive man who had been caught up in the sort of maelstrom of a situation in which he was quite bewildered and quite bemused by the drugs he'd had.

Professor Haward's closing comment on the programme was:

> There has been a considerable body of research evidence made available in the last two years on false confessions and in virtually every case there is a great deal of anxiety and desire by the person making the confession to escape from the immediate short term effects of police imprisonment and interrogation, quite regardless of the long-term consequences and Armstrong's case fits this pattern almost exactly.

The programme pointed out that the sheer detail of the confessions seemed impressive. They revealed knowledge of Guildford, some familiarity with explosives and where the actual bombs had been placed. The judge, Mr Justice Donaldson as he then was, concluded to the jury – 'You may think that the statements on their face at least disclose an extraordinary knowledge of the detail of the way in which these offences were committed.' 'But did they?' asked the programme.

Alastair Logan answered this question rather firmly – 'When you get to look at the actual analysis of evidence that came out, there is not a single shred of evidence in any of the statements which was not, on the points of importance, exactly what the police knew themselves from their own researches. They had been given nothing new in those statements.' Barry Irving added that in many similar cases we do not know exactly what was said by whom to whom during the process of interrogation. Details can be generated that were not there before. The end result, if it is uncorroborated, can look very convincing.

The programme confirmed that there was no disputing there were more than 100 major and minor discrepancies between the four statements – different numbers in the gang, different personnel, different times of departure from London, different drivers, even including Patrick Armstrong who could not drive. Alastair Logan cited the extraordinary situation whereby Carole Richardson had 'confessed' to bombing both Guildford pubs. The prosecution had to concede that this was impossible as she would not have had time to get to the London concert. Alastair Logan referred to what he described as 'the extraordinary scene' when in his opening speech the Attorney General, Sir Michael Havers, told the jury that Carole Richardson had lied when she admitted she had bombed both public houses and that she had in fact only bombed one. The Attorney General had then said this was 'deliberate disinformation by the gang – a new counter-interrogation technique by IRA terrorists.' Alastair Logan commented that, in practice, the IRA were given to saying exactly what they had done themselves, without mentioning anyone else, or nothing at all.

The programme then reviewed at length the affair of the Balcombe Street gang – or London ASU (Active Service Unit) as they were called. They surrendered in December 1975 – three months after the end of the Guildford Four trial – and were themselves on trial in January 1977. Those who surrendered at Balcombe Street were Joseph O'Connell, Edward Butler, Harry Duggan and Hugh Doherty. Brendan Dowd, arrested earlier in Manchester, had been a member of the London ASU at the time Guildford and Woolwich were bombed. In court they all declared their membership of the IRA. O'Connell, Butler, Duggan and Dowd all said they bombed Woolwich; O'Connell and Dowd said they had bombed Guildford with another man and two girls, all unnamed because they had not yet been arrested, and none of the Guildford Four was present. The programme said they had carried out, undetected, in the 18 months before they were arrested some 50 major terrorist offences – 7 London bombs in a single night, 19 deaths, 3 kidnappings, 9 shootings and incalculable damage. They all lived undercover lives in safe houses away from the Irish community. They were dedicated, professional terrorists. Significantly, the bombing campaigns in London and the Home Counties, which included Guildford and Woolwich in 1974, came to an end when the Balcombe Street ASU were arrested in December 1975. They were convicted in February 1977.

Alastair Logan then described the steps he had taken in October 1976 to obtain from the Balcombe Street ASU, who were still in prison prior to their trial, information that only they would know[1]. They had to be interviewed by somebody who had no connection with the case at all, and also in circumstances where they also had no connection with those who had been convicted of the Guildford offence.

As far as Guildford was concerned the programme gave several examples of statements by Dowd and O'Connell which would support, if not confirm, their presence at Guildford. They had hired a car for the journey from Swan National and this was checked by the police. Dowd spoke of two elderly men with shopping bags waiting in the Horse and Groom for a bus. There had in fact been two elderly men in the pub but this was not thought to be of sufficient relevance to be raised at the trial. O'Connell described a soldier in the Seven Stars asking him about the time of the last bus back to Aldershot. A statement from that soldier describing that conversation was in the unused evidence retained by the police. Consequently, Dowd and O'Connell would have had no way of knowing about the elderly men or the soldier without having been at Guildford themselves. Alastair Logan said that they were both able to pinpoint with absolute accuracy where the bombs were planted, how they were made up, what they contained by way of material, timing devices and detonators, the weight of the bombs, how they left the public house, where they went to and who got back first.

All four of the ASU were able to give similarly convincing details about the Woolwich bomb, though Dowd's account of the dummy run on the previous night varied slightly from the others. In all matters of substance the accounts were similar. The programme made the point that RARDE had said that the Woolwich bomb, which was a throw bomb with coach bolts, was similar to others used in explosions known to have been carried out by the Balcombe Street ASU. They had previously prepared a statement of incidents revealing this. However, for the trial of the Balcombe Street ASU, they had been told to remove Woolwich from the statement. This order had come from the Bomb Squad following instructions from the Director of Public Prosecutions.

Speaking of the Guildford and Woolwich bombings, James Still, former Chief Superintendent, who conducted the interviews, said to camera:

> I was satisfied that they were the four people who committed the offences and I took statements which were as long as they could possibly be – several pages of them – getting them to describe details of the scene, the cars they travelled in, methods of making the bomb, methods of leaving the bomb, and as a result I believe

[1]See Chapter One, page 7

> I got as much detail as I could possibly have got from them, and which they could not have transferred one to the other. I did not think that people of that calibre could give me the details that they gave unless they had been personally concerned with what they had done. If a person had been scripted to act the part I don't believe they could have given all the answers and all the details these people had given – and not from imagination. It would have to have been from experience. I personally was satisfied in my mind that Dowd and O'Connell were the persons who had been concerned with the Guildford bombing with others who were not in custody.

In spite of their admissions, the Balcombe Street ASU were never charged with the Guildford and Woolwich bombings – the Guildford Four had been convicted of these three months before the Balcombe Street arrests. The account of the bombings they had provided to Alastair Logan and James Still in October 1976, more extensively recorded in the TV programme than above, was not used by the prosecution at their own trial in which they were convicted in February 1977. That information was to form the basis of the appeal by the Guildford Four which was heard in October 1977.

In the last section the programme highlighted some of the main points which came out of the appeal. The crown and the judges finally accepted that Joseph O'Connell, Harry Duggan and Edward Butler had indeed bombed Woolwich. The Court was also content to assume that O'Connell and Dowd had been at Guildford. However this was not enough to free the Guildford Four because of apparent errors in Dowd's evidence about the dummy run the previous evening. The programme then listed them:

> Dowd said the gang assembled in Knightsbridge, but the others had said Sloane Square.
>
> Dowd said the car was a Corsair – the others a Cortina.
>
> Dowd said he had stayed in the car at Woolwich – the others said he had got out.
>
> Dowd said the car had been abandoned north of the river, the others said south of the river.

At this point Alastair Logan intervened to say that the apparent confusions by Dowd were no doubt accounted for by the fact he had just come out of two and a quarter years in solitary confinement. In any event he added – 'the confusions were very minor and did not affect the substance of what he had to say – and it was the substance of what he had to say that could not be attacked by the Court of Appeal.' The programme cited Lord Roskill who had said that Dowd was a deplorable witness and that the whole thing was a cunning plot to free the Guildford Four. The Court took Dowd's errors as proof that he was lying. Yet, as the programme said, they had accepted the errors in the statements of the Guildford Four. Having condemned Dowd as a liar, the judges said the others must have lied about Dowd and, as liars, no credence should be given to their evidence.

However, everything was not entirely straightforward. The programme went on to say that, while it was accepted members of the Balcombe Street gang had been at Guildford and Woolwich, there had been no explanation by the Crown as to how the Guildford Four could still have been involved. Specifically, as it had been accepted that Brendan Dowd had been at Guildford, how could Patrick Armstrong have been there when, after their extremely thorough detective work, the police had said there was only one man they had been unable to trace in the Horse and Groom? No evidence was produced at any stage to link any of the Guildford Four with any of the Balcombe Street ASU. Yet the appeal failed. There would be no retrial and so the new evidence would not be heard by a jury because 'there was no lurking doubt.'

At the end of the programme the two politicians made their concluding points. Lord Fitt said – 'I know there will be great opposition from members of the establishment, particularly in the Home Office, who will not want to admit that an error was made in the convictions of those individuals. I believe that would be a very wrong attitude to take.'

Merlyn Rees gave his final thoughts:

> I think the time has come to look again at the legislation and at the procedures to have a broader basis rather than a narrow question – is there new evidence? I suspect there is more than new evidence in the strict judicial sense of the term that ought to be able to be taken into account by the Home Secretary.
>
> . . . There may be people in jail for long periods – for life – who should not be there. And therefore it raises doubts in my mind – doubts – but doubts are good enough to look at these cases again.

The Guildford Time Bomb was a powerful and courageous programme. It made a considerable impact. It fortified in their pursuit of justice those who were concerned there could have been a miscarriage of justice. It raised in the minds of many others, including the general public, doubts as to whether justice could be seen to have been done.

The day after its screening the Home Secretary announced there was to be an internal Home Office review of the Guildford Four case. Presumably this was to be based on all the points made in the TV programme, and consideration would also be given to the reports by Dr James MacKeith and Dr Gisli Gudjonsson on Carole Richardson which the Home Secretary had received in April. No indication was given as to when the outcome of the review would be announced.

There was a seminal event in October 1986 – the publication by Robert Kee of his book *Trial and Error*, which served as a reinforcing platform for those with an interest in ensuring that justice must be seen to be done. Cardinal Hume was to say – 'This book articulates the serious anxieties I and many others have had about a possible miscarriage of justice, not only in the Maguire case but also in the convictions in the Guildford bombings trial.'

The Maguire Seven had been convicted solely on the scientific evidence, the Guildford Four solely on their confessions. In both cases the defendants had made allegations of improper methods of interrogation. In both cases these allegations were refuted by the police, and the denials had been accepted by the jury and the judge. Towards the end of his book Robert Kee identified an important difference between the cases:

> . . . It lies in the fact that the allegations [of police wrong doing] made in the Maguire trial were of no material relevance to the defence . . . what they said under interrogation formed no significant part of the case against them. Re-investigation of the case of the Maguire Seven does not therefore immediately involve any need to reopen one highly sensitive area of evidence. This may spare the Home Secretary certain immediate difficulties.

The Home Office had resolutely resisted suggestions that there should be a re-assessment by independent scientists of the forensic evidence which convicted the Maguire Seven. As to the Guildford Four, their supporters had hitherto been unable to assemble what the Home Office would consider 'new evidence or consideration of substance'. The combination of the TV programme *The Guildford Time Bomb* and Robert Kee's book brought home forcibly to those concerned about the cases the urgent need to leave no stone unturned in seeking ways to advance the cause. When Robert Kee presented a copy of his book to Cardinal Hume, they discussed possible ways forward. The Cardinal said there were many groups at grass roots level, such as 'Free the Guildford Four', doing good work but none of these efforts was likely to result in a referral back to the Court of Appeal by the Home Secretary. There was a need now for operations at a higher level. It so happened that a sequence of events which would facilitate all this was about to unfold.

On 7 October, 1986 Lord Scarman wrote to *The Times*:

> You are clearly right in commenting (third leader, October 2) that prosecuting in England and Wales has now undergone a sea change.
>
> Some of us wonder, however, whether the process of criminal trial and appeal is even yet sufficiently supported by our pre-trial procedures. Until the recent reforms introduced by the Police and Criminal Evidence Act 1984 there was in our system a dangerously low level of supervision of the processes of arrest, interrogation, and charge. Even today the critical phase, interrogation, is in reality conducted and supervised only by the police within a police station.
>
> The trial and appeal process, which is open and judicial, has shown itself an uncertain instrument for uncovering irregularities, and worse, in the pre-trial process. And judges, confronted at trial for the first time with medical or scientific evidence, have not always been able to detect its weaknesses.
>
> There is in our pre-trial procedures even today fertile ground for the development of injustice which can, and sometimes does, escape detection during the subsequent trial and appeal process. The Confait[2] case, to which you refer, is a good example: and there would appear to be grounds for querying the justice of the convictions in the Guildford bombing case and in the Maguire explosives case.
>
> These cases were under the old law. Can we be sure that the reforms in police procedure and in prosecution will suffice? I am not sure. Meanwhile, let us consider the possibility of judicial control of the pre-trial process, as in France and other civil law countries.
>
> The cry of 'inquisition' will go up. Maybe, however, an inquisition process in the control of a judge is the logical conclusion to the welcome reforms of the last few years.

A follow-up letter from Cardinal Hume was published by *The Times* on 10 October, 1986:

> We are indebted to Lord Scarman (October 7) for drawing attention to the shortcomings of pre-trial procedures prior to the recent reforms introduced by the Police and Criminal Evidence Act 1984.

[2]Maxwell Confait was murdered and three young men were convicted. In 1976 another view on the time of death came to light. The case was referred to the Court of Appeal by Roy Jenkins, then Home Secretary, under the alternative approach to the Court of a 'consideration of substance' which he had instigated. The sentences were quashed.

He adds that the trial and appeal process has shown itself 'an uncertain instrument' in uncovering irregularities.

This undoubtedly widens anxieties over the convictions in the Guildford bombings and the Maguire explosives cases to both of which Lord Scarman drew attention. My concern in this matter arose first from my contact with Patrick Joseph Conlon whom I visited on a number of occasions in Wormwood Scrubs before his death in 1980. I became absolutely convinced of his innocence and because of that had developed profound doubts about the justice of the Maguire convictions.

Since 1978 I have raised this matter with three different Home Secretaries, both Labour and Conservative, and with the Prime Minister herself.

Robert Kee's book *Trial and Error* articulates the serious anxieties I and many others have had about a possible miscarriage of justice not only in the Maguire case but also in the convictions in the Guildford bombings trial.

I would strongly urge that in the interests of justice the Home Secretary should exercise the rights available to him under Section 17 of the Criminal Appeals Act 1968 whereby 'if he thinks fit' he can refer such cases back to the Court of Appeal.

On 10 October, 1986, the same day as Cardinal Hume's letter was published, *The Times* ran a first leader – 'On Dubious Evidence' – covering the case of the Maguire Seven. Those who had been pursuing justice from before the time when Giuseppe Conlon died while serving his sentence, nearly seven years earlier, would have found themselves in full accord with the observation in the leader that 'wrongful convictions have a habit of forcing themselves on to public attention time and again; rightful convictions, even if at first hotly contested, generally fade from public memory with the passing of time.'

The leader then highlighted three reasons why this particular case was all the more disturbing, and all the more difficult for the Home Secretary:

the Maguire Seven were all convicted on a single strand of scientific evidence which destroyed the samples

although the Guildford Four and Maguire Seven cases were technically separate, there was a close relationship in that, following a tip-off, Mrs Maguire's home was believed by the police to be the factory from which the Guildford bomb came. Add to this the claim by the Balcombe Street ASU that they were responsible for Guildford. If the Guildford convictions were wrong, where does

> this leave the Maguire convictions? Grave doubts arise when the cases are looked at together which could not be done by a court but may need a special inquiry outside the formal processes of the courts
>
> however, some of the reasons for questioning the course of justice in these cases, although convincing, have no value as strict evidence –constant claims of innocence; pattern of behaviour after convictions as compared to that of known IRA terrorists; insistent disowning by the IRA.

The leader concluded that, while these reasons would not justify overturning the convictions, rather than further appeals the Home Secretary might consider the appointment of a senior lawyer to investigate and report upon all the aspects and interrelationships of the worrying Maguire Seven case.

By now Roy Jenkins, former Home Secretary from 1965 to 67 and 1974 to 76, was in touch with Lord Scarman, Cardinal Hume and Robert Kee. Merlyn Rees had already publicly expressed his doubts and concerns in *The Guildford Time Bomb*. Lord Devlin had earlier raised his concern about the outcome of the Guildford Four appeal in 1977 and, on 15 October, 1986, he, too, wrote a letter to *The Times*:

> Cardinal Hume's letter (October 10) and the leader in *The Times* which accompanies it are of clarion quality.
>
> I have seen only a little of the material in the Maguire and Guildford cases in which convictions were obtained for revolting acts of terrorism, but enough to make me doubt whether the right men were caught.
>
> In the Guildford case an IRA gang subsequently claimed sole responsibility for the crime. Their evidence was heard by the Court of Appeal, which had power either to reject it out of hand as beyond belief or to order a new trial by jury of the whole case. Instead of this they treated it as an issue which they had had power to determine themselves and which they decided against the accused. Thus what was truly an indivisible case was tried in two parts, one by a jury and the other by judges.
>
> The authority for this extraordinary procedure is said to be the decision by the House of Lords in Stafford v DPP (1974) (AC870). In a lecture at All Souls (now printed in The Judge, OUP (1979), p178) I criticized this decision as contrary to all earlier law and expressed the hope that the House would some day look at the point again. If there has been any rebuttal of my criticism, I have not seen it.

> So I welcome the Cardinal's request that these cases should be referred back to the Court of Appeal. But there is more to it than this.
>
> Protestations of innocence by prisoners are common enough. Support for them by distinguished persons is not unknown. But the total effect must be mountainous before it can command attention.
>
> Here it is as high as Everest. It has been tested by a number of others besides the Cardinal himself. It is strengthened by all the other considerations mentioned in your leader. It confronts what on paper looks to be a weak case.
>
> None of this can be admitted and weighed by a court of law. But to do justice in every individual case is sometimes beyond the reach of the law: it is the very thing that in the last resort the royal prerogative is fashioned to attain.

The whole matter of possible miscarriages of justice was now rapidly gaining momentum. On 4 November, 1986 Channel 4 TV screened a programme *Beyond Reasonable Doubt.* The programme opened with a short appearance by Lord Scarman in which, speaking of the Guildford Four and Maguire Seven cases, he said:

> It certainly looks possible that there has been injustice done to some or all of the defendants in the two cases. I choose my words carefully because the whole matter requires investigation.

The programme went on to say one of the most sensitive issues facing the British legal and political establishment was the contention that no less than 17 people convicted of terrorism and bombings in IRA cases dating back to 1974 were in fact wholly innocent – that the police and the courts had got the wrong people, and that the real bombers had escaped detection. This was in reference to the Guildford Four, the Maguire Seven and the Birmingham Six. The programme then said that three earlier films on television (*Aunt Annie's Bomb Factory*, *The Guildford Time Bomb*, both on the *First Tuesday* series of Yorkshire Television, and a World in Action film on the Birmingham Six), had prompted the Home Office to announce reviews of the three cases. In concluding the opening remarks the programme said updated versions of the three films would be shown and these would be followed by a discussion on the options open to the Home Secretary and the political considerations. Taking part in the discussion were Sir Edward Gardner QC MP, Ludovic Kennedy, Christopher Price MP, Clive Soley MP and Mary Robinson (as a senior counsel of the Irish bar before she became President of Ireland).

In introducing the discussion the programme said that they had invited the Home Office to discuss these cases but unfortunately none of the Ministers was available. They did however receive this statement:

> 'All three cases are being carefully reviewed by the Home Secretary in order to determine whether there is any action which he should properly take in respect of the convictions.
>
> The Home Secretary is well aware of the concerns which have been expressed about the safety of the convictions and will of course take this fully into account.

The programme added that the Home Office review of the Birmingham Six case had been announced in October 1985, that on the Guildford Four on 2 July, 1986, and on the Maguire Seven in September 1986.

During the discussion some of the main points made were:

> Even allowing for the fact people were outraged at the offence, that there were feelings of anger, and that the need to get someone as soon as possible was strong, most had no doubt there had been miscarriages of justice.
>
> A most convincing thing the law does not take into account is the kind of letters those who had been convicted have written, also the kind of things they say to their solicitors, and to visiting people. These were all enormously impressive. Guilty people do not go on year after year protesting their innocence.
>
> If the cases were referred to the Court of Appeal it would probably be unlikely that the reputation of the judiciary would be damaged but not so that of the police.
>
> In all the cases, particularly where forensic evidence was concerned, the police deluded themselves into thinking on the short evidence they had got the right people. A recent survey of miscarriages of justice showed that in 90% of the cases police delusion played a part.
>
> It is vital we get away from the police doing these investigations unless they are under the supervision, as they are in France, of a legal neutral figure – the juge d'instruction.
>
> In the Confait case there were confessions and forensic evidence and three young men were convicted. There was no 'new evidence' but the first trial had not been sensibly conducted especially with

regard to expert evidence. This gave rise to the new term 'consideration of substance' so enabling a retrial. The defendants were acquitted.

The view was that in the three cases considered in the two books and three films there were 'massive areas' which constitute 'considerations of substance.'

From past experience, rather than a referral back to the Court of Appeal, the cases should be the subject of an inquiry by a judge with two lay assessors.

Although the Home Office might be expected 'to be the first to leap to set right an injustice' they tend to resist. A distinguished solicitor had said he did not know of a single case of miscarriage of justice to have been originated by the Home Office.

There was an urgent need to set up an independent review body as had been recommended by the Home Affairs Committee in April 1983 but was not accepted by the Government.

Two of the responses to a last quick question as to what should be done now were

> The Home Office should 'do something next week and not wait six months.'
>
> Delay defeats justice. The Home Office 'should not try the details of the book but should take a decision to take steps in the matter.'

On 15 January, 1987 Cardinal Hume wrote again to the Prime Minister, Mrs Thatcher, referring to the two books *Trial and Error* and *Error of Judgement* (about the Birmingham case), several television programmes, and leaders and feature articles in responsible newspapers. He explained that he was in touch with Lord Scarman and Roy Jenkins and they were all disturbed by press reports about the possibility of action being taken only on the Birmingham case. He went on to say:

> All three of us hold the view that the interests of British justice might not be best served by such action and, indeed, it might be detrimental to that justice which we all want to see upheld.
>
> We consider that, on all counts, the most satisfactory way forward, rather than reference of the Birmingham case alone to the Court of Appeal, would be for all three cases together to be referred

> to a Senior Judge heading an ad hoc committee consisting possibly in addition, of two eminent laymen.

Cardinal Hume concluded by saying that they would welcome an opportunity to discuss the matter with her, and that he was sending a copy of the letter to the Home Secretary. In her reply the Prime Minister declined the request for a meeting saying – 'Allegations of miscarriages of justice in particular cases are not customarily matters in which I have a role, nor are they discussed by Ministers collectively. They are personal decisions for the Home Secretary of the day.'

There can be no doubt that *Beyond Reasonable Doubt* added to the momentum of the cause. It increased even further the number of people with doubts and concerns about the cases. On 7 January, 1987 an all party delegation of MPs and Peers pressed the Home Secretary to review the Guildford, Maguire and Birmingham cases. But on 20 January the Home Secretary, Douglas Hurd, made a statement in Parliament which came as a relief to some but a bombshell to others. He had decided to refer the Birmingham Six case to the Court of Appeal, but not the Guildford Four or the Maguire Seven cases. Robert Kee reflected the views of many when, writing in *The Times* on 22 January, he said:

> In agreeing at last to reopen the case of the six Irishmen apparently wrongly imprisoned for 12 years for the 1974 Birmingham pub bombings, the Home Secretary may seem to have done something to help maintain the high standard of British justice.
>
> But by refusing to reopen the cases of the four people serving life sentences the Guildford pub bombings of the same year, and of the seven members of the Maguire household jailed in the aftermath, he has dealt it a damaging blow.

The Home Secretary gave an oral statement to the House and supplemented this by placing in the library two Home Office memoranda in amplification of his decision not to refer the Guildford Four and Maguire Seven cases. He had sent copies of these to Cardinal Hume on the morning of 20 January.

It was not long after this that two distinguished former Home Secretaries, Roy Jenkins and Merlyn Rees, and two of probably the greatest Law Lords of the twentieth century, Lord Devlin and Lord Scarman, all came together with Cardinal Hume, each of their own volition and for their own reasons, to form what came to be known as the 'Deputation'. They were all convinced it was very likely that there had been a miscarriage of justice in the Guildford Four and Maguire Seven cases.

The first task to be undertaken by Archbishop's House at this stage was to assemble all the material required to enable an assessment to be made of the position of the two cases. Inevitably, this included examination of the oral statement by the Home Secretary on 20 January, 1987 and of the accompanying Home Office memoranda.

3

THE ASSESSMENT (1)

THE TWO cases of the Guildford Four and the Maguire Seven, in fact, started as one. Following interrogation the police obtained from the Guildford Four – Paul Hill, Gerard Conlon, Patrick Armstrong and Carole Richardson – confessions that they had taken part in the Guildford bombings. They were charged with terrorist murder. During interrogation Paul Hill and Gerard Conlon also implicated four others in the bombings – Anne Maguire, Brian Anderson, Paul Colman and John McGuinness. They, too, were charged with murder. However, they all resolutely refused to confess and continued to deny all knowledge of the bombings as, indeed, the Guildford Four had originally done.

Some three months later, as there was no other evidence that they had been at Guildford, apart from what the police had obtained from Paul Hill and Gerard Conlon, which in the absence of confessions could not constitute evidence, the murder charges against the four others had to be dropped. Brian Anderson, Paul Colman and John McGuinness were released, but not so Anne Maguire. She was told she would now be charged with unlawful possession of an explosive because, according to the Government laboratory at Woolwich, there were traces of nitroglycerine on a plastic glove which the police had collected from her house on 4 December, 1974. This was the day after they had also arrested Giuseppe Conlon, Paddy Maguire, Pat O'Neill and Sean Smyth for unlawful possession of nitroglycerine. On the day of the arrests, 3 December, 1974, trained explosives officers, police dogs and a hand-held 'sniffer' device had failed to detect any traces of nitroglycerine in the house or on Anne Maguire's plastic gloves. On 24 February 1975 the murder charge against her finally had to be dropped but, on the same day, the police arrested and charged her two sons, Vincent and Patrick, for unlawfully handling explosives on the strength of the swab tests taken three months earlier. Thus the one case became two trials, one of the Guildford Four for murder, and the other of the Maguire Seven for unlawful possession of nitroglycerine.

Towards the end of 1986, following publication of *Trial and Error* and the showing of the television programmes *The Guildford Time Bomb* and *Beyond Reasonable Doubt*, the Deputation gave further thought to the factors identifying possible miscarriages of justice. The danger signals emerged as:

> Persistent challenging of 'confession' evidence.
>
> Continuing protests of innocence.
>
> Ill-match of the character of the crime and the accused.
>
> New evidence or matters of substance – others committed the offence, alibis.
>
> Suppression or omission of evidence for the defence.
>
> Substantial points of law.

In the introduction to his oral statement to Parliament on 20 January, 1987, before dealing with specific cases, the Home Secretary, Douglas Hurd, said:

> Over the years all kinds of changes may come to alter the view which some people may take of a particular case. The enormity of the crime committed may cease to dominate the scene; those convicted may continue to protest their innocence; police procedures may be improved; new scientific tests may be developed; individuals may write books or produce television programmes which summarise days or weeks of evidence in a way which reflects their genuine conviction that the verdict was wrong or open to considerable doubt: as a result a body of distinguished opinion may grow up to the same effect. *All that has happened here*. (Home Secretary's emphasis).

The same emphasis could be accorded to the danger signals listed above.

The Home Secretary went on to say:

> A different situation arises of course if new evidence or some new consideration of substance is produced which was not available at trial or before the Court of Appeal. In any civilised system of justice there must be a means whereby a case can be reopened so that new matters can be assessed alongside the old evidence by due process of law.

Seemingly for the first time for eight years, since the case of Giuseppe Conlon was first taken up, the word 'new' was introduced to qualify 'consideration of substance.'

Towards the end of his introduction the Home Secretary said:

> . . . this House and the public would rightly become deeply suspicious of a convention which enabled politicians to throw a verdict into doubt simply because they had developed, *without any fresh evidence*, (Home Secretary's emphasis) a view that the verdict may have been mistaken . . .
>
> I believe that my predecessors were right to take a principled view of the circumstances in which it is proper to exercise the power of reference to the Court of Appeal. After much thought I mean to follow them.

The announcement that he would be referring the case of the Birmingham Six to the Court of Appeal was well received, but not so the decision not to refer the Guildford Four and Maguire Seven cases. The press were distinctly critical and some suggested there was an element of 'politics' in the decisions because they thought the circumstantial evidence in the Guildford and Maguire cases viewed in the round was, in fact, stronger than that in the Birmingham Six case. The fact that no jury had been given an opportunity to pronounce on the evidence of the Balcombe Street ASU came in for particular criticism. Reference was also made in the press to alterations to statements of offences whereby the police had instructed the scientists to omit the Guildford and Woolwich bombings from the list attributable to the Balcombe Street ASU. It was noted, too, that the Home Secretary did not accept that the scientific evidence in the Maguire Seven case could be faulty, and some said he had deliberately fettered his own powers so as to prevent an avalanche of cases.

The Home Secretary had concluded his statement by saying he had placed in the Libraries of both Houses Home Office memoranda on the Guildford Four and Maguire Seven cases which set out in greater detail the reasons for his decisions. It would be appropriate here to recall some of the provisions of the Criminal Appeal Act 1968. Under Section 17 of the Act, the Home Secretary is empowered to send back to the Court of Appeal 'if he thinks fit' a case which has already been heard in the prescribed manner. There are no qualifications or reservations. Perhaps for understandable reasons, successive Home Secretaries have used as a yardstick for considering cases for referral whether or not there is 'new evidence.' The criminal justice system is operated by humans and therefore fallible. Thus it was inevitable, though possibly on rare and exceptional occasions, that cases would arise in which it was questionable whether justice would be done, and would be seen to be done, if there was total and inflexible adherence to the 'new evidence' proviso which was, in fact, a self-imposed restriction – a procedure whereby, as Lord Scarman would say, 'an administrative rule of practice is elevated into a 'principle''.

Such a case was to arise in 1975, fairly soon after the passing of the Act. This was the Confait case, already mentioned, in which three very young men had been found guilty of murder in 1973, solely on the basis of their confessions. In 1974 a second opinion arose as to the time of death of the victim. This was not strictly new evidence because the time of death had been a central issue at the trial. To accommodate this problem, in 1976 Roy Jenkins, then Home Secretary, introduced an alternative condition for reference to the Court of Appeal – 'a consideration of substance.' His action was entirely vindicated by Lord Scarman's judgement at the Court of Appeal. Lord Scarman did not reject Crown Counsel's submission that the grounds of appeal were inadmissible under the clause in the 1968 Act governing new evidence, but he referred back to the 1907 Appeal Act, making the point that the court had discretion to hear any evidence at all if it served 'the interests of justice.' The Confait convictions were quashed. There was a later judgement by Lord Diplock in 1983 in which he made clear that it is 'the whole case' that is to be referred to the Court of Appeal, that 'this must include all facts and law involved in it, and that cogent arguments not properly developed at the previous hearing would be relevant for the court's consideration.'

It is not clear from the two Home Office memoranda – on the Guildford Four and Maguire Seven cases – which accompanied the Home Secretary's oral statement, whether or not account was taken in these two cases of the origin of 'consideration of substance', and of the judgements of Lord Scarman and Lord Diplock. Certainly there is no reference to the two judgements, fulfilment of which could well have served 'the interests of justice.' As to a 'consideration of substance', as illustrated by the Confait case, in the memoranda the Home Office went through representations which had been made to them point by point, arguing that each representation on its own did not amount to a 'consideration of substance.' Such a treatment ignored the basic fact that there were so many points of representation that, taken together, they formed compelling 'considerations of substance.' Bearing in mind the Confait case, the question arises whether, by the insertion of the word 'new' before 'consideration of substance', the Home Secretary was now seeking to establish a different interpretation of the term.

The memoranda listed the main points that had been made in the various representations the Home Office had received, and then commented on each in turn. By and large the selected main representations were reasonably presented, but the same cannot be said of several of the 'comments'. Some people considered that the general tone reflected the philosophy that where difficult and disturbing doubts over the previous verdicts arose they could be resolved by reaffirming the previous verdicts. Others thought there was a tendency in places to reassess evidence in a light confirmatory of the court's decisions. There was also recourse to the argument that because a defence point had been considered by the jury, and found wanting, there was no cause for it to be considered afresh.

In short, some of the many people outside the Home Office who considered the cases should be looked at again thought that certain 'comments' could be described as tendentious and misleading, and also that others were incomplete or not wholly accurate in places. The Home Office memoranda were understandably designed to support the decisions that had been taken. Another approach would have been to list the representations which had been made, then to draft the document in a form whereby, in a patently objective fashion, all possible 'considerations of substance' were identified, carefully considered and evaluated. They could then be selected for acceptance or rejected. Those accepted, when taken in the round, could well have led to different decisions being made.

It is extraordinary that, in drafting the two Home Office memoranda, officials do not appear to have consulted any of the solicitors acting for the Guildford Four or the Maguire Seven at the time. If they had consulted Alastair Logan about the Guildford Four case, he would certainly have reminded them, amongst other things, of the reports by Dr J MacKeith and Dr G Gudjonsson on Carole Richardson.[1] The reports, which had been requested by the Home Office, were prepared by the two doctors after they had interviewed and examined Carole Richardson on 30 April 1986. As already recorded, at the end of his report Dr MacKeith stated – 'I conclude that the statements that resulted in her conviction on the several charges were very probably unreliable.' The reports were submitted to the Home Office in May 1986. Seven months later, in December 1986, one month before the memorandum on the Guildford case was drafted, the Home Office gave Dr MacKeith permission to send a copy of the reports to Alastair Logan.

In his covering letter Dr MacKeith stated – 'I have profound doubts about whether the statements given by Carole Richardson to the police were voluntary and whether the self-incriminating contents were reliable.'

There can be no doubt that if the reports by the two doctors had

[1]Chapter Two – pages 30 to 33

been available and known to the jury at the trial in 1975 there would certainly have been a 'lurking doubt' about her guilt. It is inexplicable that not only was there no reference whatsoever to the reports in the Home Office memorandum on the Guildford Four, but also that in the preparatory stages they were apparently not even identified as 'a consideration of substance.' No reason was offered for the omission. Collapse of the case against Carole Richardson would, of course, have brought into question the convictions of the rest of the Guildford Four because they had all implicated each other in their confessions, later retracted, which were riddled with self-contradictions and contradictions of each other's statements.

There were examples of statements in the CASE SUMMARY section of the Guildford memorandum which were incomplete or not wholly accurate. It is implied that Paul Hill's admission of complicity in the murder of Brian Shaw (an ex-soldier in Northern Ireland) came after the confessions on Guildford. In fact it was the other way round, the sequence being important when examining his possible motivation for the Guildford confession. It is stated that the Court of Appeal rejected the evidence of the Balcombe Street ASU as 'a cunning and skilful attempt to deceive the Court by putting forward false evidence.' In fact, the Court was 'content to assume that O'Connell had been at Guildford and that Dowd may have been there.' The reference by the Court to 'false evidence' was in relation to the Balcombe Street gang's denial of any knowledge of the Guildford Four and not to their own presence at Guildford.

In an early section of the Home Office memorandum covering arrests and confessions, it is stated that it was known by security forces in Northern Ireland from as early as 29 August, 1974 that Paul Hill had gone to England to carry out bombings. But there is no reference to any surveillance of him during the time between his arrival in England and his arrest on 28 November, 1974 which was some seven weeks after the Guildford bombings. No explanation is offered for this. Dealing with Paul Hill's motives for confessing, one 'comment' is – 'The question posed by the judge was why, if Hill had confessed to the Guildford bombings to save his girlfriend, did he also confess to the Woolwich offence when she was clearly not involved? . . .' The question was unanswered by the judge, but Paul Hill probably confessed to Woolwich because the police wanted him to. If, as Paul Hill had alleged, his girlfriend was threatened with arrest the threat would have covered everything the police wanted from him. His girlfriend was clearly not involved in either bombing.

On the unlikelihood of the Guildford Four being suitable candidates as IRA bombers the 'comment' is – 'The fact that some people may think it unlikely, on the grounds of his or her character, that a particular person could ever have been involved in a crime of which he or she has been convicted is not an *evidential* point' (Home Office emphasis). That may be so, but it is certainly circumstantial and its importance is further enhanced by the absence of any hard evidence other than the retracted confessions. There are also further important considerations. By 1987, as compared to 1975 when the trial took place, the improbability of such people being recruited as IRA bombers on mainland Britain was a much more overwhelming consideration, particularly in the light of the arrest of the Balcombe Street ASU. These were sufficiently highly professional, dedicated terrorists to be used by the IRA and the Guildford Four bore no resemblance to them. Moreover, in all the IRA operations after 1974, no drug-addicts, squatters, or people known to the police were identified as having taken part in bombing operations other than the Guildford Four. Coupled with other matters, this could well have constituted a 'consideration of substance' – or even a 'cogent' argument under the Diplock judgement.

Still under the heading of 'Unlikely Candidates for IRA bombers', there was only one reference to Paul Hill. The comment is – 'Hill was convicted, while on remand in respect of the Guildford charges, of the murder of Brian Shaw, a British ex-soldier, in Belfast in 1974.' In drawing this to the attention of MPs and Peers in this way it was invidious for the Home Office to omit key facts of the case. Paul Hill had pleaded not guilty, there was no evidence against him other than his retracted confession, and the judge had explicitly stated that he had not pulled the trigger. He was said to be an accomplice to a killing. Details of his precise role in the affair are not known but, in the circumstances, it is questionable to present his position baldly as having been 'convicted of murder.'

As regards Patrick Armstrong and Carole Richardson, it had been represented to the Home Office that two weeks after the Guildford bombings they went on a 10-day hitch-hiking holiday during which they went to Folkstone police station to report that she had been assaulted by a drunk. They both gave their correct names and addresses. It was extremely improbable that two people who had carried out murder on the Guildford scale, and who must have known there was a nationwide search for the culprits, would have contacted the police in such a way over a minor incident.

The response by the Home Office is remarkable:

> The comments made about Armstrong and Richardson's action in seeking help from the police assume that people always behave in what others would regard as a rational and logical manner.
>
> . . . In relation to the hitch-hiking incident it appears that Armstrong had reason to get away from the squat because he was being

threatened by two men to whom he had failed to supply drugs for which they had paid.

There are two aspects of the second sentence. The first is that it is misleading in that it is not the 'getting away from the squat' which is the relevant consideration, but the fact that Patrick Armstrong and Carole Richardson were actually anxious to contact the police. The second is more serious. It would appear that the Home Office assumes that, if it is true, someone who failed to supply drugs to other people for payment would be a likely candidate as an IRA bomber.

One comment on the effects of drugs is – 'Richardson was examined on the evening of 4 December. The doctor found her to be in an hysterical state. She told him she was addicted to LSD and tuinal. By the end of the examination he found her to be calm and gave her a tuinal tablet.' Her interrogation had continued beyond 4 December. The reliance seemingly placed by the Home Office on this comment about Carole Richardson is questionable, particularly in the light of Dr MacKeith's views on the adequacy of the police doctor's assessment. Dr MacKeith's report had been in the Home Office since May 1986, well before the Home Secretary's decision. That report throws a very different light on the circumstances surrounding Carole Richardson's confession as presented to the jury at the trial in 1975 and, as such, must surely have constituted a consideration of substance, if not alone then in conjunction with other matters.

As to the circumstances in which the statements of all of the Guildford Four had been obtained, it had been represented to the Home Office that they were made as a result of assault, abuse and threats by the police. It had also been represented that, because of the circumstances in which the statements were made, they would not be admissible in evidence today. The Home Office response is that the Home Secretary noted in his oral statement that the whole question of the manner in which the statements had been obtained was aired before the courts, including the allegations of abuse, threats and assault by the police. In a later comment, after referring to the judge's summing up, the Home Office states – 'The general point about the possibility of false confessions was therefore clearly and specifically brought to the jury's attention.'

Some considerations arise from all this. It is interesting to note that allegations about improper behaviour by the police had also arisen in the case of the Birmingham Six. The Home Secretary did not confirm to Parliament in his own oral statement – nor was it confirmed in the Home Office memorandum – that in the course of the review assurances had been obtained from the Surrey Police that not a single instance of impropriety had occurred. The police officers concerned had denied at the trial there were any improprieties but, as was observed at the time, they would do that anyway. Amongst those who had been named in public as having allegedly behaved improperly were Assistant Chief Constable Rowe, Detective Chief Superintendent Simmons, Detective Chief Inspector Style, Detective Chief Inspector Longhurst, Detective Sergeant Donaldson, Detective Constable Attwell and Detective Constable Wise. There appears to be no record of any of them suing for libel.

A more compelling consideration arises over the question of false confessions. Since the trial in 1975, and by 1986, there had been substantial advances made in psychological and psychiatric knowledge about the circumstances of false confessions. Dr MacKeith and Dr Gudjonsson were amongst the leaders in this field and their report on Carole Richardson was held by the Home Office. These advances had reformed the circumstances in which confessions are taken in police custody and are reflected in the Royal Commission on Criminal Evidence and the Police and Criminal Evidence Act of 1984.

Not only this, but the scientific reports of Professor Haward and Barry Irving of the Police Foundation, both of whom had considered the case of Patrick Armstrong, were available to the Home Office.[2] In the memorandum the Home Office conceded that since 1974 the police had been advised that suspects apparently suffering from the effects of drink or drugs should not be questioned in the absence of legal representation.

It is then stated – 'The fact that this advice has been issued does not invalidate statements taken before that advice came into effect.' It is not clear to what depth all these matters were explored in the Home Office review as officials did not seem to regard them as considerations of substance. At issue was the fact that the Guildford Four were all serving life sentences solely on the basis of uncorroborated confessions obtained under a system which was now acknowledged to be defective.

The Home Office apparently accepted the prosecution argument that the inconsistencies and contradictions in the statements of the Guildford Four were 'the product of a deliberate counter-interrogation technique designed to cause confusion' as contended by Sir Michael Havers at the trial. It would appear that this was a scenario resorted to by the prosecution to account for the contradictory elements in the statements. It also provided them with a vehicle to jettison those parts which did not suit their case. Even if it was true, the question arises whether drug-addicts, squatters and building site labourers could be trained in sophisticated counter-interrogation techniques.

A further question was whether a technique which involved telling

[2]Chapter Two, pages 35 & 36

the truth in part was either sophisticated or a counter-interrogation technique. The Home Office, apparently without further investigation, accepted the contention that the statements were in no way obtained under threat or duress. It remains to be asked why the Guildford Four did not simply deny altogether, rather than engage in 'counter-interrogation', their own presence at Guildford and Woolwich, as did Anne Maguire, John McGuinness, Brian Anderson and Paul Colman. These were all equally accused of being there but the murder charge had to be dropped on the basis of their denials and the lack of any supporting evidence.

Some seven pages, out of 27, of the memorandum on the Guildford Four are devoted to their alibis and, significantly, four and a half of these seven pages cover Carole Richardson's alibis. Carole Richardson's alibi that she had been at the Jack the Lad pop concert at the South Bank Polytechnic was by far the most compelling. Before considering that, Paul Hill's alibi for Woolwich and Gerard Conlon's for Guildford merit a brief reference.

Paul Hill's alibi for Woolwich, 7 November, 1974, was that he worked daily with his uncle, Mr Keenan, and returned to the Keenans' flat at about 6.30 pm. He had supper and watched television. At 9.00 pm he went out to telephone his girlfriend Gina Clarke in Southampton from a public telephone box and returned to the flat between 9.30 pm and 10.00 pm when he watched television again. Mr and Mrs Keenan supported his alibi. The Home Office states that there was disagreement between Mr and Mrs Keenan as to when Paul Hill was with them. That is incorrect – their statements are mutually consistent.

A more important aspect, not examined in the Home Office review, was that the Keenans, a family friend and Paul Hill himself were adamant that he returned to the house well before the News at Ten. The Woolwich bomb was a throw bomb, it exploded at 10.17 pm and was announced on the news at 10.26 pm. The Crown did not attempt to show how Paul Hill could have made the journey from the Keenans' house in Camden to Woolwich and back in the timescale. Moreover, the Court of Appeal accepted the Balcombe Street ASU account of how, after the Woolwich throw bomb, they dumped a stolen Cortina in New Cross and returned to North London by public transport. The possibility that Paul Hill was with them and could have returned to Camden by public transport within the timescale becomes even more implausible. The missing link is that no jury heard the evidence of both the Guildford Four and of the Balcombe Street ASU. Had they done so, the outcome might have been different. None of all this was explored by the Home Office. Their comment on Paul Hill's alibi for Woolwich – 'it was before the jury, it appears they did not accept it.'

As the judge, Mr Justice Donaldson, had pointed out at the trial, it is a normal state of affairs for any given citizen to have difficulty in proving absolutely what his or her movements at a given time might have been after a lapse of seven weeks. This was the root of Gerard Conlon's problem. The two years before 1974 were spent, in his own words, 'stealing, drinking, gambling and now and again the odd job.' In September 1974, and up until 11 October, 1974, when he returned to Northern Ireland, he had been working on a building site with Paul Hill. They were both accommodated in a ground floor room shared with two other people in the Irish Centre hostel in Quex Road, Camden. The hostel, called Conway House, looked after homeless new arrivals, who were mainly from marginalised backgrounds, with the object of assisting them to become integrated into the local society. It was regularly visited by the police and was therefore not suitable for use by the IRA which, in any case, would never have been countenanced by the priest in charge.

In evidence at the trial in 1975, Gerard Conlon had stated that on 5 October, 1974, the day of the Guildford bombing, he had left the hostel at about 12 o'clock and, after some shopping, went to two pubs with Paul Hill. They separated at about 3.00 pm as Hill was going to Southampton to see his girlfriend Gina Clarke. He had been drinking pints and shorts and, after visiting a bookmaker, went back to his room in the hostel to sleep it off. The Home Office memorandum states that he said Paul Kelly (it was in fact Patrick Carey) visited him at about 6.00 pm and left at 7.45 pm. He had then watched television for the rest of the evening. The memorandum adds that Gerard Conlon had sought to present Kelly (Carey) as a witness at the trial but he did not appear.

The Home Office's comment is that – 'Conlon was unable to present any evidence or witnesses in support of his account, and none has since been offered.' It seemed strange to many at the time of the trial, and even more so by January 1987, that no member of the staff, or other residents, visiting police, or police investigating the case had been found who could confirm whether or not Gerard Conlon was in the hostel for the whole of the evening of 5 October, 1974.

The central issue in the case of Carole Richardson was whether or not the timings given in the alibi evidence by Lisa Astin and Frank Johnson, and in the evidence by prosecution witnesses, confirmed that she could have planted the bomb in the Horse and Groom at Guildford and then got to the South Bank Polytechnic in time for the pop concert. Whichever way the matter is looked at, in the words of the judge 'times could be crucial' – and they were because it was mainly on the outcome of the timings as presented by the prosecution that she was sentenced to life imprisonment. Other than her retracted confession, there was no other evidence against her.

Some of the points, listed in the memorandum, from the representations which had been made to the Home Office are:

> In her statement from the dock Carole Richardson said that she and Lisa Astin arrived at the Charlie Chaplin public house at the Elephant and Castle at 7.00 pm. There they were met by Frank Johnson who had invited them to a concert that night at the South Bank Polytechnic. The three of them had left the pub at about 7.30 pm, walking to the Polytechnic and arriving there between 7.45 pm and 8.00 pm.
>
> Frank Johnson had made a statement on 20 December, 1974 in which he said that he had met Carole Richardson and Lisa Astin at between 6.15 and 6.30 pm. He made another statement on 22 January, 1975 giving an account which meant that Carole Richardson would not have arrived at the Charlie Chaplin pub earlier than 7.45 pm. He said he made this statement to secure his release from police custody.
>
> At the trial it was suggested by the Crown that Carole Richardson's alibi might have been a deliberate concoction. It was represented that if that were so it would have been offered immediately on arrest, rather than allowed to emerge gradually.
>
> It was also asked in the representation why, if an alibi had been prepared for Carole Richardson, the only non-Irish member of the 'team', alibis were not also prepared to protect the others? Also, whether 'sophisticated professionals' would have failed to produce any alibi at all when first arrested, and then clumsily sought to produce them. It was suggested the judge should have put this point to the jury in his summing-up.
>
> On the planting of the bomb in the Horse and Groom, the Crown case was that it could have been planted by an unidentified 'courting couple', who had left the pub a little before 7.00 pm. Witnesses who had arrived at the pub at about 6.45 pm referred to a couple who had left seven or eight minutes after they had arrived.
>
> Evidence was also given by a party who arrived at 7.00 pm that a young couple had arrived between 7.20 and 7.30 pm, and stayed for half an hour. The judge noted that Carole Richardson could not have been one of that couple because the Crown accepted that she was at the concert at the South Bank Polytechnic by 7.45 to 8.00 pm.

> The question for the jury was whether or not she had had time to assist in planting the bomb at the Horse and Groom and reach the concert at the Polytechnic at the time she was seen there (around, or just before 8.00 pm). It was contended in the representation that she did not. The prosecution had said that a police car, observing the speed limits in force in 1974, made the journey in 52 minutes, and in 48 minutes ignoring speed limits. The defence said that a solicitor's clerk, observing the 1975 limits, had taken 64 minutes.

The main 'comment' by the Home Office on these representations as far as the trial was concerned is significant and it needs to be quoted in full:

> Some accounts of the evidence given at trial give the impression that times, in particular the time at which the 'courting couple' left the Horse and Groom and that of Richardson's arrival at the Polytechnic concert, were precise and firmly fixed. The time of 6.53 pm for the 'courting couple' leaving the Horse and Groom comes from the evidence of two soldiers who said they arrived in the pub at '6.45 pm or thereabouts and [who] spoke of a couple who departed not very long after they arrived. One of them said seven or eight minutes afterwards.' The time of Richardson's arrival at the concert was *not* firmly given as 7.45 pm. The accommodation officer of the Polytechnic gave the time of the arrival of Johnson, Astin and Richardson (though he did not name them) as between 7.45 and 8.00 pm. One member of the pop group at the concert said that Johnson appeared with the two girls at approximately quarter-to-eight but that 'the times are plus or minus quarter of an hour.' Another member of the band said 'we got back to the [concert] hall at about 7.45 pm. I was sitting outside. I knew Frank Johnson. I saw him no more than ten minutes after we got back, say 8.00pm. He was with two girls.' It does not appear, therefore, that the journey must have been made in such specific time such as 45, 48 or 52 minutes.

Some important issues arise from the above 'comment' by the Home Office and the first concerns timings. The Home Office accepts that the 'courting couple' left the Horse and Groom at 6.53 pm. This is a precise time and is based on the evidence of two soldiers 'who spoke of a couple who departed not very long after they arrived – one of them said seven or eight minutes afterwards.' This time was at the most advantageous to the Crown's contentions over the journey time to the concert. Having accepted this precise time the Home Office then endeavours to weaken the validity of the time of arrival at the concert by saying that it 'was *not* firmly given as 7.45 pm.' A contrary view is that arrival at the Polytechnic at 7.45 pm is the only fair basis of any calculation of the timing for Carole Richardson's alibi. Two independent witnesses allow that she could have arrived as early as 7.45 pm – in one case possibly 15 minutes earlier. On the principle of guilt being established beyond reasonable doubt, and in fairness to Carole Richardson and in natural justice, there is a strong case for 7.45 pm as arrival time being accepted by the Home Office with the same confidence as they accept the precise time of 6.53 pm for the time of departure.

Another aspect of the timings issue is that the Home Office referred to the question of timings being part of Carole Richardson's grounds for appeal. They quote the Court of Appeal as saying – 'If she had been at the Polytechnic at or about 8 o'clock on the evening of Saturday 5 October, it was argued that it was unlikely, to put the matter no higher, that she could have left the Horse and Groom . . . as late as about 6.50 pm.' The Court of Appeal also noted that 'the time involved was barely an hour.' They also observed that 'both O'Connell and Dowd gave one hour as the time to and from Guildford on the night of the Guildford bombings.' It is surprising that the Home Office did not observe that Lord Roskill had declared the time of arrival at the Polytechnic to be 'at or about 8 o'clock.'

In fact, on the evidence of witnesses accepted by the Crown as reliable, the time of arrival was 7.45 pm and had accordingly been entered in the grounds of appeal by Carole Richardson's QC. Also, they might have observed that having rejected the credibility of Dowd and O'Connell, the court then appeared to rely on their estimates of journey times in support of their dismissal of her appeal on the matter. The Home Office's final quotation from the Court of Appeal is – 'If the story about visiting the Charlie Chaplin public house [part of Richardson's alibi account, reported by Johnson and Lisa Astin] is false, the margin of time becomes larger and, in any event, none of the times we have mentioned can be precise.'

The Home Office comment at this point is:

> Review of the evidence and comments on this aspect of the case does not offer grounds on which to doubt the judgement the jury must have made, in the light of all the relevant information available, that Richardson, if she was one of the courting couple who had left the Horse and Groom around 6.53 pm, had had sufficient time to assist in planting the bomb and to reach the concert by the approximate time she was seen there. No new evidence or new consideration of substance have been presented on this aspect of Richardson's

case. Accordingly there are no grounds for any action on the Home Secretary's part.

Before leaving the issue of timings, there are three relevant considerations on this comment. The Home Office does not mention at all the allegations by Frank Johnson of the physical violence used against him to change his statements. Reference might also have been made to the fact that the police arrested Frank Johnson on two occasions. Consideration might have been given to why pursuit of the truth should have required such action. The Home Office makes no mention of 'end times' all of which could have had a considerable affect on the acceptability of journey times. There was the time required to walk from the Horse and Groom to the alleged parking place of the getaway car; to walk from the parking place in London to the pop concert; and the time to walk from the Elephant and Castle to the Polytechnic entrance. The timings were indeed very fine.

Another issue relates to the 'courting couple.' Having assumed in one comment that Carole Richardson was one of the 'courting couple', in another comment the Home Office states, 'if she was one of the courting couple.' It is a serious omission not to make the point that, apart from her retracted confession and the fine timings, there was no other evidence whatsoever whereby the prosecution could have proved, which they failed to do, that she was ever in the Horse and Groom. The police tried hard enough to make a connection but totally failed. She was put on an identification parade but was not recognised by any of the eight people who the Surrey Constabulary had established should have been able to do so. After that signal failure, they did not risk putting Hill, Conlon or Armstrong on parade. The one description of a wanted couple which the police had circulated was quite different from the description of those who were convicted.

A third issue relates to the evidence which came to light in the appeal of the Guildford Four in 1977 at which the Balcombe Street ASU gave evidence. Joseph O'Connell and Brendan Dowd said they had bombed Guildford with another man and two girls whom they would not name because they had not yet been arrested. They said that none of the Guildford Four was present. Dowd had given evidence about the two elderly men with shopping bags waiting for a bus which he could only have known about if he had been at Guildford. The Surrey Police had been adamant that they had accounted for everyone who had been in the Horse and Groom except for the 'courting couple'. There was, therefore, only the one man from the 'courting couple' missing. If, as the Court of Appeal accepted, Dowd had probably been at Guildford, the question the Home Office does not ask is how could Patrick Armstrong have been there. They might have gone on to consider that, if there was doubt about that, so also there must be doubt, or at least a lurking doubt, about Carole Richardson having been there.

The Home Office's final 'General Comment' on the whole of the alibi section of the memorandum is:

> 'No new points or evidence have been raised in connection with any of the alibis, which were fully aired at the trial. There are therefore no grounds on which the Home Secretary could properly refer the case to the Court of Appeal.

There were many outside the Home Office who firmly held the view that the confessions of Brendan Dowd and the Balcombe Street ASU – Joseph O'Connell, Henry Duggan, Edward Butler and Hugh Doherty – were the clearest evidence of the innocence of the Guildford Four. Maybe it was in recognition of this view that some three pages of the memorandum are devoted to 'Balcombe Street Confessions (1)' and 'Balcombe Street Confessions (2) – Inconsistencies in Dowd's Account.' In the latter section the four main points from the Court of Appeal are used, to which the Home Office adds six of their own. For an independent review of the whole case of the Guildford Four, it is significant that the Home Office does not list one comment which could be regarded as favourable to the defence in either section.

Of the 'representations' listed under the first heading above, 'Balcombe Street Confessions (1)', one argued that the prosecution case rested on proving that the Guildford Four were part of the same IRA unit as the Balcombe Street gang but that they did not succeed in proving any link; another representation made the point that the fact that the Court of Appeal accepted that members of the Balcombe Street gang could also have been involved in the Guildford and Woolwich bombings produces more inconsistencies in the story. A third representation was 'how the Balcombe Street gang could have provided such detailed accounts of events two years later if their admissions were not true.' The memorandum adds that it is suggested that they provided more detail than the Guildford Four were able to do. The fourth representation concerned the handling of scientific evidence. This fourth representation is of such importance that it will be dealt with separately later.

In commenting on the three remaining representations above in the first section, the Home Office says that 'there is no reason to suppose that only one ASU operated in the South-East in the mid 1970s'; that the Court of Appeal 'rejected the Balcombe Street men's evidence that they did not know the four;' that 'the only inconsistency which is mentioned is that if Dowd and O'Connell were in the Horse and Groom, this left no room for Armstrong.' The memorandum adds it is not certain that the police succeeded in tracing everyone who had been in the pub (apart from a courting couple and another man); and that the Court of Appeal 'assumed that the Balcombe Street men and Dowd had been able to coordinate their stories sufficiently to produce a coherent account, apart from Dowd's.' These 'comments' give rise to some important observations:

The comment that there is no reason to suppose that only one ASU was operating in the South-East is irrelevant. The point is that the prosecution failed to prove that the Guildford Four, either as part of the Balcombe Street ASU or as a separate ASU, were at Guildford on the night of the bombings. No evidence of any link between the two groups either on the night of the bombings or at any other time was ever produced. This supports the Balcombe Street ASU assertion that they did not know the Guildford Four, which was rejected.

The comment in which reference is made to 'the only inconsistency' is somewhat confusing. It has never been represented that O'Connell was in the Horse and Groom. Dowd was in the Horse and Groom where he saw the two elderly men waiting for a bus. O'Connell was in the Seven Stars and his evidence on this is not dealt with at all by the Home Secretary.

On the matter of the police tracing the customers in the Horse and Groom, the Home Office is in error in saying it is not certain that the police succeeded in tracing everyone and that apart from the 'courting couple' there was 'another man' who had not been traced. This does not accord with the prosecution case at the trial. Moreover, on 26 October, 1974, on the ITV programme *Police Five*, Detective Chief Superintendent Wally Simmons of the Surrey Police said they had narrowed the suspects down to a couple seen sitting in an alcove. He stressed that they were the only two people at the Horse and Groom at the relevant time who had not been eliminated from the inquiry.

It is extremely important to note that the Balcombe Street ASU made their admissions prior to their own trial, and some almost immediately after their arrest. There is no evidence that there was ever an opportunity for the Balcombe Street ASU to coordinate their stories.

The point about the information provided by the Balcombe Street ASU is not only that it was more detailed than that of the Guildford

> Four but that it was more *precise*. The Home Office does not comment on this point. None of this was known at the trial of the Guildford Four. There was also the independent verification by former Chief Superintendent James Still on the quality of the detail and its matching with the forensic evidence supplied by Mr Higgs and Mr Lidstone of RARDE.
>
> At the appeal the Crown accepted that O'Connell and Duggan went to Woolwich. The judges were prepared to accept that Butler also went, and that all three of them were at Woolwich on both the night of the dummy run and of the bombing. The Court of Appeal was 'content to assume' that O'Connell and Dowd may well have been at Guildford.

As regards the scientific evidence, many serious and important points arise. However, there is a need first to consider, in full, the representation which had been made to the Home Office and their comments thereon. The representation as presented in the memorandum is:

> It is noted that, in cross-examination in the Balcombe Street trial, one of the scientific experts for the Crown (Mr Higgs) admitted that, on the instructions of the police, reference to the Guildford and Woolwich bombs had been left out of an account of the pattern of, and relationship between, various bombings. Furthermore, the Commander of the Bomb Squad, Mr Jim Nevill, had said under cross-examination that the Director of Public Prosecutions Office had advised him to tell Mr Higgs to leave the two bomb offences out of his evidence.

The 'comment' by the Home Office is:

> The suggestion appears to be that the scientific evidence proved that all the bombing incidents originally mentioned were carried out by the same team (ie. The Balcombe Street gang). This is not the case. There was no scientific evidence to link the Balcombe Street gang with the Guildford and Woolwich bombings. The only link was some similarity in the methods used for Guildford and Woolwich bombings and certain counts in the indictment against the Balcombe Street men. It does not follow from this that the same people were responsible for all the offences mentioned.

Before considering this comment it would be helpful to recall certain key dates. The Guildford time bomb explosions were on 5 October 1974, and the throw bomb at the King's Arms, Woolwich was on

7 November, 1974; the Guildford Four were arrested in late November/ early December 1974; they went to trial on 16 September, 1975; the Balcombe Street ASU were arrested on 12 December, 1975 and went to trial in January 1977; the four members of the ASU and Brendan Dowd were interviewed in October 1976 by the former Chief Superintendent James Still and Alastair Logan while in prison awaiting trial; they went to trial on 27 January, 1977; the Guildford appeal hearing was from 10 to 28 October, 1977.

There were serious omissions from the 'comments' by the Home Office on the scientific evidence. Some relevant background on developments and revelations from the Balcombe Street ASU trial need to be borne in mind. The arrests of the Guildford Four by early December 1974 did not bring to a halt the wave of bombings in London which had taken place during October and November. The Balcombe Street ASU surrendered and were arrested in December 1975 by Detective Chief Superintendent Imbert, as he then was, of the Metropolitan Police Bomb Squad, who had previously questioned Paul Hill and Gerard Conlon. Joseph O'Connell and Edward Butler had told him and Commander Nevill in December 1975 of their respective involvement in Guildford and Woolwich, and they said that the four people who had been convicted were not known to any of them and had nothing to do with either operation. The part played by members of the Balcombe Street ASU in Guildford and Woolwich was never investigated by DCS Imbert and Commander Nevill. Nor did they, or the Surrey Police, seek information from the Guildford Four about the wave of bombings in London apart from those at Guildford and Woolwich.

Significantly, the bombing campaign in London and the Home Counties came to an end on the capture of the Balcombe Street ASU in December 1975. By the time of their trial, in January 1977, it was known by Douglas Higgs, a principal scientific officer at RARDE, that the period of the IRA bombing campaign from August 1974, which included three throw bombs before Guildford in October 1974 and extended to the night of the seven London bombs in January 1975, constituted Phase One of the campaign. The IRA had announced a cease-fire on 9 February, 1975. There were no further explosions until a time bomb at the Caterham Arms in Caterham, Surrey on 27 August, 1975.

The period from the Caterham Arms bomb to the arrest of the Balcombe Street ASU in December 1975 became known as Phase Two. After the Caterham Arms bomb Detective Chief Superintendent Wally Simmons of the Surrey Police Bomb Squad said at a press conference – 'It is too early to say yet who is responsible – but the bombing is consistent in size, type and method with the blasts at two Guildford pubs last October.' His impressions were borne out by the forensic scientists at RARDE – the Caterham Arms device was, indeed, a carbon copy of the two time bombs at Guildford.

At their trial the Balcombe Street ASU had refused to plead to any of the charges because Guildford and Woolwich had not been included. The jury acquitted them on five of those charges which appeared to be linked forensically to the Guildford explosions. In their comments the Home Office make no reference to the fact that the police and the Director of Public Prosecutions had failed even to investigate, let alone charge, the Balcombe Street ASU on the basis of their freely given confessions on Guildford and Woolwich. The Guildford Four had been convicted solely on their contested confessions.

The most serious revelation at the trial concerned the handling of the scientific evidence. In the stand Mr Higgs of RARDE stated that over the period 22 October, 1974 to 22 December, 1974 he had examined and listed four bombing incidents which all had common features – the bombs weighed about five pounds; they were all packed with a mixture of nails, bolts, nuts and washers; they were all aimed at windows; all had short non-mechanical fuses; they all occurred within a two month period. His list was dated 17 June, 1976. He admitted that one conclusion that could be drawn was that the same team that did Woolwich had also been responsible for the other throw bombs. On cross-examination Higgs also admitted he had prepared a similar list dated 26 January, 1976 which included Woolwich but it had been deleted from the list of 17 June, 1976. During the trial it came as a surprise to many to hear Commander Nevill confirm it was at the direction of the Director of Public Prosecutions that he had instructed an officer to tell the forensic science experts to make alterations to their lists.

On being recalled to the witness stand Detective Chief Superintendent Hucklesby of the Metropolitan Police was asked if, in his opinion, he had sufficient evidence, both from the forensic experts and the Balcombe Street ASU alleged admissions, to prosecute at least some of the Balcombe Street ASU for the Woolwich bombing. He replied, 'I submitted it to the Director of Public Prosecutions as such, yes.'

Turning to Guildford, the defence then established that, even while the Guildford trial was proceeding, Higgs had signed a statement that linked the two Guildford pub bombings with the Phase One series of time bomb attacks. The statement, dated 10 October, 1975, was an up-dated version of an earlier one prepared in July 1975. Its existence was unknown to the defence. In it Higgs had stated:

> the latter (Guildford) incidents are linked with the remainder by virtue of a nitroglycerine-based explosive and the identification of many components from a Smith's pocket-watch at the Seven Stars and fractions of a similar watch bezel from the Horse and

> Groom. . . . In my opinion, the extensive use of Smith's pocket-watches, particularly the combat variety . . . and, above all, the great similarity of explosive types are too much of a coincidence to be other than a reflection of an underlying common source of supply, information and expertise . . . The general absence of certain peculiarities consistently present in other areas of attack only strengthens my opinion that the incidents considered herein form a connected set.

Mr Higgs confirmed at the Balcombe Street ASU trial that this statement had never been part of a deposition at either the Guildford trial or the Balcombe Street ASU trial. In the statement he proffered to the latter the conclusions were the same but there was no reference whatsoever to Guildford. Donald Lidstone, who was also a principal scientific officer at RARDE, then gave evidence. He agreed that forensic debris from the Horse and Groom time bomb at Guildford, which was in Phase One, showed common features with the Caterham time bomb at the beginning of Phase Two in September 1975 – method and location of placement; type of explosive; the type of Smith's watch; and the timing of detonation. It is to be noted that the Guildford Four had been arrested in December 1974, some nine months before the Caterham bomb, which in turn was three months before the arrest of the Balcombe Street ASU.

The Home Office opening comment in this section of the memorandum is – 'The Court of Appeal examined at considerable length the admission made by members of the Balcombe Street gang and Dowd. None of the points now being raised provide grounds for a reference . . . There was no scientific evidence to link the Balcombe Street gang with the Guildford and Woolwich bombings.' This was the impression with which Peers and Members of Parliament were left.

The six most important aspects of the Guildford Four case on which the Home Office does not comment, all of which, taken together, could be regarded as considerations of substance, are:

> There was compelling evidence from the Government's own scientists at RARDE to link the Balcombe Street ASU with the Guildford and Woolwich bombings.

> There had been suppression of parts of the scientific evidence at the Guildford trial by RARDE scientists. Documents which they had prepared showing forensic details of links between the Guildford and Woolwich bombs, and other incidents which occurred while the Guildford Four were in custody, were not made available to the defence. Such suppression was a serious matter.

> There was some manipulation of scientific evidence at the Balcombe Street ASU trial whereby the scientists deleted some incidents from their list on the instructions of the Director of Public Prosecutions and the police. This was also an extremely serious development.
>
> The failure by Commander Nevill and DCS Imbert to follow up the confessions of the Balcombe Street ASU and to investigate the part played by them in the Guildford and Woolwich bombings; the failure by the Bomb Squad and the Surrey Police to investigate the part the Guildford Four might have played in the other bombings in London and the Home Counties; and the failure by the Surrey Police to interview the Balcombe Street ASU about Guildford.
>
> No bomb making equipment was found in the Maguire house. In February 1975, four months after the Guildford and Woolwich bombs, the police discovered a 'safe house' at 39 Fairholme Road, Hammersmith. It was full of bomb making material and Commander Huntley of the Bomb Squad described it as 'the most important bomb factory we have found.' After the arrests of the Balcombe Street ASU the police located their two 'safe houses' at 61 Crouch Hill and 99 Milton Grove in North London. Materials identical to those used at Guildford and Woolwich were recovered from them. There were no fingerprints of the Guildford Four at any of the 'safe houses.'
>
> No one jury had heard the evidence given at the Guildford Four trial together with the evidence of the Balcombe Street ASU given at the Court of Appeal hearing of the Guildford Four case.

Before moving on to 'Balcombe Street Confessions (2) – Inconsistencies in Dowd's Account,' it would be appropriate to refer to Joseph O'Connell's address from the dock at the end of the Balcombe Street ASU trial. He was the most able member of the gang. Those present said it was intense, but controlled and lucid. It was lengthy, but the first section was delivered without interruption from the judge, Mr Justice Cantley:

> We have recognized this court to the extent that we have instructed our lawyers to draw the attention of the court to the fact that four totally innocent people – Carole Richardson, Gerard Conlon, Paul Hill and Patrick Armstrong – are serving massive sentences for three bombings, two in Guildford and one in Woolwich. We and another man [Dowd] now sentenced have admitted our part in the Woolwich bombing. The Director of Public Prosecutions was made

aware of these submissions and has chosen to do nothing. I wonder if he would still do nothing when he is made aware of the new and important evidence which has come to light through the cross-examination by our counsel during this trial.

I will refer to three of those witnesses who gave evidence at this trial and whose evidence was also dealt with in the conviction of those four innocent people . . . Taking Mr Higgs first, he admitted in this trial that the Woolwich bomb formed part of the series of those bombings with which we are charged; yet when he gave evidence in the earlier Guildford and Woolwich trial he deliberately concealed that the Woolwich bomb was definitely part of a series carried out between October and December 1974 and that people on trial were in custody at the time of some of those bombings. Mr Lidstone in his evidence for this trial tried to make little of the suggestion that the Guildford bombing had been part of the Phase One offences with the excuse – and this appeared to be his only reason – that the Guildford bombing had occurred a long time before the rest. When it was pointed out to him that the time between the Guildford bomb and the Brook's club bomb which followed Guildford was 17 days, and the Woolwich bomb which followed that was 16 days, and that many of the other incidents with which we are charged had equal time gaps, Lidstone back-tracked and admitted that there was a likely connection. Those two men, Mr Higgs and Mr Lidstone, gave evidence at the Guildford and Woolwich trial which had no place in their true conclusions as scientists; they gave evidence which they must have known was untrue. The evidence which they gave was completely following in line with police lies so as to make the charges stick against those four people.

Then we come to Commander Nevill. He said he only wanted to get the truth concerning Guildford and Woolwich in fact when he gave evidence in this trial; yet he has not done. Why? Because Nevill knows that the truth means the end of the road for him and many other senior police officers and because his superiors know it would be a dangerous insight into how corrupt the British establishment really is.

The full title of the second section of the memorandum dealing with the Balcombe Street ASU is 'Balcombe Street Confessions (2) – Inconsistencies in Dowd's Account.' This comes as no surprise as at the Court of Appeal hearing Lord Roskill had said – 'We regard the touchstone by which the credibility of all the new evidence in the relevant respects is to be judged to be that of Dowd.'

The grounds of appeal were that three of the four members of the Balcombe Street ASU – Joseph O'Connell, Harry Duggan and Eddie

Butler, together with Brendan Dowd – had claimed that they, and they alone, had bombed Woolwich; that Dowd and a young woman he refused to identify had bombed the Horse and Groom at Guildford; that O'Connell, another man and another woman whom he refused to identify had bombed the Seven Stars at Guildford; and that they had no connection with and no knowledge of the Guildford Four. They had refused to identify the others who had taken part in the bombings because they had not yet been arrested. Additionally, Carole Richardson sought to have her conviction for Guildford overturned on the basis of the evidence of her original alibi witnesses.

The sole representation given by the Home Office in this section of the memorandum is – 'It has been suggested that it was inconsistent of the Court of Appeal to reject the account and confessions of the Balcombe Street ASU and Brendan Dowd on the basis of 'four points of detail [on which] he differed from the other three,' when there were allegedly many more contradictions in the statements by Hill, Conlon, Armstrong and Richardson.' The rest of the section consists of the Home Office 'comments' on the four points cited by the Court of Appeal, all of which related to Woolwich, together with a list of their own additional six points, four of which related to Guildford and two to Woolwich.

In summary, the first of the four points cited by the Court of Appeal was that they found it wholly incredible that, if Dowd had taken part in an abortive trip to Woolwich and had brought the bomb back by public transport, he would not have remembered details more accurately than he did in the witness box. The Home Office has repeated what the Court of Appeal said but makes no comment. The fact is that Dowd had taken part in many missions and travelled regularly with bombs as the police knew and he had admitted. He knew how to handle them in a safe manner.

The second point was that the Court of Appeal concluded Dowd was lying about his participation because his description of the scenes and events in Frances Street near the King's Arms differed in detail from that of the three Balcombe Street men. The third point was that Dowd told a circumspect story of the journey back after the car had been abandoned which was inconsistent in its detail with the account of the other three witnesses. Again, on these two points the Home Office adds no comment to their repetition of what the Court of Appeal said.

The fourth point made by the Court of Appeal, repeated without comment by the Home Office, was that Dowd had said that on the day of the bombing 'the four men had met in a public house in Knightsbridge,' while the others had said it was Sloane Square. The Home Office might have made the observation that this point is incorrect. Dowd's marginal mistake related to the dummy run on the

Wednesday and not the night of the bombing which was a Thursday. Dowd had said they met on the south side of Knightsbridge which is linked by Sloane Street to Sloane Square about half a mile away. This is even less of a minor error when it is recalled that Dowd also said they had met in a pub some 30 yards from an underground station exit. That was the pub in Sloane Square where O'Connell and Duggan said they had all met.

In summary, the four points relating to Guildford on the Home Office's own list are, first, that Dowd said he and O'Connell left London for Guildford at 6.00pm because they had to be in the pub by 7.00pm to get seats, but O'Connell had said they arrived 'shortly before 6.00pm'; second, O'Connell had said after returning to London he and Dowd had dropped off the two unidentified women on the way to North London, but when talking to James Still Dowd had said only that they 'dropped some people off'; third, after leaving Guildford Dowd could not remember where he went or what he did on what was his first operation; and fourth, Dowd had told James Still there were four people in the car, but at the appeal he said five. The Home Office's two points on Woolwich were, first, that on a reconnaissance trip to Woolwich O'Connell and the others had said that he and Dowd had taken a look at the pub, but Dowd could not recall whether or not he had; and, second, Dowd had made no mention to James Still of an abortive attempt on Woolwich.

The 'General Comment' on this second section of the 'Balcombe Street Confessions' by the Home Office consists of repeating parts of the conclusion by the Court of Appeal:

> The Court of Appeal concluded, in respect of the Balcombe Street men's and Dowd's confessions, that 'there [had] been a cunning and skilful attempt to deceive the Court by putting forward false evidence.' As the Home Secretary noted in his statement, those confessions were fully considered by the Court of Appeal, and no new points of substance have been raised. Accordingly, there are no grounds for any action on the part of the Home Secretary.

It would have been helpful if the Home Office had made clear that the above quotation about 'a cunning and skilful attempt to deceive the Court . . .' referred only to the claim by the Balcombe Street ASU and Brendan Dowd that they had had no connection with the Guildford Four and did not know them. The Home Office might have also noted that the Court of Appeal described the evidence by the Guildford Four as 'the partially true intermingled with the deliberately false.' This comment related to the sole evidence on which they had been convicted – their retracted confessions.

There were inconsistencies by Dowd in the points cited above by the Court of Appeal and the Home Office. But, considering them carefully, many formed the view that they were of such a nature as not to outweigh the many points of substance on which Dowd's evidence was fully or broadly in accord with that of the rest of the ASU. There were also matters on which he was completely and uniquely accurate such as the two elderly men with shopping bags at Guildford, and driving off after Woolwich without lights until being 'flashed' by an oncoming car. Both of these were corroborated by police witnesses. Those present at the trial of the Balcombe Street ASU and at the Guildford appeal recognised Dowd as being the least impressive performer of the group in the witness box. Sir Michael Havers, prosecuting counsel, clearly appreciated this and understandably made the most of it.

As far as operations by the ASU were concerned, Brendan Dowd was the most experienced of the group. He had taken part in over 50 missions, and also many reconnaissances and dummy runs. It was, therefore, reasonable that he would not necessarily have total recall on details relating to each mission. There were also other factors which merit consideration. There was a time lapse of nearly two years between the Guildford and Woolwich bombings and his arrest. When he arrived at the Old Bailey for the Guildford appeal he had spent 27 months in custody as a Category 'A' prisoner. For all but seven weeks of that time he had been in solitary confinement in isolation units and punishment blocks. He had had a lot to remember and memories of many incidents no doubt blended in with others with the passage of time. An aspect which is overlooked by the Home Office is that, taking Brendan Dowd's evidence as a whole, the quality of his recollection is far more significant in its similarities than in its inconsistencies with that of the other three.

He was described by Lord Roskill as a 'deplorable witness.' At no point was the Court invited to consider comparisons between Dowd's inconsistencies and the total of 153 inconsistencies in the Guildford confessions. The concentration on Brendan Dowd as a witness at the Guildford appeal led Lord Roskill and his fellow judges to the conclusion:

> Our conviction that Dowd was lying in relation to the Wednesday night, of course, inevitably casts the gravest doubts as to his veracity regarding the events of the Thursday . . . If, as we conclude without hesitation, Dowd was not there on either the Wednesday or the Thursday nights, it follows not only that Dowd has lied to the court in this respect but that O'Connell, Duggan and Butler have also lied in asserting that he was their companion and was the fourth

> man on each of those two occasions. We have no hesitation in concluding that each of them has so lied.

This led, in turn, to the 'clear conclusion' that they were all also lying in denying knowledge of Paul Hill and Patrick Armstrong with regard to Woolwich. The final words by Lord Roskill in the appeal judgement were:

> In the end we are all of the clear opinion that there are no possible grounds for doubting the justice of any of these four convictions, or for ordering retrials or, in Richardson's case, for quashing her convictions in their entirety. We therefore propose to dispose of all those applications for leave to appeal by refusing them.

Members of the Deputation started to come together during the early months of 1987. They had all received copies of the Home Secretary's oral statement and the Home Office memorandum on the Guildford Four. The Deputation had not yet had formal meetings but initially were in touch by telephone and letter. Having seen the Home Office documents they all remained resolutely convinced that the possibilities of there having been a miscarriage of justice were too strong for the case not to be pursued with vigour.

By January 1987, when the Home Secretary made his statement, the Guildford Four had been in prison for some 12 years. Lord Devlin had already expressed in the past his concern at how the Court of Appeal had handled the case, and both he and Lord Scarman renewed this concern. No one jury had heard the evidence of both the Guildford Four and the Balcombe Street ASU; no jury had heard the evidence of the Balcombe Street ASU. Cardinal Hume dubbed the Guildford Four case at that stage as 'the case that won't go away.' Unknown to him and to the Deputation, this was to be the title adopted by another forthcoming television programme in which some members of the Deputation were to take part.

4

THE ASSESSMENT (2)

BEFORE WE consider the Home Office memorandum on the Maguire Seven, it might be appropriate to stand back from the Guildford Four and Maguire Seven cases and review the differences and similarities. The first general point is that by January 1987 all the Maguire Seven had served their sentences but the Guildford Four were in their thirteenth year of imprisonment.

The Guildford and Woolwich pub bombings in 1974 were appalling crimes in which 7 people were killed and some 84 injured. The whole country had been in a state of shock, feelings were running very high, and there was a desire for speedy retribution. At the Guildford trial the court decided that the Guildford Four had committed the crimes at Guildford and that Paul Hill and Patrick Armstrong had bombed Woolwich – verdicts arrived at solely on the basis of their retracted confessions. The Court of Appeal decided that the Guildford Four, and some of the Balcombe Street ASU together with Brendan Dowd, were responsible for both bombings, and their appeal was rejected.

The situation with the Maguire Seven was quite different. Nobody had been killed or injured but the Maguire Seven also suffered from public emotional antagonism and even hate campaigns. Not one of the Maguire Seven confessed. No bulk or trace of explosive was found in the house or neighbourhood. They were all convicted of being in possession of nitroglycerine solely on the evidence of the forensic scientists. The only reason why the police were able to get on to them was because Anne Maguire had been alleged to be a bombmaker in the retracted confessions of Paul Hill and Gerard Conlon of the Guildford Four.

There were two notable similarities between the cases. Both of the trials were presided over by Mr Justice Donaldson (later to become Lord Donaldson and Master of the Rolls), while Sir Michael Havers (later to become Attorney General and Lord Chancellor) led the prosecution in each case. During the trial of the Guildford Four, which took place three months before the trial of the Maguire Seven, Sir

Michael Havers had already described Anne Maguire in graphic detail as a bombmaker. The Guildford Four had been sentenced by Mr Justice Donaldson on the basis of statements which so described her. However, at the opening of the Maguire Seven trial Sir Michael Havers asserted there was no connection whatever between the two trials.

Another similarity was that the forensic science evidence at both trials was given by scientists from the Government's Royal Armament Research and Development Establishment (RARDE). Mr Higgs admitted in the Balcombe Street trial in 1977 that before the Guildford trial he had signed a statement that linked the two Guildford bombs with the Phase One series of time bombs. The statement was not disclosed to the defence. At the Balcombe Street ASU trial it was also established that, at the direction of the Director of Public Prosecutions given to Commander Nevill of the Bomb Squad, he had instructed a junior officer, Sgt Doyle, to tell Higgs to delete Woolwich from a list showing thrown bomb incidents with common factors. Higgs had agreed to do this. At the Maguire Seven trial it was established that Mr Elliot of RARDE had prepared a report on an explosive Pentaerythritol Tetranitrate (PETN) which showed that the performance of nitroglycerine in the Thin Layer Chromatography (TLC) test was not unique as had been claimed by the prosecution. The scientists from RARDE who gave evidence at the trial of the Maguire Seven all knew this.

In the Home Office memorandum on the Maguire Seven frequent refuge is taken in the decisions of the Courts. There is no acknowledgement of the widespread concern about the quality, reliability and validity of some aspects of the positive Thin Layer Chromatography tests on which, alone, the Maguire Seven were convicted.

There is one sentence in the cover sheet to the memorandum which bears repetition – 'Moreover, a reference to the Court of Appeal without new evidence or a consideration of substance would be futile; the Court would be bound to dismiss an appeal based simply on the proposition, argued without fresh evidence, that the Courts had been mistaken.' This seems directly to contradict Lord Scarman's statement in the House of Lords on 20 December, 1986, one month before the memorandum was published, that '. . . the Court of Appeal can look into the whole case again in order to ensure that justice, however belated, is done.' It also seems to be in contradiction of Lord Diplock's judgement of 1983 (R. v. Chard) on which that statement is based.

The Home Office does not appear to have responded fully and publicly to the submissions prepared by Dr Brian Caddy and Christopher Price MP, or to the suggestions made in Parliament that an independent scientific committee be set up to report on the scientific evidence. It would appear that there is no record of a public statement being made by either the Home Secretary, Douglas Hurd, or the

Minister of State at the time, David Mellor, explaining why it seems to have been decided not to set up such a committee, who made the decision and on what grounds it was based. There will always be the thought that it might well have been possible, if the will was there, to prepare a suitable reference to the Court of Appeal.

In the CASE SUMMARY, and elsewhere in the document, there is reference to Anne Maguire's rubber gloves. They were plastic. As in the Home Office memorandum on the Guildford Four case, some of the 'representations' which had been made to the Home Office are listed and 'comments' by the Home Office are made on them. Amongst the 'representations' on the validity of the TLC test are that it does not provide 100% proof that nitroglycerine is present and other confirmatory tests should be used; that nowadays a prosecution would not proceed solely on the basis of positive TLC test results; that the significance of the fact that the TLC test could not distinguish between nitroglycerine and PETN was not properly drawn to the jury's attention; that expert witnesses for the Crown exaggerated the discrimination provided by the TLC test.

It needs to be recalled that the Maguire Seven had been charged with 'being in possession of nitroglycerine.' No other explosive had been mentioned because, as investigation had proved, all the bombs in the campaign were nitroglycerine based. The 'comment' by the Home Office is 'the question which the jury had to consider was whether they found the matter proved beyond reasonable doubt.' The Home Office then quotes the Court of Appeal as saying 'the essential question for the jury was whether the single TLC test in toluene was conclusively shown to have excluded any realistic possibility of the samples tested having contained some substance known or unknown other than nitroglycerine.' That is so, but the Home Office overlooks a further consideration which was that if the samples tested could be accepted as showing nitroglycerine, did the nitroglycerine come from the hands of the accused?

In commenting on the representation that nowadays a prosecution would not proceed solely on the basis of positive TLC results, the Home Office says, 'this is probably true.' This is misleading. It would have been more open if the Home Office had admitted that it is now 'standard practice' to use a confirmatory test. This was disclosed in a letter written by Mrs C. J. Ruffler of the Home Office dated 21 April, 1986, eight months before the memorandum was published. The point is that a jury in 1987 would undoubtedly have taken this into account when assessing whether the TLC test alone disposed of all 'lurking doubt.' The Northern Ireland Forensic Science Laboratory had abandoned TLC several years before 1974 because of its unreliability and the introduction of more reliable tests, and RARDE knew this.

As regards the PETN situation having been drawn to the attention of the jury, the Home Office says 'the arguments concerning PETN were considered by the Court of Appeal who did not think that they affected the safety of the convictions.' This was the point made to the jury by the judge but it was not what counsel had asked him to say in the absence of the jury. Counsel's incontrovertible point was that the discovery that PETN could give the same results in toluene as nitroglycerine destroyed the Crown's central argument that the position of nitroglycerine in toluene was unique. The Maguire household had been charged specifically only with handling nitroglycerine. The judge told counsel in the jury's absence that he would put it to them in this way when they returned. The Home Office has not mentioned that he did not do so.

The representations on 'Innocent Contamination' were that the suspects might have become innocently contaminated with nitroglycerine; that the swabs taken from the suspects might have been accidentally contaminated by nitroglycerine; and that an unidentified non-explosive substance was responsible for the positive TLC test results. A further representation on 'Fabrication of Test Results' suggested that the results might have been produced by the police deliberately contaminating the hands of the suspects with nitroglycerine; or by the swabs being deliberately contaminated; or by contaminated swabs being substituted for those taken from the suspects; or by false results being reported.

The 'comment' on Innocent Contamination is that 'all the points were raised at trial.' However, the Home Office confirms that one police officer admitted that he had not washed his hands after swabbing but says that he had changed his gloves. The sole comment on Fabrication of Test Results is – 'None of these arguments was put forward by the defence at the trial, and no evidence of any kind to support them has been presented.' The fact that the arguments were not put forward at the trial is of no relevance to their consideration at a review in January 1987.

Considering the importance the police attached to the case it seems remarkable that the swabs and the gloves were not handled with more dispatch while being transferred from Scotland Yard to RARDE. A jury sitting in January 1987 might have considered the delays to be of some significance. They would no doubt have wished to hear evidence from those police officers who were concerned with the handling of the material – Detective Sergeant Kenneth Day, Detective Sergeant Lawrence Vickery, Detective Sergeant Lewis, and Police Constable David Faw. Counsel might also have wished to hear the evidence of Detective Chief Superintendent Wally Simmons of the Surrey police, who had organised some of the arrests and interrogations of the Guildford Four, relating his movements between Guildford and Scotland Yard during the periods before the material was transferred to RARDE.

It had been represented that some of the TLC tests were carried out by a trainee scientist at RARDE. Also that this might have been engineered by the police so that they would have a reason to dismiss the tests as unreliable if, for any reason, they had not wished to proceed with the charges. The Home Office comments that this was raised at trial; that the trainee was not in charge of testing and did not analyse the results. The Home Office goes on to say the tests he carried out were mostly from furniture and fittings, that he was supervised, and that the tests he did on Anne Maguire's plastic gloves were duplicated by an experienced scientist. As to the police having arranged for the tests to be carried out by an inexperienced scientist, the Home Office says 'the police were not in a position to influence such decisions as to who should undertake the tests.'

The Home Office is clearly satisfied with the answers they have received from RARDE on these representations, but there are two worrying aspects about their comments. Anne Maguire's gloves arrived at RARDE after some delay. Following the confessions of Paul Hill and Gerard Conlon, she was regarded by the police and the prosecution as the chief bomb-maker in the Maguire household. Considering the criminal justice system was dealing with the first major bombing incident on the mainland which involved the deaths of 5 young people, it seems strange that the tests on Anne Maguire's gloves were entrusted to a trainee even though, as RARDE assured the Home Office, those tests were duplicated by a senior scientist.

The second comment by the Home Office is rather more significant. They say the police were not in a position to influence decisions on tests. Yet at the Guildford trial, and subsequently at the Balcombe Street ASU trial, they clearly were in a position to tell the scientists to delete Guildford and Woolwich from their statements. This left open the impression that the offences could have been committed by the Guildford Four rather than some of Balcombe Street ASU and Brendan Dowd – which they knew to be the case from their analysis of certain IRA 'safe houses' which they had found in 1975.

As regards the TLC test results on samples taken from Patrick Maguire Snr, it was represented that one of the results was odd. The dry swab taken from his right hand showed the presence of nitroglycerine (as did scrapings from his fingernails), whereas none of the other swabs, in particular those taken using ether, showed any nitroglycerine. This representation on the matter of TLC test results is of considerable importance since it was solely on those results that all of the Maguire Seven were convicted. The Home Office 'comment' is significant:

> The matter was considered at trial and covered in the judge's summing up. He reminded the jury that Mr Yallop, the defence expert witness, concluded that the results meant that Mr Maguire could not have been in contact with nitroglycerine. The judge suggested to the jury that 'what you have got to consider is whether it really casts doubt on the whole case or whether it is not just an odd result.' The matter was clearly before the court, and nothing new has been raised which would provide any ground for a reference in relation to this point or the TLC test results as a whole.

This is an example of the general tone of much of the memorandum. Where a difficult and disturbing point remained unresolved in the courts it is assumed to be sufficient merely to recapitulate the court's seeming inability to be disturbed by it. The fact remains that it was a very 'odd' result indeed. It is interesting to note that, although no 'representation' was listed as having been made about the middle son, John Maguire, having tested clean, the Home Office makes no reference whatever at any time to this equally odd result which might have been considered during their review of the case. Taken into account in the different atmosphere of 1987, together with a number of cogent arguments not properly advanced before the courts, all this might well have been less easily dismissed in a jury's mind.

Throughout the period 1981 to 1986 the validity and safety of the scientific evidence, and particularly the TLC tests, became, in a relentless fashion, ever more important in the minds of many people. It is hardly correct to say that since the trial 'nothing new has been raised which would provide any ground for a reference.' During the period 1982 to 1983 Christopher Price submitted Dr Caddy's evidence to the Home Office, and there were suggestions in Parliament that an independent scientific committee be set up to advise the Home Secretary of any possible grounds for a reference. As has already been noted, for some reason unknown to the general public at the time, neither of these two possibilities seems to have been fully explored. In the event of them having been fruitful, even if the damage to the criminal justice system could have been considerable, at least justice would have been seen to have been done. In the end that could only have enhanced public confidence in the system, which at that time was already beginning to ebb.

If one turns again to Anne Maguire's gloves, two further representations had been made specifically about them. Her conviction was based solely on the fact that a plastic glove (or rubber as the Home Office described it), which she was said to have used, was found to have nitroglycerine on it when subjected to a TLC test. She said at trial that she only wore the gloves around the house when she put ointment on her hands to treat her skin complaint. It was further represented that the glove might have become contaminated after it was taken by the police for testing.

As regards the first representation above, the sole comment by the Home Office is that 'The Court of Appeal specifically considered the nature of the evidence against Mrs Maguire. It did not find the convictions against her or any of the other defendants to be unsafe or unsatisfactory.' The Home Office comment on the second representation about the glove is – 'This point was raised at trial. The question of how the gloves became contaminated with nitroglycerine, and whether that could have occurred once they were in police custody, was specifically put to the jury in the judge's summing up.'

This comment is misleading. The possibility that the glove had become 'innocently contaminated' in police custody had been looked at more as an afterthought by Mr Justice Donaldson. In the only reference to the possibility he said 'It is a matter for you, members of the jury, but you may think it is somewhat unlikely, to say the least of it, that those gloves became contaminated in police custody.' Lord Roskill at the Court of Appeal raised the possibility that the glove might have become 'innocently contaminated' while they were in Scotland Yard and before reaching RARDE. However, he covered it simply by saying that Mr Justice Donaldson had 'dealt fully' with the point among others brought forward in Anne Maguire's defence, and added 'we see no force in any of these complaints.' The trial judge had 'dealt' with the point by saying it was 'somewhat unlikely.'

Considering the gloves related to Anne Maguire, the alleged 'chief bomb-maker', and originally implicated by the police in the Guildford bombing, it is surprising that the Home Office relies solely on the findings of the courts, particularly in the light of subsequent developments. The facts are that Anne Maguire had a large number of plastic gloves in a drawer. On 3 December, 1974, the night the Maguire Seven were arrested, the 'sniffer' dogs and 'sniffer' device failed to detect any trace of explosives, let alone nitroglycerine, from the drawer. Her hands had tested clean.

Late on 4 December, 1974 the gloves were seized and taken to Scotland Yard. They remained there for some days before being sent to RARDE. As already mentioned, no trace of nitroglycerine had been found anywhere in the Maguire house and no bulk of any explosive had been found in the house or neighbourhood. In view of this, many people considered at the time, and have done so since, that the possibilities of innocent, accidental, or even deliberate contamination, particularly as regards the gloves, had not been fully explored and examined in depth at the trial. All this could well have constituted a consideration of substance in January 1987, particularly in connection with other aspects of the scientific evidence.

Under the heading 'Handling of Bulk of Explosives' the main representation was that there was no evidence of the existence of any bulk of explosives or bomb-making equipment, and that the judge directed the jury that without evidence of some bulk of explosives they could not convict. The Home Office comment is – 'It is clear from the judge's summing up that he did *not* direct the jury that the existence of a quantity of explosives must have been directly and separately proven.' They then go on to quote from a comment by the Court of Appeal. It is, however, noteworthy that the Home Office does not quote what the trial judge actually said and, as a consequence, their comment could be misleading. In his summing up the judge at the trial said:

> Now in order to satisfy you of the guilt of any of the accused in such a charge the prosecution has to prove that the accused concerned had an explosive substance – in this case nitroglycerine – in his or her possession or control or actively assisted someone who had the explosive substance in his or her possession or control and, of course, as you have been told before, when we are talking about possession or control or an explosive substance we are not talking about traces of it on the hands of any of the accused, if there are traces on their hands, we are talking about the bulk from which the prosecution say that these traces came.

Seemingly in support of their comment on the representation they had received, the Home Office reproduced only the comment by the Court of Appeal:

> The judge's direction made it absolutely plain that before [they] could be convicted not only had the presence of traces of nitroglycerine on the hands . . . to be conclusively proven, but that the jury had to be certain that the presence of nitroglycerine if proved, was consistent with and only with each of [them] having knowingly handled and thus had in his or her possession a quantity of nitroglycerine – the corpus, to use counsel's phrase – from which those traces came.

It is to be noted that, whereas the judge at the trial stressed that traces of nitroglycerine were not in themselves sufficient to substantiate a charge of unlawful possession of explosives but that the bulk of the material had to be shown to exist, he did not draw attention to the fact that such a bulk of material had not been shown to exist. At the next stage the Court of Appeal praised the trial judge for mentioning the former consideration, but made no reference to his failure to mention the latter.

The final representation referred to 'Continued Protestations of Innocence.' It made the point that all of the Maguire Seven had protested their innocence at the time they were arrested and six of them had continued to do so over a period of 13 years during and after serving their sentences, while the seventh, Giuseppe Conlon, had continued to protest his innocence to his death bed in 1980. At his funeral in Ireland there was no IRA or para-military presence whatsoever.

These were no routine protestations of innocence. The general demeanour of the Maguires had an immediate impact on the millions who saw them on television after their release from prison. Perhaps more significantly, they also impressed all members of the Deputation – Cardinal Hume, the two Law Lords, Lord Devlin and Lord Scarman, and the two former Home Secretaries, Roy Jenkins and Merlyn Rees; and also other public figures who had got to know the Maguires personally – Lord Fitt, Sir John Biggs-Davison MP, Christopher Price MP, and John Wheeler MP. The Home Office's only comment on this representation is:

> Protestations of innocence, however strenuously sustained, cannot of themselves provide grounds for referring a case to the Court of Appeal. It is understandable that defendants who have protested their innocence up to the point of conviction might continue to do so afterwards even though guilty.

No one was suggesting that even such impressive protestations, which, in spite of the Home Office observations, were very unusual, would alone give grounds for referral. However, taken with some of the many other aspects of the Maguire Seven case, including the scientific evidence which had arisen by January 1987, they would have made a contribution towards possible considerations of substance.

As we have seen, the Home Secretary announced in January 1987 that he would not be referring the Maguire Seven or Guildford Four cases to the Court of Appeal. At that time the Ministers in the Home Office who were, and had been, dealing with the cases were the Home Secretary, Douglas Hurd, and the Minister of State, David Mellor. The Division within the Home Office responsible for handling the cases was C3, part of whose responsibilities included what, it is believed, was then described as 'Wrongful Imprisonment.' The more graphic title of 'Miscarriages of Justice' could have served well to add some impetus to the handling of cases such as the Guildford Four who by then were in their thirteenth year of imprisonment and with no end in sight.

Any attempt to re-open either of the two cases over the years, particularly the Maguire Seven case, had met with the blunt response that there could be no reference to the Court of Appeal without 'new evidence or consideration of substance.' The Home Office guideline of 'new evidence' for referral to the Court of Appeal – 'an administrative rule of practice elevated into a 'principle' ' as Lord Scarman described it – was subject to some variations as the years went by. Initially it was Roy Jenkins who, as Home Secretary in 1976 at the time of the Confait case, and in pursuit of justice, expanded the criteria for referral of 'new evidence' by adding 'or consideration of substance.'

By 1985 Lord Glenarthur, a junior Minister at the Home Office, was reported as referring to 'significant new evidence or material consideration of substance.' In 1986 David Mellor, Minister of State at the Home Office, was speaking of 'new evidence or some new and material consideration of substance.' In his oral statement in January 1987 Douglas Hurd spoke of 'new evidence or new consideration of substance.' It seemed as if the stakes were being raised progressively by the Home Office as pressure for a review of the scientific evidence in the Maguire Seven case continued to intensify.

The two cases were politically sensitive and both had now become highly controversial. One of the many reasons for this was the rigid adherence by the Home Office to the self-imposed restriction of 'new evidence.' Robert Kee made a highly pertinent observation in *Trial and Error* when he referred to the intentions of the 1968 Act – 'But the intention of the Act is plain. The pursuit of truth is the end of all justice and, if technical formalities of justice stand in the way of that pursuit, then the pursuit must take precedence over the formalities.'

Ministers over the years will obviously have taken into account the views and recommendations submitted to them by officials in C3 Division. What was not known was the extent to which those views and recommendations influenced Ministers' final decisions. The defendants had every right to expect, from Ministers and officials alike, an instinctive and objective search for the whole truth, and so justice, when their cases were being considered.

A puzzling aspect of the cases was the apparent failure of the Home Office to consider during their review two highly significant judgements in the Court of Appeal, by Lord Scarman and Lord Diplock, both of which have already been mentioned. If they had been considered during the review they were not referred to in the two memoranda, as were several other judgements and verdicts.

On 3 March, 1987 Yorkshire TV broadcast another powerful programme in their *First Tuesday* series called '*The case that won't go away*. Reference was made in this to new witnesses, and both Cardinal Hume and Lord Devlin took part.

The programme opened with a reference to *The Guildford Time Bomb* broadcast on 1 July, 1986 in which it had been asked if the right people had been convicted for the Guildford bombings. The programme then referred to the Home Secretary's 27-page memorandum on the Guildford case which had been laid before both Houses of Parliament, and which supported the decision not to refer the case to the Court of Appeal 'because there was nothing new.'

The programme was to concentrate on, as they put it, 'significant evidence known to the Home Secretary but omitted from his memorandum, and also an alibi witness who has never been heard by the courts and whose evidence relates directly to the guilt or innocence of one of the four convicted.' The programme showed how the throw bomb had been used at Woolwich. It then referred to the first TV newsflash of the explosion at 10.26 pm, at which time Paul Hill had maintained he was with his family, Mr and Mrs Keenan, 12 miles away in Camden. Turning to the Guildford Four, the programme then emphasised that all four had always claimed they were totally innocent. The only evidence against them was their confessions.

The programme moved to the Home Secretary's decision not to refer the case, and Cardinal Hume was asked to comment:

> I am very disappointed indeed because I and many other people are quite convinced that the Guildford Four are innocent. It is a question of the integrity of British justice. That I think is one of the values in our society which has to be upheld and many people are saying, and have said, that it is justice which has suffered in these cases. And I would say that perhaps, as much as justice, it is common-sense. And I think common-sense dictates that these cases be looked at again.
>
> . . . It is not surprising that people were very shocked and very angry and to some extent, of course, this can condition one subconsciously – the jury or a judge, the police – to get a conviction quickly, and perhaps to go too quickly without examining everything very carefully. I think this is what might have happened. I am not accusing anyone of malevolence, but the situation, I think, made it very difficult for both the police and everybody else to approach the situation calmly.

Lord Devlin then spoke to camera:

> It was what I would call a thin case. That is to say all the evidence against them was their own confessions, that was the sole evidence, there was no corroboration of it, no other evidence – they denied it – they said the confessions had been, putting it bluntly, beaten out of them, and that was the sole issue.

The programme turned to the confessions and the discrepancies and inconsistencies between them. The defendants did not prove any improprieties by the police who had always denied them, and the jury believed them. Lord Devlin remarked:

> I am not very happy myself about the idea of convicting only upon confessions that have been given to the police – and in some other jurisdictions a confession without corroboration would not be regarded as sufficient – in Scotland for example, – but there it was.

There had been no identification and no forensic evidence. All the statements were taken before the defendants saw a solicitor. They contained, on material points, only information the police already knew. Barry Irving of the Police Foundation recalled his work in analysing, after the trial, the confessions of Patrick Armstrong which he had explained in *The Guildford Time Bomb*. He went on to say that his – '. . . conclusion after reading them was that without corroboration in a case of this kind, one is on very dangerous ground . . . where there are additional problems about the way in which the interrogation was handled then one is on more difficult ground still.' The programme added that 'today the Guildford Four confessions would be inadmissible.'

In response to a reference to Carole Richardson, Cardinal Hume said:

> I am very convinced that Carole Richardson is an innocent person. She was a very young girl at the time and she seemed to have personal problems about drugs and the rest. The whole of her story seems to make it highly improbable either that she would be involved in IRA activities or, much more importantly, that they would use a person like that for a highly sophisticated operation from an IRA point of view.

The programme then gave some details of Carole Richardson's background, her state at the time of interrogation, and referred to the reports by Dr MacKeith and Dr Gudjonsson which, they said, had not been made public although they had obtained copies. They quoted some of the conclusions of the reports in which it was stated that the validity of the 1974 confessions must be seriously questioned; and observed that there was no reference at all to the reports by these two doctors in the Home Office memorandum on the Guildford Four, in spite of the fact that they had been commissioned by the Home Office.

Reference was made to the Criminal Appeal Act of 1968 and the

Home Secretary's interpretation of his powers and how they can be used. David Mellor gave his justification for the interpretation of the powers by successive Home Secretaries. The programme outlined the important revelations stemming from the capture and evidence of the Balcombe Street ASU, concluding with their firm affirmation that they had carried out the Guildford and Woolwich bombings and that the Guildford Four had nothing to do with them.

Lord Devlin was interviewed and said in relation to the Guildford Four:

> They asked for a new trial and they didn't get it. What they got instead was the three judges who were in the Court of Appeal saying that – we, and not a new jury, will decide this – we will hear what you have to say – we will make up our minds whether you are telling the truth or not – and if you are not – if the Balcombe Street lot are not telling the truth – then the convictions will stand . . .
>
> That I think is fundamentally wrong. It is fundamentally wrong because questions of that sort are for the jury and not the judge. And they were entitled therefore on this issue to the new trial for which they asked.

The programme related how at the appeal the Balcombe Street gang supplied unique detail to show that they were the real bombers. So much so that the prosecution and Lord Roskill were content enough to assume that three of the gang had bombed Woolwich, and that two of them had been at Guildford. Nevertheless, the appeal was dismissed. Reference was made to an 'opinion' Lord Devlin was preparing for the defence in which he was to state that the Court of Appeal decision to judge the credibility of the Balcombe Street gang itself rather than let a jury hear it was wrong on three counts.

Lord Devlin gave his three reasons:

> First – no trial by jury. Half the case was not tried by jury – that means no trial. Second, the case was split – whether it had been by judges or jury, it was split in two parts. Third, no appeal – because you cannot have the judges deciding an appeal for themselves.
>
> Each of these three points constitutes a procedural flaw, which should lead by itself to a quashing of the convictions. But it is the middle one – the central one – that is a violation of justice on any basis – however you look at it – in whatever form of procedure. You cannot split a case in half. You can't make the defence deploy half his witnesses before one tribunal and half his witnesses before another.

Moving on, the programme outlined the bombing at Woolwich, how a fourth man had to be accounted for and how Brendan Dowd was able to give telling details, including the car driving off without lights which was later confirmed by a prosecution witness. However, Dowd's account of the dummy run the previous evening differed in some details from that of others. Lord Roskill had said Dowd was a 'deplorable witness', and called him a liar whose whole evidence therefore had to be dismissed. Paul Hill's confession had been short and sketchy compared to Brendan Dowd's.

In court Paul Hill had relied on alibi witnesses. He was working at the time on a building site with Frank Keenan and had spent the evening of the Woolwich bombing with Mr and Mrs Keenan in their flat in Camden. He said he had only gone out for 20 minutes to telephone his girlfriend, Gina Clarke. Paul Hill claimed that he and the Keenans saw the newsflash about Woolwich at 10.26 pm. At the trial, Keenan confirmed all this but the jury did not believe him.

The programme then introduced a new witness, Mrs Yvonne Fox, who had not given evidence at the trial. She explained that she had spent most of the evening at the Keenans and confirmed that Paul Hill was there. The Keenans were also interviewed on the programme and were adamant that Paul Hill had been with them all the evening, apart from 20 minutes or so when he was making his phone call, and that he had returned before the newsflash at 10.26 pm. In two separate interviews Alastair Logan said that Yvonne Fox's statement was new evidence not heard by a jury and should be acceptable to the Home Secretary. He also confirmed that he had always thought from the outset that the Guildford Four whom he represented were all innocent and that he would never give up the fight.

At the end the programme returned to Cardinal Hume, who said:

> It always needs immense courage to say I am wrong. And all possible ways of re-opening the case have to be examined closely. And I like to think that the anxiety which is in many people's minds – they will go on expressing it, because where there has been an injustice – those cases do not go away.

The final word was left to Lord Devlin. He was asked what sort of overall justice did he think they had received. He replied:

> None – perhaps that is putting it a bit strongly. But either you have justice whole and complete, or you have no justice. You can't have a bit of justice here and a bit of justice there.

Reverting briefly to the Maguire case, apart from the hard core of the scientific evidence, and how representations on it had been handled in the Home Office memorandum, there were still other aspects of the case which were causing concern and were even disturbing. It will be recalled that the police were only able to get on to the Maguire household because of the contradictory and inconsistent 'confessions' of the Guildford Four. Anne Maguire and the rest of the Maguire Seven must have been the most unlikely IRA bomb-makers ever to cross the paths of the Metropolitan Police, or any other force. It is remarkable that this was not realised at the time of their arrests by senior police officers and others, and it must have been realised by the whole country after their interviews on television in 1985 following their release from prison. It is even more remarkable that Giuseppe Conlon who was gravely ill and suffered from breathlessness at the time, and who had died in 1980 while serving his sentence, could have been envisaged, as he was by the Crown, as joining 'all hands to the pump' in frantic kneading and disposal of a bulk of explosive, which was never shown to have existed.

As already mentioned, the scientific witness for the defence at the Maguire Seven trial was John Yallop who had developed the TLC test in the first place and was Mr Higgs' predecessor as a Principal Scientific Officer at RARDE. He said he had never contemplated the test being used as sole evidence in a case, and he explained some of its weaknesses in relation to the swabs taken from some of the Maguire Seven. He added that by 1974 it was common practice to carry out confirmatory tests. But in cross-examination Sir Michael Havers attempted to ridicule Yallop's 'sudden conversion' and accused him of selectivity. In contrast the scientific evidence of Higgs and Lidstone of RARDE was accepted by the Crown without question. They did not consider that in these cases a further test was necessary. They were, in fact, acting contrary to their own established scientific principles.

We should now turn to a review of the salient points and central issues relating to the Guildford Four case. The time bombs at the Horse and Groom and the Seven Stars on 5 October, 1974 were the first major incidents, in terms of loss of life and damage to property, during Phase One of the IRA mainland bombing campaign. As the weeks went by with no arrests after the Guildford explosions there was increasing pressure on the Surrey Police. Within hours of the Birmingham pub bombs on 21 November, some six weeks after the explosions at Guildford, the West Midlands police had arrested six men; they charged them three days later. But the Surrey Police were still no further forward.

It was rumoured at the time that by then there were some Surrey Police officers working with the West Midlands Police, but the purpose of this collaboration was not known, if indeed it was true. After the tip-off from Northern Ireland, the Surrey Police indulged in a frenzy of some 50 arrests, including the Guildford Four, starting on 28 November 1974. All this had clearly been organised at the highest level within the Surrey Police. They denied at the trial allegations of impropriety in securing, within a few days, uncorroborated confessions from the Four. It is not surprising that the court believed the police rather than the Guildford Four with their background of drifting, drugs and living in squats.

What is surprising is that when, after the arrests, senior officers of the Surrey Police saw the accused and read the four confessions with over 150 discrepancies, they did not suspect that the wrong people might have been arrested. Maybe they did suspect. However, it was alleged at the time of the arrests that there was a possibility the policemen concerned were convinced they had the right people, but could not prove it, and so they 'helped' the evidence. Only the Surrey Police at the time, from the highest ranks downwards, would know whether or not all this was true.

The Guildford Four went to trial in October 1975, were convicted, went to appeal in October 1977 and that was rejected. In addition to the distinct unlikelihood that the IRA would use such people for bombing missions, and the nature of their uncorroborated confessions, the central issues of the whole case emerged as the alibis, the medical reports on Carole Richardson, the evidence of the Balcombe Street ASU and Brendan Dowd at their own trial as well as at the Guildford appeal, and the alterations made by forensic scientists to their own statements.

As there was no evidence whatsoever against the Guildford Four other than their retracted confessions, their alibis were of supreme importance. The weakest case of the Four was that against Carole Richardson. It must have been clear to the Director of Public Prosecutions and the police that, if the case against Carole Richardson collapsed, so too would the case against the remaining three. And, if that had happened, the forthcoming trial of the Maguire Seven would have been brought into question.

Carole Richardson had two witnesses at the trial – Frank Johnson and Lisa Astin. Also two members of the Jack the Lad pop group had made statements. Later in 1987, Maura Kelly was another alibi witness. Her solicitor claimed that they had been treated more as suspects rather than witnesses, and were not properly protected during the course of the interviews. There was some justification for this claim because the police apparently found it necessary to arrest Frank Johnson on two occasions, between which he changed his statements.

Gerard Conlon was unable to produce an alibi witness at the trial, which seemed strange to many people at the time. He was living at the Conway House Hostel on 5 October, 1974 and said he spent the evening there. It was odd, to say the least, that no member of staff, resident, local police who visited the hostel frequently, or police who were investigating the case, could confirm whether or not he was at the hostel that evening. The police took all the records from the hostel.

As to medical evidence on Carole Richardson, it was remarkable that the Home Office should have made no reference whatsoever, in the memorandum on the Guildford Four, to the reports on her by Dr J MacKeith and Dr G Gudjonsson which the Home Office had received in April 1986. By 1987 these two doctors were leaders in research in the field of false confessions. As already recorded, at the end of his report Dr MacKeith had stated – 'I conclude that the statements that resulted in her conviction on the several charges were very probably unreliable.' In the minds of many these reports alone constituted 'a consideration of substance.'

The trial of the Balcombe Street ASU and Brendan Dowd was in January 1977 and they gave evidence at the Guildford Four appeal in October 1977. Their trial was something of a contrast to that of the Guildford Four. They openly admitted membership of the IRA, made no attempt to defend themselves and gave impressively accurate and precise evidence as to the layout of the pubs, the make-up of the bombs and where they were planted. They refused to plead to any of the charges against them because they had not been charged with the Guildford and Woolwich bombings which they had admitted. The Director of Public Prosecutions scaled down the counts on the original indictment and eliminated some of the offences committed during Phase One (August 1974 to February 1975). These included the Guildford and Woolwich offences for which the Guildford Four had been convicted. The jury refused to find the Balcombe Street ASU and Dowd guilty of any specific offences during Phase One of their operations. This caused considerable embarrassment for the Director of Public Prosecutions, the forensic scientists and the police, particularly Commander Nevill and DCS Imbert who had arrested them and to whom they had made their admissions.

It can only be assumed that the jury took such unexpected action because of revelations about the scientific evidence at the Guildford trial, and at the Balcombe Street ASU trial, which emerged at the latter only after a great deal of cross-examination of Higgs and Lidstone of RARDE regarding statements they had made. Higgs dealt mainly with time bombs, as at Guildford, while Lidstone worked mainly on throw bombs as at Woolwich.

By the middle of 1975 Lidstone had completed a thorough history of throw bombs but it was not published. For purposes of the Guildford and Woolwich trial he produced simply a statement which related to the Woolwich offence. He gave no details of any other similar offences, including the three thrown devices before Guildford, relating to the modus operandi, the material, or any other idiosyncratic factor of a forensic nature. As regards Woolwich, Higgs told the court that he had made two statements. The first, dated 26 January, 1976, had linked the Woolwich explosion to a series later attributed to the Balcombe Street ASU. The second, dated 17 June, 1976, omitted all mention of the Woolwich explosion.

In relation to Guildford, he had signed a statement dated 10 October, 1975 (before the end of the Guildford trial and not made available to the defence) which included a diagram linking the Guildford bombings to a series of explosions which had occurred after the arrest of the Guildford Four. At the Balcombe Street ASU trial he made a second statement dated 12 July 1976 which was identical to the earlier statement but all reference to Guildford had been removed. As we have seen, it came to light at the Balcombe Street ASU trial that it was at the instigation of the Director of Public Prosecutions that Commander Nevill had instructed Higgs to remove reference to Guildford and Woolwich from the lists.

All this emerged after Higgs and Lidstone were asked questions in cross-examination designed to find out why they had not, apparently, made the connection forensically between the Woolwich and Guildford offences and the remainder of the offences with which the Balcombe Street ASU were charged. The Director of Public Prosecutions, and the police, must have been aware of the connections which had been made by Higgs and Lidstone. They also knew that some 19 sets of fingerprints were found in the two Balcombe Street ASU 'safe houses', located after their arrest, but none of the prints was of the Guildford Four. Many were, however, of known IRA members.

No answers to key questions arising from this summary of central issues concerning the Guildford Four case were forthcoming after the rejection of their appeal in October 1977. Some questions still remained unanswered in January 1987 when the Home Secretary decided not to refer the case:

> Why was it necessary to present the Guildford and Woolwich offences at the Guildford trial as isolated acts of terrorism whereas in reality they were part of a connected series of offences for which there were strong, positive and idiosyncratic forensic links showing these connections?
>
> Why did the Surrey police and the Bomb Squad not question the Guildford Four about the other connected offences which preceded Guildford and came before Woolwich?

Why did the Bomb Squad carry out only a very 'surface' interrogation of the Guildford Four in the aftermath of the alleged freely made confessions by them to the Surrey Police who believed they had in their custody persons who had been engaged in terrorist activity?

Why did the Surrey Police fail to ask questions about the Guildford bombings when they interviewed the Balcombe Street ASU about the Caterham bombing?

In view of this would it be right to conclude that the Bomb Squad did not believe that the Guildford Four and those who were originally charged with them, but whose charges were subsequently dropped, were members of an IRA ASU?

Also, in view of the failure to ask the Balcombe Street ASU about the Guildford bombings, would it be right to conclude that the police were anxious that the links between the various bombings should remain concealed?

If the Balcombe Street ASU and Dowd were believed by the scientific expert witnesses to have committed the Guildford and Woolwich offences, and the police were correct in their assumption that they never got all the people who were responsible, why was it necessary to go to the extent of manufacturing new statements in which this important evidence was omitted?

If the evidence was sufficiently strong to charge the Balcombe Street ASU with the other offences forensically linked with Guildford and Woolwich in the absence of admissions by them in relation thereto, why was it thought impractical to charge them with the Guildford and Woolwich offences for which full and detailed confessions were available to the prosecution?

Against the background of this review of the main issues in the Maguire Seven and Guildford Four cases, the search was on in Archbishop's House, during the early months of 1987, for a way through the impasse with which all those who supported the two cases were now confronted. Three members of the Deputation – Cardinal Hume, Lord Scarman and Roy Jenkins – were able to have a preliminary meeting on 3 February, the object of which was to review the present situation and discuss possible ways forward. At later meetings all members of the Deputation were able to be present, as was Robert Kee.

At the meeting on 3 February, the wide-ranging discussion included consideration of the relative merits of finding a way through to the Court of Appeal; of proposing to the Home Secretary that a Tribunal under the 1921 Act should be set up; or suggesting that a senior judge, possibly a Scottish Law Lord, should be appointed with lay assessors in the form of an ad hoc public inquiry. Another matter discussed was the important underlying factor of the possible effects of the climate of opinion at the time of the bombings and trials on the various constituent parts of the criminal justice system. It was agreed that, as a first step, Cardinal Hume should have exploratory discussions with the Home Secretary.

By mid-February word was received from Alastair Logan, who at the time was acting for all of the Guildford Four, that some new witnesses concerning Paul Hill's alibi for Woolwich might be forthcoming. It has already been mentioned[1] that it was not generally known at the time that throughout the period from 1974 right up until 1998, by which time he was still in the final stages of completing some of the compensation arrangements for the Maguires, Alastair Logan had continued to represent all or some of the Guildford Four and the Maguire Seven for long periods without any remuneration.

It was in 1987 that Lord Devlin and Lord Scarman were to pay him a fitting and moving tribute. Lord Devlin was doing some early drafting on 'Justice and the Guildford Four' which was to be published jointly with Lord Scarman in 1988. After referring to the interviews with the Balcombe Street ASU which Alastair Logan had arranged, he wrote – 'Alastair Logan was, and is, a Guildford solicitor working on his own. Offered the case by the Legal Aid Panel he refused it as too heavy. When no one else would take it, he did. He is one of those pilgrims of the law who, when justice beckons, pick up the staff and the scrip and walk. Legal aid has long since dried up. He is walking still.'

The period February to May 1987 saw much activity in Archbishop's House in the way of meetings preparing material for consideration by members of the Deputation, some of whom attended some of the meetings. By May 1987 things were taking shape and Cardinal Hume had received confirmation from the Home Secretary that he would meet the whole 'Deputation' when they were ready.

Meanwhile, further new evidence in the form of statements was being made ready by Alastair Logan and passed to the Deputation. Lord Devlin had drafted a paper on the legal implications of the action taken by the Court of Appeal at the Guildford Four hearing. The final document was to be in the form of a 'Joint Opinion' by Lord Devlin and Lord Scarman. In addition to the new evidence on which Alastair

[1]Chapter Two – pages 21 to 22.

Logan was working, which related only to the Guildford Four case, other papers covering both cases were being prepared.

Cardinal Hume had undertaken, on behalf of the Deputation, to send a copy of the whole 'submission' to the Home Secretary some days before the proposed meeting.

5

THE SUBMISSION

BY 20 January, 1987 when he gave his oral statement to Parliament and published the two Home Office memoranda, the Home Secretary, Douglas Hurd, had made clear his current position. He considered that individual opinion, whether his own or that of others, was irrelevant to the question of whether the cases of the Guildford Four and Maguire Seven should be referred to the Court of Appeal. He could not see his way to departing from the self-imposed administrative procedure whereby 'new evidence' or a '*new* consideration of substance' were essential pre-conditions before a reference to the Court of Appeal could even be considered. Hurd did not think it would be appropriate to refer the cases to a Tribunal of Inquiry set up under the 1921 Act. He, therefore, felt unable to refer the cases to the Court of Appeal. He gave no indication as to whether or not he might have had doubts about any or all of the Guildford Four and Maguire Seven convictions.

The Home Secretary's decision not to refer the cases clearly followed consideration of advice tendered to him over a period by the Minister of State, and officials in C3 Division. At that time Mr Brian Caffarey was Head of C3 Division and Mr P.A. Stanton was the official with responsibilities for the cases. Some of the advice the Home Secretary received stemmed from the outcome of the internal review of the Guildford Four case which he instigated within days of the showing of the Yorkshire TV programme *The Guildford Time Bomb* on 1 July 1986. He had also set up internal reviews of the Maguire Seven and Birmingham Six cases and he reported on all three cases in his statement to Parliament on 20 January 1987. All this must have put considerable pressure on officials in C3 Division which, in turn, could have affected the scope, depth and quality of the reviews.

During April and May 1987 position papers were prepared in Archbishop's House, with much outside help from Robert Kee, Alastair Logan and others. These papers were for consideration by the whole Deputation which had now come together. The purpose of the papers was to examine the arguments of the Home Office, as revealed in the Home Secretary's oral statement and the two Home Office memoranda, and so provide data on which the Deputation could decide what form their forthcoming 'submission' to the Home Secretary should take. Inevitably there was speculation in many circles about the forthright statement made by Lord Fitt on the *Aunt Annie's Bomb Factory* programme.[1] The question arose whether or not there was, indeed, a possibility that the political establishment feared it might lose public confidence if any, or all, of the convictions were quashed. It was known at the time that there was a view in some circles that where evidence has come to light to show that witnesses who were previously relied upon should not have been, it would be better not to rake over old embers. Within various parts of the criminal justice system this, in turn, could have led to a desire not to have to admit a mistake taking precedence over a genuine belief that justice was being best served.

During this preparatory phase, one object of which was to endeavour to get into the mind of the Home Office, discussions were held with a variety of people who had experience of dealing with C3 Division. Reports were variable. It did, however, come to light that responses to letters and telephone calls were not always prompt or helpful. Some people detected a reluctance, and even resistance, to seeing the other side of events and evidence from the past. It is necessary to take a temporary step forward into 1988 for an illustration of some of the difficulties being encountered during 1987. On 9 September 1988 Alastair Logan had occasion to write to Mr Stanton concerning Carole Richardson. He enclosed copies of an exchange of correspondence between himself and Dr MacKeith asking for them to be placed with papers about Carole Richardson he had already sent to the Home Office. The second and only other paragraph of the letter read:

> Could I also draw your attention to the correspondence that took place between myself and Mr Caffarey and in particular my letter to him of 15 January 1987, and the reminder of 25 August 1987, which have still not been replied to. I also refer to my letter to Mr Caffarey of 1 September 1987 and my letter to yourself of 5 November 1987 which does not appear to have been replied to either.

[1]Lord Fitt had said: 'I know that there is an official mind in connection with this case. I know many members of the police in London, and, indeed, throughout Britain. I know many of the Ministers in the Home Office. I have no doubt that at the back of their mind there is a feeling that Giuseppe Conlon and others may be innocent of this crime for which they have been convicted. But if we find them not guilty then it will open up the floodgates to other people who have been sentenced on very much the same evidence.'

All this was part of the background to the decision taken by Archbishop's House staff in April 1987 to continue to have no direct discussions or correspondence with C3 Division.

Meanwhile, the papers being prepared in Archbishop's House embraced the salient points and central issues which were causing concern after the Home Secretary's refusal to refer the two cases to the Court of Appeal.[2] The fundamental pivot on which the pursuit of justice hangs is the oath taken in court by witnesses – 'The truth, the whole truth, and nothing but the truth.' Whether or not justice was done in the Guildford Four and Maguire Seven cases depends almost entirely on the extent to which the prosecution and their witnesses, the police and forensic scientists, told 'the whole truth.' Not to tell 'the whole truth' is a denial of justice, whether it happens in court or elsewhere, as well as constituting perjured evidence, for the oath has been broken and it matters not that the evidence given as part of the truth is true.

As the papers continued to be drafted, many new facets of the main issues came to light as did further omissions and errors in the Home Office's two memoranda. These should be briefly reviewed.

There can be no doubt that by the time of the Balcombe Street ASU trial in 1977, let alone by 1987, the Director of Public Prosecutions, the scientists at RARDE and the police knew that all the bombings and shootings in Phases One and Two of the IRA campaign in London and the Home Counties were the work of one gang. Phase One extended from August 1974 to February 1975 and included the time bombs at Guildford and the throw bomb at Woolwich. Phase Two started with the time bomb at the Caterham Arms in Caterham in August 1975 and continued until the Balcombe Street ASU were captured in December 1975. The Caterham Arms time bomb was regarded as a carbon-copy of the Guildford bombs.

The question arises whether the juries could safely have relied on what was presented to them as scientific facts by the prosecution scientists. The jury at the trial of the Balcombe Street ASU showed their suspicions, and even distrust, about the scientific and police evidence by failing to find the accused guilty of specific charges in Phase One. The jury were clearly aware that Guildford and Woolwich had been deliberately omitted from statements by the scientists in the Balcombe Street Four trial on instructions from the police as directed by the DPP.

It was the same scientists from RARDE who had also given evidence at the Maguire Seven trial. They did so knowing that the prosecution's central argument that the TLC test using toluene could uniquely iden-

[2]See Chapter Four – pages 94 to 95 for major points

tify nitroglycerine was not, in fact, true. There was no mention of this in the Home Office memorandum on the Maguire Seven. Nor was it acknowledged that Anne Maguire's hands had actually tested clean as did those of her son John Maguire who was not charged. It was on a test done on one of many pairs of Anne Maguire's gloves which were collected later that the scientists and the police relied.

In the absence of any bulk of explosive to be kneaded in the Maguire household, it is difficult to see how the scientists could explain to the prosecution, and in turn to the jury, how traces of nitroglycerine could have been found on the hands of some of the Maguire Seven. Higgs relied on bulk to justify both the level and extent of contamination, and yet the household had been searched by police, sniffer dogs and again by hand-held sniffer devices, as well as being under police observation for over two hours before the arrests. In the same memorandum the Home Office was in error. They stated categorically that the judge 'did *not* direct the jury that the evidence of a quantity of explosives must have been directly and separately proven.' The judge did so direct the jury, but what he did not do was to remind them that no bulk of explosive had been found.

Turning to the memorandum on the Guildford Four, the Home Office omitted any reference to Carole Richardson's doll. The police appeared to have made determined efforts to undermine her alibi evidence, as instanced by their treatment of Frank Johnson and Lisa Astin. She and Carole Richardson said that on the afternoon of 5 October, 1974, the day of the Guildford bombing, when they went to the pop concert at the South Bank Polytechnic in the Elephant and Castle, London, Carole Richardson had bought two dolls, giving one to Maura Kelly. A member of the band at the concert confirmed she had a doll and she was even photographed with it.

In fact, the DPP knew, prior to both the trial and the appeal, that Carole Richardson's solicitors had taken proof of evidence from the five members of the Jack the Lad group who gave the pop concert. One of the group, Philip Murray, who did not give evidence at the trial, said in a statement to the police on 10 January, 1975 that Carole Richardson 'had a little plastic doll about 5' or 6' long, with a green, pointed hat on it'. So, if the prosecution was to be believed, Carole Richardson took the plastic doll to Guildford and back on her 'bombing mission.' Moreover, she would have been seen in the Horse and Groom pub with it on her lap as one of the 'courting couple'.

In the same memorandum the Home Office made a major error in their 'General Comments' on the Balcombe Street ASU admissions at the Guildford Four appeal in October 1977. They quoted the Court of Appeal as saying in relation to the admissions 'there had been a cunning and skilful attempt to deceive the Court by putting forward false evidence.' Those remarks by the Court of Appeal referred only to the claim by the Balcombe Street ASU and Brendan Dowd that they had had no connection with, and did not know, the Guildford Four, and not to their own admissions to the offences which the court accepted, as being true, save in relation to Brendan Dowd's evidence on Woolwich. This error in the memorandum had not only been carried forward to the Home Secretary's oral statement but it also appeared in a letter to *The Times* on 23 January 1987 from David Mellor, Minister of State at the Home Office.

There was yet another facet relating to the Balcombe Street ASU admissions which the Home Secretary may or may not have considered during his review. If he did, he makes no reference to it. Most people with a deep knowledge of the cases regarded the Balcombe Street ASU admissions, and those of Brendan Dowd, as being a very strong indication indeed that the Guildford Four had not been responsible for the bombings. Sir Michael Havers, prosecuting counsel at the Guildford appeal, admitted to the Court that the evidence of Dowd and the ASU had 'a ring of truth' and showed a 'very close personal knowledge of both bombings.' Brendan Dowd had said he had hired a car for the team of five in the Guildford operation in the name of Moffit from Swan National. He had, in fact, used a stolen driving licence in that name which was in the possession of the ASU and which was found amongst the property of the Balcombe Street ASU on their arrest. Swan National confirmed the hiring and that the signature was in Dowd's handwriting. The prosecution, and others, were well aware of the significance of the admissions by the Balcombe Street ASU and Brendan Dowd. This may have accounted for the subsequent attacks made on Dowd's credibility.

Because of his insistence now that both the Guildford Four and the Balcombe Street ASU had been at Guildford, Sir Michael Havers found he needed a second car to accommodate the enlarged gang. A further trawl of Swan National's records showed a second car, but in the name of a Mr R.C. Moffat, had been hired during the same period. The hire form was clearly in a different hand and bore no similarity to the Moffit form. The handwriting was not Dowd's. However, the Crown proceeded on the assumption this was the second car used for the bombings. The admissions of the Balcombe Street ASU had a substantial impact on the Guildford case in that if the Guildford Four had been shown to have been wrongly convicted, the police raid on the Maguire household would have emerged as a less than clever operation.

During those early months of 1987 it was not at all clear what documentation had been available to C3 Division when they undertook the review of the cases. If they did not have access to the reports and notebooks of RARDE scientists, to police statements and notes on interviews undertaken, and to the evidence given in the Court of Appeal by the Balcombe Street ASU, then the comparatively limited scope and depth of the Home Office memoranda emerging from the review would not have been surprising. If they did have such access, then in the view of many people, the outcome of the memoranda was surprising. As the Home Office would not accept Dr Caddy's reports on the scientific evidence as had been given at the trial, and would not set up an independent scientific committee to advise the Home Secretary, it can be argued that in the circumstances they should have insisted on such access, particularly to documents from RARDE.

All members of the Deputation were determined that there was now an urgent need for them to present a 'submission' to the Home Secretary. They were very conscious that by 1987 all of the Maguire Seven had served their long sentences, with Giuseppe Conlon having died after serving six years of his sentence, and that the Guildford Four were now in their fourteenth year of imprisonment. Alastair Logan was making considerable progress in obtaining what could be regarded as 'new evidence'. He was seeking to obtain statements from Fathers Ryan and Carolan, who were the two priests who ran the Conway House Hostel in Quex Road, about Paul Hill and Gerard Conlon; from Mrs Fox and Mr and Mrs Keenan about Paul Hill's alibi for Woolwich; and from Maura Kelly relating to Carole Richardson's alibi for the Guildford Bombing. Cardinal Hume wrote to the Home Secretary on 9 April ,1987 mentioning the new evidence which was being assembled and saying the Deputation would like to come and see him when their work was completed. In commenting on the Home Secretary's decision not to refer cases except on the basis of new evidence or matters of substance, the Cardinal went on to say:

> Although I can acknowledge the reasoning behind the principle, nonetheless I cannot get out of my mind that such an approach can be too restrictive. This is particularly so in respect of the Maguires where the case for the Crown was very narrowly based and, it seems to me, the context within which the specific judgement was made ignored the background and customary behaviour of that family.

Meanwhile, after receiving copies of the memoranda, Cardinal Hume had started to develop what could be described as a philosophical approach to the two cases. It became known as the 'concentric circles.' In essence, the 'outer circle' consisted of the general improbability of guilt for various reasons; the 'middle circle' comprised matters of substance which had arisen since the trials or were not presented at the trials; and the 'inner circle' was to consist of new evidence as and when it became available.

For some considerable time, measured in years, Lord Devlin had been greatly concerned about how the case of the Guildford Four had been handled by the Court of Appeal in October 1977. He considered there had been an error in law. The general public became well aware of his views in 'A case that won't go away' which had been screened on 3 March, 1987[3]. Lord Scarman shared his views and they were both preparing a 'joint opinion', supported by background material. This point of law was to be part of the 'submission' to be presented to the Home Secretary.

In May 1987 two important events took place. The first was that a general election had been announced for 11 June. The Deputation immediately decided to seek their meeting with the Home Secretary, whoever he or she might be by then, in July after the general election. The date was subsequently arranged for 23 July, 1987. Work on the submission continued with this date in mind. The second important event was the progress which Alastair Logan had been able to make in assembling new evidence. He had succeeded in obtaining new statements, including some not heard at the trial, and these were to become the main part of the 'inner circle' of Cardinal Hume's concentric circles. Under the same heading, in addition to the statements, reference was also to be made to the reports of Dr MacKeith and Dr Gudjonsson which were already in the possession of the Home Secretary. Copies of the whole 'concentric circles' document were circulated to all members of the Deputation and they all agreed it should form part of the forthcoming 'submission.'

By mid-July the submission was nearing completion. It was to consist of a covering letter from Cardinal Hume; an 'AIDE-MÉMOIRE' which was a brief statement of the major submissions; APPENDIX 1 to the AIDE-MÉMOIRE which was the JOINT OPINION of Lord Devlin and Lord Scarman with an accompanying MEMORANDUM; APPENDIX 2 to the AIDE-MÉMOIRE, which was developed from the original 'concentric circles' paper – was to be a document now headed 'The "Guildford Four" and the "Maguires"'; and attached to APPENDIX 2 were statements by Maura Kelly, Yvonne Fox, Mr and Mrs Keenan, Father Ryan and Father Carolan. Attached to the MEMORANDUM which accompanied the JOINT OPINION was an ANNEX as a supporting document. This was a lengthy, and inevitably technical, detailed examination of a long line of authorities as well as of several sections of amending statutes. As the submission was a key document in the history of the Guildford Four and Maguire Seven cases it is recorded in full below, other than the technical ANNEX attached to the MEMORANDUM which

[3]Chapter Four, pages 86 to 90

accompanied the JOINT OPINION. However, in the interests of completeness this ANNEX is reproduced as APPENDIX I to the book.

Before we turn to the submission, reference needs to be made to two important decisions taken by the Deputation before Cardinal Hume, on their behalf, sent the documents to the Home Secretary on 20 July 1987, three days before the meeting was to take place. The first decision was that the Deputation would adopt a self-imposed restriction of not revealing any details of the new evidence, or other matters being considered within the Deputation, which were not already in the public domain. The second decision was that the sole channel of communication between the Deputation and the Home Office would be from Cardinal Hume to the Home Secretary.

In his covering letter to the Home Secretary, Cardinal Hume explained the attachments and re-iterated his serious and continuing anxieties about the justice of the convictions:

> I am grateful to you for arranging to see our Deputation on the Guildford Four/Maguire cases which includes Lord Devlin, Lord Scarman, Roy Jenkins and Merlyn Rees. Robert Kee and my Assistant for Public Affairs, Patrick Victory, will be 'in attendance' on the Deputation.
>
> On behalf of the Deputation I now enclose an 'Aide-Mémoire' with accompanying papers. The 'Aide-Mémoire' is not intended to be a definitive document but, taken with Appendices I and 2 attached to it, we submit that, even as it stands, it constitutes a powerful and compelling case.
>
> Members of the Deputation will be speaking to various parts of the enclosed papers at the meeting.
>
> It remains here now only for me to re-iterate my concern about the cases which I have discussed with you and with your predecessors. My concern in this matter arose first from my contact with Patrick Joseph Conlon whom I visited on a number of occasions in Wormwood Scrubs before his death in 1980. I became absolutely convinced of his innocence and because of that developed profound doubts about the justice of the Maguire convictions.
>
> Information which has been published and broadcast over the past year articulates the serious anxieties I and many others have had about a possible miscarriage of justice not only in the Maguire case but also in the convictions in the Guildford bombings trial.

The AIDE-MÉMOIRE, had been prepared by Lord Scarman –

AIDE-MÉMOIRE
'The Guildford Four' and the 'Maguires'

1 The purpose of this note is to state briefly, without recapitulating the detail now to be found in the extensive documentation available to the Secretary of State, the major submissions which we ask the Secretary of State to take into consideration.

2 In our view a substantial miscarriage of justice may well have occurred in the two trials resulting in the wrongful conviction of the accused. In the Criminal Appeals Act 1968 provision is made which enables the Secretary of State, if he thinks fit, to refer cases to the Court of Appeal for review. If the Secretary of State so decides, the Court reviews the whole case, fact and law; it is not confined to 'new evidence or matters of substance': see R v Lattimore and others 62 Cr. App. R.53, and R v Perry and Harvey (1909) 2 Cr. App. R.89, 92, and R v Chard (1983): 3 All E.R. page 637 at page 641.

3 We understand that a practice or convention has developed in the Home Office under which the Secretary of State refers cases only if satisfied that *new* matter (i.e. evidence or other matters of substance) has arisen or emerged since the conclusion of the judicial process. Any such convention fails to measure up to the wide powers possessed by the Court if a reference is made. If upon a reference the Court can review the whole case, the Secretary of State should be able to refer if of the opinion that there is a strong likelihood that there has been a substantial miscarriage of justice whether the likelihood arises from some incident or omission or other error in the judicial proceedings resulting in conviction or from new matters arising thereafter. In the Lattimore case the true ground for referral was mistake at trial either in the medical evidence or in the judge's understanding of its effect.

4 Further, the statute itself does not, upon its true construction, confine the Secretary of State to 'new' matter. The power to refer arises if he thinks the case fit to refer. It would be wrong to confine the width of the power which Parliament has conferred by an executive practice or convention.

5 But, if the Secretary of State chooses in this case to require new evidence or matter of substance, we submit that such matter exists in both cases. Put broadly, for the reasons which we have already developed in documents available to the Secretary of State the convictions of the 'Guildford Four' based as they were exclusively on 'confessions' were unsafe at the time and are now demonstrably unsatisfactory and unsafe. The Court of Appeal fell into grievous error when, instead of ordering a new trial so that *a jury* could

decide whether in the light of the evidence, which had become available, of Dowd and of the Balcombe Street men the guilt of the accused was established beyond reasonable doubt, it formed, and acted upon, its own assessment of the new evidence. The paper by Lord Devlin and myself (Appendix I) refers.

6 In our view, therefore, the Court's failure to order a new trial in the light of the new evidence available was a fundamental denial of the right of the four accused to trial by jury. Nevertheless, if this be deemed insufficient for a reference, there are new matters of substance which reveal the unsatisfactory and unsafe nature of the verdicts. They include the new evidence listed in Appendix 2 relating to the Richardson alibi (Maura Kelly); the opinions of those who have assessed the reliability of her admissions in the light of her character, her habits prior to trial, and her record and protestations of innocence since conviction (Report of Drs MacKeith and Gudjonsson); statements by Mr and Mrs Keenan and Yvonne Fox (relating to Paul Hill); statements by Father Ryan and Father Carolan (relating to Hill and Conlon). Robert Kee has produced a useful analysis of these matters within a scheme of approach which was first adopted by Cardinal Hume and is now Appendix 2 to this note. (The analysis, of course, includes much else of importance.)

7 If the statements of the 'Guildford Four' can now be seen to be an unsafe and unsatisfactory basis for conviction (as we believe a jury would find them to be), then the Maguire verdicts must be extremely suspect. The Maguires and those who were arrested with them were arrested in the first instance because Anne Maguire was implicated in the Guildford pub murders by Hill and Conlon. If Hill's and Conlon's statements can now be seen to be unreliable, one is left with the extraordinarily flimsy case based on the findings of nitroglycerine upon the hands and fingers of the accused other than Anne and upon the gloves of Anne. We say 'flimsy' not only because of the queries raised as to the validity of the tests but also because of the evidence (astonishing if they were really guilty) that no nitroglycerine was found in the Maguires' house or in the surrounding neighbourhood (which was searched). We would add also the extraordinary omission by the defendants' counsel to explore the possibility of contamination of the swabs from other sources.

8 The conduct of the seven accused in their persistent protestations, post-trial, of innocence including the death-bed protestation of 'Giuseppe' Conlon, is surely in the strange circumstances of this trial significant and persuasive new matter suggesting an appalling miscarriage of justice. Not one of the accused ever admitted guilt, despite pertinacious attempts by the police to obtain confessions of guilt.

9 This note assumes a knowledge of the detail of the cases. We believe that no system of criminal justice should be without an effective review process where there are strong grounds for believing that there has been a substantial miscarriage of justice, whatever its cause or causes.
10 Properly interpreted and applied, the Criminal Appeals statute provides a review process which, if unencumbered by administrative rules of practice or decision-making formulae, does enable the Court of Appeal to carry out the broad review that is necessary if the miscarriage is to be corrected and justice ultimately done. The Secretary of State is in criminal matters the nation's Minister of Justice. 'Fiat justitia' is his inescapable duty: the consequences will be not the collapse of the heavens (no need to cry 'ruant coeli') but the vindication of the British criminal process as one capable of recognising and correcting injustice, even when the injustice has arisen through its own errors but has emerged or won recognition long after the conclusion of the trial.

15 July, 1987 (Signed): Scarman

The point of law was dealt with at APPENDIX I to the AIDE-MÉMOIRE. It consisted of two parts. The first was the JOINT OPINION by Lord Devlin and Lord Scarman, and the second was the supporting MEMORANDUM also signed by them–

APPENDIX 1 to AIDE-MÉMOIRE

JOINT OPINION

In our opinion the judgement of the Court of Appeal in this case raises an appealable point of law in a matter of substance. By an 'appealable point of law' we mean a point which, if it had been placed before the Appeal Committee of the House of Lords, would have been likely to result in the grant of leave to appeal. By 'a matter of substance' we mean that the point is not a mere technicality: in the respects set out in para 2 of the attached Memorandum it alleges a failure of due process fatal to the judgement.

The point is as follows. The Appellants tendered to the Court of Appeal fresh evidence which, if truthful, constituted a complete defence. The power and duty of the Court was to decide whether the evidence tendered was 'capable of belief and, if placed before a jury, might be believed': see para 8 of the Annex to the Memorandum attached. The Court heard the witnesses tendered. But instead of deciding as an inter-locutory matter whether or not the evidence was 'likely to be credible' (Criminal Appeal Act 1967 Section 23), themselves rejected the evidence as untruthful. In so doing they exceeded their power. It is submitted that the authority of the judgement in the House of Lords in Stafford v D.P.P. (1974) A.C. 878, on which the Court of Appeal relied, does not extend beyond the facts of that case in which there was no issue as to the truthfulness of the evidence tendered.

(Signed): DEVLIN
SCARMAN

16 July, 1987

MEMORANDUM BY LORD DEVLIN AND LORD SCARMAN

GUILDFORD BOMBERS

1 On 16 September 1975 the trial began of four persons, whom we shall call the Guildford Bombers, charged with the murders of the victims of a bomb which exploded in a Guildford pub on 5 October 1974. The only evidence against them was their own confessions made to the police. Their defence was that the confessions were untrue and had been extorted; there was also some alibi evidence. The trial continued until October. In October, after deliberating for over a day, the jury found them all guilty and they were sentenced accordingly. They appealed. While the appeal was pending, their solicitor came into contact with O'Connell and Dowd who were in prison charged with a similar murder at Woolwich. They told the solicitor that they were responsible for the Guildford bombing and that the Guildford convicts had nothing to do with it. They were allowed by the Court of Appeal to give evidence to this effect in the Guildford appeal but the three appeal judges disbelieved them and refused to order the new trial for which the appellants had asked. So the appeal was dismissed and the Guildford convicts are still in prison.
2 In our opinion the refusal of a new trial violated three fundamental principles of British justice.
First, it split the trial arbitrarily into two parts. Over what may be called the first half of the case the jury had deliberated for more than a day before rejecting the defence. Who can say that if the evidence in the first part had been fortified by the second, the jury would inevitably have rejected both?
Second, it deprived the defendants as to 50% of the trial of their constitutional right to a jury.

Third, it deprived them of their right of appeal. An appeal requires a review. Judges cannot review their own findings of fact. If judges are going to substitute themselves for the jury at the trial, there must be a second lot of judges for the review.

3 These violations were of course not deliberate but the consequence of a deep misunderstanding of the law. The function of the Court of Appeal in relation to new evidence was left undetermined by statute and the efforts of the judges to formulate a workable code have not proved altogether satisfactory. It would indeed be astounding if any of their formulations compelled any of the three results set out in the preceding paragraph. It is easier to say that than to identify the points at which the reasoning began to stray. That task involves the detailed examination of a long line of authorities as well as of several sections of amending statutes. We leave it to an ANNEX which will inevitably be technical.

(Signed): DEVLIN
16 July 1987 SCARMAN

The technical ANNEX to the MEMORANDUM referring to authorities and statutes is, as already mentioned, at APPENDIX I to the book.

APPENDIX 2 to the AIDE-MÉMOIRE was the final development of the original 'concentric circles' approach devised by Cardinal Hume and completed by Robert Kee–

APPENDIX 2 to AIDE-MÉMOIRE

'THE GUILDFORD FOUR' AND THE 'MAGUIRES'

This paper has been prepared in pursuance of Cardinal Hume's philosophic approach to the cases as under: –

Outer Circle

The general improbability of guilt for various reasons.

Middle Circle

Matters of substance which have arisen since the trials or were not presented at the trials.

Inner Circle

New evidence.

OUTER CIRCLE:
(General improbability of guilt for various reasons).

Guildford:
No evidence whatever other than confessions to connect the Four with the bombings.

Confessions self-contradictory and mutually inconsistent.

Confessions say four others were with them at Guildford (McGuinness, Anderson, Colman and Anne Maguire) but, since these do not confess, the murder charge against them has to be dropped. (Another charge found for Anne Maguire).

Except as alleged in this case by the Crown, I.R.A. have never operated from squats or hostels – for obvious security reasons. (Police actually visited squat and hostel in question in weeks before bombing).

Except as alleged in this case by the Crown, I.R.A. have never used drug-addicts or petty criminals – for obvious security reasons. (Armstrong was actually on remand for several weeks on burglary charge in 1974). (Richardson was a shop-lifter and drug-addict).

Improbability of I.R.A. using a very young *English* girl, and particularly one who was a shop-lifter and drug-addict.

Improbability, if Richardson's alibi was concocted as alleged by the Crown, of I.R.A. concocting such an alibi and *not* including in it other members of team.

Improbability, if Richardson's alibi was concocted as alleged by the Crown, of her not producing it on arrest and in interrogations in following days.

Improbability of Richardson and Armstrong contacting police and giving their correct names and addresses, after Folkestone telephone box incident, if they had carried out the Guildford bombing 3 weeks before.

Tone and content of all letters home of those convicted over a period of more than twelve years since their arrest.

Maguires:

Extreme improbability, given the court accepted movements of Maguire household that day, and given complete absence of any bomb-making equipment or body of explosives in the house or neighbourhood, that the nitroglycerine on the swabs as tested can have come from the hands of those arrested and subsequently convicted.

Extreme improbability, if the Maguire household had been handling explosives, of Paddy Maguire going to the local police station to enquire about his missing brother, as he did, in the period in which the Crown alleges explosives were being handled in his house.

Failure of the Crown to explain how, if explosives were being handled in the house as alleged between 6.30 pm (approx.), when Smyth and O'Neill arrived, and 7.00 pm, when the police put the house under observation, the bulk of the explosives can have been disposed of without trace.

Absurdity of Judge's suggestion that it might have been disposed of while the men were on their way to the nearby pub, while under police observation, without the disposal being observed by the police.

Extreme unlikelihood, if O'Neill had been handling explosives as alleged by the Crown, of him not taking advantage of the three days' liberty allowed him by the police before the result of the tests on his hand swabs were known, to leave the country.

Demeanour of Giuseppe Conlon until his death (1980) and Maguire household for past 12 1/2 years.

MIDDLE CIRCLE:

(Matters of substance which have arisen since the trials or were not presented at the trials).

Guildford:

New information has emerged since the Guildford trial (1975) which, if available to the defence at the trial, could have enabled them to advance a cogent argument in support of their clients' innocence which might have persuaded the jury to bring in a different verdict.

At the 'Balcombe Street' trial (1977) government forensic experts testified that, before the Guildford trial, they had prepared statements showing forensic links between the explosions at Guildford and Woolwich and other I.R.A. explosions with which the accused could not be associated.

But they further testified that, on orders from the Director of Public Prosecutions communicated to them by the anti-terrorist squad, they had subsequently altered these statements to omit all reference to the links with Guildford and Woolwich, for the purposes of the Guildford and Woolwich trial.

They also testified that in this, the Balcombe Street trial, they had omitted all reference to the forensic links between the offences being tried there and the Guildford and Woolwich offences.

Commander Nevill of the anti-terrorist squad testified that he had received instructions from the Director of Public Prosecutions to instruct the forensic scientists to do this.

Leaving aside the propriety or otherwise of such instructions, it can be seen that at the Guildford trial the defence was deprived of evidence which could have seemed significant to the jury. The manner in which it was so deprived could further have added to the jury's doubts about the integrity of the prosecution case.

Other information, elicited only after the Balcombe Street arrests and therefore unavailable to the jury at the Guildford trial, was extended and confirmed at the Guildford Appeal. The Court accepted that one member of the Balcombe Street unit had probably taken part in the Guildford bombing, together with another I.R.A. man arrested elsewhere, both of whom strongly denied that the four sentenced for Guildford had had anything to do with that offence or indeed had ever been known to them.

The Appeal Court decided as a question of fact that this denial was untrue. But a jury, particularly in the light of the above forensic testimony, might not have decided this question of fact in the same way, had the evidence been available to them.

Far from the jury system being challenged by a call for review of these cases, it can be seen that it is the refusal to review them which diminishes the proper powers of a jury.

Maguires:

The scientific T.L.C. test, on the results of which alone the seven people from the Maguire household were found guilty, is no longer accepted by the Home Office as satisfactory unless supported by a confirmatory test. The Maguire Seven could not today be found guilty on the basis of the evidence produced at their trial.

There is no other known case of a similar type in which the evidence of the actual sample of allegedly contaminated swab has been deliberately destroyed, thus making it impossible to check the evidence of the Crown.

Proper scientific practice demands that part of the sample be retained, a procedure which presents no problem since in solution it is capable of multiple division.

A cogent defence argument not developed at the trial was that, even if the jury were to become convinced that the T.L.C. test, unsupported by confirmatory test, were accurate in revealing, as alleged, nitroglycerine on the swabs, this did not necessarily mean that nitroglycerine had been on the hands and gloves when swabbed. Accuracy of the T.L.C. test came to be equated with the guilt of the Maguire Seven.

At the Guildford trial no attempt was made to protect the name of Anne Maguire against hearsay evidence alleging her to be a bombmaker, an offence with which she had been charged though not tried.

She was so named at the Guildford trial by the same prosecuting counsel who was later to prosecute her, before the same judge who was later to try her, as having committed the offence for which she was to be tried.

In view of the wide publicity which this received at the time, the assurance by both prosecuting counsel and judge at the second trial that the Maguire trial had no connection with any other must have carried reduced impact.

A 'piece of chalk' was referred to in a statement to police by Vincent Maguire as having been handled by him in the Maguire house. A Crown witness at the trial suggested this might have been a 'stick of gelignite'. Vincent Maguire claims that he showed the stick of chalk to the police officers who returned him home after making the statement. The evidence was not heard at the trial.

INNER CIRCLE:

(New evidence)

The MacKeith-Gudjonsson report, which also constitutes new evidence and is already in the possession of the Secretary of State, concluded that Carole Richardson's confession statements were probably unreliable.

16 July, 1987 (Signed): ROBERT KEE

Copies of the statements listed below, which constitute new evidence, were attached to the submission. They are reproduced as APPENDICES to the book as shown:

APPENDIX II
Statement of Maura Kelly, substantiating Carole Richardson's alibi.

APPENDIX III
Statement of Yvonne Fox about Paul Hill on the night of the Woolwich bombing.

APPENDIX IV
Statement of Mr Keenan about Paul Hill on the night of the Woolwich bombing (which includes points not obtained from them at the trial).

APPENDIX V
Statement of Mrs Keenan about Paul Hill on the night of the Woolwich bombing (which includes points not obtained from them at the trial).

APPENDIX VI
Statement of Father Ryan about Hill and Conlon (Gerard) while staying in Quex Road hostel, Conway House, in the period before and after the Guildford bombing.

APPENDIX VII
Statement of Father Carolan about Hill and Conlon (Gerard) while staying in Quex Road hostel in the period before and after the Guildford bombing.

The next step was to be the meeting with the Home Secretary, Douglas Hurd, on 23 July, 1987. All members of the 'Deputation' were present, with Robert Kee and Patrick Victory in attendance. Douglas Hurd was accompanied by John Patten MP, who was now Minister of State, and by several civil servants, including no doubt officials from C3 Division. As already mentioned, Cardinal Hume had sent the whole of the 'submission' to the Home Secretary three days ahead of the meeting. This took place at 4.00 pm and lasted, as scheduled, for some 45 minutes. It had never been the intention that there would be a full and detailed discussion of the submission at the meeting. The purpose was to present the submission to the Home Secretary by highlighting some of the main aspects of the cases which had been sources of concern to the Deputation over a long period.

All members of the Deputation took part in the discussion that followed a brief introductory summary by Cardinal Hume of the main points to which the Deputation wished to draw particular attention. Amongst the many points discussed were the significance and importance of the evidence of the Balcombe Street ASU and Dowd, and the error in law whereby at the Guildford appeal the Court formed and acted upon its own assessment of the new evidence; that the convictions of the Guildford Four, based as they were exclusively on 'confessions', were unsafe at the time and were now demonstrably unsatisfactory and unsafe; the weakness of the case against Carole Richardson, particularly in the light of the medical evidence; bearing in mind their image as a family at the time, and their behaviour since the trial, the extreme improbability of the Maguire family being involved in bomb making; if the statements by Paul Hill and Gerard Conlon could now be seen to be unreliable, the extraordinarily flimsy case against the Maguires; Section 17 of the Criminal Appeal Act of 1968 enabled a Home Secretary to refer cases to the Court of Appeal 'if he thinks fit' but a convention had been adopted in the Home Office whereby cases would only be considered for reference if new material had emerged – such a convention failed to measure up to the wide powers possessed by the Court if a reference was made; the new evidence now included in the submission; and finally the need to review both cases in the round against the background of the many representations which have been made over the years from which 'considerations of substance' could emerge. During the meeting, Douglas Hurd gave the background on the Home Office convention relating to the 'new evidence'[4] proviso and also explained his own position with reference to Section 17 of the 1968 Act. As the meeting drew to a close members of the Deputation said that they thought there was growing concern, both in the public and amongst politicians of all parties, about the two cases. This concern could only increase and become more vociferous as time went by.

On 27 July 1987 Cardinal Hume wrote to the Home Secretary, on

[4]See Chapter Four – Page 86

behalf of the Deputation. After thanking him for the time given to hearing what the Deputation considered to be a powerful and compelling case in support of the view that there could have been a miscarriage of justice in the Guildford Four and Maguire Seven cases, he went on to say:

> I understand the reasoning you advanced in support of the need for you to adopt a 'principled' approach in the use of your powers for determining the right course of action to follow in such cases.
>
> Members of the Deputation welcomed the opportunity both to make a positive, and constructive, response to the reasoning in the light of the particular circumstances of the Guildford Four/Maguire cases, and also to draw attention to matters of substance which were either new or resulted from deficiencies in presentations made at the trials.
>
> We were particularly encouraged by your undertaking to examine these matters of substance, and also, as I understood it, to re-consider the use of Section 17 in what has now emerged as the special situation relating to these trials.
>
> It has been a particular concern of mine that a narrow interpretation of Section 17 could, in fact, exclude the consideration of matters of substance which would seem to me to be self-evidently supportive of the claim by our Deputation that there was likely to have been a miscarriage of justice.
>
> You will appreciate, I know, that we were not covering old ground in our discussion with you but it is vitally important, as I am sure you will agree, to consider the intervention we made last Thursday against the background of many considerations which have been published in different ways over the last few years and were referred to in our papers. In other words, there was much more that we could have said.

Word got around (not from the Deputation) that the Home Secretary would be considering the Guildford and Woolwich bombings case. This prompted a powerful leader in *The Times* on 28 July 1987 entitled 'Mr Hurd Looks Again'. The central thrust was 'Mr Hurd's decision is overdue. Even now he is not saying that he will refer the cases to the Court of Appeal. But a referral must not be delayed much longer.' After recalling that the Home Secretary had referred the Birmingham Six case in January 1987, and having reminded readers that 'the Home Office line has been that, in cases such as this, only "new evidence" justifies referral to the Court of Appeal', the leader went on to say:

> The suspicion was that the Home Office was simply trying to minimise the amount of damage involved in admitting that all 17 convictions [Birmingham Six, Guildford Four, Maguire Seven] might be unjust – and so had referred one group in the hope that people would forget about the other. But they will not be forgotten.

It came as a surprise to an ever-widening circle of people that the Home Office had not yet accepted that the cases 'will not go away.'

On 30 July, 1987 the Home Secretary wrote a lengthy letter to *The Times* in response to the leader. He was at pains to explain, as he had done in his oral statement to Parliament on 20 January 1987, why the Home Office had adopted a procedure whereby cases could only be considered for referral on the basis of 'settled principle.' In effect, this meant only on 'new evidence.' In a letter to *The Times* published the following day, Robert Kee made two telling points. The first was that it was curious that, in clarifying his power to refer the Guildford Four and Maguire Seven cases to the Court of Appeal, Douglas Hurd had omitted the only words in which Parliament had defined his power – 'if he thinks fit.' The second point was – 'since in his letter to you the Home Secretary chooses to argue one of the most important points in dispute, namely the worth of the Balcombe Street gang evidence, it is necessary to state that this is indeed new in the sense that no jury has ever been called on to decide its credibility.'

On 6 August Lord Scarman's letter to *The Times*, referring to the leader and the Home Secretary's response, was published. He made three important points:

> As a member of the Deputation led by Cardinal Hume I had intended to make no public comments on the Guildford and Woolwich pub-bombing case or the Maguire explosives case while the Home Secretary was considering our submissions. But his letter (July 30) in response to your leading article of July 28 is too disturbing to let pass.
>
> First, there is his emphasis on the need for new and substantial matter not before the original court as a condition to be met if a case is to be referred to the Court of Appeal. The condition is not to be found in the statute which empowers him to make the reference: and the case law shows that once a case is referred the Court of Appeal is not confined to a consideration of the new matter but reviews the case as a whole.
>
> Secondly, it would appear that if refusal is to be conditional upon the emergence of 'new' matter our system of criminal justice is deprived of the possibility of judicial review of a conviction which can be demonstrated to have been obtained by mistake of law or

fact which for one reason or another was uncorrected in the original proceedings, either in the course of trial or in the Court of Appeal. This would be serious indeed.

I confess that I am fearful when an administrative rule of practice is elevated into 'a principle'.

On 7 August Douglas Hurd wrote to Cardinal Hume saying – 'I am very glad to have had the opportunity to listen to the views that were powerfully expressed by yourself and other members of the Deputation. I am, as I said, giving the most careful consideration to all the points which were raised, legal and factual, against the background (as you rightly point out) of other representations which have been made in the last few years. I am not replying to the points raised by Lord Scarman and Robert Kee in *The Times* because I believe that these points and indeed my own position were fully covered in our discussion.' The Home Secretary went on to say that the Deputy Chief Constable of Avon and Somerset, Mr Sharples, would be leading an inquiry into the new statements by Mrs Fox, Mr and Mrs Keenan, Maura Kelly, and Fathers Ryan and Carolan. He concluded his letter by saying that the inquiries were to be carried out swiftly so that he could decide as soon as practicable whether to refer the case to the Court of Appeal.

Following on from this, on 14 August, in a brief statement, the Home Office officially confirmed that the Home Secretary had asked James Sharples to examine the new evidence he had received (from the Deputation) concerning alibis relating to the Guildford and Woolwich bombing case. The announcement was widely reported in the Press.

There was relief at, and a general welcome to, the response by the Home Secretary to the presentation of new evidence, but it was noted that the police inquiry concerned only the Guildford Four case. There was some concern amongst the press about the omission of the case of the Maguire family. They had all served their sentences by then, but were still fighting to clear their names. Some asked – where were they to go from here? They had been convicted solely on the basis of forensic evidence. But RARDE had destroyed the swabs and the Home Office had refused to accept the reports of Dr Caddy on the scientific evidence as presented at the trial, or to set up an independent scientific committee to examine again the evidence.

In the circumstances, there was also considerable concern within the Deputation at that stage as to what the next steps should be in the Maguire case. As one newspaper had put it – 'it would be impossible to believe that a false tip-off led by pure chance to the true culprits – to a bomb factory in which no explosives were found.' It came to be recognised by the Deputation that, for the time being anyway, the only way forward might be dependent on the final outcome of the Guildford Four case. If, after a possible referral to the Court of Appeal, their convictions were to be found unsafe and unsatisfactory, then this would immediately bring into question the convictions of the Maguire Seven.

The Maguires were not the only concern that emerged at that time. Alastair Logan was reported in *The Guardian* as saying that he hoped there would be no undue delays in the police investigation, and that the inquiries would not attract the sort of criticisms that had been levelled at the Birmingham investigation. This was a reference to the investigations being undertaken at the time by the Devon and Cornwall police after the Home Secretary had decided in January 1987 to refer the Birmingham Six case to the Court of Appeal. They were looking into a claim by the former West Midlands police officer, Tom Clarke, that the six men were mistreated in police custody where they made confessions which they later retracted.

The background to these anxieties was that earlier Chris Mullin MP and Sir John Farr MP had said that the 30 police officers from the Devon and Cornwall police inquiring into the evidence of Tom Clarke had, between them, taken 'more than 700 statements from every conceivable witness.' Chris Mullin, who had recently published a book, *Error of Judgement*, on the Birmingham bombings, claimed that he had twice been interviewed by senior officers and had formed the view that, 'as is common with inquiries of this nature, they are displaying an unhealthy preoccupation with discrediting Mr Clarke rather than establishing how the convicted men came by their injuries.'

By September 1987 the investigation by James Sharples was getting under way. At an early stage some problems arose from inquiries by solicitors about his precise terms of reference. Also, some difficulties were to be encountered during the course of the early interviews the police wished to undertake and the methods they adopted. But September 1987 onwards was to mark the beginning of a long period in the Deputation's activities which, for want of a better term, could be regarded as 'The Struggle.'

6

THE STRUGGLE

THE HOME SECRETARY had dealt with the cases of the Birmingham Six and the Guildford Four in different ways.

In the Birmingham Six case a former police officer had stated that he had been in the police station on the night when the Birmingham Six were held there and had himself seen violence meted out to them. On the strength of this new evidence the Home Secretary had referred the case to the Court of Appeal. He had also arranged for the Devon and Cornwall Constabulary to undertake further inquiries into these new allegations.

When, six months later, the Home Secretary received the new evidence relating to the Guildford Four and Maguire Seven cases from the Deputation in July 1987, he did not refer them to the Court of Appeal. Instead, before taking any such action, he first arranged for the statements comprising the new evidence relating to the Guildford Four case to be investigated by the Avon and Somerset Constabulary. He made a public announcement to this effect on 14 August.

In the Birmingham Six case, in relation to the scientific evidence, the Home Secretary included in the grounds for referral 'the report of a reappraisal of the Greiss text which was conducted at my request by the Aldermaston Forensic Laboratory.' This contrasted with his refusal over a period of five years to set up an independent appraisal of the scientific evidence in the case of the Maguire Seven. The view held by many was that if the case against the Maguire Seven had collapsed the convictions of the Guildford Four would have been brought into question.

The Devon and Cornwall Constabulary chose to interpret their instructions to investigate the new evidence in the Birmingham case as giving them authority to interview just about everybody who was connected in any way with the case in 1974/75. However, all statements taken by the police during the inquiries were to be made available to the defence because the case had already been referred back to the Court of Appeal.

In the Guildford Four case James Sharples, of the Avon and Somerset Constabulary, had been asked by the Home Secretary to investigate, and report to him on, the new statements which the Deputation had presented to him. The defence would not be entitled, as of right, to see the report or to be informed of the results, particularly of any statements that might be taken.

Having seen how the Devon and Cornwall police had interpreted their instructions, solicitors for the Guildford Four became anxious as to how the inquiry into the new statements on the Guildford Four case would be handled by the Avon and Somerset Police, as it was known that the Devon and Cornwall police had conducted over 700 interviews on the Birmingham case. It is therefore not surprising that the nature and scope of the terms of reference of the Avon and Somerset Police inquiry came to the fore.

In the event, it emerged that a *precise* statement of the terms of reference for the Avon and Somerset inquiry could not be traced. If they had been prepared by the Home Office, they had not been made public. It is also questionable whether such a statement had been given to Sharples. It came to light from a perusal of various items of correspondence at the time that there were variations in the interpretation of the tasks he had been requested to carry out.

In writing to Cardinal Hume in August 1987 the Home Secretary said '. . . I have asked the Chief Constable of Avon and Somerset to inquire into the new statements by Mrs Fox, Mr and Mrs Keenan, Maura Kelly and Fathers Ryan and Carolan which you presented to me.' Continuing, he said, 'The inquiries will be carried out swiftly, so that I can decide as soon as practicable whether to refer the case to the Court of Appeal.' In view of the apparently limited scope of the inquiry, it was hoped at the time that it would be completed, and a decision reached, by Christmas 1987. This was not to be.

During August and September 1987 Alastair Logan wrote to both Sharples and Caffarey of the Home Office explaining that those to be interviewed could be contacted through him. He made it plain that he would not be prepared to advise his clients to go ahead with any interview until all material from interviews carried out in 1974/75 on those to be interviewed had been made available. He was also clearly anxious about how the nature and extent of the inquiry might develop, being concerned that he would not have any access to any part of the report.

Consequently he inquired in writing of both Caffarey and Sharples as to the precise nature and scope of the inquiry. He was particularly anxious to know what Sharples would be enquiring into and the full extent of his authority. Caffarey wrote on 10 August, 1987 saying – '. . . You ask about the purpose of the police enquiries. It is simply to ascertain as far as possible the facts concerning the relevant matters mentioned in the new statements so that the Home Secretary can then decide whether there are grounds for referring any of the convictions to the Court of Appeal. . . . it is common for us to ask police to undertake enquiries where new material is presented to the Home Secretary.' Logan responded by saying 'to undertake enquiries' could cover a large number of things, and he sought more precise information. None was forthcoming.

After telephone conversations, Sharples wrote to Logan saying his officers . . .'are currently engaged in studying the papers in relation to this case and in due course will be contacting you with a view to seeing your clients . . . the police enquiry will move forward at as quick a pace as possible.' Logan sought more precise information on the scope of the enquiry and Sharples responded on 9 September, 1987. '. . . I have been asked by the Home Office to examine the statements in question and to seek to establish if there is any further supportive evidence.' It is surprising that, after their extensive review of the case, the Home Office did not appear to have defined more precisely the scope and extent of the inquiry but, of course, it is not known what, if any, supplementary matters might have been discussed by telephone or even personal contact.

Meanwhile, Sharples had written to Cardinal Hume on 4 September 1987 saying he was aware of the Cardinal's interest in the case, and that he would be pleased to receive any communication on the subject either by letter or, if preferred, by personal meeting.

Cardinal Hume arranged to meet Sharples, who was accompanied by his deputy, Superintendent Coates, at Archbishop's House on 12 November, 1987. At the beginning of the meeting Sharples explained that it was a courtesy call and his inquiry was restricted to the new evidence plus anything else he considered relevant, pointing out that he was familiar with the whole case. He went on to say that the Home Secretary had seen a group of Irish MPs and had told them he would be examining the whole case. In response to a question from Cardinal Hume, Sharples said he saw his task as being to say whether or not the new evidence was 'acceptable' and 'credible'.

Cardinal Hume said that he and the Deputation stood by the new statements and accompanying evidence they had submitted to the Home Secretary. They considered it was sufficient to merit a referral back to the Court of Appeal. He then highlighted some of the key points in the submission additional to the new statements. These included details of the weakness of the case against Carole Richardson, having particular regard to her alibis and the car timings for the journey from Guildford; the handling of the forensic evidence by the scientists acting on the instructions of the Director of Public Prosecutions and

Commander Nevill; the various 'considerations of substance' in the submission which, when taken together, would require the criminal justice system to face up to the question of whether they got the right people.

Sharples agreed that Carole Richardson could be a 'consideration of substance', and added he might see her himself. It later became known that members of the Sharples team subsequently interviewed various prison officers about Carole Richardson. Sharples emphasised that he had never been involved in any bomb cases, he did not know the police involved in this case, and that his commitment was to produce a fair report, unaffected by political considerations.

Earlier in the year Gareth Peirce, of Birnberg & Co, had started to represent Gerard Conlon of the Guildford Four. At the time Gareth Peirce was still also representing four of the Birmingham Six. Their case was being investigated by the Devon and Cornwall Police having been referred to the Court of Appeal in January 1987. Gareth Peirce was still working on the case and hoped it would be taken by the Court about the end of the year. Meanwhile, in view of her new responsibilities to Gerard Conlon, and as it was made public in August 1987 that the Deputation had presented a submission to the Home Secretary, she sought a meeting at Archbishop's House.

The meeting with Archbishop's House staff was held on 4 September. It took the form of a briefing on the submission on the Guildford Four, and an indication of the present thinking and future plans of the Deputation. Gareth Peirce had started reading herself into the Guildford Four case. She said at the meeting that her main anxiety and immediate concerns were that at his trial in 1975 Gerard Conlon had been unable to call any alibi witnesses. She was convinced there must have been something radically wrong during the preparatory stages of the trial. Her point was that on Saturday 5 October, 1974, the day of the Guildford bombing, Gerard Conlon had spent most of the day visiting pubs with Paul Hill until Hill left for Southampton at about 3.00pm to visit his girlfriend. After that Conlon visited more pubs and a betting shop and then went back to sleep it all off at the Conway House Hostel where he was living at the time.

Gareth Peirce believed that some member of staff or a resident who had seen Conlon at the Hostel that evening could be found. Moreover, it was known that the Surrey Police, and possibly the Metropolitan Police as well, had taken statements from some residents and members of staff. She saw her immediate and urgent tasks as being to locate any person who had seen Conlon, and also to find those who had made statements to the police. If the Birmingham Six appeal was dismissed Gareth Peirce's concern was that it would not bode well for the Guildford Four case. On the other hand, if the Birmingham Six convictions were quashed it could be very difficult for Sharples not to recommend that the Guildford Four case should be referred to the Court of Appeal. Significantly, on 29 October, 1987 the Relatives Action Group handed in to the Home Office a 55,000-signature petition calling for a re-trial for the Guildford Four.

The Deputation was to benefit greatly from a flow of information from solicitors representing the Guildford Four, particularly Alastair Logan who had been so helpful in the past, but now also from Gareth Peirce. In the course of their day to day work on the cases they had dealings with many people – sources which the Deputation itself could not tap directly but from which came valuable information. During the period from October 1987 onwards, Gareth Peirce continued to be involved in the Birmingham Six case, and also in searching for alibi evidence for Gerard Conlon. However, by that time Alastair Logan, representing Patrick Armstrong and Carole Richardson, and Michael Fisher, representing Paul Hill, were both heavily engaged in making arrangements for interviews with the Avon and Somerset Police. The word was that some difficulties were being encountered, but none that could not be resolved.

However, in fact by December 1987, things were apparently not going as smoothly as would have been wished by either the solicitors or the police. On 17 December, 1987 Mr Hurd wrote to Cardinal Hume. He said he was concerned to hear that the Avon and Somerset Police had met difficulties in pursuing their enquiries into the new statements given to him by the Deputation. He spoke of problems concerning documents and proposed interviews relating to Mrs Fox's alibi for Paul Hill, and the interviewing of three members of Paul Hill's original defence team. He added that Michael Fisher had informed the police that consent would be given to interviews subject to five pre-conditions.

He went on to say that, after the police had written formally to the two solicitors involved, he now understood exchanges were continuing between the Avon and Somerset Police and the solicitors. He confirmed that, in the last few days, Fisher had given the police access to some of the documentation which they had been seeking. He added that, as a result of the problems, the police enquiries would unfortunately now take longer than had been expected.

A trawl by the staff of Archbishop's House of copies of some of the correspondence available, which had taken place between solicitors acting for the Guildford Four and the Force Solicitor of the Avon and Somerset Police, revealed that the Home Secretary's concerns were partially understandable. However, it became apparent that he had not been apprised of all sides of the situation. These included the nature of some of the correspondence from the Force Solicitor, and also the considerable anxieties of solicitors and those being interviewed about the approaches and methods being adopted by the police.

In a letter to Michael Fisher on 27 November, 1987, the Force Solicitor complained about 'the lack of cooperation' by, in particular, two witnesses who had refused to speak to the police without his consent. The first was Mr D Melton who was employed by Paul Hill's solicitors at the time of the trial. The second was Mrs Eugina Tohill (now in Northern Ireland) who was formerly Gina Clarke, Paul Hill's girlfriend in Southampton. These had been referred to, but not by name, in the Home Secretary's letter to the Cardinal.

In replying to the Force Solicitor on 3 December concerning Mr Melton, Mr Fisher explained that when Superintendent Coates visited his office on 11 November a memorandum was drawn up setting out five requests he made on behalf of his client. One of the five requests was that he should be present at the interview. He went on to say that his firm did indeed claim that communications between Mrs Fox and Mr Melton were privileged but, as he had told Superintendent Coates, he had instructions that this privilege should be waived. He added that it came as no surprise to him that Mr Melton required the consent of Paul Hill in order to discuss matters with the police.

As regards Mrs Eugina Tohill, Michael Fisher's firm wrote:

> We have spoken to this witness who informs us that officers recently went to her home address accompanied by RUC officers and two jeeps full of soldiers with rifles. Needless to say this caused considerable distress to her and her family. She tells us she did not inform your officers that she required permission before being interviewed but she did inform them she wished to be interviewed by Mr Fisher first.
>
> ... She will be in London in the next few days ... so that the necessary arrangements for an interview with your officers can take place ... we would wish this to be in our offices so that Mr Fisher can be present.
>
> ... A telephone call or a letter to this witness before the officers went to Belfast would have saved the public expenses that you refer to.

Alastair Logan was also mentioned in the Home Secretary's letter and he, too, had problems relating to the handling of witnesses. Applications for copies of statements of witnesses were refused by the Avon and Somerset Constabulary, and no explanation for this was offered. The Surrey Constabulary had previously freely provided copies of statements against written authorities by the makers of the statements.

The root of the problem as far as his client's witnesses were concerned was self-evident. He knew that the Home Secretary was under no obligation to publish the inquiry, and those who were the subject of the inquiry would get no opportunity to explain or contest any assertions that might be made of them in the report. Consequently those whose names appeared in the report could possibly find themselves without credibility as far as the Home Secretary was concerned. All this is clearly illustrated by the way in which the police dealt with two of Carole Richardson's alibi witnesses – Maura Kelly and Lisa Astin.

Taking Maura Kelly first, Alastair Logan wrote to the Avon and Somerset Constabulary on 6 November, 1987 saying he understood they wanted to interview Maura Kelly and her mother, and that this could be done by arrangements made through him. This letter was neither answered nor even acknowledged. In seeking the whereabouts of Maura Kelly and her mother the police went ahead and first of all contacted Mrs Kelly's former husband. That was extremely undesirable as far as Maura Kelly and her mother were concerned.

Moreover, it seems a strange approach, not only because of Alastair Logan's letter of 6 November, but also because Robert Kee had written to Mr Sharples on 21 September, 1987 saying he had talked to Maura Kelly and her mother for about an hour and a half and gave the address at which they were living. The Force Solicitor wrote, somewhat abruptly, to Alastair Logan on 27 November, 1987, saying Mrs Kelly and Maura Kelly refused to be interviewed without his consent and presence at the interviews. Then followed the curt question – 'On what basis do you claim to be entitled to be present at the interviews? If you attend, what do you hope to achieve?'

In his reply on 8 December, Logan sought, amongst other things, an explanation as to why the Force Solicitor seemed to think it would be a hindrance to enquiries if a solicitor was present. However, from the penultimate paragraph of the Force Solicitor's letter of 27 November it was clear that there was a sensing of the anxieties there might be amongst witnesses:

> I can assure you that enquiries will be carried out lawfully. For example, any well founded claims of privilege will be respected. However, the Chief Constable considers it essential to the interests of justice that his officers are free to carry out their enquiries. They cannot be fettered by spurious claims of privilege or other unjustified obstacles.

The riposte in the final paragraph of Alastair Logan's reply did much to explain the difficulties being encountered –

> As to the remainder of your letter I object very strongly to the tone of it and do not intend to dignify it with a reply. If witnesses had been treated in 1974/75 in a manner set out in the penultimate paragraph of your letter they might not now be insisting on the presence of a solicitor or independent third party.

The second witness who had been discussed was Lisa Astin. She was a strong alibi witness for Carole Richardson and had never deviated from her first statement. It is to be noted that there was not a new statement from her in the submission by the Deputation. Lisa Astin was a properly accredited visitor to Carole Richardson at HM Prison, Styal. As such she had been interviewed by Special Branch and had to complete a number of forms which included her home address, her home telephone number, her work address and telephone number, and much more information about her personally. In spite of all this the police approached her brother. He said she did not want to be interviewed and refused to give them her address. On hearing this Lisa Astin telephoned Alastair Logan and said she was prepared to be interviewed but, after her earlier experiences in 1975, wished a third party to be present and suggested Alastair Logan or Dr James MacKeith. Logan passed on all this information by letter to the Force Solicitor on 10 December. He added – 'We cannot at the moment think why it would be necessary for your officers to interview Miss Astin who was extensively interviewed by the Surrey Constabulary, and gave evidence both at the Committal Proceedings and the trial.'

It was against the background of the Home Secretary's letter to Cardinal Hume of 17 December, 1987, and of all of the above research, that arrangements were made for a second meeting at Archbishop's House between Cardinal Hume and James Sharples. The meeting took place on 13 January, 1988, and Superintendent Coates was again present.

Cardinal Hume referred to the letter he had received from the Home Secretary. He said he was concerned that the impression could be gained from the letter that the veracity of Mrs Fox's statement was being queried. Sharples explained that some difficulties had arisen but they were mainly legal problems and not all lack of cooperation. He briefly reviewed the present position regarding interviews and said he accepted that legal representatives could be present at interviews. The remaining interviews would be starting shortly and he hoped to report to the Home Secretary within the next two months.

Sharples referred to the statement by Mrs Fox as being the crux of the matter, and Cardinal Hume emphasised that the Deputation stood by her statement as, indeed, they did the whole of the submission. He referred also to the strange way in which the police had apparently tried to trace Maura Kelly through her mother's former husband. He went on to say that the Deputation considered Carole Richardson was the key to the whole case, and if she was proved to be innocent the whole Guildford Four case would collapse. Hence the importance of her alibi witnesses and their integrity. The Cardinal emphasised the need to look at the case as a whole and cited the evidence of the Balcombe Street ASU, and the alterations made by scientists to their statements. Sharples commented that such matters were not within his remit.

Towards the end of the meeting Sharples said that they were making progress and he did not want Fisher and Logan to feel the inquiry team was complaining. In response to a question whether the Deputation might see papers before the Home Secretary made his decision, Sharples said he thought the Deputation might be informed of certain information before the decision was made.

Cardinal Hume wrote to the Home Secretary on 14 January, 1988, the day after the meeting, in response to his letter of 17 December, 1987 regarding difficulties being encountered by the Avon and Somerset police:

> I was concerned to hear there had been difficulties and took the liberty of asking Mr Sharples to call in to talk them through, and to see if there was anything I could do to facilitate his task.
>
> Most of the problems seem to stem from the fact that, not only did Mr Hill change his solicitor last summer and retained Mr Fisher but, also, Mr Logan, who acted for him previously, has had a long-standing relationship with some of the witnesses over the years during which he undoubtedly attracted their confidence.
>
> '. . . Mrs Fox made her statement which we forwarded to you with our submission, which also included the Maura Kelly statement relating to Carole Richardson. Our contention, as you know, is that the new evidence by Mrs Fox and Maura Kelly has to be seen within the context of the whole case and would, surely, have made an impression on the jury at the time of the original trial . . . We believe the convictions cannot be regarded as being safe on the knowledge of the case which we now have.
>
> . . . I appreciate our Deputation has no right as such to see Mr Sharples' report before any final decisions are made, but I am wondering whether it might be possible for the Deputation to see the report and be allowed to give you our comments before you make your decision.

The Home Secretary responded to the letter from Cardinal Hume on 27 January, 1988 –

> . . . I think it is only right that I should say now, though, that I shall not be able to make Mr Sharples' report available to you. It is a long established principle that reports of police investigations are confidential. This is because the reports are generally used to help senior police officers and the Crown Prosecution Service in taking decisions on such matters as whether or not to bring prosecutions. If the right decisions are to be taken, officers who prepare the reports must feel free to be completely frank in their assessments of the available evidence and of the reliability of witnesses. This can be achieved only if the complete confidentiality of the reports is guaranteed. While Mr Sharples' report will not be used for decisions on prosecutions, the same principle applies and he is preparing it on that basis. But of course at the right time I will be glad, if you wish, to go over with you the ground covered by the report.

Copies of this important letter were circulated to all members of the Deputation and to solicitors acting for the Guildford Four. There was considerable concern at the concept that police preparing reports for the Home Secretary must feel free to be completely frank 'in their assessments of the available evidence and of the reliability of witnesses.' Further, the suggestion that they might be for the purpose of prosecutions was disquieting. These concerns were enhanced on receipt in Archbishop's House of an updating report from solicitors which had been requested one week after Cardinal Hume's meeting with Mr Sharples on 13 January, 1988.

The note was dated 21 January, 1988. Many points were made but there is a need to refer to only two to illustrate the concerns of witnesses, their solicitors and members of the Deputation. The first point was that neither Alastair Logan nor Michael Fisher had yet received confirmation that they could be present when witnesses relating to their clients were interviewed.

The second point was that the Avon and Somerset Constabulary appeared to have extended widely the circle of interviews in that they were interviewing most, if not all, of Mrs Fox's workmates, and were continuing to try and interview members of the extended family of Lisa Astin and Maura Kelly. It was the latter which was giving particular concern.

On the morning of 21 January the police arrived unannounced at the house of Maura Kelly's brother who had by that time left to go to work. Her sister-in-law was at the house and they demanded to see the brother. The sister-in-law was very upset and did not know why the police wanted to interview her husband. The sister-in-law found out from Maura that her brother knew nothing about her involvement in the Guildford Four case.

Maura Kelly's brother was five years older than she was. Eventually the police interviewed him in a car outside his house. He had refused to allow them into the house because of the distress it would cause his wife. They asked him such questions as, 'did Maura go to Ireland in 1975?' He could not remember. He said if she did go she was more likely to have stayed with her grandmother rather than her uncle. In fact, she did go to Ireland and spent nine months there. When Maura spoke to him about this later he was oblivious of the fact.

Such an episode indicates the problems that can arise when police arrive unannounced at houses of persons connected with witnesses and demand answers to questions they have not had sufficient time to think about, and which relate to matters fourteen years previously. It is easy to see the possibility that Maura Kelly's evidence might be regarded as suspect on the basis of what her brother had said. Such possibilities were at the root of concerns being experienced by solicitors and the witnesses towards the end of January 1988. But there was yet another one to come.

On 28 January, 1988 the Court of Appeal gave its judgement on the Birmingham Six case. The appeal was dismissed. The Six applied for leave to appeal to the House of Lords but on 14 April, 1988 three Law Lords rejected the application. The Six, and all their supporters who included MPs, were devastated. Dismissal of the appeal on 28 January, though half-expected by some, was badly received by the media. There were those who said that 'to have quashed the Birmingham convictions would have meant admitting that fraud and perjury had been permitted by police officers ranging in rank from detective constable to assistant chief constable. It would also have meant admitting that our legal system has been bent from top to bottom to achieve and sustain these convictions[1].' Some recalled Lord Denning's, by now notorious, 'appalling vista' statement in dismissing the civil action against the police by the Six.[2]

A statement by Lord Lane, the Lord Chief Justice, at the end of the Birmingham Six appeal judgement was to cause concern, and even dismay, in many circles – 'As has happened before in references by the Home Secretary to this Court, the longer this hearing has gone on the more convinced this Court has become that the verdict of the jury was correct.' There was some speculation as to how this dictum would be received and interpreted by Ministers and officials in the Home Office. The general view was that it could only retard their efforts to seek ways and means of justifying referrals of cases in which doubts had arisen. Of particular interest to many was the immediate question

[1]The Observer 31 January 1988 [2]Chapter One, page 6

as to what effect the judgement might have on the Guildford Four and Maguire Seven cases.

So far, the Home Secretary had felt unable even to refer the cases to the Court of Appeal, though he had arranged for the Avon and Somerset Police to investigate the new evidence in the Guildford Four case given to him by the Deputation. Some argued that he would now feel fortified by the Birmingham decision in his refusal to refer them and, even if he did, they would now have even less of a chance of being successful. Others thought that, leaving aside the Maguire case, at least the Guildford Four case might now have a better chance of being referred because political considerations of one shade or another might call for a balance to the Birmingham decision. However, after the Birmingham judgement, many people had lost confidence in, and even respect for, the Court of Appeal. Indeed, some people who had attended daily went so far as to suggest that the handling of the case had brought the Court into disrepute. Similar sentiments had been expressed in 1977 when the Guildford Four appeal was heard at which the Balcombe Street ASU gave evidence.

The Guildford Four themselves, their solicitors, the witnesses, and those supporting the case including the Deputation, all hoped and trusted that the Home Office would be guided by the decisions in 'The Government Reply to the Sixth Report from the Home Affairs Committee' of April 1983. In essence, the Committee had put a case to the Government for the need to set up an independent review body to review possible miscarriages of justice, rather than referring them to the Court of Appeal. The Government rejected the proposal for an independent review body, but was quite clear and specific as to what should be done instead:

> As to greater use of the procedure, the Home Secretary will in future be required to exercise his power of reference more readily; and the Lord Chief Justice, who has been consulted about this reply, sees room for the Court to be more ready to exercise its own powers to receive evidence or, where appropriate and practical, to order a retrial.

As far as the Guildford Four case was concerned, all hopes were now to be pinned on the Government Reply of 1983.

Since September 1987, the Deputation had conducted its affairs by arranging, when necessary, meetings of the two or three members who might be available at the time, by position papers keeping other members informed, and by correspondence and extended telephone conversations. The Deputation had always had it in mind that there should be a full meeting after the outcome of the appeal by the Birmingham Six was known. It had also always been appreciated that, by that time, other factors would have come to light requiring consideration. Indeed, that proved to be the case and by March 1988 important replies to letters from Cardinal Hume to the Home Secretary had been received; there had been meetings between Cardinal Hume and James Sharples, and correspondence about the latter's terms of reference; it had also become known that the Home Secretary was likely to receive the report by Sharples in April 1988 and could be making a decision shortly after that.

The meeting took place on 10 March and consisted of a full review and assessment of the current situation. It was appreciated that the report by Sharples might facilitate a decision being made by the Home Secretary not to refer the Guildford Four case. It was therefore decided that a comprehensive, self-contained letter should be sent to the Home Secretary re-iterating the views of the Deputation, and incorporating comments on some of his responses to Cardinal Hume, particularly that referring to the police report.

It was also agreed that there should be an ANNEX to the letter highlighting in semi-tabular form and re-emphasising the salient points concerning Carole Richardson, the Maguires, the Commander Nevill incident and the 'Balcombe Street admissions.'

As the timing in the probable Home Office decision-making process was becoming crucial, the letter was despatched on 16 March, 1988. The Deputation attached the highest importance to this letter and so it is reproduced in full below, together with its ANNEX:

> I am replying to your letter of 27 January, 1988 regarding the Guildford and Woolwich pub bombings and the Maguire cases and I note that, at the right time, you would be prepared to go over with me the ground covered by the report being prepared by the Avon and Somerset Police.
>
> In the meantime the Deputation which came to see you on 23 July, 1987 has met to review the situation in the light of recent events, and we thought we should write to you again to bring to your attention at this stage the result of our deliberations.
>
> In addition to the 'Aide Mémoire', the submission we presented to you on 23 July, 1987 consisted of two parts. The first, at APPENDIX 1 to the submission, was a Joint Opinion by Lord Devlin and Lord Scarman, two former Lords of Appeal in Ordinary, concerning a point of law. The second part, APPENDIX 2 to the submission, consisted of new evidence and new matters of substance.
>
> In the Memorandum attached to the Joint Opinion referred to above, it is stated that three fundamental principles of British justice were violated and that this was not deliberate but the consequence of a deep misunderstanding of the law.

In essence the point of law is that the appellants tendered to the Court of Appeal fresh evidence which, if truthful, constituted a complete defence. The power and duty of the Court was to decide whether the evidence tendered was 'capable of belief and, if placed before a jury, might be believed.' Instead of deciding whether or not the evidence was 'likely to be credible' the Court themselves rejected the evidence as untruthful, so exceeding their powers.

We understand that when the appellants in the Birmingham Six case applied for leave to appeal to the House of Lords, the Lord Chief Justice certified that the case raised a question of general public importance, although he refused leave to appeal. We further understand that the appellants in that case are applying to the House of Lords for leave to appeal. The certified question of law is very similar to that which we have raised with you. We agree with the Lord Chief Justice that it is a question of general public importance, and we believe that it arises in the Guildford and Woolwich bombing case more appropriately than in the Birmingham Six case.

A possible course which you might consider is that the Birmingham appeal should be adjourned and our case referred so that the question could be considered in both cases by the House of Lords in one hearing. But in any event, whatever decision is taken in the Birmingham Six case, we are asking you to consider the question in our own case where it is appropriate and could be decisive.

Before turning to the second part of our submission covering new evidence and matters of substance, we have noted with considerable interest recent events in Gibraltar. On this occasion the IRA, as is their custom, admitted responsibility even before the car containing the explosives was found. Moreover, it appears the operation took some four months to plan and those executing it were clearly of high calibre. These features were none of them present in the case of those convicted for the Guildford and Woolwich bombings. On the contrary, the 'Balcombe Street admissions' were admissions by senior IRA personnel that those convicted had nothing to do with the Guildford and Woolwich bombings.

We remain convinced, and know in this we are articulating the views of many others, that the convictions in the Guildford Four/ Maguire cases cannot be regarded as safe and satisfactory. There are many reasons why we adhere firmly to this view.

Apart from the point of law, our present argument rests on the new evidence we presented to you in our submission on 23 July, 1987, together with the important 'matters of substance' which were covered in some detail in APPENDIX 2 to our submission. We have noticed that the Appeal judges in the Birmingham Six case accepted that 'the appellants before us are not confined to the grounds upon which this reference is made.' It could therefore be argued that 'other grounds' are themselves sufficient for a reference to the Court of Appeal.

We acknowledge the reasoning behind your principle that cases are not referred except on the basis of new evidence or matters of substance. This principle is not consistent with the wide powers possessed by the Court if a reference is made. If upon a reference the Court can review the whole case, we are of the opinion that the Secretary of State should be able to refer it if he is of the opinion that there is a likelihood of the convictions not being safe and satisfactory. We believe this to be so whether the likelihood arises from some incident or omission or other error in the judicial proceedings resulting in conviction or from new matters arising thereafter.

We have been somewhat exercised by the reference in your letter to me of 27 January, 1988 that police officers who prepare the report being submitted to you must feel free to be completely frank 'in their assessments of the available evidence and of the reliability of witnesses.' It is, of course, right for police officers to report their views on the credibility of evidence, i.e. as to whether it can be believed, but we consider that assessment of the available evidence and of the reliability of witnesses is a matter for the Court or a jury.

We have argued the point of law which we consider is reason enough to merit a referral. In addition we believe that the new evidence and matters of substance we have given you are strong enough to merit a referral which would be consistent with the principles under which you operate, but our case does not rest alone on these. We attach at the ANNEX to this letter 'Some comments on the Pub Bombings and Maguire cases.'

Although they were tried separately we consider the Guildford Four and Maguire cases are inseparable in that, if the Guildford Four convictions were found not to be safe and satisfactory, the Maguires' convictions would immediately be brought into question. Anne Maguire was originally arrested and, with Carole Richardson, was charged with five counts of murder at Guildford. The Maguires were convicted on a TLC test, carried out by an assistant and not confirmed, which is not now considered to have been reliable by forensic scientists and, in the view of Government scientists, would not be accepted by a Court or jury today. The likelihood of the convictions in the Maguire case not being safe and satisfactory is, in our view, very strong indeed.

Continued protestations of innocence over thirteen years by the Guildford Four and the Maguires which, prima facie, seem to be intrinsically credible, and the widespread suspicions among many persons that the original convictions were not safe and satisfactory, constitute, in our view, both separately and together, 'matters of substance' of considerable import.

We are most concerned that there has been a recent reiteration in the media of the philosophy behind the view expressed at the time of the rejection of the Birmingham Six civil suit against the police that success would open an 'appalling vista' of official embarrassment. We would wish to dissociate ourselves entirely from such a view. The need to uphold public faith in the processes of the law is paramount. If earlier decisions are flawed, and suspicion that this is so is widespread, then public confidence in the administration of justice is seriously undermined. This matters in all parts of Britain as well as in both parts of Ireland.

ANNEX: SOME COMMENTS ON THE PUB BOMBINGS AND MAGUIRE CASES

Carole Richardson

1 On 1 September, 1987 an up-dated psychiatric report on Carole Richardson dated 7 August, 1987, prepared for the Home Office by Dr James MacKeith, was sent to Mr Caffarey and the 'Summary of Conclusions' was as follows: –

> The probability is that her mental state during the interrogations of 1974 and her enduring psychological qualities made her statements unreliable. The probability is that she was not capable of making a truly voluntary statement of reliable content. The psychological and psychiatric information briefly outlined in this report supports the view that Miss Richardson's admissions to police during interviews and in her voluntary statements should not have been relied upon at her trial. No medical, psychiatric or psychological evidence was given at her trial concerning whether the record of interviews and voluntary statements could be relied upon so that the court could decide whether or not to depend on her self-incriminating admissions. From the scientific viewpoint, the research and experience gained since 1975 amounts to a matter of substance.'

2 Other salient points are: –

(a) after the Folkestone telephone box incident, the improbability of Richardson and Armstrong contacting the police and giving their correct names and addresses if they had carried out the Guildford bombing three weeks before;

(b) the fact that the leader of the 'Jack the Lad' pop group saw her at the concert with a doll;
(c) for the timings of the car journey from Guildford to the pop concert at the South London Polytechnic to have held against her, the journey would have to have been completed in forty-eight minutes. The Court said a police car, observing the 1974 speed limits, had done it in fifty-two minutes. A police car observing no speed limits at all had done it in forty-eight minutes;
(d) the improbability of the IRA using a very young *English* girl, particularly one who was a shop-lifter and abused drugs and alcohol on a regular basis;
(e) if, as alleged by the Crown, her alibi was concocted, the improbability of the IRA concocting such an alibi and *not* including in it other members of the team;
(f) if her alibi was concocted as alleged by the Crown, the improbability of her not producing it on arrest and in interrogations in the following days.

The Maguires

3 The main considerations are: –
(a) given the Court accepted the movements of the Maguire family on the day, and given the complete absence of any bomb-making equipment or body of explosives in the house or neighbourhood, the extreme improbability that the nitroglycerine alleged to have been found on the swabs as tested can have come from the hands of those arrested and subsequently convicted;
(b) the TLC test, on the results of which alone the seven members of the Maguire household were convicted, was carried out by an assistant and was not confirmed. The evidence of the actual sample was destroyed, thus making it impossible to check the evidence of the Crown. Proper scientific practice demands that part of the sample be retained;
(c) in the view of Government scientists, the unconfirmed test on which the Maguires were convicted would not be accepted by a Court or jury today.

The Commander Nevill incident

4 The following facts were revealed at the 'Balcombe Street' trial in 1977 and, if available at the Guildford trial, could have enabled the defence to advance a cogent argument in support of their clients' innocence: –

(a) Government forensic experts testified that, before the Guildford trial, they had prepared statements showing forensic links between the explosions at Guildford and Woolwich and other IRA explosions with which the accused could not be associated;
(b) they further testified that, on orders of the Director of Public Prosecutions communicated to them by the anti-terrorist squad, they had subsequently, for purposes of the Guildford and Woolwich trial, altered these statements to omit any reference to any forensic links between the Guildford and Woolwich explosions and any other IRA bombings;
(c) they also testified at the 'Balcombe Street' trial that they had omitted all reference at that trial to the forensic links between the offences being tried there and the Guildford and Woolwich offences;
(d) Commander Nevill, of the anti-terrorist squad, testified that he had received instructions from the Director of Public Prosecutions to instruct the forensic scientists to do this.

The 'Balcombe Street' admissions

5 The main points are: –
(a) the Balcombe Street ASU came up for trial in January 1977;
(b) O'Connell, who had taken part in the Guildford and Woolwich bombings, and Butler and Duggan, who had taken part in the Woolwich bombing, refused to plead on the grounds that, dishonestly, they had not been charged with the Guildford and Woolwich bombings as well to which they had admitted;
(c) in spite of statements by O'Connell and Butler under interrogation to Commander Nevill and Detective Superintendent Imbert that those convicted at Guildford had nothing to do with them, no further police investigation had taken place, notwithstanding expressions of concern by Commander Nevill and Detective Superintendent Imbert, contained in the record of those interrogations, that innocent persons may have been convicted for these offences;
(d) when the appeal of the Guildford Four was finally heard later in 1977, the Court regarded as relevant only that part of the evidence in which O'Connell, Dowd, Duggan and Butler said that none of the appellants had been involved in the Guildford and Woolwich bombings;
(e) both the Crown and the Court of Appeal were content to accept that Dowd and O'Connell were present at Guildford, but they tried to assert that they were there together with the Guildford Four when there was no evidence in possession of the Crown

which showed any link between the Guildford Four and the Balcombe Street ASU.

Towards the end of March 1988, further evidence of possible benefit to the defence started to come to light. In December 1974, after both Paul Hill and Gerard Conlon had been arrested, many of the records and rent books from the Conway House Hostel, Quex Road, where they were both living at the time, were confiscated by the police. They were, consequently, never available to the defence in preparing for the trial in September 1975 or the appeal in October 1977.

In spite of repeated requests the police would not return the records to the hostel. Father Ryan was the priest in charge of the hostel at the time of the Guildford bombings. During the first months of 1988, knowing that the police inquiry was under way, Father Ryan arranged for solicitors to the hostel to threaten legal action for the return of the records. After they had been returned, he wrote to a large number of people who had passed through the hostel at the time of the bombing. He asked them if they could recollect whether Paul Hill or Gerard Conlon were in the hostel at the time. He received a reply from a Michael Kennedy saying Gerard Conlon was in the TV room at the hostel when the newsflash about the bombing came on television.

On 29 March Cardinal Hume sent a copy of the correspondence he had received from Father Ryan to the Home Secretary, explaining the background as to how it had been obtained. Douglas Hurd responded on 6 April 1988 saying he would take account of Kennedy's letter when reaching a decision on whether any further action was called for in the light of the police report which he expected shortly.

At the time of his trial in 1975, Gerard Conlon had spoken of 'Paul – the greengrocer' as a resident in the hostel who might provide alibi evidence for him. In late March 1988 Gareth Peirce searched thoroughly the records which had now been returned but no trace could be found of a 'Paul' filling that description. However, there was a record of a Charles Burke who was an assistant manager in a greengrocer's shop. He had occupied one of the beds in the four-man room to which Gerard Conlon had returned on 5 October, 1974 to sleep off his pub visits. Charles Burke had left the hostel on his return from work late in the evening of 5 October, 1974. There was no record of where he had gone. By early April 1988 Gareth Peirce succeeded in tracing his family but they had not seen him for ten years. The search for Charles Burke, and other possibles, was now on. Many methods were used in trying to trace Burke including advertisements in newspapers.

On 29 March, 1988 the Home Secretary replied to Cardinal Hume's comprehensive letter of 16 March. The Deputation intended that this important letter should be in the Home Secretary's hands just before or at the time he received the police report. The Home Secretary gave an assurance he would consider what was said very carefully but he did not think it would be helpful to reply in detail to the points made. He did, however, wish to offer comment on two points. The first point related to the suggestion that consideration might be given to arranging matters in such a way as to provide the House of Lords with an opportunity to consider the argument raised by Lord Devlin and Lord Scarman in the Guildford case at the same time as it considered that presented in the Birmingham case. He had concluded it was not open to him to take action on such lines.

His second point related to the Deputation's comments on his interpretation of how the police report could be used. He said:

> I note also your concern about what I said in my letter of 27 January about the preparation of the police report. I think, from what you say, that you appreciate that my reference to the police assessing available evidence and the reliability of witnesses does no more than indicate what the police, in practice, must be expected to do in reporting on any investigation regarding inquiries into offences. Clearly, the decision as to whether or not I find grounds for referral to the Court of Appeal is a matter for me, and the action that the court may decide to take regarding any new evidence presented to it is a matter solely for the court. Decisions by me and by the courts will not be restricted by any observations the police might feel it right to offer in their report.

It is probable that this response did not wholly relieve the concerns of solicitors and some of their witnesses who had made statements. Reference has already been made to the culture and tradition of courts in the 1970s which were accepted at the time by most juries and some, but not all, judges. It was apparent from the outcome of most trials – including the Guildford Four and the Maguire Seven – that evidence by police officers, prison officers and expert witnesses was very likely to be completely accepted.[3] Even by 1987 it could be said that there had been very few proven miscarriages of justice to diminish this likelihood of acceptance. Which is not to say that the Home Office would necessarily react as most courts were inclined to do. The real problem is that such acceptance weakens the position of those senior officers who are aware of improprieties and wish to stamp them out.

It was generally known at the time that the Home Secretary was

[3]Chapter One page 6

likely to receive the police report in April 1988. There was some speculation in the press about what it might say and how it might be handled. There was a large and informative feature in *The Guardian* on 9 April by David Pallister entitled 'Enigma at the heart of the Guildford bombing case.' It was not clear whether the piece was directed at the police before making their report, or at the Home Office after receiving it, but a central feature of it was:

> Together the four of them made more than a dozen statements. If all that was written on them was true, then the expedition to bomb the two Guildford pubs was an absurdly confusing and chaotic affair. Up to 12 people, some of them quite befuddled by drugs, were involved; two cars were used, but their makes kept changing and they were driven by people who could not drive; different people in different combinations planted the bombs.
>
> The police had to work out a rational scenario. 'Their separate stories fitted neatly together like a jigsaw', Sir Michael [Havers] was able to tell the jury.

The weeks went by with no word from the Home Office. Inevitably, many surmises had to be made; maybe C3 Division does not agree with the recommendations of the police report; or the Home Secretary does not agree with C3's recommendations. Cynics were even suggesting that as the time for decision approached the fact that some of the main players in the cases were now in high positions was beginning to raise its difficult head.

Over the next few months Alastair Logan and Gareth Peirce were engaged in correspondence with C3 Division in the Home Office. They kept Archbishop's House informed so that the Deputation was always abreast of developments. On 22 June, 1988 B.M. Birnberg & Co sent a letter (instigated by Gareth Peirce) to C3 Division giving a comprehensive and detailed review of the case for Gerard Conlon. This letter was to achieve some fame in future discussions and correspondence in that it became generally known as 'The Birnberg letter.' Copies were sent to all members of the Deputation.

Birnbergs said they had been led to believe that the police report submitted to the Home Office indicated that no action should be taken to re-open the case. The letter gave much new information and cited key aspects covering which new witnesses could be produced. They had found eight witnesses, unnamed in the letter at that stage, who could give important evidence supporting the extreme unlikelihood of Gerard Conlon having been involved in the Guildford bombings. They had hoped to have more time to interview, investigate and trace witnesses. They had not yet found an alibi witness to cover the crucial period of approximately 6.00pm to, say, 8.00pm on 5 October 1974. They were convinced that some, or at least one, existed and could be found given more time.

They went on to request that if an announcement adverse to Gerard Conlon's case being re-opened was about to be made, the Home Office should not so decide until they had heard the full arguments and had seen the witness statements to be submitted to them. The final request was that the letter should not be rejected out of hand and, if it was thought there was merit in the letter, an early meeting might be arranged to discuss next steps. The letter was undoubtedly a compelling document and lent more than a lurking doubt to the assertion that Gerard Conlon had been in Guildford on the crucial evening. In the event, for reasons which were not to unfold until later, it was some considerable time before a meeting took place. (Allegedly, the Home Office said subsequently that the delay had been caused by the Birnberg letter of 22 June having been sent to the wrong address.)

An interesting event did, however, take place on 12 July, 1988. There had been a spate of violence, muggings, football hooliganism and attacks on policemen in many parts of the country. Against this background Ludovic Kennedy had a wide ranging interview with the Commissioner of the Metropolitan Police, Sir Peter Imbert, during which many current problems were reviewed. The interview was published under the 'Spectrum' banner in *The Times*.

At one stage, during which the handling of police evidence was being discussed, Ludovic Kennedy raised the question of the Guildford pub bombings. He recalled that in that case guilt was proved solely on police evidence of alleged confessions. As Sir Peter Imbert had played some part in this, Ludovic Kennedy asked if he had ever had any doubts about the correctness of those convictions. Sir Peter Imbert answered – 'I haven't had any doubts about the convictions. What I have had doubts about is the length of the sentence of the girl who was involved in it . . .'

When asked if he believed the claim of the Balcombe Street gang, when he had interviewed them, to have taken part in the bombings the Commissioner replied – 'Oh, I believed the Balcombe Street gang all the way through . . .' When he was reminded that the Balcombe Street gang said those who were convicted were innocent he went on – '. . . Yes, that's right. The Balcombe Street gang obviously knew a lot about the Guildford bombings and the Woolwich bombing . . . The only thing I can conclude is that they all knew each other, or in some way the Balcombe Street gang were told about it in fine detail.'

The last answer led to the question by Ludovic Kennedy whether he still held that justice was done in the Guildford case, 'although a lot of people today, judges and politicians and indeed myself, doubt the convictions of those convicted?' Sir Peter Imbert's response was – 'I can only speak about the questioning at Woolwich because I was there. The questioning was fair and objective, and the admissions made without any pressure whatsoever. I wasn't part of the questioning where Guildford was concerned.'

It was, of course, generally known that the Balcombe Street gang had freely admitted all their offences, including Woolwich and Guildford, in accurate detail. The last response could, perhaps, have given the impression that, at that time anyway, he was distancing himself from the Guildford convictions. Ludovic Kennedy related that as they walked to the door, to his surprise, the Commissioner spontaneously said to him something that he himself had believed to be true for years . . .' I think we policemen are far too ready to assume a suspect's guilt in the early stages when we should be assuming his innocence.'

As already mentioned, Alastair Logan, as well as Gareth Peirce, was to have substantial correspondence with C3 over the months following early July. By then Robert Baxter had taken over as head of C3 from Caffarey and started to make reasonably prompt responses to letters. However, much of the correspondence was conducted with Stanton. It consisted mainly of substantial additional information about Patrick Armstrong and Carole Richardson. As to the latter, copies of letters from Dr MacKeith, concerning the effects of the pethidine injection which Dr Makos, the police surgeon, had now admitted to having administered to Carole Richardson before her interrogation, were also included.

One of Alastair Logan's main points was that the Avon and Somerset Police had access to documents which the defendants and their solicitors had never seen and so could not comment on. Consequently, the Home Secretary would see only the police view on such matters. Logan had offered to have meetings with C3 to discuss the aspects he had written about but there was no response. Interestingly, in the course of an extended telephone conversation, Stanton said he would suppose the police would have regarded investigations of statements by the Balcombe Street gang as being part of their brief. Sharples had told Cardinal Hume that they were not in his remit.

In July 1988 the book *Time Bomb* by Grant McKee and Ros Franey became available. They had made, in the *First Tuesday* ITV series, the three powerful TV programmes which had been screened during the preceding three years – *Aunt Annie's Bomb Factory*, *The Guildford Time Bomb*, and *A Case that Won't Go Away*. The book was exceedingly well researched and was able to carry further, after the passage of two years, the convincing analysis of the cases by Robert Kee in *Trial and Error* published in 1986. The book had a considerable impact.

Towards the end of August 1988 an intriguing possible scenario of indeterminate origin wafted along the airways, passing by Archbishop's House as it did so. It ran something like this. Much thought has been given to the problem of the Guildford Four case. It could well be that a reference to the Court of Appeal might not achieve the outcome that is being sought. The likelihood of this happening can only have been enhanced by the dismissal of the Birmingham appeal and the accompanying comments by the Lord Chief Justice. If there was a prospect that Carole Richardson would be released by Christmas, would consideration be given to easing down and withdrawing from activity on behalf of the Guildford Four? This would have to be on the basis that it would probably not be possible to do anything about the three men or the Maguire Seven.

Such a scenario did not reach the Deputation even in either an unofficial or an off the record fashion. Had it done so, there is little doubt that the pursuit of truth and justice in respect of all the defendants would have continued relentlessly by one means or another.

The Home Secretary, unaccompanied by officials, saw Cardinal Hume at Archbishop's House on 8 September, 1988. He said he had now received the police report, had looked at the evidence, and had decided not to refer the case. He would be making an announcement before the end of the month.

Douglas Hurd then made some specific comments on the evidence. Neither Mr and Mrs Keenan nor Paul Hill had mentioned the presence of Yvonne Fox in the flat. Also there were discrepancies in the timings in her statements. In a statement in 1975 Maura Kelly said Carole Richardson saw her in the shop before lunch. In 1988 she said it was after lunch. As regards medical evidence the timings were such that Carole Richardson could have been lucid at the time she confessed. It was agreed the convicted were not really 'IRA types' but such a point was not absolute. Finally, he said the point of law by Lord Devlin and Lord Scarman had been settled by the highest court in the land.

In an immediate response, Cardinal Hume refuted his reasons and said he and the Deputation stood firmly by their submission and the statements it contained. He would respond in writing to some of the assertions made. Meanwhile, he asked Douglas Hurd if he had seen the MacKeith/Makos correspondence about the pethidine injection given to Carole Richardson before interrogation which was also revealed in the book *Time Bomb*. A jury could well have taken a different view if they had known that. He went on to say he was still deeply concerned about the suppression of forensic links between the Guildford and Woolwich offences, and other bombings for which the Guildford Four could not have been responsible, all of which came out at the Balcombe Street ASU trial.

When Cardinal Hume emphasised the importance of the 'Birnberg letter', the Home Secretary appeared to be not yet wholly familiar with it. The last point made by the Cardinal was what appeared to be the very convincing evidence about Carole Richardson's doll which she was seen with at the pop concert. The meeting concluded with Douglas Hurd undertaking to look again at the points raised by Cardinal Hume, and in doing so he added . . . 'a state of finality has not yet been reached.' It was as well that this was his final thought because the public would not have understood the lack of justice from the man who has the only key to the door and keeps it locked.

Before relating subsequent urgent action by Cardinal Hume and the Deputation, an initial comment on the 'point of law' issue might be appropriate. The joint opinion of Lord Devlin and Lord Scarman, which had formed part of the Deputation's submission, was a quite exceptional, indeed unique event. It had probably never happened before that two former Law Lords, of such eminence, should have combined to give an opinion to a Home Secretary on one specific case.

It could reasonably have been assumed that, in such circumstances, the Home Secretary is likely to have consulted the Attorney General and sought his views. Indeed, this might well have been done but, in the absence of confirmation, it is not surprising that, on hearing what the Home Secretary had said, Lord Devlin's swift and lucid response on the telephone was:

> Whoever has advised him is not even on the threshold of an understanding of the point if he feels that it has been dealt with by the Court of Appeal, let alone the House of Lords . . .
>
> May we be informed of the name of the distinguished legal adviser who thought fit to recommend to the Home Secretary that the opinion of two former Lords of Appeal should be rejected without consultation.

The position of the two former Law Lords on the 'point of law' had been argued fully and clearly in the submission.[4] As to the 'facts', at the meeting the Home Secretary was, initially anyway, not of a mind to refer the case. Whatever it was that had figured sufficiently prominently in his personal assessment of the case to lead him to this conclusion was a matter for speculation – the police report, the recommendations of C3 or the advice of his new Minister of State, John Patten? It was generally believed at the time, whether true or not, that his predecessor as Minister of State, David Mellor QC, as the only legally qualified Minister, had allegedly not considered a reference

[4]Chapter Five – pages 109 to 110

justified since he had been involved in the cases from 1983. He had rejected at that time an assessment of the scientific evidence as given at the trial of the Maguire Seven by Dr Caddy and Christopher Price which would have led to a detailed re-examination of the evidence. In any event many thought that there were those who could have had their own reasons for not agreeing the cases should have been referred. It was to be regretted that consideration of the submission over the past thirteen months, during which the Guildford Four were serving their fourteenth year in prison, had produced only a so shallow response.

In writing to the Home Secretary on 9 September, 1988, after thanking him for his courteous visit, Cardinal Hume went on to say that he appreciated the difficulties of being certain that right and just decisions are reached. It was, in fact, pursuit of this latter aim that had brought the Deputation together in the belief that the need to uphold public faith in the processes of the law was paramount. Widespread acknowledgement and recognition that every step had been taken to ensure that justice had been done would be a major contribution towards the building up of confidence in both parts of Ireland in British justice. He added that he would be writing again responding to the points raised in the meeting but that meanwhile he would say now that the two former Law Lords in the Deputation would most certainly not accept that the point of law had now been settled.

He concluded by saying:

> You would be looking further into the medical opinion (which I believe constitutes 'evidence') of Drs. MacKeith and Makos, the question of the dolls, and also the Birnberg letter of 22 June, 1988 in which reference is made to further witnesses. There is also the very worrying question of the suppression at the Balcombe Street trial of forensic evidence relating to Guildford and Woolwich.

Meanwhile, Cardinal Hume had been perturbed to hear from the Home Secretary that doubts were being expressed concerning the testimony of Maura Kelly. She was 16 years old at the time. There seemed to be a suggestion of a discrepancy in statements made by her in 1974/75 and what she was supposed to have said to the Avon and Somerset Police. He instructed the staff at Archbishop's House to investigate all this further without in any way referring to his meeting with the Home Secretary, but on the basis that some queries appeared to be arising within the Home Office.

The investigation resulted in an immediate and most revealing response to the staff by fax on 9 September 1988 from Alastair Logan who was acting for Carole Richardson. It became apparent that the report which had been made to the Home Secretary by the Avon and Somerset Police was incorrect. Maura Kelly was never interviewed by the police in 1974. She was interviewed in 1975 but did not make a statement. Significantly, missing from the police record of the interview, but confirmed by both Maura Kelly and her mother, was the fact that during the course of the interview the female police officer struck Miss Kelly on the face. There were other disturbing aspects relating to interviews and statements. These were recorded in Alastair Logan's report (a copy of which is at APPENDIX VIII). Cardinal Hume considered the report to be of such importance that he sent it to the Home Secretary without delay on 9 September.

Meanwhile, without in any way linking it with the meeting between the Home Secretary and Cardinal Hume, the staff at Archbishop's House asked Alastair Logan to assist them in checking that the information they held was correct 'by setting down your understanding of the situation so far as Paul Hill's witnesses are concerned.' The Home Secretary had specifically commented that neither Mr and Mrs Keenan nor Paul Hill had mentioned the presence of Yvonne Fox in the flat, and that there were discrepancies in the timings in her statements. It was thought that expressing the request to Alastair Logan in such unspecific and broad general terms would best produce a comprehensive and thoroughly objective review of the specific points raised by the Home Secretary. This, indeed, proved to be the case. The report gave an illuminating account of how Mr and Mrs Keenan had been treated by the police and the effect it had on their references to Yvonne Fox. There were some disturbing revelations as can be seen from the copy of the report at APPENDIX IX.

The 'Birnberg letter' of 22 June, 1988 had listed eight witnesses, unnamed in the letter at that stage, who could verify between them Gerard Conlon's own account of how he had spent the whole of 5 October, 1974. The only gap was the important 'window' between 6.00 pm and 8.00 pm covering the Guildford bombing. On 16 September, 1988 Gareth Peirce had a lengthy meeting with the new Head of C3, Robert Baxter, and Mr Stanton. She handed over to them the actual statements of the eight unnamed witnesses in the 'Birnberg letter.' In addition she gave them medical evidence that Gerard Conlon had been suffering from an untreated illness at the time he confessed. She also explained she was still searching for other possible witnesses, including a Charles Burke, who might be able to make statements about the 'window' period.

By mid-September members of the Deputation had much new material to consider – the points made by the Home Secretary on his visit to Cardinal Hume on 8 September; the views of the two Law Lords in the Deputation on the point of law; the revealing report by

Alastair Logan on the statements by Maura Kelly; the pethidine injection given to Carole Richardson by Dr Makos; the comprehensive, and in places disturbing, report from Alastair Logan concerning evidence by Mr and Mrs Keenan, and Yvonne Fox; the report by Gareth Peirce on her meeting with C3. The Deputation recognised that things were moving to a head, with the Home Secretary apparently disinclined to refer the case. It was decided that a comprehensive letter should be sent as soon as possible to Douglas Hurd.

The letter was to be so designed as to set out in the clearest terms the Deputation's assessment of the present situation; their responses to the Home Secretary's points, making full use of the reports they had received; and their firm views on what, in the interests of truth and justice, should be the way forward.

Accordingly, Cardinal Hume wrote to the Home Secretary on 22 September, 1988:

> I am writing to you following our meeting on 8 September 1988 and further to my letters of 9 and 13 September 1988 concerning the Guildford Four/Maguire cases.
>
> At our meeting you gave as the reasons for the unlikelihood, at that stage, of a referral of the case to the Court of Appeal alleged discrepancy in statements made by Maura Kelly, the failure of Mr and Mrs Keenan and Paul Hill to mention a 'fourth person' (i.e. Yvonne Fox) in the flat, that the point of law had now been settled by the highest court in the land, and that in the medical evidence the timings were such that Carole Richardson could have been lucid at the time of her confession. You added that you would agree the convicted were not real 'IRA types' but that such a conclusion was not absolute in itself.
>
> Having looked again at the points you raised, to which I refer below, I have to say at the outset I am now even more convinced than ever that the convictions in these cases cannot be regarded as safe and satisfactory. This view is shared by the whole of our Deputation. Unless a reference is made now to the Court of Appeal, or to a Tribunal set up under the 1921 Act, the country will have to face up to the fact that, not only will the Deputation continue what it regards as the pursuit of justice, but your successor, and probably mine, will be left to continue grappling with the problem.
>
> I turn first to the testimony of Maura Kelly. In my letter of 13 September 1988 I said how perturbed I was at the suggestion of a discrepancy in statements made by her in 1974/75 and what she is supposed to have said to the Avon and Somerset Police. With that letter I sent to you a report by Mr Alastair Logan, the solicitor

acting for Carole Richardson, a copy of which I attach at Annex 1 for easy reference. [APPENDIX VIII to book].

Some very serious matters arise from this report. In addition to this, not only does it refute any allegation of discrepancies in Maura Kelly's testimony, but would also seem to indicate that had the Avon and Somerset Police accepted all the documents offered to them they might have arrived at a different conclusion regarding discrepancies. Having seen this report, I cannot help having substantial reservations about the alleged conduct of the enquiry by the police. I am sure you would agree that full account would have to be taken of the report at Annex 1 [APPENDIX VIII to book] before any public statement could be made advancing discrepancies in Maura Kelly's evidence as a reason for non-referral.

Your next point related to the 'fourth person' (Yvonne Fox). On the same basis as in my letter of 13 September, 1988, I asked my Staff to investigate the situation in the short time available. This has resulted in a further report from Mr Alastair Logan, a copy of which is at Annex 2. [APPENDIX IX to book].

Section A of the report, on pages 1 and 2, gives important background on the treatment of Mr and Mrs Keenan at the hands of the police in 1974. This traumatic experience undoubtedly coloured their attitude towards the possible exposure of their best friend, Mrs Yvonne Fox, to similar treatment. The rest of the report outlines the situation up to the trial and the calling of witnesses. From Section G of the report it would appear that the files of the solicitors, Woodford and Ackroyd, to which my staff do not have access but presumably the Avon and Somerset police did, contain information that Mrs Fox was present in the flat on 7 November, 1974.

Again I would assume any public statement that, based on the Avon and Somerset Police report, Mrs Fox was not present in the flat would be accompanied by publication of the contents of the report at Annex 2 [APPENDIX IX to book]. In the last resort the Deputation would have to consider doing this if they find they have to publish their account of the negotiations, including the original submission and subsequent correspondence.

On the matter of the point of law I can only reiterate my initial statement in my letter of 9 September, 1988. The two Lords of Appeal in our Deputation most emphatically will not accept that the matter has now been settled in 'the highest court in the land'. Their first reaction to this – and it is best that I give it to you quite frankly – is that those who have tendered this advice have failed completely to understand the points raised in our submission of 23 July, 1987, and they do not appear to understand the true function of the Committee of three Law Lords which deals with applications for leave to appeal. Nothing has occurred since the Birmingham judgement that would prevent the House of Lords examining the point of law raised in our original submission.

As to the medical evidence, I was surprised when you said to me that the timings were such that Carole Richardson might have been lucid at the time of her confession. I do not think that medical opinion would support this in the light of present scientific knowledge. So the revelation about the pethidine injection constitutes a fundamental and major issue not known to the jury at the trial. I do not know whether the Avon and Somerset Police saw Dr Mackeith or, failing that, if your officials have seen him. I understand that in the light of the knowledge now available to him, including the information about the giving of the pethidine and the prescribing of the tuinal, his medical opinion, with the benefit of hindsight, would certainly be that the interviewing of Carole Richardson should not have continued until she was physically and mentally in a healthy state.

In the light of this, I would have thought that the view of Dr MacKeith must be ascertained, and given full weight, before any aspect of the medical evidence can be used as a rebuttal for reference of the case.

The above covers the responses you made at the beginning of our meeting on 8 September to some of the points made in our submission on 23 July last year, and in subsequent correspondence. I have no knowledge of what was in the Avon and Somerset Police report. However, I would hold the view that our original evidence, looked at in the light of the two reports by Mr Logan at Annexes 1 and 2 to this letter, [APPENDICES VIII and IX to book], and also, in particular, in the light of the 'pethidine' evidence submitted by Dr MacKeith, together with the crucial letter from Dr Makos, all now consolidates into sufficient new evidence to merit a referral. There has been a precedent for this. The Confait case was referred solely on new medical opinion.

You will recall that at our meeting I raised with you the medical evidence, the convincing evidence about the two dolls, and the Birnberg letter, all of which you undertook to look into. There was also the very worrying question of the suppression of forensic evidence relating to Guildford and Woolwich which came out at the Balcombe Street trial.

I look forward to hearing your responses on these matters but, in particular, I would like to refer again to the Birnberg letter of 22 June, 1988 to which I attach considerable importance. It is very significant that at the trial not one single witness, not even as to character, appeared for Gerard Conlon. This letter represents a painstaking attempt by his new solicitor to build up a case for him, and it reveals the existence of several witnesses, all of which constitutes new evidence. When you were giving me your reasons for being disinclined to refer the case, I was not entirely clear to what extent you had had an opportunity to consider the implications of the Birnberg letter of 22 June, 1988.

The Birnberg letter reveals evidence which has not been before a jury. But, almost more importantly, it emphasises an important aspect of this case which may have escaped the notice of some. I had originally thought that it was unlikely that there would be one single piece of evidence which on its own would be strong enough to justify referral. I now think differently. I believe that the evidence that could be given before a jury today by Maura Kelly, Yvonne Fox, Dr MacKeith, Dr Makos and the witnesses cited in the Birnberg letter, each taken singly and separately, would be strong enough grounds for referral. Furthermore, I hold the view that the evidence in our original submission, supplemented not only by the reports at Annexes 1 and 2 [APPENDICES VIII and IX to book] to this letter relating to Maura Kelly and Yvonne Fox, but also by the recent medical evidence about injections, and by the Birnberg letter, all taken together, present an overwhelmingly strong case for referral in some form or another.

None of the above witnesses appeared and gave evidence before the jury at the trial. If any of them, singly, were to appear before a jury today, I am convinced that jury would not find the defendants guilty. It is a chilling thought when one reflects that not all that long ago three of the four convicted for Guildford (Carole Richardson was under eighteen) would have gone to the gallows on the grounds that guilt was beyond reasonable doubt.

Annexes 1 and 2 [APPENDICES VIII and IX to book] to this letter illustrate all too clearly the dangers of decisions on referral being based solely on the police comments on our original submission. Indeed, if the decisions were so based they could have been made last May. It would surely be unwise, and indeed would expose the whole legal process to widespread, adverse comment, if the substantial material submitted to the Home Office since the completion of the Avon and Somerset Police report was not taken into full account before any decisions are made.

Towards the end of our discussion we thought, for different reasons, that referral to the Court of Appeal might not be the right answer. If the case went to the Court of Appeal, and was turned down, it would be some eighteen months before the matter could be revived again. This would lead to an intolerable position whereby the convicted, whose convictions are rapidly becoming less safe and satisfactory as more evidence comes to light, would be moving into the sixteenth year of imprisonment.

You referred to, but rejected, the possibility of a Tribunal under the 1921 Act. On reflection, I am becoming convinced that the cases themselves, as cases, are now matters of public importance.

In view of this, and your doubts about the merits of a reference to the Court of Appeal, it has to be recognised that if there is no referral, pressure will continue for further investigation of a matter which has caused, and continues to cause, public misgiving. Inevitably, in this event, consideration would have to be given to a Tribunal being set up under the 1921 Act. This would ensure that at least all the facts are brought to light, and are fully considered and assessed. Such a step would have the merit of satisfying all the many interests in England and Ireland, and indeed North America, who are concerned about these cases.

An alternative, and perhaps even better, solution might be to put Dowd and O'Connell on trial for Woolwich and Guildford, and Butler and Duggan for Woolwich. They all refused to plead at the Balcombe Street trial because they were not also being charged with Guildford and/or Woolwich. Such a step would also bring to light the very worrying suppression of evidence that there was a forensic link between the Guildford and Woolwich bombings and other bombings which had taken place after the arrest of the Guildford Four.

Turning to the Maguires, as you know from my letter to you of 16 March, 1988, the Deputation considers the Guildford Four and Maguire cases are inseparable in that, if the Guildford Four convictions were found not to be safe and satisfactory, the Maguires' convictions would immediately be brought into question. No bulk of explosive substance whatsoever was ever found. The Maguires were convicted solely on a TLC test which, in the view of Government scientists, would not be accepted by a Court or jury today.

Ever since the Deputation presented the submission to you on 23 July, 1987, we have been meticulous in the preservation of confidentiality. We have taken extra special steps to ensure that there were no disclosures of details of the point of law or new evidence in the papers we presented for your consideration. The same has applied to the very important material sent to the Home Office during the past five months. The mere fact that the Deputation exists has done much, together with additional positive encouragement from us, to assist in restraint being exercised by the several organisations and groups with a special interest in these cases.

As I said earlier, these cases are now a matter of public importance. It is for this reason that once a decision has been taken we

> would wish to release ourselves from our self-imposed confidentiality. We are not given to releasing material to the media, and would be reluctant to do so, but the importance of these cases is such that, in certain circumstances, it would be undesirable, and indeed wrong, for the Deputation to withhold information on the original submission and the subsequent correspondence.
>
> Finally, as a Catholic Bishop, I would like to make a personal reflection. My deep interest in these cases stems not only from a wish to play a part in seeing that justice is done, but also from a wider interest in the problems of Northern Ireland and the need for a solution. Our constant expressions of disgust at, and condemnation of, IRA terrorist activities, about the evils of which I feel so deeply, must always be accompanied, I am sure you would agree, by the most scrupulous attention to the total integrity of British justice.

Unknown to the Deputation at the time, this letter was to prove to be the end of the beginning of the struggle to secure justice for the Guildford Four.

In writing to Cardinal Hume on 30 September, Douglas Hurd said he understood the potential importance of the issues raised in the Cardinal's letters of 9 and 22 September. He added that, in addition to the 'Birnberg letter' of 22 June, they had also now sent further material with a request that it be considered before a decision was made.

By late October, even allowing for time to consider the further material from Birnbergs, concern started to mount about the seemingly inordinate delay in reaching a decision. Moreover, there was a 'sensing' abroad, to put it no higher than that, that the delays were likely to result in a decision not to refer the case. As had happened before in times of delay and indecision, there were those who were beginning to think that the enormous human, political and practical implications that could flow from a referral were winning the day. There could have been concerns in all parts of the criminal justice system – the judiciary, prosecution lawyers, the police, forensic scientists, and even in the Home Office itself.

Against this background, it was decided to have a full meeting of the Deputation on 14 November at which recent developments would be assessed and the whole situation reviewed. Press releases covering three possible eventualities were approved – release of Carole Richardson only; referral of the whole case to the Court of Appeal; no referral. The appropriate release was to be made by Cardinal Hume on behalf of the entire Deputation. In the event of no referral, after saying the Deputation 'was both disappointed and disturbed', the release would have ended:

> Throughout the period since seeing the Home Secretary on 23 July, 1987 we have been resisting pressure from the media to disclose the nature of the submission and all members of the Deputation have, at all times, maintained strict confidentiality.
>
> However, it is the firm belief of myself and all members of the Deputation that it is in the public interest we should now release the relevant papers.

There was also discussion of possible action plans in the event of no referral, or the release only of Carole Richardson. Two further important decisions were taken. The first was that a letter should be sent immediately to the Home Secretary and released to the press. The letter was to be a clear statement of the position of the Deputation, and it would highlight three key considerations of compelling importance to which the Home Secretary would be urged to give the most careful consideration in forming his own judgement. It was to be so worded that the Deputation would not be departing from their self-imposed restriction of not revealing any details of the new evidence which were not already in the public domain through recent publications. The second decision was that arrangements should be explored to publish in the national press the comprehensive paper examining the 'point of law' by Lord Devlin and Lord Scarman entitled *Justice and the Guildford Four*.

The letter was sent on 16 November. It attracted very wide publicity indeed in both the broadsheets and the tabloids. Many papers quoted substantially from the letter and some specifically included the three key considerations. In view of this the letter is reproduced in full below:

> You will, I know, be aware of the increasing and renewed public interest in the possible decisions on the Guildford Four and Maguire cases, which in themselves are matters of public importance. This is understandable given that the Home Office received the Avon and Somerset Police Report in May this year, and that additional new evidence has been submitted subsequently to you by our Deputation and by solicitors representing the convicted persons.
>
> We find that many individuals and bodies are seeking reassurance from us that all possible steps are being taken to ensure speedy progress in the necessary procedures.
>
> You last wrote to me on 30 September 1988, saying that you would take full account of the representations made by our Deputation and others in the period since we presented our original submission on 23 July, 1987. Subsequently on 5 October a press release from the Home Office indicated that you would not be in a position to take a decision for 'at least some weeks.

I know you will share our concern at the continuing delays in taking a decision on these cases and that you are as conscious as we are that the Guildford Four, whose convictions seem to us and others to be increasingly less safe and satisfactory, will shortly be moving into the fifteenth year of imprisonment.

As you will recall, our original submission consisted of a point of law and additional facts constituting new evidence and matters of substance to be considered in the context of the whole case. Our Deputation met on 14 November 1988 to review the whole situation. We surveyed afresh the point of law and all the new evidence which was submitted to you in our original submission, together with the several additional items of new evidence which have been submitted to you over the past five months by solicitors acting for the prisoners.

We are now even more convinced than ever that there is an overwhelmingly strong case for the Guildford Four and Maguire cases to be re-investigated and re-appraised. Justice can only be seen to have been done if this course is taken.

Our assessment of recent developments is such that we now feel impelled to release this letter to share our anxieties with the many who are looking to us for progress. I know you will appreciate that in so doing we are not departing from our self-imposed restriction of not revealing any details of the new evidence which are not already in the public domain through recent publications.

We trust that you will shortly be coming to a conclusion yourself and, as a Deputation, we decided that at this stage we should put to you three key considerations. These are of compelling importance and we would urge you to give them the most careful consideration in forming your own judgement.

The first is that items of new evidence have to be considered both individually and then collectively in the context of the case as a whole. Of course it is necessary to test each fragment of evidence separately to assess its significance. And some pieces of new evidence – such as the new medical opinion in relation to the injection of pethidine which Carole Richardson was given shortly before making the confession on which alone she was convicted – are matters of substance which in themselves unquestionably warrant a re-investigation of the case. But this is not all. Having examined each piece of evidence separately, it is then equally necessary to stand back and assess the whole scene. And when all the evidence is taken together, the cumulative weight of probability points to the very great unlikelihood of any of those convictions being 'safe and satisfactory.'

The second consideration is this. The Guildford Four were convicted solely on their own confessions. The Court of Appeal in 1977

> described the confessions as 'the partially true intermingled with the deliberately false.' Yet they were the only evidence for the prosecution at the trials. Not a scrap of circumstantial evidence corroborated anything they said. This damaging criticism of the confessions by the Court of Appeal was made of what was the only evidence for the Crown. How could a verdict reached in such circumstances and based on evidence which contained many falsehoods be accepted as safe and satisfactory?
>
> The third consideration is the evidence of O'Connell and Dowd considered by the Court of Appeal in 1977. At the appeal the testimony they gave, in particular their command of details which they would have known only by participation, compelled acceptance that their evidence that they committed the Guildford and Woolwich bombings could be true. But the Court of Appeal refused to believe the other part of their evidence in which they claimed that the Guildford Four were not also involved. The question remains whether a jury, whose purpose is to decide the facts, would have believed them. The Guildford Four have yet to be tried by a jury on that evidence. This is one of the main aspects of the point of law in our original submission.
>
> You will appreciate that in making these three points we have in our minds one question: namely, would a jury have convicted the Guildford Four and the Maguires if all the evidence now available had been presented at the trial? In the view of each and all of us it is highly unlikely they would have done so.

As regards the paper *Justice and the Guildford Four*, it was decided that an essential condition of handing it over to a newspaper for publication would be agreement that it must be reproduced in full with no editing whatsoever. After some negotiations, *The Times* agreed to publish it as soon as they could allot to it the whole of the 'Op-Ed' page – opposite the editorials. It was published on 30 November, 1988.[5] In their detailed analysis of the trial of the Guildford Four, and its aftermath, Lord Devlin and Lord Scarman said that what was now at stake was the integrity of the English criminal justice system.

On 24 November Douglas Hurd replied to Cardinal Hume's letter of 16 November about the Guildford Four and the Maguire Seven cases:

> Since you mention the Maguires, I should perhaps say that I regard the material which has been submitted to me by your Deputation and by solicitors acting on behalf of the Guildford Four as

[5]The full text is at APPENDIX X.

> concerning only the convictions of Patrick Armstrong, Gerald Conlon, Paul Hill and Carole Richardson. I have received no representations other than repetitions of those I considered before my statement of 20 January last year, which appear to bear directly on the safety of the convictions in the Maguire case. So in line with the principle which I have consistently followed about new and substantial matters, I am considering only the case of the Guildford Four, not the Maguires.

He went on to say he understood the weight the Deputation attached to the arguments they had advanced, and he would be taking them into consideration in reaching his decision. He shared the concern about the length of time the review had taken but had deferred a decision at the request of solicitors acting for the Guildford Four as they were still submitting further material. He hoped to be able to announce his decision early in the new year.

It should be noted that, in nearly every single letter he had written over many years to the Home Secretary on behalf of the Deputation, Cardinal Hume had invariably referred to the Maguire Seven case as well as the Guildford Four. This letter was the first occasion on which the Home Secretary specifically stated he was not considering the Maguire Seven case. After brief consultations the Deputation decided they would not pursue the matter at this stage. They remained confident that, if the Guildford Four convictions were not found to be safe and satisfactory by the Court of Appeal, then all the convictions in the Maguire Seven case would be brought into question.

By December 1988, there had been some concern about the apparent failure of the Home Office to fulfil the Government's response in 1983 to the Home Affairs Select Committee whereby the Government said the Home Secretary would be more ready to use his power of reference to the Court of Appeal, and that the Lord Chief Justice had been consulted and would be more ready to make full use of the powers of the Court of Appeal. In the ten years prior to the report of the Select Committee in 1982, the Home Secretary referred back an average of five cases a year. However, in the four years since the report there had been an average of only four cases a year. It has already been mentioned that at the end of the Birmingham Six appeal, which was dismissed in January 1988, Lord Lane, the Lord Chief Justice, implied that the Home Secretary had wasted the court's time by referring it back.

Furthermore, although the Guildford Four and Maguire Seven cases were legally separate, in the eyes of many, including the Deputation, they were closely interconnected. If the convictions of the Guildford Four were found to be unsafe and unsatisfactory by the Court of

Appeal, because none of the Four had had anything to do with the bombings, then it was extremely unlikely that they could have known where the bombs came from. This could only lead to the conclusion that there must have been something wrong with the scientific evidence against the Maguire Seven.

It was during late December 1988 that further rumours, again of an indeterminate source, were detected. The word was that, in the light of the circumstances prevailing at the time, it was becoming increasingly unlikely that the Guildford Four case would be referred. Based on hard information available at the time, it was not possible to assess the reliability of such murmuring. However, arrangements were then made for the Deputation to meet on 17 January, 1989 to review such situation as might have developed by that time.

During early January 1989 it so happened that Cardinal Hume was attending a meeting of bishops in the North West of England. Finding himself near the prison at Styal, he took the opportunity to see Carole Richardson whom he had never met on any previous occasion. On his return to Archbishop's House he wrote to the Prime Minister, Mrs Thatcher, on 13 January, 1989. After referring to his visit to the North West, and to Styal prison, he referred to the work of the Deputation and then went on to say:

> . . . To meet Carole Richardson is to be convinced of the passionate sincerity of her consistent protestations of innocence. The circumstances surrounding her confession are really quite disturbing. The fact is that this girl was on drugs and was given at the time a pethidine injection. According to the best medical opinion, this would make her confession quite unreliable as evidence. There was no other evidence at the trial against the girl.
>
> . . . If the Home Secretary decides to review the case, as we sincerely hope he will, some might claim that it thereby impugns British justice. But of course the opposite is true: a reinvestigation would demonstrate the capacity of British justice to take full account of any possible miscarriages and give the lie to any suggestion that there cannot be justice for all in this country.

Meanwhile the Home Secretary had written to Cardinal Hume on 16 January saying that he had now considered fully all the matters that had been put to him and had come to a decision on the case of the Guildford Four. He enclosed a copy of a Written Reply to a Parliamentary Question which was to be published in the House of Commons that day. He had decided to refer the case to the Court of Appeal for the reasons given in the Written Reply.

The beginning of the end of the struggle had at last been reached.

The next stage was for the Deputation and solicitors acting for the Four to study the Home Secretary's reasons, and for the solicitors to prepare their cases for the Court of Appeal.

7

THE QUASHING

THE REFERRAL of the Guildford Four case to the Court of Appeal was received with satisfaction, indeed relief, by the Deputation. It was regarded as the first major step towards securing justice for the Guildford Four, and ultimately the Maguire Seven.

The next day, 17 January 1989, a Catholic priest, who quite by chance happened to be giving the *Thought for the Day* broadcast on BBC Radio 4, made a telling point – 'A hatred of evil without a passion for truth quickly turns a blind eye to inconvenient facts. In its zeal it can begin to choose victims at random.'

The 'broadsheets' – *The Times*, *The Daily Telegraph*, *The Guardian* and *The Independent* – all gave wide coverage to the Written Reply on the same day. All these newspapers had played an important role in reporting on various aspects of both the Guildford Four and Maguire Seven cases since the publication of Robert Kee's book, *Trial and Error*, in October 1986. This coverage included, in many cases, strong and perceptive leaders. During that period it was generally agreed, and was visible to all, that *The Independent*, no doubt reflecting editorial policy, had consistently made a major contribution to the cases in terms of lengthy and informative coverage.

There were reports in the press that there was always the possibility that Douglas Hurd would have taken the decision to re-open the case with some reluctance, and that the Court of Appeal would hear it with a certain built-in scepticism. There were also press reports which went further, saying that the Court of Appeal must not act as 'judge and jury.'

Apart from the potential complication resulting from the close connection between the Guildford Four and the Maguire Seven cases, already referred to, there were other considerations aired in the press. If the Court of Appeal quashed the convictions, serious doubts would be raised about the prosecution and the police investigations. Moreover, if the verdicts were overturned, it would be the first IRA trial where the prosecution had been proved wrong. For all these, and undoubtedly other reasons too, it could be said that the Home Secretary had, in the end, made a courageous decision in referring back, albeit belatedly, the Guildford Four case.

It had been well established that, when a case is referred to the Court of Appeal, the appellants are not restricted to the grounds on which the reference has been made and are free to raise any relevant and permissible matters connected with the whole case. Before reviewing the grounds for reference listed in the Written Reply it is interesting to recall the reasons given to Cardinal Hume by the Home Secretary, during their meeting on 8 September 1988, for his decision not to refer the case. In brief, the reasons were – neither Mr and Mrs Keenan nor Paul Hill had mentioned the presence of Mrs Fox in the flat; discrepancies in the timings in her statements; in a statement in 1975 Maura Kelly said she saw Carole Richardson in her shop before lunch, but in 1988 she said it was after lunch; as regards medical evidence the timings were such that Carole Richardson could have been lucid when she confessed; the point of law by Lord Devlin and Lord Scarman had been settled in the highest court in the land.

Section 17 of the Criminal Appeal Act 1968 states clearly that a Home Secretary can refer a case to the Court of Appeal 'if he thinks fit.' There are no qualifications or reservations. The following extract from the Home Secretary's introductory remarks in his Written Reply illustrates the position adopted by successive Home Secretaries and their officials in C3 over the preceding nine years for all cases, including those of the Guildford Four and Maguire Seven. In particular, the last sentence of this extract could be seen as neutralising, as far as these two cases were concerned, the clause 'if he thinks fit':

> The Home Secretary is an elected politician representing the executive. The judiciary is and must be seen to be independent of the executive. It follows that the power of the executive over decisions of the judiciary needs to be exercised with very great care. Those who are seriously concerned about civil liberties in this country should be particularly chary of urging the Home Secretary to use these powers. I believe that the Home Secretary should only exercise the power of referral within stiff constraints. He should resist the temptation to substitute his view of the case for that of a court of law. The opinions of those who make representations to him, however distinguished, on whether the jury or the Court of Appeal dealt correctly with the evidence before them should not be decisive. Nor should his own personal opinions. This rules out at a stroke many of the matters raised in this case, because they were before the jury or the Court of Appeal.

Rigid adoption of this administrative rule of procedure, which as Lord Scarman had said appeared to have been elevated to 'a principle,' had not been helpful in the pursuit of justice for, in particular, the Guildford Four and the Maguire Seven. The full significance of the evidence of the Balcombe Street ASU together with the associated alteration of scientific statements; and the widely held view of the need to arrange for an independent re-appraisal of the validity of the scientific evidence given at the trial of the Maguire Seven, on which alone they had been convicted, both come to mind. The rigidity of the approach to referrals to the Court of Appeal gave rise to some suggestions in the press at the time that the Home Secretary had deliberately fettered his own powers to prevent an avalanche of cases.

Before giving in his Written Reply the three specific grounds for the referral, the Home Secretary dealt with the point of law which had formed part of the Deputation's submission to him on 23 July, 1987. When Douglas Hurd visited Cardinal Hume on 8 September, 1988 to explain why he would not be referring the Guildford Four case, he said that the point of law had been settled by the highest court in the land. The immediate telephone reactions to this by Lord Devlin have already been recorded.[1] Reference was also made to this comment, in the following terms, in the comprehensive Deputation letter which Cardinal Hume sent to the Home Secretary on 22 September, 1988,[2] after the visit on 8 September:

> . . . those who have tendered this advice have failed completely to understand the points raised in our submission of 23 July 1987, and they do not appear to understand the true function of the Committee of three Law Lords which deals with applications for leave to appeal. Nothing has occurred since the Birmingham judgement that would prevent the House of Lords examining the point of law raised in our original submission.

The nub of the point of law was this. Lord Devlin and Lord Scarman considered that a jury should have been given the chance to reach a conclusion on the convictions of the Guildford Four by a previous jury in the light of the confessions of the Balcombe Street gang about which the previous jury knew nothing. The above comments in the letter of 22 September, 1988 do not appear to have reached the Home Secretary's advisers because, still dealing with the point of law, he went on to say in his Written Reply that a similar point of law was raised in the context of the Birmingham bombings, but the Appeal Committee of the House of Lords refused leave to appeal. He concluded it would

[1]See Chapter Six – page 145. [2]See Chapter Six – pages 148 to 153.

not be sensible to base a reference to the Court of Appeal on a point of law which the Appeal Committee had recently declined to consider.

As Lord Scarman observed to the Deputation when he saw the Written Reply, the point of law raised by Lord Devlin and himself had not yet been considered by the House of Lords. The fact that the Appeals Committee had turned down Birmingham, whose case anyway was weaker than that of the Guildford Four, did not mean that the point had thereby been dealt with: refusal of leave to appeal did not constitute a judgement on the point of law. Consequently, Lord Scarman concluded that the Home Secretary was mistaken in believing that it had already been considered by the House of Lords.

Having given his view on the point of law, the Home Secretary went on to list 'the three main points which seem to me to bear directly on the safety of the convictions. These points were not available to the jury or the Court of Appeal. They need to be tested in Court.'

The first point was the matter of the use of drugs by Carole Richardson, and the medical treatment given to her while in custody:

> Dr Makos, the police surgeon who saw her in 1974, volunteered in August 1987, and repeated to the Avon and Somerset police in November 1987, that he had administered an injection of pethidine to Carole Richardson. Later, in December last year, in a letter and subsequent statement to officers of Avon and Somerset, he withdrew this admission. Dr Makos' recollections may be uncertain or unclear, but it does appear that pethidine might not have been a suitable treatment for someone in Miss Richardson's apparent condition, that is suffering from withdrawal from barbiturates. Even if she was not given pethidine, at least some of her confessions would appear to have been made at a time when she was suffering from withdrawal to a greater degree than has hitherto been thought. The admitted administration of the drug tuinal to Miss Richardson would appear, in medical opinion now, to have had the effect of prolonging and increasing withdrawal symptoms. The possible effects of these drugs on the reliability of her statements were not adequately exposed to the jury or the Court of Appeal;

This statement was of some significance, bearing in mind that the Home Secretary had decided not to refer the case in January 1987. In their submission to the Home Secretary in July 1987, the Deputation had referred to the reports by Dr MacKeith and Dr Gudjonsson on Carole Richardson which had been received by the Home Office in April 1986.[3] Because of her medical state following the use of drugs,

[3]See Chapter Three, pages 54 to 55.

and the administration of the drug tuinal, the doctors did not believe that reliance could be placed on her confessions. The Deputation had considered that those reports, probably alone and certainly in conjunction with other matters, constituted considerations of substance meriting reference to the Court of Appeal.

The announcement of the decision not to refer the case was accompanied by a memorandum[4] giving the reasons supporting the decision. There was no reference whatsoever in the memorandum to the reports by the two doctors, although the Home Office had commissioned the reports.

There were other revelations in the Written Reply which hitherto had been unknown to the Deputation. The Home Office had apparently known from the Avon and Somerset Police since November 1987 that Carole Richardson had been given an injection of pethidine by Dr Makos. Nevertheless, amongst the reasons given by the Home Secretary, at the meeting with Cardinal Hume on 8 September, 1988, for not referring the case was that from the medical evidence Carole Richardson could have been lucid at the time she confessed. Presumably this point had been made in the report to the Home Secretary in April 1988 by the Avon and Somerset Police.

In July 1988, before the meeting between the Home Secretary and Cardinal Hume on 8 September, Alastair Logan had sent to C3 a further comprehensive report by Dr MacKeith. In this he stated that 'an intravenous injection of pethidine could certainly have so influenced her mental state, her perceptions, her judgement and her self control that her disclosures would certainly be regarded as unreliable testimony.' In the Written Reply, Dr Makos had apparently made another statement to the Avon and Somerset Police in December 1988 withdrawing his admission about the pethidine injection.

Nonetheless, the Home Secretary was now conceding that even if Carole Richardson had not been given pethidine, 'at least some of her confessions would appear to have been made at a time when she was suffering from withdrawal to a greater extent than has hitherto been thought.' There was still no reference to the original reports to the Home Office in April 1986 by Dr MacKeith and Dr Gudjonsson which had cast doubts on the validity of Carole Richardson's confessions. The Deputation had referred to these reports in their submission in July 1987.

The second point by the Home Secretary in the referral was:

The alibi given by Maura Kelly in March 1987 for Carole Richardson, alleges that during the afternoon of the Guildford bomb, 5

[4]See Chapter Three – pages 54 to 55.

> October 1974, she was visited at the baker's shop where she worked by Richardson and her friend Lisa Astin, at about 2.30pm. The two left and returned to the shop some time later, when Richardson gave Maura Kelly a doll. When Maura Kelly closed the shop at around 5pm, the two girls were still with her. She walked with them to the bus stop when they separated. Maura Kelly had left the country before the trial and the defence were unable to call her to give evidence. Neither a jury nor the Court of Appeal have therefore had the opportunity to assess the value of her evidence alongside the alibi presented by Carole Richardson, that during the course of the afternoon she had no opportunity to make any journey to Guildford;

A statement by Maura Kelly had formed part of the submission made by the Deputation. One of the reasons for not referring the case, given to Cardinal Hume by the Home Secretary at their meeting on 8 September 1988, was that there seemed to be a discrepancy in statements made by Maura Kelly in 1974/75 and what she was supposed to have said to the Avon and Somerset Police in 1988. Cardinal Hume gave a robust response to this assertion. He attached to his letter of 13 September, 1988 to the Home Secretary a copy of a most revealing report which Archbishop's House staff had obtained from Alastair Logan.

This report was to become Annex 1 to the Cardinal's main and lengthy response of 22 September, 1988 to the Home Secretary following the meeting on 8 September 1988[5]. (The report is reproduced at APPENDIX VIII to the book.) In his letter of 22 September, 1988, Cardinal Hume had said that this report illustrated all too clearly the danger of decisions on referral being based solely on police comments on the Deputation's original submission. It was apparent from the Written Reply that the statement by Maura Kelly which had been part of the Deputation's submission on 23 July, 1987 had now, in January 1989, become the second of the Home Secretary's main points for making the referral.

The third point in the Written Reply completing the Home Secretary's reasons for referring the case, was:

> the alibi by Mrs Fox for Paul Hill, produced on 15 July, 1987 states that on the evening of the Woolwich bombing, 7 November, 1974, she was at the flat of Mr and Mrs Keenan, where Paul Hill was living. Mrs Fox says she was with Mr and Mrs Keenan between 7 pm and 10.15 pm. During that period Paul Hill was present except for a period of about 20 minutes when he left to make a telephone

[5]Chapter Six, pages 148 to 149.

> call to his girlfriend. Mrs Fox attended the trial but did not give evidence, and Mr and Mrs Keenan and Paul Hill, who did give evidence, made no mention of her. In statements of 15 July, 1987, both Mr and Mrs Keenan now confirm that Mrs Fox had been at their flat that evening.
>
> Paul Hill said he left Mr and Mrs Keenan's flat only to make a telephone call. This was supported by the Keenans in their evidence. The account Mrs Fox offers appears to add weight to the alibi evidence, but neither the jury nor the Court of Appeal have had the opportunity to consider it.'

The submission made by the Deputation to the Home Secretary in July 1987 included statements by Mrs Yvonne Fox, Mr Frank Keenan and Mrs Anne Keenan. A similar situation to that over the Maura Kelly statement subsequently arose. At the meeting with Cardinal Hume on 8 September, 1988 the Home Secretary gave as one of his reasons for not referring the case that neither Mr and Mrs Keenan nor Paul Hill mentioned the presence of Yvonne Fox in the flat, and that there were discrepancies in the timings in her statements. These comments were presumably based on the report of the Avon and Somerset Police.

Following research by the staff at Archbishop's House, Cardinal Hume again responded in a robust fashion. An illuminating and disturbing report on the situation regarding evidence by Mr and Mrs Keenan and Yvonne Fox was received by the staff from Alastair Logan. This report was attached as Annex 2 to Cardinal Hume's comprehensive letter of 22 September, 1988 to the Home Secretary, following their meeting on 8 September, 1988. (A copy of the report is at APPENDIX IX to the book.)

In the body of the letter of 22 September, 1988[6] Cardinal Hume said he would assume any public statement that, based on the Avon and Somerset Police report, Mrs Fox was not present in the flat would be accompanied by publication of the contents of the report at Annex 2 to the letter. (APPENDIX IX). He added that, in the last resort, the Deputation would have to consider doing this if they found they had to publish their account of the negotiations, including the original submission and subsequent correspondence.

The above main three points which the Home Secretary considered justifying referral were, therefore, all part of the original submission by the Deputation in July 1987. This raised again the different ways in which the Home Secretary dealt with the Birmingham Six and Guildford Four cases. In his announcement in January 1987 he referred the case of the former to the Court of Appeal on the basis of the

[6]See Chapter Six, page 149.

evidence of the former policeman, Tom Clarke, and then asked the Devon and Cornwall Constabulary to examine the new evidence.

Six months later, in July 1987, the Deputation presented their submission. This included the three main points on the basis of which the Home Secretary had now referred the case which he had declined to do in July 1987. Instead of a referral at that time he arranged for the Avon and Somerset Constabulary to investigate the new evidence given by the Deputation.

The essential difference was that the Devon and Cornwall Constabulary would, presumably, report to the Director of Prosecutions, so assisting the Court of Appeal in their consideration of the case, while the Avon and Somerset Constabulary would report to the Home Secretary who would then decide whether or not to refer the case.

On 17 January, 1989, the day after the Written Reply had been received, the meeting of the Deputation, which had been planned in December 1988, duly took place.[7] It will be recalled that this meeting had been arranged to assess and review the situation, against the background of 'murmurings' at the time, that it could be unlikely that the Guildford Four case would be referred. In the event, of course, with the meeting taking place the day after the referral had been made, the matters actually discussed at the meeting were somewhat different to those which had been on the original agenda.

It is of interest to recall that the main item on the original agenda would have been proposed action to be taken by the Deputation in the event of there being no referral of the Guildford Four case. The Deputation would have called an early press conference at which as many as possible of them would be present. Depending on the contents of the Home Secretary's statement giving reasons for not referring the cases, the main thrust at the press conference would have been:

Details of the alibi evidence available at the time in respect of Carole Richardson, Gerard Conlon, and Paul Hill.

Forceful emphasis on the evidence (to be listed) which had NOT been before a jury.

Simplified explanation of the 'point of law' in the Guildford case, sufficient for those present to grasp the main points as to why there could have been a miscarriage of justice.

Bearing in mind no bulk of explosives whatsoever was found in the Maguire home, the need for the *whole* of the Maguire Seven

[7]See Chapter Six, page 158.

> case to be looked at again, with particular emphasis on the scientific evidence on which alone they had been convicted.

As the Guildford Four case had now been referred, the meeting of the Deputation on 17 January, 1989 took a totally different form. It was agreed that, as a Deputation, they would wish some tribute to be paid on their behalf to Alastair Logan and Gareth Peirce for the substantial contribution they had both made in the pursuit of justice. In particular, they noted that Alastair Logan had been with the cases since 1974, without remuneration for much of the time. After the meeting personal letters of appreciation, reflecting their respective contributions, were sent to Alastair Logan and Gareth Peirce by Cardinal Hume on behalf of the Deputation.

It was further agreed that the Deputation would remain in being, but would lie dormant until the appeal had been heard. Meanwhile, they should be kept appraised, on an informal basis, of progress in work towards preparation of the appeal, and of any major developments that might arise. Lord Scarman referred again to the fact that although the Appeals Committee had refused leave to appeal to the Birmingham case, which was similar to that of the Guildford Four but not as strong, that did not constitute a judgement on the point of law.

In response to a question as to what would happen if the case was rejected by the Court of Appeal, Lord Scarman said that in that event the point of law ought to go to the House of Lords. Given the support of the two Law Lords, he thought the House would probably consider the point on this occasion.

Returning to the Written Reply, towards the end of it the Home Secretary had said:

> Little purpose would be served by setting out in detail here the other points put to me. The three main points I mention seem to me to bear directly on the safety of the convictions. These points were not available to the jury or the Court of Appeal. They need to be tested in court.

The Home Secretary had had the greater part of the three main points since July 1987 when the whole Deputation presented their submission to him. It had been hoped he would refer the case then. However, following receipt in April 1988 of the report by the Avon and Somerset Constabulary, he had clearly turned his mind against referral by the time he went to see Cardinal Hume on 8 September 1988. It can, therefore, only be assumed that 'some of the other points put to me' also contributed to the change of mind. There were, indeed, two other very important points – the 'Birnberg letters',[8] sent by Gareth Peirce

[8] See Chapter Six, page 141.

Andes Press Agency

I . CARDINAL HUME

Cardinal Basil Hume, OM – Archbishop of Westminster, 1976–99.

'It always needs immense courage to say "I'm wrong," and all possible ways of re-opening the case have to be examined very closely . . . When there's been a miscarriage of justice, those cases don't go away.'

Universal Pictorial Press Agency

II . LORD DEVLIN

Lord Devlin – Law Lord 1961–64.

On being asked during a TV broadcast what sort of overall justice did he think the Guildford Four had received –

'None. Perhaps that's putting it a bit strongly. But either you have justice whole and complete, or you have no justice. You can't have a bit of justice here and a bit of justice there.'

Universal Pictorial Press Agency

III . LORD SCARMAN

Lord Scarman OBE – Law Lord 1977–86.

'The convictions of the Guildford Four and the Maguire Seven were as great a miscarriage of justice as any known to have occurred in the twentieth century in the United Kingdom. The cases will be seen as milestones in the history of British criminal justice.'

Universal Pictorial Press Agency

IV . LORD JENKINS OF HILLHEAD

Lord Jenkins of Hillhead OM – Home Secretary 1965–67 and 1974–76.

'Associated with the mood of the time (1974–75) there occurred some of the worst miscarriages of justice in the recent history of British criminal law. Guildford and Birmingham became notorious names in this context. There was I fear a certain atavistic desire to get any Irish man and convict him which affected police, prosecuting counsel, judges and juries. As a result it required a great campaign to right some appalling mis-convictions.'

Universal Pictorial Press Agency

V . LORD MERLYN-REES

Lord Merlyn-Rees – Home Secretary 1976–79.

'Looking at this case afresh, years afterwards, it raises doubts in my mind about the way the confessions were made. There may be people in jail who should not be there. We must find a way of looking again – were we clouded by emotion at the time – understandable emotion?'

VI . ROBERT KEE

Robert Kee – Writer and Broadcaster, author of *Trial and Error*.
Consultant to the Deputation 1986–95.

'The Home Secretary of the day said he was "satisfied" that the case should not be looked at again, despite concerns expressed. There was, he said, "no new evidence." But there *was* new evidence – not to be found for another two years, lying where it had been for the past ten years, because the criminal justice system had failed to look for it.'

VII . PATRICK VICTORY

Patrick Victory OBE MC KCSG.
Assistant for Public Affairs to Cardinal Hume, 1986–99.
Coordinator of activities to the Deputation 1986–95.

'It is fervently to be hoped that the individual deficiencies, failings and mistakes which came to light within all parts of the criminal justice system will help to safeguard against possible future miscarriages of justice.'

From the Archbishop of Westminster and others

Sir, For many years we have, with others, regarded the Guildford Four case as a grave miscarriage of justice. Our initial reaction to Sir John May's final report is one of disappointment.

We are glad that he has confirmed that there was a miscarriage of justice and that serious mistakes were made in the handling of the case at various stages. Some of these, as he indicates, could have resulted from over-reliance by police and prosecution on the validity of the confessions of the Guildford Four.

Following on from that there is the likelihood that some components of the criminal justice system were being driven at the time by an anxiety not to undermine the validity of the confessions as they saw it.

A penetrating and more robust examination of these possibilities was, we believe, required. The weakness of the report is that it does not go far enough in exploring and attributing the extent of responsibility and blame for the miscarriage of justice which Sir John recognises did occur.

The whole truth has not yet been revealed.

Yours faithfully,
BASIL HUME,
ROY JENKINS,
SCARMAN,
MERLYN-REES,
Archbishop's House,
Westminster, SW1.
July 4.

Photocopy of Deputation letter on the Final Report of the May Enquiry, published in *The Times* on the 6th July, 1994.

on 22 June, 1988, and the submissions by Barry Irving, Director of the independent Police Foundation, sent to the Home Secretary in early December 1988.

There was something of a mystery about the handling of the 'Birnberg letter' of 22 June 1988 which was sent to C3. Having heard at the meeting on 8 September that the Home Secretary would not be referring the case, Cardinal Hume referred to, amongst other things, the 'Birnberg letter.' The Home Secretary did not appear to be wholly aware of its contents. In writing to Cardinal Hume on 30 September, Douglas Hurd explained he had 'not been able to reach a view on the letter at the meeting on 8 September 1988 mainly because of its late arrival.' Allegedly, it had been wrongly addressed. It was, in fact, an extremely important letter and it was unfortunate the Home Secretary had not had an opportunity to study it before the meeting.

In the same letter of 30 September, 1988 the Home Secretary referred to the visit to the Home Office by Birnbergs to deliver more material. They had asked that he consider this before making a decision. This was, in fact, a reference to the visit to C3 by Gareth Peirce on 16 September, 1988.[9]

Reference has already been made to the work of Barry Irving, Director of the independent Police Foundation.[10] In 1974 he had started to investigate a number of psychological issues which included confessions, and interrogation techniques and their effects. These were of crucial importance to the just administration of the criminal law. His early studies included the Guildford pub bombing case. His understanding of the potential problems associated with custodial interrogation, and the reliability of confessions obtained therefrom, was shaped by that case, and others like it. This led to research for the Royal Commission on Criminal Procedure. The Police and Criminal Evidence Act 1984 and the Codes attached contain the great majority of the safeguards which he had recommended to the Royal Commission.

Against this background he produced by December 1988, at the request of Alastair Logan, a 'Commentary on Information provided by Potential Alibi witness Frank Johnson.' Alastair Logan had prepared affidavits from both Frank Johnson and Lisa Astin which he had then submitted to Barry Irving, together with the relevant material in the cases, and had asked him to look at this aspect of the case. The 'Commentary' is an impressive in-depth examination of the issues. It covers all possible explanations and reasons as to why and how Frank Johnson walked voluntarily into a police station in Newcastle upon Tyne in early December 1974 when he heard Carole Richardson had

[9]See Chapter Six, page 147. [10]See Chapter Two, page 35.

been arrested; gave his account of meeting her and Lisa Astin at the Charlie Chaplin pub and at the pop concert on the evening of Saturday 5 October, 1974, the day of the Guildford bombing; the timings he gave were such that his account constituted an alibi for Carole Richardson; how police officers from Guildford arrived, treated him as a suspect rather than a witness, took him to Guildford under arrest for intense interrogation; how he became more confused as the questioning went on; and in the end, according to police notes of the final interview, he agreed he had made up the story. In his own affidavit Frank Johnson said he was so confused and exhausted by the end of the three-day interrogation, with no solicitor present, that he told the police to write down what they wanted him to say and he would sign it. He had given an account of all this in the *First Tuesday* TV programme *The Guildford Time Bomb* which was broadcast on 1 July, 1986.[11]

Barry Irving said in his 'Commentary' that he believed the confessions of the Guildford Four would not have stood had the supporting investigation of potential alibi witnesses been fair and sensitive. This led him to examine the experiences of Frank Johnson and Lisa Astin, both of whom signed sworn affidavits as to their treatment as a witness and the effect this had on their witnessing. The affidavits are most revealing, disturbing in places, more particularly Frank Johnson's, and have to be read to be believed. It came to light in the affidavits that the police officers who had interrogated and mainly dealt with Frank Johnson and Lisa Astin were Detective Chief Inspector Longhurst, Detective Constable Wise, PC Lewis and WPC Mills.

Although not quoted in either the 'Commentary' or the affidavits, *The Independent* published on 28 December, 1988 the following extracts from a six-hour interview with Frank Johnson at Guildford Police station in January 1975. These illustrated the anxieties held by many people about the handling of alibi evidence:

Q The first part of what you say in your first statement is untrue, Frank. I have seen lots of people and you have got your time wrong.
A The only thing is I can't remember the time, about 6.30 pm. We went to the Charlie Chaplin, then went to the Poly and met the group at 7pm . . .
Q You have tried to alter the times back at least an hour.
A I haven't . . .
Q You never met her between 6 and 6.30 pm. You got to the Poly at 8pm?
A I don't remember . . .

[11]See Chapter Two, page 35.

Q It was 8 pm?
A I'm trying to think hard to see if it could be 8 pm.
Q You have committed yourself and told lies.
A I believe what I am telling you is true.
Q Are your friends members of Sinn Fein or the IRA?
A No, I am not sympathetic to those kind of people . . .
Q Do you know where Lisa met you that night?
A In the Charlie Chaplin.
Q No it wasn't. What do you know about bombs?
A Only that they kill people.
Q It may be you, Lisa, Carole and the others were all here in Guildford. You know the answer.
A I know I wasn't there.
Q You can't prove you were not there.
A I can't think about it . . .
Q Frank, tell me the truth.
A I made it up. I didn't think Carole was there.
Q What time was it you got to the Charlie Chaplin?
A I don't know.
Q You knew it was a lie about the time.
A Yes . . .
Q You knew when the bombs were planted and what time they went off. That's why you filled in the evening for them. You came down here to help out.
A Yes, I did.'

At the request of Alastair Logan, Barry Irving sent both the 'Commentary' and the two affidavits to the Home Secretary in December 1988. Knowledge of all this came into the public domain when, on 28 December, 1988, *The Independent* published the following as part of a feature on the case in general, and on Frank Johnson in particular. The wording is such that it must have reflected responses by the Home Office to questions put to them:

> Douglas Hurd, the Home Secretary, has agreed, in a surprise move, to extend the scope of the Guildford Four enquiry by examining claims that two key alibi witnesses were intimidated by police, and the evidence of one was deliberately discredited.
>
> The Home Office has asked for affidavits from the witnesses, Frank Johnson and Lisa Astin, and has accepted submissions on Mr Johnson's treatment from a leading criminologist, Barry Irving, director of the independent Police Foundation.
>
> Mr Hurd will be considering the documents over the holiday period, along with the other new evidence and submissions from a

Deputation led by Cardinal Hume. His decision on whether to refer the case back to the Court of Appeal is expected next month.

Towards the end of his Commentary Barry Irving came to some compelling conclusions. Amongst them were:

If Frank Johnson's alibi story was a danger to the prosecution case and had to be discredited by intimidation, then any person who could corroborate it would need to be intimidated as well.

A common prosecution argument pitched against libertarian fears about the reliability of uncorroborated confessions is that any competent police investigation will always take account of the possibility of false confession by carefully checking subsequent denials.

The power of this argument rests on the fairness and skill exercised by police interviewers in dealing with inconvenient witnesses who appear to undermine what would otherwise be an impressive confession-based case.

In view of the vital role of alibi witnesses in cases of alleged false confession, it would be wise to investigate Johnson's allegation of intimidation as carefully as all the other aspects of the case.

In the body of the Commentary it is stated that 'Frank Johnson alleges systematic intimidation from very early in his contact with the police and lasting well after his release (in fact some ambiguous event is said to have occurred in 1979).' It is apparent that the alibi value of his statements depreciated rapidly while in custody from the viewpoint of the defence. Frank Johnson had prepared notes about the evening of 5 October, 1974 and took them to a solicitor in Newcastle. The solicitor refused to help him and told him to go to the police. Verbatim records of his interrogation by the police were apparently not kept. Barry Irving said that the best record available was Frank Johnson's own notes made for his meeting with the solicitor.

These notes were discounted as evidence on the grounds that they were attempts to construct an alibi. Barry Irving went on to say that those notes should, on the contrary, have been treated as contemporaneous notes of Frank Johnson's evidence uncontaminated by the effects of police questioning.

In the light of all this, and of the submissions by Birnbergs through Gareth Peirce, it was surprising that the grounds for referral in the Written Reply consisted only of points given to the Home Secretary by the Deputation in July 1987. There was no reference at all to the submissions by Birnbergs or Barry Irving. However, the Home Secretary had made the point in his Written Reply that '... when a case is referred to the Court of Appeal by the Home Secretary he may cite grounds for such references but the subsequent hearing is not confined to those grounds. Once a case is referred ... the defence may thus seek to raise any matters of fact or law which they regard as pertinent.'

Reference has been made to the speed and scope of the arrangements made by the Surrey Constabulary immediately after the bombing at Guildford.[12] By the next day a team of some 150 detectives of all ranks was assembled. Coordination and control of the operation must have stemmed from the highest level. On reflection a question that had to be asked at the time of the referral was to what extent the very senior ranks in the Surrey Constabulary examined how it was that the value to the defence of Frank Johnson as an alibi witness diminished so rapidly while he was in police custody. When he was released from custody he reverted to his original statement, but by then he had been discredited to the extent that the court, as tended to be the culture in those days, accepted evidence given by the police rather than by him. In his Commentary, under the heading 'Frank as the failed but genuine alibi witness,' Barry Irving made this key observation:

> Had the police treated Frank Johnson as a genuine witness for long enough to obtain a full and complete account from him under the best possible circumstances, and had they then treated him as a hostile suspect, the courts could have decided on which account they wished to operate.

There can be little doubt that the submissions by Birnbergs through Gareth Peirce, and by Barry Irving, were both taken fully into account by the Home Secretary in making his decisions to refer the Guildford Four case. Presumably the defence now had it in mind that all these matters could be raised at the hearing by the Court of Appeal.

During the following months the defence were, of course, receiving very large quantities of documents, assembling and examining this additional data, specifically for preparation of the grounds of appeal, but also relating to the many aspects of the case which had never been before a jury. Over this period the Deputation adhered to their decision to lie dormant, other than in an emergency, until the appeal was heard. Meanwhile the staff at Archbishop's House limited activities to keeping open the lines of communication with the solicitors concerned. This seemingly peaceful period, although a very busy one for the solicitors representing the Guildford Four, was shortly to be shattered by a totally

[12]See Chapter One, page 1.

unexpected event. But it has to be said that the surprise was not so total in the minds of some who had spent many frustrating years with the case trying to find ways through to justice.

In May 1989 Gareth Pierce discovered that a statement had, indeed, been made by a resident in the Conway House Hostel in Quex Road to the Surrey police on 18 January, 1975. His name was Charles Burke. His statement, if true, constituted an alibi for Gerard Conlon in that it revealed that he was in the hostel, and not Guildford, on the evening of 5 October, 1974, the night of the bombing; it also lent support to Paul Hill's assertion that on Saturday 5 October he had gone to Southampton for the weekend. A copy of the actual statement, together with the Avon and Somerset Constabulary cover sheet, is at APPENDIX XI to the book. As will be seen, after briefly giving information on his background, Charles Burke went on to say:

> . . . I came back to England, on the 5th September. [1974]. I stayed in a bed and breakfast place in Cricklewood for three days, and then moved into Father CARYLYN's place in Quex Road, on the 8th of September. I was put in St. Louis Room, which has four beds in it. I have shown you on my sketch where the beds were (Exhibit C.J.B.1.). When I first moved in the beds I show Paul and Gerry in were as follows: – Paul's bed was occupied by a solicitor's clerk, and the bed I show Gerry in was empty. The bed I show Pat in was occupied by a baker from Dublin. After I had been in St. Louis room about one week, the solicitor's clerk moved out and the baker fellow went home to Ireland. That's when Paul and Gerry moved in, and Pat the labourer from Northern Ireland. While Paul and Gerry were there I went out with them on one evening only, to the Memphis Belle. They met two girls there, I don't know their names. I will describe them. (1). About 5' 7' 17–18 years, blonde, fairly plump, well built, English. Gerry was attracted it seemed to her, she knew his name. She was dressed in hippy gear, a long coat, with a big shoulder bag. (No. 2), was more attracted to Paul. She was 17 years old, built smaller, fairish hair, shoulder length. I can't remember her clothing. I never spoke to her nor she to me. Paul and Gerry, apart from this once, kept very much to themselves at Quex Road. In fact I never asked to go out with them, I met them by accident in the Memphis. They never discussed work, but I knew they worked on the buildings. I was in work all the time, seven days a week at B. & M. Fruiterers, 308, Neasden Lane. Paul was the quiet one of the two, but Gerry was mouthy. I knew he didn't like the English, for when it said on T.V. a soldier had been shot, he laughed and said something like 'Bloody good job'. On the Friday before I left Quex Road, the 4th of October, I remember Paul

> said he was going to Southampton for the weekend, to see some friends. When I left work on Saturday, 5th October, 1974, I had found a new place to live, this address, as I was fed up sharing a room. I got back to Quex Road about 7.00 p.m., because we take stock Saturday night. I packed my gear, and Gerry was in his bed. He was the only other person in St. Louis Room. He said he was broke and asked to borrow a quid, but I never let him have it. About 7.30p.m. I caught a taxi and left Quex Road for the last time. When I left he was still in bed. I came straight to this address, and I haven't seen Gerry or Paul since. As far as I know Father CARYLYN wasn't there the night I left. I never said goodbye to anybody except Gerry. I don't owe no money at Quex Road and they don't owe me any either.

This was a statement of the highest importance. There is a need to review, in the light of information available in mid-1989, how it entered the arena at this very late stage and why it had not been disclosed to the defence before they discovered it in May 1989. When in August 1987 the Home Secretary arranged for the Avon and Somerset Police to inquire into the case, they retrieved all available papers from the Surrey Police, Metropolitan Police and the office of the Director of Public Prosecutions (DPP) (by now known as the Crown Prosecution Service (CPS)). When the Avon and Somerset Police submitted their report to the Home Secretary in April 1988 it was accompanied by all the relevant documents. These included the statement made by Charles Burke to the Surrey Police on 18 January, 1975.

After the Home Secretary had referred the case to the Court of Appeal in January 1989, he sent a copy of the Avon and Somerset Police report and relevant documents to the CPS. The CPS then started to serve the relevant documents they had received from the Home Office and the Avon and Somerset Police on defence solicitors. In May 1989 Gareth Peirce of Birnbergs (representing Gerard Conlon) received her bundles of papers from the CPS. Amongst them she found a copy of a statement by a Charles Burke of 18 January, 1975. This was not only the first she knew of it but, from the examination of defence papers back to 1974/75 which she had conducted in her search for Charles Burke, it was apparent that the existence of this statement was at no time known to the defence.

But there was more to come. Having now seen a copy of what became known as the 'Burke alibi' she asked Avon and Somerset Police if she could visit their headquarters in Bristol to look through the original copies of any other documents they might have. For weeks on end these requests were rebuffed as were those from other solicitors. She was told to let them know which documents she wanted copies of and they would photocopy them for her. Her understandable response was that she had to see the documents first before knowing which she would need to copy.

Eventually the first of several visits to Bristol was agreed. These led to even more startling revelations. She discovered that the Charles Burke statement of 18 January 1975 was in a bundle which had been sent to the Home Office and was marked as not having been seen by the defence. Staff at Archbishop's House were left with the impression that the bundle had been marked in manuscript 'Not to be shown to the Defence.' On a later visit she made yet another startling discovery. She found a statement revealing that the Avon and Somerset Police had traced Charles Burke in June 1988. They had taken another statement from him in which he confirmed he did not wish to alter in any way his earlier statement of 18 January, 1975. Presumably a copy of this latest statement, taken after the Avon and Somerset Police had submitted their report to the Home Secretary in April 1988, was also sent to the Home Office, though Gareth Peirce suspected it might not have been. The defence were not informed of it until she found it.

As seen in mid-1989, the discovery of the statement of 18 January, 1975 made by Charles Burke gave rise to a very serious situation. On the face of it the position was that a statement had been taken from a witness central to Gerard Conlon's alibi by the police in January 1975. This was prior to the trial of the Guildford Four, and neither the name, nor the address, nor the contents had ever been made known to those representing Gerard Conlon prior to May 1989. Such action was in direct breach of the law which states that there must be disclosure to the defence of material witnesses not relied upon by the prosecution.

To put this extremely serious situation into immediate perspective it is necessary, as a first step, to go back to the trial of the Guildford Four in September/October 1975. In his closing speech Sir Michael Havers, who led for the prosecution, referred to the fact that Gerard Conlon had no alibi. The judge (now Lord Donaldson) reminded Sir Michael that in fact Gerard Conlon claimed he did have an alibi but had been unable to produce witnesses to support it. So while the prosecution lawyers were standing in court claiming that Gerard Conlon had no alibi, the prosecuting authorities knew very well that this was untrue.

The Surrey Police and the DPP, who both had a hand in the preparation of the indictment whereby Gerard Conlon was charged with murder, must have known of the existence of the statement by Charles Burke on 18 January, 1975 – the 'Burke alibi'. Those who did not know about it at the trial and right up until May 1989 were the lawyers for the defence. There can be no doubt whatsoever that had the defence known about the Burke alibi the trial would have unfolded in a somewhat different way.

It will be recalled that at his trial Gerard Conlon described his day on 5 October, 1974 – in and around the Quex Road Hostel all day; in the middle of the day going to the betting shop, then the pubs; late afternoon, drunk, returning to his four-bed room in the hostel to sleep it off; then went to the television room. During the crucial hours of 6.00 pm to 8.00 pm he thought that Patrick Carey and/or 'Paul the greengrocer' were around but he was confused about who might have seen him and when. Patrick Carey was called to give evidence but there was a delay in the trial. He returned to Belfast and never came back. 'Paul the grocer' was, in fact, Charles Burke but the defence did not know of his statement, or even his whereabouts, and so he was not called.

Ever since those days, it has never ceased to amaze how the police and prosecution, although they knew from the RUC of his earlier membership of the IRA, could have assumed that Gerard Conlon could have been a member of an IRA Active Service Unit. They clearly did not have, or did not wish to have, any understanding of his social milieu – living in a hostel away from home; having no diary or appointments; no planned social events; difficulty in recollecting accurate timings of his activities in the disorganised context of his movements between betting offices and pubs on Saturday 5 October, 1974 which was not a working day. Moreover, it also needs to be recalled that the reign of terror spread by the 50 speedy arrests of many innocent persons during late November/early December 1974[13] left the defence bereft of potential assistance. Most of those arrested had Irish connections but were in no way associated with the IRA.

Moving on now into the 1980s, the seriousness of the non-disclosure of the Burke alibi compounds the problem, in that a situation arose whereby the case could, and some would emphatically say should, have been referred to the Court of Appeal nearly two years before it was so referred. The following observations speak for themselves:

> The DPP and the prosecution must have known about the statement by Charles Burke taken by the Surrey Police in January 1975 well before the trial of the Guildford Four in September 1975.
>
> The Avon and Somerset Police had the Burke alibi when they retrieved all the relevant papers from the Surrey Police in August 1987.

[13]See Chapter One, page 2.

> The Home Office knew of it when C3 received the report and relevant documents from the Avon and Somerset Police in April 1988.
>
> A copy of the Burke alibi was in the Home Office when the Home Secretary saw Cardinal Hume on 8 September, 1988 and said he would not be referring the case. He did not mention the Burke alibi.
>
> On 16 September, 1988 Gareth Peirce spent some hours with Mr Baxter and Mr Stanton of C3. She handed over the statements of all those witnesses who could support Gerard Conlon's own account of his activities on Saturday 5 October, 1974 other than between 6.00 pm and 8.00 pm.
>
> She explained that she was still seeking witnesses covering the crucial period 6.00 pm to 8.00 pm but had drawn a blank. She believed that a Charles Burke could help but she could not trace him. No mention was made to her of the Burke alibi which was in the Home Office at that time.
>
> In June 1989, on one of her visits to the Avon and Somerset Police, Gareth Peirce discovered that the Avon and Somerset Police had traced Charles Burke in June 1988, three months after they had handed in their report in April 1988. He confirmed his statement of 18 January 1975. What was not known for certain at the time was whether or not the Avon and Somerset Police sent a copy of the June 1988 statement to the Home Office. It was not mentioned at the meetings on 8 and 16 September referred to above.

The Deputation regarded the Burke alibi as a major issue and attached the greatest importance to it. The statement itself, and its non-disclosure, were believed to constitute a consideration of substance. Reflecting back to January 1989 when the case was referred to the Court of Appeal, it is astonishing that the Burke alibi, and its non-disclosure to the defence in 1975, had not been included by the Home Office as a ground of reference for the Guildford Four case. This should have at least ensured that why and how it had all happened, and who was responsible, would have been examined.

As part of the agreed arrangements for keeping the Deputation informed of developments, Alastair Logan wrote to Archbishop's House on 26 July, 1989 reporting the outcome of a directions hearing held on 20 July before the Court of Appeal with the Lord Chief Justice, Lord Lane, presiding. The fixture for the Guildford Four case to be heard had previously been arranged for 9 October, 1989. Everyone was agreed that there was insufficient time to absorb the vast quantity of documentation that was being supplied. It was at that hearing that Crown Counsel, Mr Amlot, assured the Lord Chief Justice that every document of relevance had been furnished to the defence.

After hearing views Lord Lane agreed that the case should be adjourned to the first week of the Spring Term in January 1990, and that grounds of appeal should be filed by 31 October, 1989. In his letter Alastair Logan then referred to some of the information Gareth Peirce had obtained from the Avon and Somerset Police. He went on to say that they were both experiencing difficulty in obtaining from the police the custody and prison records of all four defendants on the grounds that these were privileged. They had been made available to the Avon and Somerset Constabulary, at their request, by the Home Office. The solicitors felt strongly about this and hoped the matter could be resolved.

Following the directions hearing on 20 July, 1989, solicitors and their counsel continued work on absorbing the great amount of material that was being made available to them by the CPS. Consideration was also being given by them to preparation of the grounds of appeal which were to be filed by 31 October, 1989. Meanwhile it was announced that the Guildford Four case would be heard by the Court of Appeal on 15 January 1990.

On the morning of 17 October, 1989 a veritable bombshell burst upon the scene. The Crown Prosecution Service made the following statement:

> In January this year the Home Secretary referred to the Court of Appeal under Section 17 of the Criminal Appeal Act, 1968, the convictions of Paul Hill, Gerard Conlon, Carole Richardson and Patrick Armstrong for murder arising out of the Guildford and Woolwich pub bombings which occurred in October and November 1974 respectively.
>
> Circumstances have recently come to the notice of the Director of Public Prosecutions which have caused him to conclude that it would be wrong for the Crown to seek to sustain the convictions. The Court was informed yesterday afternoon and ordered an expedited hearing.
>
> It will now take place on Thursday 19 October at the Central Criminal Court. The reasons for the Director's decision will be given.

This dramatic development came as a total surprise to everybody other than the prosecution, the Avon and Somerset Police, Ministers and selected officials in the Home Office, and, no doubt, the Prime Minister. It also meant that the defence had only two days' notice of the hearing.

Those who had been concerned about the case, together with those such as the Deputation who had been in active pursuit of justice for the Guildford Four, regarded the statement by the CPS as signalling that the end was at last now well in sight. In reflecting on this, some recalled the comments of the judge at the trial in sentencing the Guildford Four:

> You have been sentenced to life imprisonment for murder, and I want you to understand what this means. And I want your fellow members of the IRA and in particular those being sent to this country to commit these crimes to understand that these crimes have a very special feature.
>
> You may think you can expect to be released in twelve to fifteen years. I want to spell out the facts. The idea that life means twelve to fifteen years dates from the days when the sentence for murder was death. Only when there were extenuating circumstances was that commuted to life imprisonment. It was a reprieve, and reprieved murderers were released after such a period. None of you would have been in that category. You would have been executed. Sentence of life imprisonment must have an entirely different meaning.

The reference to possible future offenders was understandable in the circumstances obtaining at the time. The reference to execution was chilling. If the death penalty had not been abolished in 1965, only Carole Richardson would have lived to see 19 October, 1989 – she was too young to hang. Indeed, in that event it is questionable whether the case would have ever been referred back to the Court of Appeal. This had to be a matter of grave reflection for all constituent parts of the criminal justice system.

This discomforting thought gave rise to the expectation that the Director of Public Prosecutions would fully cover at the hearing all the circumstances which had led him to his momentous conclusion. It had been apparent to many people for a long time that the whole of the criminal justice system had spectacularly failed the Guildford Four. It was anticipated that much would be revealed. The hearing duly took place on 19 October, 1989, as had been announced by the CPS two days earlier on 17 October. Lord Lane, sitting with Lord Justice Glidewell and Lord Justice Farquharson, heard the appeal. Mr Roy Amlot QC appeared on behalf of the Crown. Counsel for the Appellants were Mr Patrick Macentee S.C.QC for Patrick Armstrong, Mr George Carman QC for Carole Richardson, Lord Gifford QC for Paul Hill, and Mr Anthony Scrivener QC for Gerard Conlon.

In the introduction to his presentation Mr Amlot made a very definite announcement:

> It is my onerous duty to have to inform the court that since the referral in January this year evidence of great significance has come to light. That evidence throws such doubt upon the honesty and integrity of a number of Surrey Police officers investigating this case in 1974 that the Crown now feels unable to say that the conviction of any appellant was safe or satisfactory.

This powerful opening statement made a direct link between the conduct of the police officers and the convictions of the Guildford Four. By calling into question their reliability and truthfulness at the very outset of his statement, Mr Amlot made clear that this was now likely to be the main basis on which the Director of Public Prosecutions would be unable to say the convictions were safe or satisfactory. Indeed the indications were that the case would now be presented to the court solely on the basis of those narrow, though extremely grave and seriously important, grounds. It would, therefore, now be for defence counsel to be prepared to raise those other issues, such as the 'Burke alibi' which, it would be submitted, also rendered the convictions unsafe or unsatisfactory. Some of those issues related to other parts of the criminal justice system.

Roy Amlot's presentation fell broadly under four headings – a summary of the original trial of 1975; the main issues at the appeal of 1977; brief reference to the Home Secretary's referral in January 1989; and the questioning of police credibility. The transcript of his presentation is a substantial document of some 22 pages. It will, therefore, only be possible to refer here mainly to those revelations which were of particular interest to the Deputation in the light of their researches and misgivings over the years.

Amlot opened the first section convening the trial by focusing on the central issue, namely that – 'The case against each appellant depended entirely upon the confessions to the police. There was no other evidence.' Each appellant was interviewed by units of two or three officers from the Surrey Constabulary. A total of 12 Surrey officers were involved in the interviews. Additionally, after that, Patrick Armstrong and Paul Hill were interviewed about the Woolwich bombing by the Metropolitan Police but at Guildford Police Station. Amlot went on to say that at the trial serious allegations were made against the Surrey interviewing officers by each appellant – 'there were allegations of brutality, threats, intimidation, inducements and concoction of evidence.' All these allegations were denied by the officers – 'and it is clear that the jury acted upon those denials and relied upon the integrity of the officers involved.'

After describing the circumstances of the bombings at Guildford and Woolwich, Amlot gave a full account of the sequence of interviews and timings for all four appellants. He also gave a very brief account of the contents of the statements which followed the many interviews which had taken place – Paul Hill was interviewed six times, Carole Richardson four times, and Patrick Armstrong three times. Amlot summarised the situation as follows:

> Therefore it is clear that during the trial in respect of the confessions these features stood out. First of all, there were many discrepancies between the accounts of the four appellants on Guildford and between Hill and Armstrong on Woolwich. For example, upon the role that each played at Guildford, Hill and Conlon said Annie Maguire went into the Horse and Groom and Paul [not Hill] and Richardson went into the Seven Stars. Conlon said he and Richardson went into the Seven Stars. Richardson said she, Armstrong and the passenger – probably Conlon – went into the Horse and Groom. Armstrong said he, Richardson and Conlon went into the Horse and Groom. So the only consistent versions were Richardson's and Armstrong's on that aspect.
>
> As to Woolwich, Hill said that he had passed the bomb to Armstrong, who threw it through the window, and Armstrong said he was not involved in the bombing, only in a reconnaissance.

Amlot said the jury obviously relied upon the integrity of the police officers in considering the Crown's explanation for the inconsistencies. That explanation was that the defendants either deliberately misled the police or minimised their roles out of self-interest. He added that at the same time the Crown alleged that amongst the inconsistency Armstrong was closest to the truth in his confession, and in fact he was placed first in the indictment. [By 'closest to the truth' the Crown presumably meant the version of events the police believed to have taken place.] Mr Amlot concluded his review of confessions by saying:

> I emphasise that because of material I shall come to relating to him. It is of course obvious that in a case dependent upon confessions the integrity of the interviewing officers was of paramount importance.

Before leaving the trial, Roy Amlot said that the alibis put forward by each appellant were 'carefully analysed and considered during the trial.' Paul Hill called on his girlfriend Gina Clarke and her sister Mrs Crosbie in Southampton for Guildford, and Mr and Mrs Keenan for Woolwich; Gerard Conlon named a Patrick Carey but he had returned to Ireland and did not give evidence. (It is to be noted that Amlot did not even mention Charles Burke whose statement of 18 January, 1975 was unknown to the defence at the time of the trial, but was certainly known to the defence and the DPP by May 1989, some five months before the hearing). Carole Richardson called on Lisa Astin and Frank Johnson.

In concluding his comments on alibis Amlot said that at the trial the Crown strongly contested the evidence of Lisa Astin and Frank Johnson and 'proved inconsistent statements by both of them to the investigating officers.' He did not mention that they had both been treated as suspects rather than witnesses. Nevertheless, it is interesting to note that, in speaking of all the alibis, he observed:

> It is right to say that no alibi was so destroyed that the learned trial judge felt able to direct the jury that it supported the Crown case against any appellant.

Turning to the appeal, Amlot said it was heard before Lord Justice Roskill (as he was then), Lord Justice Lawton and Mr Justice Boreham. He said the main issues in the hearing arose out of evidence given before the court by O'Connell, Duggan and Butler of the Balcombe Street ASU, and also by Dowd who had been arrested five months earlier. Specifically he said:

> Their evidence amounted to this. O'Connell and Dowd claimed that they were responsible with three others unnamed for the Guildford bombings. All four claimed responsibility for the Woolwich bombing. They all claimed that the applicants – the Guildford defendants – had nothing to do with either bombing. If they were right, the applicants' confessions were of course false.
>
> . . . Richardson also argued that there was at least a lurking doubt that her alibi might be true, or rather that the Crown had not shown it to be false.

In reviewing some of the evidence given at the appeal Amlot referred specifically to the fact that Dowd had given (correctly) the name and address of the firm from which the car had been hired, and that he had also accurately described the presence and position of two elderly men in the Horse and Groom. In giving judgement Lord Roskill said:

> We see no reason to decide whether O'Connell or Dowd took part in the Guildford bombings. We are content to assume that O'Connell's story of his presence and participation may indeed be true and that Dowd may also have taken part notwithstanding the doubts we have on that latter point.

Amlot then related that part of the judgement covering O'Connell's evidence which ended with:

> We are therefore content to proceed upon the assumption that he and Duggan and, though with more hesitation, Butler took part in both the abortive journey to Woolwich on the Wednesday and also the journey when the Kings Arms was attacked and the murders took place upon the Thursday. Once we have disbelieved, as we do, their evidence regarding Dowd's presence on the Wednesday and Thursday, we see no reason to give any credence whatever to their details of knowledge of Hill and Armstrong.

Towards the end of the judgement Lord Roskill said the Crown's case at the trial was based on confessions; there was no evidence whatever of identification; the descriptive evidence was of minimal weight; and there was no fingerprint evidence. He concluded that part of the judgement by saying '. . . but, if the confessions were both voluntary and true, the evidence against all the applicants was overwhelming.' The court clearly believed that the confessions were 'voluntary and true.' They rejected all four applications for leave to appeal.

Moving on to the referral by the Home Office, Roy Amlot recapitulated the three grounds of reference given by the Home Secretary. He explained that these were based on the original submissions by Cardinal Hume's Deputation to the Home Secretary who had then arranged for them to be investigated by the Avon and Somerset Police. He emphasised that, if the appeal had been confined to those issues, they would have been firmly resisted by the Crown. (It is to be noted that though making this point he still did not refer to the Burke alibi which the DPP had known about since 1975.) But, 'it did not end there,' he added, somewhat ominously. He went on to say that, after the referral, a close scrutiny of all the papers, including those which had been kept by the Surrey Police, had to be undertaken by the Avon and Somerset Police.

He added (erroneously as it turned out later,) that the Avon and Somerset Police were not asked to investigate the behaviour of Surrey police officers or the circumstances of the detention and interrogations of the appellants in 1974. In fact, at the request of Birnbergs, the Home Secretary had specifically asked in September 1988 for an investigation to be carried out by the Avon and Somerset Police into the witness statements in which allegations about police behaviour had been made and which had been handed to C3 by Gareth Peirce at the meeting on 16 September 1988[14]. Apparently the Avon and Somerset Police did produce a supplemental report. Its existence and contents were not known to the Deputation at the time in October 1989, nor was it known who had knowledge of its contents at that time. (But see CHAPTER

[14]See Chapter Six, page 147 and Chapter Seven, page 169.

NINE, pages 272 to 274, where reference is made to the Birnberg letter of 2 February, 1994 sent to the May Inquiry before publication of their Final Report in June 1994).

Moving into the fourth part of his presentation which covered the integrity and credibility of police officers, Amlot emphasised that the Guildford case papers had remained with the Surrey Police until they were collected by Avon and Somerset Police 'at the beginning of their inquiry'. By this he presumably meant the beginning of the inquiry in August 1987 as requested by the Home Secretary, though he had said earlier that the scrutiny instigated after the referral included some papers which had been kept by the Surrey Police.

This was a key section in Roy Amlot's presentation, and it was crucial in consideration of the possible quashing of the convictions. Amongst the papers that had been kept by the Surrey Police, the Avon and Somerset Police discovered rough draft notes of each of the three interviews of Patrick Armstrong over three days. He said that the set of these notes which related to the confession allegedly made by Patrick Armstrong were typewritten. The typewritten document contained a large number of alterations in manuscript. There was a second typewritten version that incorporated these alterations and that, too, contained a large number of manuscript alterations. He added that the three police officers who had interviewed Patrick Armstrong admitted that the notes, both the typing and the hand-written amendments, were theirs. He then said that the final version incorporating the second set of amendments matched almost word for word a separate set of manuscript notes used by the police officers at the trial.

At the trial the officers claimed that the manuscript notes had been recorded contemporaneously during each interview as Patrick Armstrong 'confessed'. If that were so, he went on, it is difficult to see why two sets of draft notes were brought into existence. He told the court it was impossible to see why the draft typewritten notes would take the form they did unless they were made before the manuscript notes. If they were, he said, the manuscript notes could not have been made during the interviews. The police officers could not now offer a satisfactory explanation. He summed up the situation thus:

> The inescapable conclusion is that no contemporaneous notes were made of each interview, as indeed was suggested by the defence at the trial, and that the officers seriously misled the court.

He then went on to say that 'none of these documents was disclosed to the Director of Public Prosecutions or to prosecuting counsel at the trial.' It could be that he was referring only to the draft typed and amended notes since the manuscript notes allegedly recording the interviews would presumably have been considered by the DPP in preparing the indictments. He also made no reference to who authorised this non-disclosure, or to whether the officers concerned had acted independently of their superiors, or whether there were others with greater powers of responsibility also involved.

Amlot then painstakingly took members of the court, page by page, through the relevant documents, copies of which they all held, showing how and where alterations had been made. He then said that not only did all three officers who had interrogated Patrick Armstrong:

> . . . mislead the court, but that because of the way the notes had been prepared, and because of the statements that those officers made in 1974 for purposes of the trial, it is clear that they agreed together to present their notes to the court in this fashion.

He then turned to a set of manuscript notes relating to an interview of Paul Hill, which had also been discovered by Avon and Somerset police officers, and which had been identified by one of the two Surrey officers concerned. The interview as revealed by the notes was never tendered in evidence and had not been disclosed to the DPP or to prosecuting counsel. Amlot said it was clear from the content of the notes that it took place two days after Paul Hill had been charged and it led to his fifth statement under caution.

Continuing, he said the content of the notes bore no resemblance to the evidence given by the police as to the way in which they claimed Hill 'volunteered' to make his fifth statement. This statement was of considerable significance in the trial because in it he was the first to name Carole Richardson. Amlot added that during the trial the police officers denied the defence suggestions that there was an interview on that day, and he made the point that the manuscript notes were inconsistent with that denial.

Amlot then carefully took the Court through all the relevant documents. In doing so he confirmed that the handwriting was that of the officers and it had been identified by each officer. He added that the discrepancy in timings was supported by what information could be derived from detention sheets. After going through all the notes, and amendments thereto, in a detailed fashion, he said the fact was that the interview as revealed by the notes was suppressed by the officers and:

> . . . one is driven to the inescapable conclusion that this piece of evidence was concocted, no doubt in order to circumvent the rule that because Hill had been charged, there must not be an interview unless there were special circumstances, and the concocted version

> gives the very clear impression that this was a piece of volunteering without questions by Hill.

Amlot went on to say that the discovery of the Armstrong and Hill notes led to a thorough examination of all existing documents and records relating to the detention and interrogation of the appellants and other suspects at the time. These revealed 'disquieting aspects of the case':

> The detention sheets for each appellant (which do not appear to have been either required or made available in the trial) – and they record the suspects' movements about the police station – reveal a disturbing difference between the numbers and times of interviews according to the sheets and the number and times of interviews according to the officers in evidence. Interviews are shown on the sheets which were never given in evidence or revealed to the DPP or prosecuting counsel.

He then gave detailed illustrations to the Court, all relating to Paul Hill, Patrick Armstrong and Carole Richardson, as to where interviews were shown on the detention sheets as taking place at markedly different times from those given in court by the interviewing officers. There were two sets of detention sheets, the originals and a concocted set.

He then declared – 'it is clear that a full criminal investigation of all these matters is called for, which the Director of Public Prosecutions has this week set in motion.' It was the view of the Crown that the 'Armstrong and Hill notes' showed clear prima facie evidence that a total of five Surrey officers out of the 12 involved seriously misled the court in relation to the interviewing of two of the four appellants. In the light of this material he said:

> The Crown has come to the conclusion that it would have contaminated the case for the prosecution as a whole. That case depended entirely upon the confessions and in turn upon the integrity of the officers taking them. Moreover it was a case where the confessions produced substantially inconsistent accounts between the appellants.

Amlot then referred to the separate confessions made by Paul Hill and Patrick Armstrong to Metropolitan Police officers[15] investigating Woolwich. He said that nothing had come to light to cast the slightest doubt on the integrity of any of the Metropolitan Police officers concerned, but the circumstances of the confessions needed to be put in

[15]Chapter 6 page 142 interview of DCS Imbert by Ludovic Kennedy.

perspective. These confessions were made in Guildford Police Station, following interviews by Surrey officers in which initial confessions to involvement in Woolwich had been recorded. In Patrick Armstrong's case, the Metropolitan officers did not introduce themselves as Metropolitan officers. Neither of the defendants gave the Metropolitan officers any detail of any substance which they had not already given to the Surrey officers.

The confessions to the Metropolitan officers were made after Paul Hill had been in continuous custody for seven days and Patrick Armstrong for two days in Guildford Police Station. He added that, in any event, the two defendants produced inconsistent accounts in their confessions as between themselves. Moreover, Amlot said, there was no evidence independent of either confession on Woolwich that either implicated each defendant or verified the accuracy of each confession. In the circumstances and as the Surrey police evidence was now tainted, the Crown was unable to argue that the factors undermining the reliability of the confessions recorded by certain Surrey police officers did not also undermine the reliability of the confessions repeated to certain Metropolitan police officers.

Roy Amlot concluded his presentation:

> It is therefore the Crown's considered view that the recent discovery[16] in the Surrey police files of the material I have already analysed with your Lordships throws such doubt now on the honesty and integrity of that part of the investigation which led to the confessions that it would not be right for the Crown to contend that the conviction of any appellant was either safe or satisfactory.

By this one single act the Crown ensured that justice would at last be forthcoming for the Guildford Four, but it also deprived them of a full hearing in the Court of Appeal. Such a hearing would have enabled their counsel to expose both those failings in the criminal justice system itself, and the failings by some individuals in its constituent parts, which had all resulted in wrongful imprisonment for fifteen years. These would have included the handling of the Burke alibi which had been known to the prosecution since before the Guildford Four trial in 1975.

Three observations can be made at this stage on Roy Amlot's presentation. He made reference to '. . . a thorough examination of all existing documents and records relating to the detention and interrogation of the appellants and other suspects at the time'.

[16]In fact, the material had been discovered by Avon and Somerset Police in May 1989. The question arises why the documents were not discovered earlier, and why Crown Counsel did not know about them at the directions hearing on 20 July 1989. (See Chapter Seven, pages 178 to 179).

This was undertaken by the Avon and Somerset Police after the discovery of the notes relating to Paul Hill and Patrick Armstrong. He made no mention of the position about the confessions of Gerard Conlon and Carole Richardson. This could have been because he was engaged in a damage limitation exercise, especially in the light of the Burke alibi.

A second observation could have been explained if, in fact, while making a very full though perhaps not wholly comprehensive presentation, Amlot was continuing to be partially engaged in damage limitation. It was well known that, within 24 hours of the Guildford bombings, the Surrey Police had assembled a team of some 150 detectives whose activities must have been planned, organised and supervised by very senior officers. There was no mention of their possible culpability.

A third observation relates to Amlot's statement that none of the incriminating documents 'was disclosed to the Director of Public Prosecutions or to prosecuting counsel in the trial'. Presumably a key question, to be resolved in the 'full criminal investigation' which Amlot had said was to be set up by the DPP, would be how it came about that Sir Michael Havers and his prosecuting team had no knowledge or sight of the documents which had been found in Surrey Police custody. The question also arises whether Havers or any of his team asked for production of all documents related to the confessions. If they did ask it needed to be established whether they got all that were available: and, if not, why not.

Referring again to Sir Michael Havers, it is difficult not to recall his words at the Guildford trial:

> Accusations of the most appalling kind have been made against the police during this trial. If true, there has been a really gigantic conspiracy between two police forces – the Surrey Police and the Bomb Squad – through officers of all ranks, including Commander Huntley of the Bomb Squad, the Head of Surrey C.I.D., Detective Chief Superintendent Walter Simmons, and Surrey Assistant Chief Constable, Christopher Rowe. If the allegations are true there has been a most appalling perversion of justice.

In the Court of Appeal, defence counsel representing all four defendants made brief statements. George Carman, for Carole Richardson, said the very gravely disturbing facts, involving the fabrication of evidence by police officers and lies told by them on oath at the trial, overwhelmingly inferred that there had been a grave miscarriage of justice so far as all four appellants were concerned. He added that the documents now disclosed supported the case for the appellants put for them at the trial by their leading counsel.

Turning to Carole Richardson, he said that had the matter proceeded to a full hearing of the appeal, quite independently of the grave matters raised by Mr Amlot, there were compelling and powerful arguments for saying her conviction was unsafe and unsatisfactory. Specifically he singled out medical evidence which showed that, at the time she made her four written confessions, she was in a state of drug withdrawal and consequently her statements were unreliable. He also referred to the alibi evidence of Maura Kelly, who was unavailable at the trial, in which she confirmed the evidence given by Lisa Astin as to Carole Richardson's movements on the day of the bombing. He concluded by saying '. . . for the last 15 years Carole Richardson has been protesting her innocence and through me, in public, she does so today.'

Anthony Scrivener, representing Gerard Conlon, said that his client wished to thank the many people in Britain and the Irish Republic who had supported his cause. He said that the facts, as reviewed dispassionately by Mr Amlot, revealed that the interviews which were said by the prosecution at the trial to fit together like a jigsaw puzzle had been shown to have fallen apart. One of the grounds he would have wished to urge before the court if there had been a full hearing related to an alibi witness. He said there were statements in police custody from two witnesses, both dated in January 1975 (one of whom was Charles Burke), which in fact provided Gerard Conlon with an alibi. They had not been disclosed to the defence at the trial. His last words were – 'My Lord, may I finally say, thank God we did not have capital punishment.'

Patrick Macentee, representing Patrick Armstrong, said his client wished to thank those who had stood behind him for 15 years whilst he had 'consistently asserted his innocence and today asserts it again.' He added that if the appeal had gone on he would have been in a position to advance very powerful and compelling arguments as to why Patrick Armstrong's conviction was unsafe and unsatisfactory. In particular, he would have urged upon the Court that the decision of those who were preparing the evidence for the prosecution not to reveal to the defence the fact that the idiosyncratic nature of the construction of the Balcombe Street ASU bombs was a matter relevant at the trial. His client was gravely disadvantaged by not having that evidence furnished to his advisers at the time. He concluded by saying that it was very disturbing that all these matters might never have come to light and that a possible appalling miscarriage of justice might have gone uncorrected.

Lord Gifford, representing Paul Hill, said it was a tragedy that it had taken 15 years before the material could be brought before a court of justice. He said that, first, as the court knew, fresh witnesses would have been tendered to support Paul Hill's alibi. He then corrected the statement of facts relating to train timetables as given by Mr Amlot at the hearing. He went on to say that Hill's alibi for 5 October, 1974 had been invalidated at trial by evidence relating to the train timetables. This was not correctly put to the jury by the trial judge and, in fact, it had not been put correctly by Mr Amlot at the hearing.

It would have been his contention, in a full hearing, that the evidence relating to the train timetables, when looked at correctly, did not invalidate the alibi Paul Hill's counsel had put forward. Specifically, he said there was no evidence that anyone had said to the police that he had gone to Southampton by the train which was diverted.

After a brief review of the situation relating to the conviction of Hill on another matter recorded against him in the Belfast City Court, the Lord Chief Justice, Lord Lane, closed the hearing and said 'judgement would be delivered at 2 o'clock'.

The judgement by Lord Lane is necessarily reported in a very shortened form. He began by reviewing the facts of the case in brief outline up to the hearing, and he made reference to the trial in 1975 and the appeal in 1977. There had been representations to the Home Secretary but he had declined to refer the case in January 1987. However, representations continued to be made, and new evidence emerged, following which the Home Secretary referred the case in January 1989. He then said the grounds of appeal were, for Carole Richardson, an alibi statement by Maura Kelly, and her medical condition at the time her confessions were made; for Paul Hill, a new alibi witness, Mrs Fox, with regard to the Woolwich bombing.

Lord Lane went on to say that the starting date for the hearing had originally been arranged for 15 January 1990, but earlier during the week the court was informed that the Crown would no longer seek to uphold the convictions. The grounds upon which the case had been referred were not the basis of this decision by the Crown. Indeed, Mr Amlot had said that if the grounds of referral remained the sole points of the appeal they would have been hotly contested by the Crown. Lord Lane then said:

> The reasons now put forward by Mr Amlot, which we have heard this morning, arise out of the fact that the prosecution case depended upon confessions which were allegedly made by these appellants to the police during the course of those police enquiries . . . it would, I think, be fair to say that, save in Carole Richardson's case, the alibis were not at the centre of the defence submissions.

Lord Lane then commented in turn on the case against each appellant and his or her defence. Patrick Armstrong made two statements, which amounted to confessions, saying he was involved in Guildford but not

Woolwich. His defence at the trial was that he had not taken part in either bombing. He claimed his statements were untrue, except for personal details. He had said he was high on drugs when arrested and had been treated with brutality by the police at Guildford Police Station. He asserted his first statement was done by question and answer in such a way that the answer was suggested and he simply agreed with it. As to his second statement, he said the officer started making it in the form it was eventually written and he simply answered questions. He also put forward an alibi.

Lord Lane said that Carole Richardson made four statements to the police which amounted in effect to a confession of her complicity in the Guildford bombing. The statements which it was alleged she had made to the police were, she had asserted, dictated to her by the police. This included the second statement which gave details of the trip to Guildford and the planting of the bomb. She said she had been subjected to police brutality and had signed the statements because she was frightened. She also gave evidence of an alibi which was part of the grounds on which the case had been referred. She asserted that she had been taking barbiturates and was affected by the fact that the drugs were wearing off.

Turning to the case against Paul Hill, Lord Lane said he made a number of statements into which it was not necessary to go in detail. The fifth statement (in which Carole Richardson had been implicated for the first time) was a summary of all the previous admissions about Guildford. Paul Hill's evidence was to the effect that he took no part in either bombing. He asserted he made his statements to the police because they had said they were going to charge his girlfriend Gina Clark (from Southampton) and he wanted to prevent her from being involved in the proceedings. He said the police had suggested what he should write down, and the idea that there were two teams of bombers came from the way the police had directed their questioning. He added that his final statement was put down the way the police wanted it put down, and that it was not true.

Lord Lane said that the case against Gerard Conlon was that he was part of the Guildford bombing team. He was alleged to have made a number of statements in which he was further alleged to have said that 'Hill had asked him to do a ''little job'' and there was a suggestion that he, Conlon, would be killed if he did not help Hill in the enterprise'. Gerard Conlon had also given evidence in his own defence. He had said that at the time he had been in London with a man called Paul Kelly [Carey], but Kelly [Carey], did not in fact give evidence. Gerard Conlon also said he had been assaulted by the police at Guildford; threats had been made against his family to try to persuade him to confess; and that the police tore up his first statement in which he had declined to make any confessions. Concluding the brief account of Gerard Conlon's evidence about the bombings, Lord Lane added he had said that, eventually, in effect, the police dictated the material statement and the admissions he made were not true.

Lord Lane then reviewed the main factors concerning evidence at the trial 'which Mr Amlot has meticulously described in his opening address.' He said that, in reality, everything depended on whether the jury were sufficiently satisfied to be sure that the police evidence about interviews, and the ensuing statements, could be relied upon or not:

> It follows that any evidence which casts a real doubt upon the reliability or veracity of the officers who were responsible for the various interrogations must mean that the whole foundation of the prosecution case disappears and that the convictions will in those circumstances be obviously unsafe.

He dealt with the evidence found by the Avon and Somerset Police which, he said, the Crown rightly accepted, revealed that the so-called contemporaneous notes on interviews with Patrick Armstrong were not contemporaneous notes at all. The court, necessarily speculating, thought there might be two possible explanations for the typescripts relating to Patrick Armstrong and the amendments made to them. It was possible they were a fabrication from start to finish 'invented by some fertile Constabulary mind,' were amended to make them more effective, and were then written out in manuscript so as to enable the police to produce them as 'contemporaneous notes'. A second possibility was that there was a contemporaneous manuscript note, which was reduced to typewritten form, was then amended here and there to improve it, and was then finally reconverted into manuscript so that it could be produced as a contemporaneous note.

According to Lord Lane, it was immaterial for purposes of the appeal which of the two possible versions was true, and that the officers, 'to use Mr Amlot's somewhat anodyne expression, seriously misled the court. In fact they must have lied.' He concluded the section on Patrick Armstrong by saying:

> In any event the police were not telling the truth about this crucial document in the case against Armstrong. If they were prepared to tell this sort of lie, then the whole of their evidence becomes suspect and, I repeat, on their evidence depended the prosecution case.

Turning to matters relating to Paul Hill, Lord Lane said these took the shape, as Mr Amlot had demonstrated, of a series of manuscript notes on interviews. The contents of the notes were significant and they were never disclosed to the Director of Public Prosecutions or to prosecuting counsel before the trial. If they had been disclosed it would have been shown that the fifth statement, which was of the greatest importance, was taken in breach of Judges' Rules and might well have been ruled inadmissible. He added that, as conceded by the Crown, the Surrey officers on oath denied there had been any such interview.

Lord Lane then turned to the detention sheets which were the third and final matter raised and disclosed by the Avon and Somerset Police. A schedule showed discrepancies between the detention sheets and the record of interviews, and Mr Amlot had pointed out where the detention records conflict with the officers' evidence. Lord Lane said that there were material discrepancies. If they had been known at the trial, they might on their own, let alone in conjunction with other matters, have made a grave difference to the outcome. He added that the cases against Carole Richardson and Gerard Conlon were intimately bound up with these events:

> We have no doubt that these events make the convictions of all of these four appellants in respect of the Guildford and Woolwich events unsafe.

Referring to the inquiry now being undertaken by the Director of Public Prosecutions the Lord Chief Justice added:

> We earnestly express the hope that nothing will be allowed to stand in the way of a speedy progress of these proceedings.

After commenting on the 'perspicacious efforts' of the Avon and Somerset Police which 'have salvaged something from this unhappy matter', and also after referring to the other arguments counsel for the appellants would have advanced, the Lord Chief Justice finally concluded –

> . . . so far as this Court is concerned these appeals are allowed and the convictions are quashed.

That was how the four appellants, who had all spent fifteen years in prison as a result of all that had been revealed, heard the final outcome. They were immediately released. On 30 November, 1989 Carole Richardson gave a two page interview to *The Daily Mirror*. She showed no bitterness or resentment but, as the feature concluded:

> Not once does she criticise the system which has now granted her freedom, rubber-stamped her innocence . . .

When you ask her what else she could ask from a system of justice which sliced away almost half her life, she answers simply -

'for someone to say they're sorry.''

Later in the day on which the judgement was given, 19 October, 1989, the Home Secretary made a statement in Parliament about the quashing in the Court of Appeal of the convictions of the four appellants. He explained that after he had referred the case to the Court of Appeal on 16 January 1989, the Crown Prosecution Service had asked the Avon and Somerset Police to carry out a further scrutiny of the large number of police documents. He added that the information provided by the Avon and Somerset Police led the Crown to take the view that misleading evidence had been given by officers of the Surrey Police at the trial, and that this was sufficient to undermine the reliability of the confession evidence on which the convictions had been based.

He then referred briefly to the points made by the Court relating to the record of interviews with Patrick Armstrong which could not have been a contemporaneous record as claimed by a number of police officers; to the misleading evidence by the police officers about the circumstances in which they obtained information from Paul Hill; to the serious discrepancies in the detention records; and to the status of the confessions repeated to Metropolitan police officers in Guildford Police Station.

Douglas Hurd said that, as the Court of Appeal had quashed the convictions, the four persons involved would be eligible to apply to him for compensation under the provisions of the Criminal Justice Act 1988. He also informed the House that the Director of Public Prosecutions had set in train a criminal investigation so that he could determine whether there was sufficient evidence to justify prosecuting the police officers involved.

The Home Secretary then said that he and the Attorney General had decided to establish 'a judicial inquiry into the circumstances leading to the trial of those convicted of the Guildford and Woolwich offences to establish as far as possible the details of what had occurred.' He also confirmed that the judicial inquiry would additionally look into the circumstances leading to the trial of the Maguire Seven in March 1976 for possessing explosives. He added that he and the Attorney General had considered carefully whether the judicial inquiry should be postponed until the completion of the criminal investigation. However, they had 'concluded that such is the importance of this case that it would be right to establish the inquiry straightaway, recognising that it would have to adjust or adjourn its work as the interests of the administration of criminal justice might require.'

Sir John May, who until June 1988 had been a Lord Justice of Appeal, was to preside. The inquiry was to conduct its work on a non-statutory basis, and its terms of reference were:

> to inquire into the circumstances leading to and deriving from the trial of Patrick Armstrong, Gerard Conlon, Paul Hill and Carole Richardson on charges arising out of the explosions in public houses in Guildford on 5 October, 1974, of Patrick Armstrong and Paul Hill in relation to charges arising out of an explosion in a public house in Woolwich on 7 November, 1974, and of Anne and Patrick Maguire, their sons, Vincent and Patrick Maguire, and Patrick Conlon, Patrick O'Neill and Sean Smyth on charges of possessing explosives and to report to the Home Secretary and the Attorney General.

It is to be noted that the earlier clause 'to establish as far as possible the details of what had occurred' was omitted.

At the end of his statement Douglas Hurd said:

> . . . there has been a serious miscarriage of justice which has resulted in wrongful imprisonment for many years . . .
>
> . . . we must all feel anxiety, regret and deep concern at what has occurred.

No one could deny that all parts of the criminal justice system – the Home Office, the DPP/CPS, the judiciary, prosecuting counsel, the police and forensic scientists – had all, to varying degrees and at different times, contributed to the injustices meted out to the Guildford Four. There were great hopes and expectations that the May Inquiry would expose in a thoroughly objective and forthright manner all possible failings there might have been both in the system itself and by individuals.

In his statement to Parliament in January 1987, when he gave reasons for not referring the Guildford Four case, Douglas Hurd had said '. . . individuals may write books or produce television programmes which summarise days or weeks of evidence in a way which reflects their genuine conviction that the verdict was wrong or open to considerable doubt: as a result a body of distinguished opinion may grow up to the same effect'.

The Deputation made history in that it was the first known occasion in which two of probably the greatest Law Lords of the last century, two widely experienced and distinguished Home Secretaries, and a Cardinal Archbishop of Westminster had all come together to secure justice in one case – the Guildford Four. They all did this of their own volition, and for their own strong reasons, which were a reflection of their extensive knowledge of, and experience in, the administration of justice.

It appeared to take some time before Ministers and some officials in the Home Office came to appreciate the significance of the Deputation and how totally convinced they were that certain things had gone radically wrong in the Guildford Four and Maguire Seven cases, and that there could be no diminution of the determination to see that justice was done in the end.

In illustration of this when, on 17 October, 1989, the expedited meeting of the Court Appeal was announced, the Deputation assumed that the case against the Guildford Four would be quashed. Consequently, a press release was prepared welcoming this but stating in the last paragraph the Deputation's determination to pursue the case of the Maguire Seven. It was decided not to issue the press release until the Home Secretary made his statement. On hearing that statement the last paragraph of the press release was altered to also welcome the inclusion of the Maguire Seven case in the May Inquiry.

As was to be expected, the quashing of the Guildford Four convictions and the setting up of the May Inquiry resulted in very wide coverage in the press. Various aspects of the history of the case and of the criminal justice system were subjected to examination. As far as the Deputation was concerned, arrangements were made for a meeting to be held on the earliest possible date, which proved to be 22 November, 1989. The main purposes of the meeting were to conduct a comprehensive review of the present situation, and to discuss relationships and co-operation with the May Inquiry.

There needs to be reference at this stage to an exceedingly powerful BBC *Panorama* programme entitled *Guildford – The Untold Story*. It was screened by the BBC in December 1990, a year after the quashing of the Guildford Four convictions, but during the early stages of the May Inquiry, and Cardinal Hume took part before they considered that case. The programme was researched and presented by John Ware and had obtained access to important police and RARDE documents and reports. Using this material, the programme highlighted some of the serious issues relating to the Guildford Four case which it considered would need to be addressed and resolved by the May Inquiry.

It is possible to give only a short résumé of the ground covered in the programme. After briefly interviewing each of the Guildford Four, the programme said that those who had played a part in securing justice for them wanted to know 'just how the system so catastrophically failed'. Cardinal Hume said:

> There has to be this relentless search for the truth, exactly what did happen and then not only that, but were the cases handled correctly

> at every level. The truth has to be established because there is no justice without truth. We have always had in our nation such a high regard for justice, that it is simply too important not to get absolutely to the truth so that everybody is satisfied, yes – we've got it right. If this means that a number of people have to own up to making a mistake, well then that must be so.

It was stated that the official search for the truth by the May Inquiry might be delayed for another year pending the outcome of investigations about three Surrey police officers. (As is now known it was to be some two and a half years after the programme before the Surrey police officers went to trial. This delayed publication of the Final Report of the May Inquiry on the Guildford Four case until June 1994.)

The programme then singled out and expanded on the following assertions, amongst many others, which had not so far been resolved and which would have to be fully investigated by the May Inquiry:

> All four implicated each other in making the Guildford bombs, all four said they planted them too. Hill and Armstrong also admitted to bombing Woolwich but, as soon as they left the custody of the Surrey police, all four retracted their confessions. They claimed they had been extracted under duress.

> The bombings did not stop with the arrest of the Guildford Four. In fact 'they grew bloodier and the forensic picture that unfolded raised more questions than it answered.'

> RARDE established there was a clear pattern in the way the bombs were made. Their conclusion pointed to one IRA unit being responsible for all the bombings, including Guildford and Woolwich. The Bomb Squad knew that thrown bombs made exactly like the Woolwich bomb continued to explode after the arrest of the Guildford Four.

> The trial opened on 26 September 1975 but the jury 'was to hear none of the crucial forensic evidence known to RARDE and the Bomb Squad – someone in the prosecution had failed to disclose it to the lawyers of the Guildford Four'.

> The prosecution failed to disclose further important forensic evidence, details of which were given in the programme –

>> By February 1975 RARDE had analysed thirty-two bombs. Then with the trial now seven months' away Scotland Yard made a crucial discovery in this basement flat in a drab London street

> called Fairholme Road. Inside they found drawers stuffed full of bomb-making paraphernalia, batteries, clocks, wires, bulbs and detonators. RARDE told the Yard the same components had been used in both the throw bombs and the time bombs to which the scientists connected Guildford and Woolwich. It now looked as if all the bombs were linked. RARDE's findings were written up in a statement which concluded that all thirty-two bombs including Guildford and Woolwich – were planted and made with a common source of supply, information and expertise. But as with RARDE's first statement this second and even more telling statement, was not disclosed to the defence.'

> The Bomb Squad's own intelligence on the IRA campaign was entirely consistent with RARDE's conclusion that a common source was responsible for all the bombings. A report written by Commander Roy Habershon of the Bomb Squad showed (in paragraph 55) that they believed the common source to be the IRA unit based at the safe house in Fairholme Road. [This was the base from which the Balcombe Street gang operated.]

Members of the prosecution team, who were named, had declined to appear on the programme saying the points raised were matters for the May Inquiry. The senior Bomb Squad officers, also named, also declined an invitation to appear on the programme. However, the programme understood they were likely to tell the May Inquiry they had no reason to disbelieve the confessions because they had been repeated after the trial[17] to Sir Peter Imbert (as he now was) and also to Commander Nevill. It was at this point that Cardinal Hume said:

> I think one's got to put oneself in their situation. These were terrible crimes and I don't think one ever wants to minimise that. What happened at Guildford just as what happened at Woolwich were terrible crimes, totally to be condemned – and everybody was outraged – and I was outraged at the time. They had to find somebody; they had to get the people. The fact that they got the wrong people was the tragedy, but they had to get somebody and I can see how a certain logic then begins to take over – and especially when they confessed to having done it.

This comment was added to by Gareth Peirce who also appeared on the programme:

[17] This is a reference to what came to be known as the 'Imbert Tapes' – see Chapter Eight – pages 215 to 217.

> Many miscarriages of justice appear to be when the police at an early stage have become fixated on the wrong people and thereafter have simply refused or been unable to see dramatic evidence that's pointing in a different direction towards the right conclusion. This has been the hallmark of many wrongful convictions and perhaps it happened here.

The programme then gave very extensive coverage to the whole question of the 'Burke alibi'[18] and asserted that not only was its existence known to the prosecution but there were also two statements (Sister Power and Father Carolan) which corroborated it. It was for a jury to decide the validity of the Burke alibi but it never reached the jury room. Cardinal Hume said:

> One thing that needs to be looked at very carefully is the whole question of Charles Burke as a witness for an alibi for Gerry Conlon. Now my information is that his statement actually existed at the time of the trial and certainly was not known to the defence. That needs to be looked at extremely carefully because I think Charles Burke's evidence is very, very, very important.

Lengthy coverage was given to, and made assertions about, all the major aspects of the Balcombe Street ASU – the 'real bombers' as they were termed. In particular the programme examined in some depth the forensic information available to RARDE and to the police, and the absence of proper questioning of the Balcombe Street gang and Brendan Dowd about Guildford.

It also questioned the quality and effectiveness, in terms of searching for the truth, of such interviews as the police might have conducted with them. As regards forensic evidence, the following extract from the transcript of the programme is informative:

> The Yard's Intelligence Collation Section, had compiled a chart which Panorama has obtained. It listed all the IRA people whose fingerprints linked them to terrorist activity from March 1976, going back to December 1973. It shows that the Yard has identified fingerprints not just in bombings, but shootings, kidnappings and safehouses too. The prints belong to thirty-one IRA men and women, and included the eight bombers from the Fairholme Rd unit. But nowhere did the names of the Guildford Four feature. It fell to one of the defence lawyers to do what the police had never done. Alastair Logan conducted a series of interviews with the Fairholme Road

[18]See Chapter Seven, pages 174 to 178.

unit, including a fifth member who'd been arrested separately – Brendan Dowd.[19]

The programme then dwelt on the appeal by the Guildford Four. It finally referred to those in the legal profession, including the judiciary, to whom 'contrition has not come easily – some are still in deep shock and cannot even bring themselves to acknowledge the innocence of the Guildford Four'. The programme ended with these words by Cardinal Hume:

> I think there is an instinct deep in all of us, to close ranks if anybody in our profession is in some way criticised or attacked. It's natural, and it's not a bad thing actually. But in this matter, I believe, we must believe, that among the people involved in this case, there are certainly people who'll be big enough to say, yes we were wrong. If not it will be very sad.

The extent to which the May Inquiry was to be able to establish the truth in all aspects of the case, including those raised in the *Panorama* programme, will be assessed in Chapter Nine – THE MAY INQUIRY (2) – The Guildford Four.

Immediately after the quashings on 19 October, 1989 and during the year 1990, matters had started to move ahead at a pace. The reviews in the press of the implications of the quashings had pulled no punches. They were comprehensive, forceful and highly critical of all component parts of the criminal justice system. In January 1990 Sir John May had sought a meeting with the Deputation to discuss various aspects of the Guildford Four and Maguire Seven cases. Early in 1990 the May Inquiry started work and held hearings on, initially, only the Maguire Seven case. This gave rise to the Interim Report by Sir John May which was published on 12 July, 1990. It was as a result of the Interim Report that the Court of Appeal quashed the convictions of the Maguire Seven on 26 June, 1991.

[19]See Chapter One pages 7 and 8. This refers to interviews conducted in October/November 1976 by Alastair Logan and James Still, the retired Chief Superintendent of the Metropolitan Police.

8

THE MAY INQUIRY (1)

The Maguire Seven

'A STORY FILLED WITH SHAME'
'HOW FAR DID THE CORRUPTION GO?'
'A SCANDAL THAT SHAKES THE VERY FOUNDATION OF JUSTICE'
'THE MEN WITHOUT SHAME – AND THE UNSUNG HEROES'
'WHEN PRESSURES MOUNT ON THE POLICE'
'IMBERT BELIEVED BOMB CONFESSIONS'
TOO MUCH FAITH IN THEIR OWN CONVICTIONS'
'SENIOR POLICE OFFICERS TO BE CHALLENGED OVER BOMB INQUIRIES'
'PRESS ACCUSED OF ''CRUCIFYING'' POLICE IN GUILDFORD CASE'
'WHERE IS THE JUSTICE IN THIS NIGHTMARE?'
'EARLY DOUBTS IGNORED OVER GUILDFORD FOUR – SECRET REPORTS SUGGEST PRE-TRIAL BOMB SQUAD DOUBTS ABOUT WHETHER THE GUILTY HAD BEEN ARRESTED.'
'MAGUIRES SEE FRESH HOPE IN GUILDFORD'

SUCH is a selection of the headlines with which the British public were faced by their newspapers on the days immediately following the quashing of the convictions of the Guildford Four on 19 October, 1989. An unbalanced list, some might say. Not so. There were no headlines at all favouring any constituent part of the criminal justice system itself. Truth 'the whole truth' had been the major casualty and disregard for it resulted in four young people spending fifteen years in prison for crimes they did not commit.

The Guildford Four case was both astonishing and unique. There were many other reasons for this. A number of them were disturbing because they exposed serious deficiencies in parts of the criminal justice system at that time and also serious failings by some individuals in the system.

The key factor in the case was that the convictions of all four defendants were based solely on their confessions which they later retracted. Roy Amlot had exposed how the confessions of Patrick Armstrong and Paul Hill had been handled but what of those of Carole Richardson and Gerard Conlon? He did not report on them and it was not known at the time whether the Avon and Somerset Police had done so.

The assumption at the time was that the May Inquiry would be looking into and reporting on all these matters. Before turning to the May Inquiry, however, it is important, for the record, to review some of those parts of the press coverage which were of particular interest to the Deputation in the light of their work and the views they had expressed over the years. Such press reports, were, of course, also available to the May Inquiry. The coverage by the press was immense, particularly by the 'broadsheets' which at the time also included *The Sunday Correspondent.*

By now many journalists had a very deep knowledge of the case, and they were fully familiar with the intricacies of the criminal justice system. The press coverage, which was both factual and objective, constituted a major service to the public at large during those bewildering days. No part of the criminal justice system was spared from criticism – the police, the DPP, the prosecution, forensic scientists, the judiciary and the Home Office. Advice for the forthcoming May Inquiry was also tendered by some newspapers.

In a leader on 20 October, 1989 *The Daily Telegraph* made the point that 'the public anger and bitterness that follow a terrorist outrage create the worst possible climate for cool and reasoned detective work, or the measured administration of justice'. The leader in *The Observer* on 22 October, 1989, took things a little further and captured the situation well in retrospect:–

> Those months in late 1974 were a terrible time, with IRA bombs exploding almost every few days; the police knew they had to get a result and, not surprisingly, some of them were none too scrupulous about how they went about it.

In their leader of 20 October, 1989 *The Daily Telegraph* had also gone on to say – '. . . it is a grave blot on our system of policing, and of criminal justice, that a number of officers investigating a case of the highest importance should be able seriously to mislead the court'.

The most welcome sequel to the dramatic events of 19 October, 1989 would have been the arrest and conviction of those who bombed Guildford and Woolwich. But at such a late stage this was not to be – no doubt to the distress of the families and friends of those who had been killed and injured. Nevertheless, the great majority of people would say it would be too much to ask that the difficult operating conditions, resulting from the prevailing climate at the time, could be an acceptable explanation for four people having to spend 15 years in prison. The police were to come in for some powerful and penetrating criticisms. They are best reported in the words of the newspapers themselves and a representative group is recorded below.

A leader in *The Times* on 20 October, 1989, after dealing with various aspects of the case, went on to say:

> There are several points at which injustice could and should have been prevented . . . one concerns the responsibility of senior police. It is hard to believe that supervision of officers involved could have been so lax that there is now 'clear prima facie evidence' that five police officers seriously misled the court. Senior officers must then be partly to blame . . .
>
> The most unsatisfactory feature of the case is that until the Avon and Somerset Police came on the scene, nobody looked; or, if they did look and were not prepared to act, that is worse.

Two points on the police were made on the same day in a lengthy leader in *The Independent* headed 'How far did the corruption go?' which dealt mainly with the DPP:

> This was a very important case; blame cannot rest with the junior officers involved in it . . .
>
> The judicial inquiry will have to clarify the roles played by different parts of the police, and by the then Director of Public Prosecutions, Sir Norman Skelhorn (now dead), and his staff.

By Sunday 22 October newspapers had had more time to absorb and assess all that had happened. This led to a number of perceptive features and leaders. A feature in *The Sunday Times* reported that some lawyers thought that the May Inquiry would need to examine the role of DCI Grundy as this could be central to discovering what went wrong. He and DS Jermey had arrested Gerard Conlon in Belfast. DCI Grundy's role was important because his subsequent interrogation of Gerard Conlon helped to convict the Maguire Seven. DCS Simmons was also involved in later interrogations.

On the same day *The Mail on Sunday* ran a lengthy feature in which three devastating comments were made:

> Are we to believe that the system is such that some junior officers downstairs in the cells could be both asking the questions and

> making up the answers in the safe knowledge that their senior men upstairs would never know. Or even worse the senior men upstairs would concur? . . .
>
> Does the Guildford saga really begin and end with the police officer who asked the questions and then made up the answers? Are we really saying that a few bent coppers could take on the legal majesty of Lords Havers, Donaldson, Lawton, Roskill and Boreham and get away with it? . . .
>
> And most unbelievable of all, what sort of an opinion must these policemen have had of the judicial system before which they were quite prepared to present their evidence?

The Sunday Correspondent covered the case very extensively. In a leader in the issue of 22 October, which also carried four pages of detailed analysis of the case, the writer said it had been the bleakest of weeks for the police. They would now have to 'recover from an inevitable and deserved loss of public confidence and esteem.' After referring to the enormous pressures on police to secure convictions during concentrated bombing campaigns, the leader went on:

> It is at such times that the need for the closest supervision of the more junior ranks during the investigating is most needed. Any suggestion that responsibility for rigging evidence against the Guildford Four is restricted to the more junior officers so far suspended should be dismissed.

It will come as no surprise that there were many more similar and additional comments on the role of the police in all the papers. It was inevitable that some sort of defence would be mounted. This was done within a week by Sir Peter Imbert, by then Commissioner of the Metropolitan Police, by Brian Hayes, then Chief Constable of Surrey Police, and by the Police Federation.

In an interview with *The Independent Magazine* which was later published on 4 November, when speaking of the Guildford Four and the Balcombe Street ASU, Sir Peter Imbert said 'I'm in the peculiar position of having frankly believed – or not disbelieved – both sets of admissions so that's an unusual position to be in.' He did not clarify whether he believed the assertion by the Balcombe Street ASU that they did not know the Guildford Four, and that they were not present at Guildford. Earlier, he had been reported in *The Times* on 24 October as urging people not to assume that officers were guilty of fabricating evidence until the police and judicial inquiries had been completed. He had added that the public should not fall into the trap that police officers appeared to have fallen into in 1974 when, seemingly, they convinced themselves certain people were guilty. 'I can see strong similarities. Let us not make the same mistake.' He had spoken in similar vein to *The Daily Telegraph* on the same day, but added, 'It was not only the police involved in this – it was the judicial system, the public and indeed the media as well.'

On 28 October *The Independent* reported on the Early Day Motion signed by 25 MPs calling for all officers involved in the original Guildford investigation to be suspended. The motion said:

> This House notes that Sir Peter Imbert received the Balcombe Street gang's admission to the Guildford bombing and that he subsequently became Deputy Chief Constable of Surrey and was therefore in a position of authority to see and reveal documents which eventually proved the innocence of the Guildford Four . . .

The Motion went on to ask Sir Peter Imbert seriously to consider whether he could continue in his current position and maintain credibility and public confidence in the Metropolitan Police. Scotland Yard said that Sir Peter Imbert did not wish to comment on the Motion.

On the same day, 28 October, *The Independent* reported on a letter Brian Hayes, Chief Constable of Surrey, had written to *The Surrey Advertiser*. He attacked the Press for hypocrisy and unbalanced reporting – 'the same Press who bayed for convictions in 1974 . . . and avidly recorded the guilt of the Guildford Four, now switched its attention to crucifying Surrey officers, picking up the accusations that some had distorted statements to secure convictions.'

The Surrey Advertiser might have drawn Brian Hayes' attention to the following paragraph from page 197 of Robert Kee's book, *Trial and Error*, which came after the paragraphs dealing with the sentencing at the end of the trial:

> 'On behalf of the public,' Donaldson J expressed his appreciation of the skill with which the police had undertaken their task. *The Surrey Advertiser* which was the only newspaper to report the trial fully throughout, often headlining boldly the allegations against the police, now made amends. Describing those convicted as the 'warped dregs of humanity' for whom 'the quality of mercy is strained to the limit in attempting to feel anything but loathing and revulsion'; it assured the police of 'our boundless admiration and gratitude for the vigorous and determined way they handled the case. Our confidence in them is increased, not diminished.'

Before leaving press reports on the police it would be appropriate to quote from Lord Devlin's book *The Judge* published in 1979,

> At the heart of the difficulty is the tendency of the police, once their mind is made up, to treat as mistaken any evidence that contradicts their proof of guilt. It is still to my mind a blot on our procedure that it rests upon a unilateral inquiry into crime with no clear method of ensuring that facts favouring the accused are fully presented; where there is a wrong conviction, this defect is more likely than any other to have played a part in it.

It was the police who bore the main brunt of criticisms after the events of 19 October, 1989. But other constituent parts of the criminal justice system were also severely taken to task for their actions, or indeed inaction, over the years. There is a need to quote from only a few of the features and leaders to illustrate this. They convey some of the feelings of incredulity, and even despondency, which the failings in the system had brought to the fore.

In their strong leader of 20 October, headed 'How far did the corruption go?', *The Independent* asked a series of very pertinent questions. Why did the DPP leave the Guildford and Woolwich bombings out of the indictment against the Balcombe Street ASU? Sir Peter Imbert, then a superintendent in the Bomb Squad, heard them confess to the murders of which the Guildford Four had already been convicted. Why was an attempt made to suppress forensic evidence prepared by Mr Higgs [of RARDE], evidence which connected the Guildford and Woolwich bombings to others committed when the Guildford Four were in custody? Why did the DPP withhold evidence supporting the alibi [the Burke alibi] of Gerard Conlon from his lawyers?

On the same day the *Guardian* leader also picked up the question of a key witness whom the defence could not trace but who was found by the police and interviewed. It went on to say that alibi evidence [the Burke alibi] was not passed to the defence and the defendant was prosecuted:

> There could hardly be a more damning allegation. It suggests a prosecution system so committed to securing a conviction after a horrendous bombing that fundamental principles of justice were jettisoned, even by the men at the top.

In a feature in the same issue, after dealing with the announcement of the May Inquiry, the paper said that Douglas Hurd had pointed to the non-statutory inquiry into the Confait case as the precedent for the announcement – 'not an auspicious parallel since it has been established that the Confait inquiry under Sir Henry Fisher took two years to reach the wrong conclusion.'

Peter Jenkins, writing in *The Independent* on 24 October, 1989, pulled no punches. He strongly criticised the – 'Official Establishment response to this monstrous miscarriage of justice perpetrated 14 years ago [has been] to rest its defence on the discovery by Avon and Somerset Police of the documentary evidence of fabricated confessions which were the sole evidence against the wrongfully convicted.' He then recalled the books, the television programmes and the work of the Deputation over the years. He also referred to the 'devastating indictment of the Court of Appeal's handling of the case' by Lord Devlin and Lord Scarman which had been published in *The Times*. He went on to point out that all the activity consistently drew attention 'to what everybody had known, from the start: that the Guildford Four were an unlikely quartet as members of a professional IRA active service unit.' While acknowledging that the position over the years adopted by the Home Office might be 'constitutionally proper – it was a formula which enables a Home Secretary to wash his hands of justice.' His all-embracing comment was:

> The judiciary and criminal justice system has a good deal to answer for in the original trial. Did nobody smell a rat in the case, which was brought against the unlikely four – the Director of Public Prosecutions? The Judge, Lord Donaldson, today Master of the Rolls? Lord Havers the prosecutor, subsequently Attorney General and Lord Chancellor?

On 22 October *The Sunday Correspondent* had a two-page spread headlined 'Secret reports pointed to innocence.' Apparently two secret reports had been leaked to the newspaper after the quashing of the convictions. The first report, unsigned and undated, was alleged to have been written after an IRA cell was arrested in Manchester on 10 July, 1975, and before the trial of the Guildford Four on 16 September, 1975. The second report was alleged to have been written by DS Doyle of the Bomb Squad (dead by the time of the leak) after the Balcombe Street siege. The first report was stated to have shown that before the Guildford Four had been tried the Bomb Squad at the Yard had misgivings about whether the Surrey Police had arrested the real bombers. The second report was said to have revealed that after the conviction of the Guildford Four 'the Yard had a shrewd idea of who was really involved.' The feature went on to say that neither report expressed these doubts directly but – 'as police sources have told us, it was not the job of the Bomb Squad openly to question the work of their colleagues in Surrey.'

In a major feature on 14 November *The Independent* had this to say – 'The word has spread in certain quarters of The Temple, of Whitehall, of Scotland Yard and Surrey Police that, despite it all, the

Guildford Four are really guilty.' The writer then said that word had come to them that the prosecution was not going to take 'lying down' the accusations that they got it all wrong:

> They will use the judicial inquiry under Sir John May to claw back lost ground and to justify the general thrust of the original prosecution case. Thereby they can save their own necks, vindicating everyone's role in the affair, except for the few junior officers who so far have been accused of malpractice.

The question being asked by many at the time was 'will they succeed?' Two significant statements were made after the quashings on 19 October. In *The Sunday Telegraph* of 22 October Lord Denning was reported as saying, 'British Justice is in ruins.' Speaking in the House of Commons after the Home Secretary had made his statement about the quashings, Ivor Stanbrook said – 'If we were to allow the due process of justice to be diverted at the behest of cardinals and archbishops, British Justice would be no better than that of the Ayatollah Khomeini.'

On 1 November Sir John May told the Press he was unlikely to be able to report to the Home Secretary before 1991 at the very earliest. He anticipated the report would be published and added – 'there is no sort of whitewash or anything like that. I don't think it would serve one of the purposes of the inquiry, which is to allay public disquiet.' The above press reports illustrated the extent of the problem which confronted the May Inquiry. There was much ground to be covered if they were 'to allay public disquiet'. The only certain way of achieving this would be to establish the truth as to what did actually happen.

The meeting of the Deputation, which had been arranged immediately after the quashing of the convictions on 19 October, took place on 22 November. All five members were present. As already mentioned the main purposes of the meeting were to review comprehensively the present situation, and to discuss relationships and co-operation with the May Inquiry. In an aide-mémoire on the May Inquiry Lord Scarman had clarified its position. It was not a statutory inquiry. It had no power to order production of documents, to require the attendance of witnesses, or to take evidence on oath. It had none of the powers of a tribunal set up under the Tribunals of Inquiry Act 1921 or of a 'police inquiry' such as that of Brixton set up pursuant to s.32 of the Police Act 1964. It was 'judicial' in one sense only, namely the appointment of a retired Lord Justice to conduct the inquiry.

It was noted at the meeting that in a recent press conference Sir John May had stated that the question of the innocence of the Guildford

Four was not a matter for his inquiry. Consequently amongst the many subjects discussed by the Deputation were the nature of the May Inquiry; the need for a clear statement on the position of the Deputation; the position of the Maguire Seven and the possibility of an interim report covering their case owing to the inevitable delays in the work of the inquiry because of the possible prosecution of three Surrey police officers; and co-operation with the May Inquiry. In further discussion it was noted that it was not clear from the terms of reference what in fact the May Inquiry was designed to achieve; it was thought there were elements of what could become a whitewash. It was known that some elements in the criminal justice system were feeding the public mind with a lingering doubt that the Guildford Four got off on a technicality – hence the importance of the Deputation making its position quite clear.

After the meeting, in writing on 30 November to the Home Secretary, by now David Waddington, Cardinal Hume said the Deputation welcomed the inclusion of the Maguire Seven in the May Inquiry. It was also hoped, in view of possible delays, Sir John May would be able to consider making an interim report on the Maguire Seven. The Cardinal then made clear the position of the Deputation in the terms which had been discussed at the meeting:

> It was the belief of each and all of us individually in the innocence of the Guildford Four that brought us together in the first place. We had all come to this conclusion from an overview of the circumstances of the case long before the recent disclosure that certain documents which had come to light resulted in the Crown not being able to support the convictions. We, therefore, wholly reject the view, which has been advanced by some, that the Guildford Four were merely the beneficiaries of a technical miscarriage of justice.
>
> It is a highly improbable proposition that the whole Deputation could have independently been erroneously convinced of their innocence. Moreover, the Deputation maintains that if the new evidence and matters of substance we submitted to your predecessor had come to the court, the convictions would not have been regarded as safe and satisfactory.

As regards contributions to the May Inquiry the letter ended –

> The Deputation will welcome an opportunity to make contributions to the Inquiry, some of which could initially be on a confidential basis, on the following: –

– The Maguire Seven case;

– the parts played by the Surrey, Metropolitan, and Avon and Somerset police forces; the office of the DPP; and the Home Office;

– proposals for law reform, particularly in relation to procedures for reviewing possible miscarriages of justice.'

A copy of the letter was sent to Sir John May.

Sir John wrote to Cardinal Hume on 12 December suggesting it would be helpful to him to meet, informally for the moment, the Cardinal and other members of the Deputation. The object would be to discuss generally how they could best help him in his work on the Inquiry. Arrangements were made for an informal meeting to take place at Archbishop's House on 22 January 1990. Sir John May was to be accompanied by Mrs Felicity Clarkson, who was Secretary to his Inquiry on secondment from the Home Office. Present with Cardinal Hume were Lord Scarman and Merlyn Rees. Patrick Victory, as co-ordinator of the activities of the Deputation, was also present.

In response to Cardinal Hume's enquiry as to how he thought the Deputation might best help him Sir John May said that, because of the Surrey Police criminal investigations, his Inquiry into the Guildford Four case would be delayed some months. He was therefore thinking of looking into the Maguire Seven case in the meantime and would welcome comments on that case. The main points on it made by Lord Scarman and other members of the Deputation, which included some matters unknown to Sir John May, were:

They had been convicted solely on the scientific evidence but no bulk of explosive had ever been found.

The difficulty with the case was the TLC test but it was plain that with the evidence of John Yallop the case for the defence had certain strengths. He had developed the test while still in RARDE.

The reliability of the TLC test was implicitly questioned shortly after the Maguire convictions when the Home Office issued instructions that the test should only be done in conjunction with confirmatory tests. John Yallop had always maintained it should be so used and said so at the trial.

The police were only led to the Maguires on the basis of one of the Guildford confessions, now known to have been fabricated. Being thus invalidated, its evidential value was nil.

It was considered the defence at the Maguire trial had been wrong to allow the case to go to the jury on one issue alone, namely the reliability of the TLC test. The possibility of the test results having been fabricated could not be ignored, particularly in view of what had come to light over the Guildford confessions.

It would be interesting to know whether the police who arrested the Maguires were connected with the Guildford investigation or whether they had spoken to those involved in it.

All members of the Deputation considered there was certainly a case for a reference to the Court of Appeal. In reflecting on the Maguire case Cardinal Hume said, 'it was not justice that was at stake but common sense.'

In response to Sir John May's request for comments on the Guildford Four case, the following points were made –

It was important for the Inquiry to look carefully at the evidence of Maura Kelly, Lisa Astin, Frank Johnson, Charles Burke, and other material witnesses who had important information relating not only to the initial investigation but also to the subsequent enquiries by the Avon and Somerset Police.

Indications were coming to light that the Metropolitan Police had doubts early on about whether or not the Surrey Police had got the right people. The role of DCS Imbert, as he was then, was clearly important.

The fabricated confessions of two of the Guildford Four had been discovered by the Avon and Somerset Police in May 1989. It was six months before the case came before the Court of Appeal in October 1989. This gap needed explaining, particularly as defence solicitors and the Court had been assured up to and even beyond 6 October 1989, that they had all the relevant papers.

There was a need for the Inquiry to ask how false confessions came to be given, to look at the way the Surrey Police handled the interrogations, who reported to whom, who collated intelligence and to examine carefully the conduct of the officers involved.

It would be a matter of great public importance for the Inquiry to establish at what level police misconduct occurred.

Sir John May said he did not anticipate members of the Deputation giving evidence to the Inquiry. He thought he would embark on the

Maguire case first and then, possibly, produce an interim report. Meanwhile it would be helpful if the Deputation could give him a written brief, as full as possible, on the Maguire case, which would be the basis for subsequent discussions on the case. At the end of the meeting Cardinal Hume said he could see that 'there was both a law reform aspect and a historical aspect to the Inquiry' and he expressed the hope that 'the law reform aspects would not be pursued at the expense of attributing culpability where this was due.' Preparations to assemble a substantial brief were put in hand immediately after the meeting.

A submission on the Maguire Seven case was drafted entirely by Lord Scarman and agreed with Lord Devlin. It was based on information known to the Deputation by March 1990. It developed substantially the points on the case made at the meeting with Sir John May on 22 January, 1990. The submission was discussed at a meeting of the full Deputation on 22 March. It was approved unanimously and was sent to Sir John May by Cardinal Hume, on behalf of the Deputation, on 27 March. Attached to it was an Annex prepared by Robert Kee in his continuing capacity as a consultant to the Deputation. (The submission is at APPENDIX XII together with its Annex.)

In essence, amongst other things, it developed the close connection between the Guildford Four and Maguire Seven cases; the fact that the link between the Guildford and Maguire cases was too close for comfort even before 1989, and was certainly so now; the collapse of the supposed link of the Maguires with bombers now that the convictions of the Guildford Four were quashed on the grounds of police misconduct in relation to the 'confessions'; the defence had no material on which to base a thorough or penetrating cross-examination of the police because they had emerged unscathed from the defence challenge in the Guildford Four trial; the resulting concentration at the trial on the efficacy of the TLC test to the exclusion of exploration of possible contamination of swabs which should now be investigated; the Crown case at the trial was so thin that if the jury had known of police procurement of false evidence in the Guildford case there must be a genuine doubt whether the jury could have been satisfied beyond reasonable doubt that the Maguire Seven were guilty.

By 27 March 1990, when the Deputation submission on the Maguire case was sent to Sir John May, there had been some developments. He had said at an opening hearing on 4 December 1989 that he anticipated the criminal investigations into the Surrey police would be completed in two to three months. Consequently, although there would be some delay, he anticipated being able to submit his report to the Home Secretary in 1991. Many thought his assumptions were too optimistic and this, indeed, proved to be the case.

On the same day, 4 December, 1989, *The Independent* had run a whole-page feature on the Guildford Four and Maguire Seven cases covering the police, the other players and the tasks confronting the May Inquiry. They spoke of the May Inquiry having 'to lay bare the numerous conspiracy theories which the two cases had spun in their 15-year history.' They regarded the Deputation as 'the only standard bearer of truth in the whole affair' because it had no vested interests and wished only for the truth to be established. While recognising the lapse of time may make it difficult to find all the answers, the feature suggested an outline agenda for Sir John May:

> . . . can at least ask the right questions of the right people. He can ask why Surrey Police arrested and charged the Guildford Four and how they took confessions. He can ask why the Metropolitan Police did not call for a halt to the prosecutions in the light of their suspicions. He can ask why the DPP's Office withheld evidence. He can ask why the Court of Appeal did not properly weigh up new evidence. He can ask why the Home Office failed to reopen the case for so long. He can ask why it took the Avon and Somerset Police two years to uncover wrong doing.

There was general concern as to whether the inquiry would get to the truth, bearing in mind its limitations. These included inability to compel the attendance of witnesses or to subpoena documents. Perhaps, more importantly, it could not offer immunity to police officers who had been named in return for information as to who else may or may not have been involved. Nevertheless, from the outset, the Deputation had assured Sir John May of all possible help and support in what they regarded as an Inquiry of the greatest importance. Public confidence in the criminal justice system would not be restored unless the truth was established by the Inquiry regardless of the consequences.

By March 1990 Sir John May had already formally announced that it would not be possible for him to undertake immediately an inquiry into the Guildford and Woolwich bombings because of the criminal investigations, which were still continuing, into how the alleged confessions by the Guildford Four were obtained. He recognised the close connections between the Guildford Four and Maguire Seven cases and did not yet think it appropriate to embark on a wide-ranging investigation of the trial and convictions of the Maguire Seven. He therefore decided to limit, initially, his investigations into the Maguire Seven case to the scientific evidence on which the convictions had been based.

In the event some four and a half years were to elapse before the whole May Inquiry was completed. Two reports were made on the Maguire case – an Interim Report on 12 July, 1990 covering the scientific aspects; and a Second Report on 3 December, 1992. This covered re-consideration of the scientific issues, an examination of the circumstances of the prosecution and convictions, and the handling of representations by the Home Office over the years. The Final Report covering the circumstances surrounding the convictions arising out of the Guildford and Woolwich bombings was not published until 30 June 1994.

The delays in the conduct of the Inquiry and the Final Report were both caused entirely by the inordinate amount of time taken up by the completion of the criminal investigations and the subsequent prosecution of three Surrey Police officers. These delays gave rise to an immense amount of unease and dissatisfaction, and faith in the final outcome of the Inquiry began to diminish.

Hitherto in each chapter, the activities of the Deputation have been related in chronological order within the sphere covered by successive chapters and based on what was known to the Deputation at the time. In view of the time scale of four and a half years, for purposes of this and subsequent chapters it will be assumed that the Interim and Second Reports on the Maguire case and the Final Report on the Guildford Four case have all been published. Reference will be made both to those parts of the reports of particular interest to the Deputation, in the light of their submissions over the years, and also to those revelations which had been unknown to the Deputation, some of which came as an uncomfortable surprise. A brief account will also be given of the unsatisfactory correspondence relating to the trial of the Surrey Police officers between the Deputation and Mrs Barbara Mills, the Director of Public Prosecutions, as she was then.

The May Inquiry held a preliminary meeting on the Maguire case, limited to the scientific evidence, on 13 March, 1990, and then public hearings at which evidence was called and cross-examined between 21 May and 18 June, 1990. However, in the middle of that period, on 11 April, 1990, there was a quite unusual and totally unexpected happening in *The Guardian* – publication of what came to be known as the *Imbert tapes*.

The Guardian gave extensive coverage to transcripts of these tapes and associated matters. There were allegations at the time that the story of the 'tapes' had been hawked round Fleet Street and had finally come to rest with David Rose and *The Guardian.* The coverage included half of the front page, the whole of pages 4 and 5, and a leader. The front-page section summarised the situation under the heading *Tapes rekindle Guildford Four row*. Page 4 was headed *What Conlon said on the Imbert tapes,* while the main feature on page 5 was *Imbert's role in Guildford Case.*

The two taped interviews of Gerard Conlon by DCS Imbert and DS

Lewis of the Bomb Squad, as they then were, took place in Wandsworth prison the day after Gerard Conlon was sentenced at the Old Bailey. The leader said – 'Our reporter David Rose has had full access to an independently transcribed record of what was said. So the details are published today.' Gerard Conlon always maintained he did not request the interviews with the Bomb Squad. They asserted he did. The beginning of the 'interview' which would have revealed the truth about this matter was not recorded. Gerard Conlon is said to have again admitted his alleged role in the Guildford bombings and to have volunteered a mass of information including many names. However, the leader commented – 'Many of the names were of no account; of people dead or in prison . . . they added nothing to the sum of police knowledge.' The leader concluded that the 'smouldering existence' of the tapes 'was probably one reason why the British establishment rested content, even complacent, for so long as the case against the Guildford Four crumbled.'

Gerard Conlon's defence solicitor stated he was interviewed when he was at his most vulnerable having just been sentenced. He had been wrongly convicted and was carrying a burden of remorse for the plight of his father, Giuseppe Conlon, who was to face trial with the rest of the Maguire household about three months after the interviews. Gerard Conlon knew he was partly responsible for his father being in this position. He had said on the tapes that Anne Maguire and his father were innocent. He wanted to appear on the tapes to be co-operative in the hope of helping his father. *The Guardian* ended the *Conlon tapes* section by saying – 'Aside from the hope of assisting Giuseppe [his father], no obvious motive for asking for the interviews is contained in the records of any of Mr Conlon's meetings with the Bomb Squad.'

In the feature on page 5 headed *Imbert's role in Guildford Case*, it was alleged that before the arrest of the Balcombe Street ASU the police already had forensic reports linking Woolwich to other similar attacks, although efforts had been made to suppress this evidence for the Guildford Four trial. Following the Balcombe Street trial, the feature alleged that Sir Peter Imbert's critics say he must have known from an early stage that the Guildford Four's convictions were unsafe. The argument continued that he should have campaigned in the police force for the case to be re-opened. It went on to say that he did recommend that Edward Butler (of the Balcombe Street ASU) be charged with the Woolwich bombing, but it was alleged that this was ignored by the DPP at the time. The feature went even further saying that in 1978, when he took up the post of Assistant Chief Constable of Surrey, Sir Peter Imbert should have looked at the case papers and records of the original interrogations. This section on his role in the Guildford case ended thus:

> But the true reason for the strength of Sir Peter's lack of doubt concerning at any rate Mr Conlon may now be clear. He, at least, found – and continues to find – the content of his secret prison interviews with Mr Conlon wholly convincing.

Gareth Peirce, who was representing Gerard Conlon at the time when the transcript of the tapes was published on 11 April, 1990, asserted that '*The Guardian* had effectively demanded that any commentary Mr Conlon or his solicitor might have upon the so-called 'transcripts' of interviews with police officers should be provided to its reporters'. She sent an extremely powerful statement to *The Guardian* insisting that they publish it. They did – and the last paragraph was:

> The prosecution of Mr Conlon lies in tatters, totally discredited and it was abandoned in full knowledge of the so-called material *The Guardian* seeks to publish. We do not consider it is for Mr Conlon once again to have a gun put to his head and be told that he has to prove his innocence. He does not.

The last word on this questionable episode has to rest with Robert Kee. He sent the following letter to *The Guardian* on 11 April, 1990:

> Much of your paper today dealt with 'news' of what Gerard Conlon said to the police after his conviction for the Guildford bombing (now quashed). This 'news' has been available since 1986 when it was published in summary on page 265 of my book *Trial and Error*. Significantly you omit two facts there mentioned:
>
> 1 That Conlon was not, on the tapes, cautioned to the effect that anything he said could be used in evidence against him;
>
> 2 That he subsequently withdrew these 'confessions' as he had earlier withdrawn those, which the Court of Appeal now accepts as, discredited.
>
> That the present Commissioner of Metropolitan Police should be making this material available now when he himself is likely to be questioned by Sir John May on his own wider involvement in the Guildford and Woolwich case seems curious. That he should thus by implication make public charges against Mr Conlon on the basis of a statement made not under caution seems improper. That you should give so much publicity to his material without disclosing the full facts seems at variance with the traditions of your great newspaper.

Turning now to his Interim Report, and bearing in mind the Maguire Seven case was by now of some 15 years standing, Sir John May produced it with commendable alacrity. He earned the gratitude of many. The public hearings were held between 21 May and 18 June, 1990. The Report was published on 12 July, 1990.

The May Inquiry recognised that since the trial of the Maguire Seven in 1976 there had been 'a substantial amount of criticism of the scientific evidence relied upon by the Crown'. Accordingly, the Inquiry appointed, as an adviser on these matters, Professor Duncan Thorburn Burns who was a distinguished, independent, expert, analytical chemist. The observation might have been made in the Interim Report that the Home Office had been asked to take similar action as far back as the early '80s but had declined to do so without giving reasons.

The Report then reviewed at length the history of the purely scientific aspects of the case – the taking of swabs from the Maguires and their house; the role of RARDE and their scientists Higgs (who had taken over from Yallop as Principal Scientific Officer), Elliott, Dr Hayes, Mrs Brooker and Wyndham; the nature of the TLC test and its limitations; and the scientific investigation undertaken for the Inquiry by Professor Thorburn Burns.

The Report noted that the essence of the Crown's case at trial was that traces of nitro-glycerine (NG) had been under the fingernails of six of the defendants and on the gloves belonging to and used by the seventh (Anne Maguire), and that these were inconsistent with any other explanation than that they had all been knowingly handling NG for an unlawful purpose. The investigations by Professor Thorburn Burns led to the conclusion that in the TLC test it is not possible to distinguish between NG and another explosive, PETN.[1] At the trial the prosecution asserted that the TLC test was 'specific and particular' for NG. Sir Michael Havers, as he then was, who led the prosecution, went further to say the scientists would testify that the tests were like fingerprints.[2] After a thoroughly comprehensive review of the ramifications of the NG/PETN situation both at the trial, and from all the evidence given to the Inquiry both by the prosecution and the scientists from RARDE (whose notebooks were examined), the Inquiry made important points and came to certain firm conclusions.

In the interest of brevity it is possible to identify and record only some of the many points, together with the main conclusions, which were of particular interest to the Deputation. These were either because they were matters they were already aware of, had referred to in the past and had suspected, or because they came as revelations which had remained hidden for so long:

[1]Interim Report – page 28. [2]Interim Report – page 25.

The substantial number of swabs from the house which proved on TLC tests to be negative and the absence of traces of NG on the defendants' clothing pointed strongly to there being no bulk at the house or nearby.[3]

The question of innocent contamination and whether this could have been the explanation of the traces on the defendants' hands was never properly investigated at the trial.[4]

The scientific investigations by the Inquiry demonstrated there was substantially greater scope for innocent contamination of the hands and gloves than the evidence of Crown witnesses at the trial suggested.[5]

It was amply demonstrated by the RARDE notebooks that not only did the RARDE scientists know throughout the trial that PETN was potentially confusable with NG on the TLC test in toluene, but also that their work at RARDE had taken this fully into account.[6]

If the jury had been aware of some of the scientists' notebooks, particularly relating to the failure to disclose knowledge of, and failure to disclose, the existence of PETN and its mimicry of NG in the TLC/Toluene tests, they would have viewed the evidence of the RARDE scientists very differently.[7]

The Crown cannot now be taken to have proved that the traces on the defendants' hands and upon the gloves were of NG. The TLC/Toluene test upon which the Crown relied as being specific for NG has been shown not to be so.[8]

The accuracy, reliability, fairness and credibility of the RARDE scientists were fundamental to the convictions. It was now clear that some at least of the RARDE scientists, notably Mr Elliott, who was the principal case officer, could have been accused of being selective in their evidence, and of taking extraneous 'non-scientific factors' into account in forming their conclusions.[9]

Mr Higgs said in evidence at the trial on 27 January, 1976 that he could not see how NG could be transferred under the fingernails

[3]Interim Report – page 27 (8.7). [4]Interim Report – page 27 (8.9).
[5]Interim Report – page 29 (9.6). [6]Interim Report – page 37 (11.4).
[7]Interim Report – page 51 (14.5). [8]Interim Report – page 50 (14.4).
[9]Interim Report – page 50 (14.5).

after merely clenching the hand. Mr Elliott maintained the assertion contained in his statement that NG under the fingernails indicated manipulating and kneading.[10]

It soon became clear that the TLC/toluene tests after the return of the kits to RARDE had been carried out by junior staff including Mrs Brooker and Mr Wyndham, not under the direct supervision of Mr Higgs, but merely on the basis that they reported the results of tests to him and he then gave evidence which he did at the trial. The trial judge and the Court of Appeal believed Mr Higgs was giving direct evidence of seeing the results of tests.[11]

From an examination of Mr Wyndham's notebook, it was quite clear that it was not a contemporaneous record of the results of some tests which he had carried out: it was merely a listed fair copy of some other notes somewhere else.[12]

The Report did not consider the failure by the scientists to disclose the confusion of NG with PETN was a conspiracy but it was nonetheless improper for them to exclude it. When Mr Higgs prepared a list for consultation on 13 January 1976 which purported to exclude all substances which might mimic NG, he deliberately left out PETN which could not be so excluded.[13]

A further observation on RARDE witnesses was that Mr Elliott and Mr Higgs knew the TLC test using toluene was not specific for NG when advising the prosecution team, and when giving evidence, but they failed to say so. They knew that a second system was available to resolve the two substances but they did not mention it.[14]

Towards the end of the section in the Report concerning the trial, Sir John May said – '. . . any observer considering the circumstances of the trial and convictions must ask himself where the alleged bulk of NG which had been handled could have been and when each of the defendants, together or separately, could have handled it. The question also arises why the defendants, or at least some of them, should have been doing so.'[15]

In addition to all this, there were some disturbing revelations about disclosure of evidence. The Report referred specifically to the Birnberg

[10]Interim Report – page 42 (11.20 ii). [11]Interim Report – page 45 (11.27).
[12]Interim Report – page 46 (11.29). [13]Interim Report – page 46,47 (11.32).
[14]Interim Report – page 47 (11.33). [15]Interim Report – page 26–27 (8.6).

request. In April 1975 they wrote to the DPP asking for a copy of a further statement by Elliott served at committal and asking if they could have a sight of 'any more detailed notes or reports that there are by Mr Elliott or his assistants who did the tests, to explain more precisely the procedure used and the results obtained.'[16] After a further request six months later on 9 October, 1975, the DPP finally replied on 22 October – 'On the advice of Counsel I regret I am unable to supply you with copies of any notes made by Mr Elliott. The procedure used was the normal thin layer chromatography process.'[17]

The prosecuting team was led by Sir Michael Havers QC and included Mr Michael Hill QC and Mr Paul Purnell QC. The latter was the team member involved in some disclosures and had been given notice that during the public hearings of the May Inquiry he might be criticised for the prosecution's attitude to disclosure. After recording some aspects of this Sir John May said:

> I think that this attitude to the disclosure of scientists' notebooks was both regrettable and significant . . . I believe that had the prosecution been more open minded to disclosure of the scientists' notebooks it is very possible that events would have taken a different turn . . . If the jury had been aware of some of the contents of the notebooks, particularly relating to the scientists' knowledge of but failure to disclose the existence of PETN and its mimicry of NG in the TLC/Toluene tests, the fact of second tests themselves, and the experiments carried out during the trial, I believe that they would have viewed the evidence of the RARDE scientists very differently.'[18]

In his concluding remarks Sir John May made, amongst others, three points of particular importance. The first was that he referred again to his earlier remarks that the possibility of innocent contamination should not have been excluded. The second was that Sir Michael Havers had accused Mr Yallop, the scientific witness for the defence, of being selective in his evidence.[19] (It will be recalled that Mr Yallop was Mr Higgs' predecessor at RARDE and had, in fact, invented the TLC test.) Sir John May went on to say that, in the light of the treatment of Mr Yallop by Sir Michael Havers, if any of the counsel acting for the defendants at the trial had the material he now had, they could have cross-examined the RARDE scientists effectively on precisely the same lines as Sir Michael Havers challenged Mr Yallop –

[16]Interim Report – page 48 (12.1). [17]Interim Report – page 48 (12.1).
[18]Interim Report – page 48 (12.4) and page 51 (14.5). [19]Interim Report – page 50 (14.5).

In my opinion it has been shown that the whole scientific basis upon which the prosecution was founded was in truth so vitiated that on this basis alone the Court of Appeal should be invited to set aside the convictions.[20]

Sir John May's third point was that he considered the conduct of the trial itself could be validly challenged on at least two points to which he had already referred. He did not think the jury was adequately directed on the foundation of the Crown's case, namely the exclusivity of the TLC/Toluene test for NG. He also believed that Higgs's evidence about the negative results of the tests, which he had organised on the 916 hand test kits, was inadmissible.[21]

The Home Secretary referred the case to the Court of Appeal on 12 July, 1990, the day on which the Interim Report was published. After some delays, of which Sir John May was subsequently critical, the Court allowed the appeal on 26 June, 1991, but only on the limited ground upon which the DPP had indicated that he felt unable to support the convictions, namely that at the trial the Crown had not disproved the possibility that the hands of the defendant appellants had been innocently contaminated with traces of NG. The judgement of the Court was not well received, either by the Maguire Seven, or by the many who had been seeking to obtain justice for them.

After the quashing of the Guildford Four convictions there had been comments in the press that some parts of the criminal justice system had much to answer for. Sir John May's Interim Report was comprehensive, compelling and conclusive. After seeing that Report there were those who said that, so far anyway, the Home Office, for not setting up a re-examination of the scientific evidence earlier, the scientists, the DPP, and the prosecution had all been left with much to think about.

In their leader on 13 July, 1990 *The Independent* said:

The interim report of Sir John May's inquiry is a damning document. It shows how forensic evidence was misused to secure the convictions in 1976 of the Maguire Seven for being in possession of explosives . . .

The May report is severely critical not only of the government technicians who provided the evidence on which they were condemned but also of the way the trial judge directed the jury about a key part of it; and it criticises the Court of Appeal for upholding his advice.

[20]Interim Report – page 51 (14.5). [21]Interim Report – page 51 (14.6).

Sir John May published his 'Second Report on the Maguire Case', on 3 December, 1992. Early in the introduction he referred again to the fact that the Court of Appeal had found itself unable to agree with some of the conclusions in his Interim Report. One, in particular, caused him some surprise.[22] When the Court of Appeal quashed the Maguires' convictions on 26 June, 1991 they referred to the 'clear and succinct submissions' of Counsel for the Conlon family that 'the Crown's case, as presented at trial was so improbable as to be frankly incredible . . .' and the Court said that 'in our judgement the Crown's case that all the appellants must have been knowingly handling bulk explosive was highly improbable'.

The Court added that Counsel's arguments, if deployed at trial – 'should have been sufficient in themselves to cast doubt . . . on the opinion of Mr Elliott and Mr Higgs that the findings are inconsistent with innocent contamination'. Bearing in mind that the onus of proof rested with the Crown, Sir John May found it 'surprising that the Court of Appeal were not driven by their finding of high improbability and logic quickly to the conclusion that the convictions were unsafe and unsatisfactory on this ground alone'.[23]

Referring back to his Interim Report, Sir John May said his conclusions then had been that the tests by the scientists had not been specific for NG and that the handling or kneading hypothesis could not be based on the presence of NG traces on fingernails. Indeed, Sir John went on to say that it was 'upon the ground that the kneading hypothesis as put forward at trial could no longer be supported that the Director of Public Prosecutions conceded, both before me and the Court of Appeal, that he could no longer support the convictions because the possibility of innocent contamination had not been excluded.'[24]

He added that, prior to and during the public hearings in 1990, RARDE had been invited, and encouraged, to be legally represented and to take part in them but they declined.[25] However, when all concerned were informed the Inquiry would be holding further public hearings into the Maguire case following publication of the Interim Report in July 1990, RARDE then asked to be represented. At these further hearings in September and October 1991, Mr Higgs of RARDE advanced arguments on the conclusions of the Interim Report and he belatedly sought to press them on the Inquiry. However, in doing this, RARDE fully accepted the Court of Appeal had been correct in allowing the appeal of the Maguire Seven in June 1991, and they expressly disavowed any suggestion that the original convictions of the Maguire Seven could be justified.

[22]Second Report – pages 2 and 3. [23]Second Report – page 3.
[24]Chapter Eight – page 222. [25]Second Report – page 4 (2.3).

In fairness to RARDE, Sir John May set up a Scientific Committee to advise him further on the disputed issues. The Chairman was Professor T.S. West, formerly of Birmingham and Aberdeen Universities, and of Imperial College.

The Report of the West Committee caused Sir John May 'to modify one of the conclusions I had expressed in the Interim Report and to draw certain further conclusions'.[26] These can be summarised as follows: –

(a) The kneading hypothesis was not disproved by the Thorburn Burns report, contrary to his earlier conclusion in the Interim Report. Nevertheless, the hypothesis remains unproved and should not have been advanced in unqualified terms at the trial.
(b) The Thorburn Burns experiments demonstrated that there is a possibility that some of the positive fingernail findings could have resulted from cross-contamination during the taking of the Maguire samples (without any fault in the sampler's part).
(c) There is a possibility that the positive findings from the samples resulted from accidental contamination of those samples after they were obtained from the Maguire Seven.

After the Court of Appeal had quashed the convictions of the Maguire Seven in June 1991, Sir John May felt free to investigate two other aspects of their prosecution – the circumstances in which the Attorney-General's fiat had been applied for and granted, and secondly the role of the Home Office in view of the repeated representations made to them over the years that the convictions were suspect. The Inquiry held public hearings, and closing submissions, on these two issues in September and October 1991. Higgs gave evidence. There were also witnesses from the Law Officers Department, the DPP and the prosecution, all legally represented, as were the 13 witnesses, including C3 and the Home Secretary, on the second issue of the Home Office's handling of the representations.

Sir John May said that in seeking to receive evidence in public from civil servants and Ministers he was breaking new ground. For this reason, and to achieve his objective, he changed the proceedings at hearings in that he did not allow any cross-examination of any witnesses other than by Counsel to the Inquiry (David Clarke QC) and himself. Nevertheless, those representing interested parties could suggest lines of questioning to be followed and many of these were accepted. Although various criticisms of the revised procedure were

[26]Second Report – page 10.

expressed during the hearings, Sir John May said – 'I am quite satisfied that these had no real substance'.

The first of the two further issues to be investigated by the Inquiry was – 'the circumstances in which the Attorney General's fiat had been applied for and granted'. This was covered at considerable length. Reference will be made only to some key points in the four main parts which were the Statement of Facts, the doubts of the Attorney General (Sam Silkin QC MP), the statements and evidence by Roger Maitland (Law Officers Department), and the conclusions reached by the Inquiry.

Up until February 1975 the Maguire Seven and Guildford Four cases were still being treated as one. Michael Hill QC, Treasury Counsel, was instructed in the case. He produced a first draft Statement of Facts. On 7 February, 1975 Hill, together with his colleagues in the prosecution team (Sir Michael Havers QC, Paul Purnell, Philip Havers), some members of the DPP's staff, and three Surrey police officers (Messrs Rowe, Underwood and Hopkins), visited RARDE. Elliott gave a demonstration of the TLC procedure, and Higgs joined the ensuing discussion. Following this, some additions were made to the Statement of Facts. This statement included the sentence – 'The expert evidence will be that to get nitroglycerine under fingernails it is necessary to 'knead' and that its presence under nails is indicative of breaking sticks of explosives into smaller pieces.'[27]

The Attorney-General's fiat was sought for both the Guildford Four case, and for charges against the whole of the Maguire household for 'conspiracy to cause explosions' and 'possession of explosives'. The Attorney-General signed those fiats relating to the Guildford Four but expressed some doubts about the Maguire Seven case in a minute, dated 17 February, 1975, to the DPP, Mr Hetherington, as he then was. The minute opened with – 'The evidence seems to be confined to nitroglycerine traces under fingernails and plastic gloves'. He went on to comment on the absence of any bulk of explosive, and recognised the difficulty in proving that all the Maguire Seven were breaking up and disposing of NG. He observed that the statements of the Guildford Four who implicated Anne Maguire were not evidence. He concluded, – 'It seems to me there is some evidence to support the charge at para 19(v) ('possession of explosives') but only just. I cannot see what there is to establish para 19(iv) ('conspiracy to cause explosions')'.

The Attorney-General went on to suggest that the Solicitor-General (Peter Archer QC MP as he then was) should see Mr Hill and should 'consult with Mr Maitland (Law Officers Department), particularly as he seems to have serious doubts about the TLC test used at Woolwich'.[28]

[27]Second Report – page 18. [28]Second Report – pages 20 and 21.

Sir John May's assessment of the situation so far was straightforward and precise:

> It is clear that Mr Silkin was concerned about the adequacy of the evidence against the Maguire Seven. He recognised that this was limited to the NG traces under their fingernails and on the plastic gloves. He also recognised the evidential difficulty in seeking to prove that the seven proposed defendants were breaking up and disposing of NG when no trace was later found in the Maguire's house.'[29]

At the request of the Attorney-General, Mr Hetherington arranged a meeting on 18 February 1975 which was attended by Sir Michael Havers and Mr Hill of the prosecution, two representatives from the office of the DPP, and Mr Maitland of the Law Officers Department (LOD). Three notes of this meeting were put before the May Inquiry in evidence – two very short ones from Mr Hetherington and Mr Hill, and a lengthy one from Mr Maitland (LOD) describing the meeting more fully. Sir John May had some regard for Mr Maitland, describing him as '. . . quite clearly a concerned and caring member of the LOD staff who was more sceptical about the worth of the material scientific evidence than his colleagues'.[30] In addition to his note of the meeting on 18 February 1975, Mr Maitland also gave evidence to the Inquiry.

Mr Maitland's note is quoted in full in the Second Report[31]. It was of particular interest to the Deputation because it tended to confirm their doubts over many years about the safety and validity of the scientific evidence. The first two paragraphs of Maitland's note are revealing –

> At the meeting on 18 February the A.G. was particularly concerned about the Maguire group, who had been arrested and charged on the basis that so-called traces of nitroglycerine were found upon the palms and under their nails.
>
> Sir Michael Havers and Mr Michael Hill emphatically assured the A.G. that the Woolwich method of analysis provides conclusive proof of the presence of nitroglycerine. **They said it was comparable to fingerprint identification**'.[32]

This was a very significant, and indeed bold, statement by the prosecution team. It carried the weight of absolute certainty, and when presented in such a manner it was virtually impossible to discredit.

[29]Second Report – page 20 (5.8). [30]Second Report – page 22
[31]Second Report – pages 22–23. [32]Second Report – page 22 (Author's heavy type).

Sir John May sought the origin of the assertion that TLC is comparable to fingerprint identification (in the context of specificity). He went on:

> Mr Maitland has it coming from counsel, and Sir Michael Havers certainly put it to the jury in opening the Maguire trial. Asked about it during the public hearings in 1990, Mr Hill did not recall its use but said that the prosecution's opening comments as to specificity would, he believed, have drawn upon what had been learned from the RARDE scientists. The analogy may well have been mentioned on the 7 February visit . . . Mr Higgs is sure it did not come from him or Mr Elliott. Dr Marshall of RARDE told me in a statement prepared for last year's hearings that he does not believe that either Mr Higgs or Mr Elliott would have used such an analogy'.[33]

Sir John May concluded that it was an unhelpful analogy in that it overstated the specificity of the TLC test. 'There I fear I must let it rest', he said. The Deputation and other readers of the May Report were left to come to their own conclusions.

There were further, and indeed disturbing, revelations in Roger Maitland's note. In reference to the under-nail traces he said:

> Havers and Hill advanced the usual Woolwich theories i.e.
>
> (a) That under-nail traces cannot be obtained unless the defendant has been kneading gelignite, like dough
>
> (b) That the finding of under-nail traces suggests that the defendant has forced a detonator into gelignite with his fingers. (RM understands that bombers often use a pencil to make a hole).'[34]

Later in the note he said –

> 'No one explained that: –
>
> (i) In other cases there has always been other cogent evidence, e.g. admissions.
>
> (ii) That the Woolwich theories (a and b) have been strongly challenged by retired experts from Woolwich

[33]Second Report – page 23 (5.11). [34]Second Report – page 22.

(iii) That, when they retired, the challengers were honoured for their services to science and the public service'.[35]

A final disturbing revelation was:

> The A.G. was informed that Mrs Maguire's 18 pairs of rubber gloves were found in a pile and that, due to a blunder by the police, cross-contamination was probable. The gloves had been tested as a batch and traces of nitroglycerine were found.

After subsequently hearing his evidence, Sir John May said that Mr Mailtand's doubts 'were genuine and broadly based'. They arose principally from a concern that the procedures for both swabbing and subsequent analysis were not fool-proof or had not been properly followed, so that cross-contamination could have occurred. Maitland told the Inquiry that he had always thought that the TLC test was, in fact, a very good test, but that it all depended on whether or not it was properly carried out.

Maitland's note had gone on to say that the Attorney-General asked Sir Michael Havers and Hill whether they had studied the Judith Ward evidence. They both made an affirmative reply. The significance of this question by the Attorney-General at the meeting on 18 February 1975 was not apparent from Maitland's note, and only became so in later sections in Sir John May's Second Report entitled 'Further consideration of the kneading hypothesis', and 'The Judith Ward Appeal'.[36]

The background to the Judith Ward case was summarised in these two sections. Judith Ward and two others were arrested and their hands were swabbed after bombs exploded at Euston and King's Cross on 10 September, 1973. The hand tests were processed by Elliott at RARDE. He found all three were positive for NG, though the record of the tests relating to Judith Ward stated only faint traces were found. All three were released. Judith Ward was arrested again on 13 February, 1974 in connection with the M62 coach bombing. She then allegedly made admissions in respect of the Euston and M62 blasts.

Sir John May referred to a Metropolitan Police Report[37] of 2 April, 1974, only about eight months before the arrest of the Maguires, which recommended that Judith Ward be prosecuted for the two offences. However, it also explained why she and the other two had not been prosecuted earlier for the bombings at the railway stations in the following terms –

[35]Second Report – page 23. [36]Second Report, pages 41–42. [37]Second Report – page 30.

It will be appreciated that positive traces of explosives on hands and nails alone is not sufficient evidence of handling explosives due to contamination which can be caused by other means'.

It will be recalled that there were no admissions whatsoever at any time by any of the Maguire Seven.

Sir John May deduced that the 'kneading hypothesis' originated in the preparation for the trial of Judith Ward in 1974, and in the evidence which Elliott and Higgs in particular gave at that trial. He therefore explored further the history of the hypothesis in a long section. Amongst the points he established and the conclusions he came to were: –

> It is reasonable to conclude that the formulation of the kneading process by the scientists was unlikely to have pre-dated the Metropolitan Police Report of 2 April, 1974 and the Ward case.
>
> It would seem that when Mr Hill came to draft the Statement of Facts he had already studied the Ward transcripts because there was some similarity between the terms he employed and Mr Higgs' evidence.
>
> Prior to the visit to RARDE on 7 February, 1975 by the prosecution team, the DPP's staff and the Surrey Police Officers,[38] the only relevant test before that date was carried out on 6 February, 1975 by Mr Elliott and was designed to check the validity of the kneading hypothesis.
>
> The test revealed that even when a hand had been handling bare explosive with the fingertips, pressing it as if shaking it or inserting a detonator, a negative result was obtained from the fingernails.
>
> Mr Hill confirmed to Sir John May in his 1991 evidence that on the visit to RARDE there had been discussion of the significance of positive findings under the fingernails and of the basis on which the experts' evidence would exclude innocent contamination.

Sir John May came to the view that 'there was not a shadow of doubt in the minds of counsel, following the visit to RARDE, about the soundness of the kneading process'. Nevertheless he recorded that Counsel to the Inquiry pointed out that 'the responsibility of the scientists should not be overstated, because, after all, they did not make the

[38]Chapter Eight – page 225.

decision to prosecute'. It can only be assumed that when, at the meeting on 18 February, 1975,[39] the Attorney General asked Sir Michael Havers and Mr Hill whether they had studied the 'Ward evidence', he had some anxieties about the scientific evidence. It would appear that the prosecution team did not share these concerns and they went ahead seeking a fiat.

Although he was not to know it at the time, the Attorney General's possible 'concerns' were to be vindicated some 18 years later by both the May Inquiry and the Court of Appeal in its judgement on 4 June 1992 on the Judith Ward case. Sir John May said:

> The submission on behalf of Mr Higgs that the intention of the scientists was to advance an opinion in qualified terms to the effect that the presence of NG under the fingernails only 'tended to show' rather than 'showed' that the subject had knowingly handled explosive, is in my view wholly at variance with the evidence given at the Maguires' trial.
>
> . . . I believe that the kneading hypothesis was left in unambiguous and unqualified terms' in the Maguire trial and '. . . there never was any justification for stating the hypothesis in these terms'.

In their judgement on the Judith Ward case on 4 June, 1992 the Court of Appeal 'were highly critical of Mr Higgs and the late Mr Elliott.' The Court found that they 'withheld important information which might have weakened the prosecution case or which might have encouraged investigation by the defence.' The Court went on to say:

> Given the fact we have found that Mr Higgs and Mr Elliott allowed their objectivity to become clouded by partisanship, the question arises whether we can have faith in their supervision and interpretation of test results . . .
>
> . . . it seems more realistic to accept that the lack of objectivity that subsequently characterised the conduct of Mr Higgs and Mr Elliott may also have affected their judgement on the earlier interpretation of the TLC tests.

In drawing together his 'conclusions' on the prosecution, Sir John May said that the Attorney-General's note[40] of 17 February, 1975 demonstrated that he was 'mindful of the inherent improbability of the prosecution case, the TLC test notwithstanding, but he could not have had a full appreciation of all the facts as they were to develop at the trial'. Sir John May also referred to the question of speculation which was

[39]Chapter Eight – page 228. [40]Chapter Eight – page 225.

graphically described at the trial as 'all hands to the pump' by Sir Michael Havers. He made the point that there is a fine line to be drawn between proper and improper speculation.

Three telling points in his final paragraphs in this section were –

> At the end of this part of my Inquiry I remain troubled by the underlying improbability of the prosecution case against the Maguire Seven.
>
> I believe that the underlying 'bomb factory' assumption pervaded the entire case and was allowed to obscure the improbability of what was alleged against the Maguire Seven.
>
> I have reached the conclusion that the Maguire Seven were the victims of a serious miscarriage of justice.

His concluding sentence before moving on to the section dealing with the Home Office was '. . . if the Attorney-General had been aware in 1975 of the matters of which I am now aware affecting the reliability and credibility of the scientists upon whose evidence the prosecution depended, I do not think he would have granted even the limited fiats which he did'.

The Second Report was some 94 pages long of which 47 were devoted to various aspects of the role of the Home Office. These included, amongst others, an introduction, history, innocent contamination, the kneading hypothesis, and scientific committees and advice. The public hearings on the Home Office phase were held between 23 September and 7 October, 1991, with closing submissions on 23 September, 1992. Amongst those from the Home Office who gave evidence were two former heads of C3, Caffarey and Watts, and Stanton who was the case officer. The Home Secretary, Douglas Hurd, also gave evidence.

In both his Interim and Second Reports, Sir John May paid tribute to his secretariat. In particular he mentioned David Clarke QC, who was Counsel to the Inquiry, and Felicity Clarkson who had been seconded from the Home Office to act as Secretary to the Inquiry. He said he could not have had better advice than that from David Clarke QC who had continually pointed him in the right direction in the investigations. Felicity Clarkson, he said, had given unstinting assistance in arranging programmes for evidence and providing all the papers required.

There can be no doubt that both were held in high regard for the way in which they carried out their respective duties by all outside the criminal justice system who had dealings with the Inquiry. Felicity

Clarkson was seen to be, and was respected as being, 'an Inquiry person' rather than 'a Home Office person' and, no doubt as a result of this, she readily attracted co-operation from those outside. In October 1991, after the hearings on the Home Office in September and October, she was promoted elsewhere and so left the Inquiry. She was replaced by Tim Morris also from the Home Office, to whom Sir John May also paid tribute, and who was also co-operative.

It is probably fair to say that relations with the Home Office between, initially, Cardinal Hume and subsequently the Deputation were not sufficiently fruitful at an early enough stage in the cases of the Maguire Seven and the Guildford Four.

It will be recalled that Cardinal Hume wrote the first of some 19 letters over a period of five years to the Home Secretary on 26 March, 1979 about the case of Giuseppe Conlon.[41] By 1984 this case had widened to the whole of the Maguire Seven. During the early '80s several representations were made to the Home Office about the scientific evidence at the Maguire trial, and the matter was also raised in Parliament. Publication in 1986 of Robert Kee's *Trial and Error* led to attention now being directed at the case of the Guildford Four as well as the Maguire Seven. Whatever the niceties of the law, the two cases were clearly interconnected. Prior to 1986, as well as the Cardinal, individual members of the Deputation – Lord Devlin, Lord Scarman, and Roy Jenkins and Merlyn Rees – had all expressed their personal concerns about the cases. It was by early 1987, after the Home Secretary had decided in January 1987 not to refer either of the two cases, that they all came together as a Deputation. In July 1987 they presented a submission to the Home Secretary.[42]

From the very first letter by Cardinal Hume on 26 March 1979 to the then Home Secretary, Merlyn Rees, right up to but excluding the submission in July 1987, everybody who had any dealings with the Home Office on the cases received the same stock reply. As far as the submission by the Deputation was concerned, the eventual response was when the Home Secretary, Douglas Hurd, visited Cardinal Hume on 8 September 1988 to say he would not be referring the Guildford Four or the Maguire Seven cases.[43]

It is noteworthy that, up until 1985, letters from Cardinal Hume to successive Home Secretaries, and to the Prime Minister, referred only to the Maguire Seven case. Thereafter, in his many letters, he invariably referred to both the Maguire Seven and the Guildford Four cases. The Maguire Seven case was also referred to in the submission by the Deputation in July 1987. It was not until his letter to Cardinal Hume of 24 November, 1988 – some two months after he had told the

[41]Chapter Two, page 15. [42]See Chapter Five, page 105. [43]Chapter Six, page 144.

Cardinal he would not be referring the Guildford Four case – that the Home Secretary clarified his position on the Maguires.

After saying that he regarded the material submitted by the Deputation as concerning only the convictions of the Guildford Four, he went on to say that in relation to the Maguire Seven:

> I have received no representations other than repetitions of those I considered before my statement of 20 January last year, which appear to bear directly on the safety of the convictions in the Maguire case. So in line with the principle which I have consistently followed about new and substantial matters, I am considering only the case of the Guildford Four, not the Maguires.

The stock response over the years to all other representations had been words to the effect that '. . . cases cannot be reconsidered on the basis of facts already considered by the courts, but only where some relevant new evidence or consideration of substance has come to light'. The Deputation, and many people before them, frequently made the point to the Home Office that Section 17 of the 1968 Bill states:

> (1) Where a person has been convicted on indictment . . . the Secretary of State may, if he thinks fit, at any time either: –
> (a) refer the whole case to the Court of Appeal, and the case shall then be treated for all purposes as an appeal to the Court by that person . . .

It is necessary to consider Sir John May's key comments on this section of the Act before referring to specific aspects of the Maguire case which were of particular interest to the Deputation. It is on these comments that he based his apparent vindication of the role played by the Home Office during the lengthy period 1979 to 1989, which was so frustrating and dispiriting for all the defendants and those who were seeking to obtain justice for them.

After referring to the above quoted Section 17, Sir John May went on to say that although the terms of it 'are unrestricted and on their face give a Home Secretary an unfettered discretion to refer a case to the Court of Appeal 'if he thinks fit,' in practice he and the civil servants advising him on these matters operate within strict self-imposed limits'. He went on to say that these limits 'rest upon constitutional considerations and upon the approach that has been demonstrated by the Court of Appeal itself to its own statutory powers'. Home Office witnesses, including the Home Secretary himself, expressed the same views in evidence.

Sir John May then said he had no doubt that the reasoning of the

Home Office on 'the point of construction', as he put it, was soundly based in both law and logic and that 'no criticism can properly be made of that Department in setting up and applying the criterion which it did'. In the very next paragraph he commented:

> . . . there is no doubt that the criterion so defined was and is a limiting one and had resulted in the responsible officials within the Home Office taking a substantially restricted view of cases to which their attention has been drawn as was the case in the Maguires.[44]

There were shades here of Lord Scarman's frequent comment at meetings of the Deputation that he was 'fearful when an administrative rule of practice is elevated to a principle'.

After saying that the very nature and terms of the self-imposed limits on the Home Secretary's power to refer cases have led the Home Office only to respond to the representations which have been made to it rather than carrying out its own investigations, Sir John May then declared:

> In the light of such constitutional reasoning I think that most of the public criticism that there has been of what with hindsight have been miscarriages of justice, and the alleged failure of the authorities to do anything about them, has been unjustified.

It is fair to say that these views were not widely shared in the '80s, particularly by those who were striving for justice for the Maguire Seven. It would be appropriate at this stage, as no reference was made to it at this point by the Inquiry, to recall the Government Reply in April 1983 to the Home Affairs Committee Report on *Miscarriages of Justice*,[45]

> As to greater use of the procedure, the Home Secretary will in future be prepared to exercise his power of reference more readily; and the Lord Chief Justice, who has been consulted about this reply, sees room for the Court to be more ready to exercise its own powers to receive evidence or, where appropriate and practical, to order a retrial.

There was one central fact concerning the Maguire Seven. They were convicted solely on scientific evidence as given by the expert witnesses from RARDE. There were no confessions, no disputed oral statements to the police, no witness statements of any kind, no documentary

[44]Second Report – page 50. [45]Cmnd.8856.

evidence of any sort and no fingerprints. They had been picked up and arrested by the police for the sole reason that in confession statements, which were later retracted, two of the Guildford Four had said Annie Maguire made bombs. All this was known by members of the Deputation, even before they came together, and also by the Director of Public Prosecutions, by the prosecution teams, and by the Home Office.

The Second Report covered at great length how the many representations on the scientific evidence were handled in the Home Office. This included extensive quotations from long minutes. The two aspects which were of particular interest to the Deputation were how the representations by Christopher Price MP and Dr Caddy in 1982 and 1983 were handled, and the reasoning behind the refusal to set up a scientific committee as had been done later by the May Inquiry.

In February 1982 Price sent to the Home Secretary a report by Dr Brian Caddy on the evidence presented at the trial of Giuseppe Conlon by Mr Yallop, one of the defence scientists. He expressed the opinion that a single TLC test as performed by RARDE was insufficient, without a confirmatory test, to make an unequivocal finding of NG. At the request of Patrick Mayhew, then Minister of State, the matter was referred to the Home Office Forensic Science Service (FSS). In replying to the Minister on 7 April 1982, Dr Alan Curry, head of FSS, said he had discussed the matter with the experts at RARDE –Higgs and Elliott. He had concluded the simple TLC procedure involved many other criteria which 'all the experts are agreed' add up to the finding of NG. However, in closing the note he said:

> Because of the furore raised in the Conlon case additional tests are now carried out but nothing has come to light to throw doubt upon the evidence given in 1975.

Sir John May went on to say that Dr Curry told him that although he had discussed the case with Higgs and Elliott, he did not inspect the notebooks. Sir John May observed that, in his reply to Patrick Mayhew, Dr Curry did not refer to the fact that in June 1976 he had commented on a copy of a report he had been sent on the Maguire trial prepared by the Metropolitan Police. In a note to the Police Department in the Home Office he had said he was at a loss to explain why it appeared that only the TLC test was used. He agreed with the defence experts view that a confirmatory test using a different method was needed. In November 1976 he wrote to Dr Carver at RARDE:

> I am particularly concerned with the analytical procedures and the evidence your scientists give before the courts. A very serious point

of identification arises with the TLC method and I would not consider a single chromatographic parameter as proof of identity.

It is to be noted that the Maguire trial took place in January 1976 and the first appeal, which was dismissed, was heard in July 1977, some nine months after the letter to Dr Carver.

It is possible to make only the briefest references to first, the subsequent representations in May 1983 by Price and Caddy, and secondly, to the scientific advice sought by the Home Office and their reactions to proposals made in Parliament and elsewhere that they should set up a scientific committee. It has to be assumed that the wide-ranging discussion in various lengthy minutes quoted in the Second Report led to and supported the final recommendation made. Brief reference will therefore be made only to some of those recommendations relating to the above two specific aspects, which were of particular interest to the Deputation, and also to subsequent decisions made by Ministers.

It has to be said at the outset that some of the revelations in the Second Report relating to the internal workings of the Home Office, hitherto totally unknown to either the Deputation or the public at large, are highly significant. In February 1983 Price sent a second report from Caddy to Patrick Mayhew. Dr Caddy considered that the TLC test could not have distinguished NG from PETN and EGDN and that a confirmatory test should have been carried out. Price considered that Caddy's report was a consideration of substance. As such, he said it should enable the Home Secretary to regard the verdict against Giuseppe Conlon as unsafe and unsatisfactory and to grant him a free pardon[46]. Mr Cook of C3 division sent the report to both the FSS and to RARDE. Miss Pereira (the Controller of the FSS) chaired a meeting at the Home Office on 10 March 1983 to discuss Caddy's report. Higgs attended. Sir John May commented that a manuscript note of the meeting recorded that 'in the absence of proof of level of spot on Conlon it is difficult to say it could not be contamination.'[47]

A reply to Dr Caddy's report was prepared by the FSS in consultation with RARDE and sent to C3 Division by Miss Pereira on 17 March, 1983. Sir John May was critical of two aspects of the terms of the reply.[48] He then said that Miss Pereira informed the Inquiry that 'the purpose of the meeting was to ascertain whether the science was reasonably reliable, to check what RARDE had done and what precautions they had taken'. She went on to say that she had been unaware of the importance to the Crown case of the kneading hypothesis, nor did she know the results of the individual TLC tests. Also, she was not aware of how PETN had been dealt with in court, although she

[46]Second Report – page 60. [47]Second Report – page 61. [48]Second Report – page 62.

said she thought the position should have been made clear in the original statements. Sir John May's comment was:

> It is clear to me that the FSS were not supplied by C3 Division with sufficient information about the scientific evidence and course of events at the trial to enable them to look critically at advice given by RARDE at the meeting.[49]

In May 1983 Price and Sir John Biggs-Davison sent a final report[50] from Dr Caddy to the Home Office. Three of the main points covered were –

> Whether the TLC tests used by RARDE could differentiate between NG, PETN and EGDN
>
> How long NG remained on hands after they had been contaminated with it
>
> The extent to which each contamination could result from handling objects themselves previously touched by handlers of explosives

Dr Caddy's experiments confirmed that the TLC systems used by RARDE could not distinguish NG from PETN and EGDN, and that secondary contamination could indeed take place through the handling of door knobs and similar objects. Sir John May went on to say the report was sent to RARDE by FSS on 24 June, 1983, and that Dr Carver, Head of Home Office Branch of RARDE, responded 'somewhat dismissively'.[51] He referred briefly to Dr Twibell's paper[52] but gave no details. At this point Sir John May said:

> It is clear from all the evidence and material that I have received that nobody appreciated the potential significance of its findings in the context of the Maguire convictions.

Sir John May then referred to a lengthy submission to Ministers on 22 August, 1983 by Mr Varney, then head of C3 Division, on the 'troublesome, involved, long standing and notorious case' of Giuseppe Conlon. One conclusion was – 'even if the case could be referred we

[49]Second Report – page 63. [50]Second Report – page 63. [51]Second Report – page 63.

[52]Dr Twibell sent a paper to RARDE in June/July 1977. It was ultimately published in 1982. It was considered by the Inquiry's 'West Committee' as it was relevant to, but not conclusive on, the kneading hypothesis. Nevertheless, the Inquiry considered that the paper showed that the hypothesis was open to serious question and cast doubt on the certainty with which it had been advanced at the trial.

do not think the new evidence or the arguments adduced would justify it' – 'Dr Caddy's findings do not seem to us to call these convictions seriously into question or to add at all significantly to the issues contested at the trial and the appeal'.[53] After the general election in June 1983, David Mellor took over from Patrick Mayhew. On 5 December Mellor informed the Home Secretary, following discussions with Varney and Cook of C3 Division, that he agreed with the advice in the submission of 22 August, 1983 by Varney. He then wrote to Sir John Biggs-Davison on 20 December, 1983 saying he saw no grounds to recommend the granting of a free pardon to Giuseppe Conlon. Sir John May's comment was:

> I have seen nothing in the documents nor heard any evidence which explains the delay which occurred between August and December 1983 . . . I do not know why the decision on this submission was not taken until December.

Turning now to the proposals to the Home Office that they should re-examine the scientific evidence, they were made on three separate occasions. The first was in August 1980 when John Biggs-Davison raised the Giuseppe Conlon case in Parliament and asked that it should be studied afresh by expert opinion – scientific as well as legal. He was supported in the same debate by Christopher Price who called for 'a reinterpretation of the scientific evidence'. On the second and third occasions the proposals were specifically for an independent scientific committee to be established. One occasion was in the House of Lords debate in May 1985 where it was initiated by Lord Fitt and supported by Lord Mischon, the other was at meetings with the Home Secretary on 7 and 12 January, 1987. All three proposals were rejected by the Home Office.

The May Inquiry carefully reviewed the appropriate lengthy minutes within the Home Office on these proposals over some 14 pages from page 67 onwards in the Second Report. As they were all rejected it would be sufficient not to repeat the reasoning but to quote only some of the recommendations made by C3 Division. Watts was head of C3 Division at the time of the Fitt/Mischon proposal. In a lengthy minute he said:

> We see no real merit in this suggestion . . . (after referring to Dr Caddy's views in 1983, which were not deemed to justify a referral, and to views expected from other scientists which can be considered in consultation with RARDE and the FSS, he concluded) '–We do

[53]Second Report – page 64.

> not need an independent scientific enquiry to help us reach that point'.

In giving evidence to the May Inquiry Watts said –

> ... we did not need an independent committee looking into the whole of the evidence much of which had not been questioned as to its reliability by representations.

Sir John May went on to say that Watts thought it would be awkward if the scientists supported the views already expressed by Dr Caddy, which had been considered insufficient in the Home Office to justify a referral to the Court of Appeal. Sir John May's comment[54] was:

> It is not easy to reconcile the oft-repeated claim by the Home Office to openness in this and other similar matters and to its readiness to receive and consider any new material with its reluctance on this occasion to seek the views of the fresh scientists who were mentioned.

He said this reluctance stemmed mainly from a strict application of the criteria adopted in the Home Office to which he had already referred. Later, after repeated requests to establish a scientific committee, Sir John May quoted a minute by Stanton:[55]

> These approaches must continue to be resisted. We do not know what conclusions, if any, a committee of scientists might arrive at. There would be pressure for the Secretary of State to act on the basis of any recommendations (e.g. referral) it might make, leaving potentially awkward decisions to be made, and setting a dangerous precedent. Arguably it remains up to the Maguires and their supporters to demonstrate a case, not for the Secretary of State to explore it himself.

Other minutes in a similar vein were quoted in full, including a very lengthy one by Caffarey, then head of C3 Division, in December 1986. This minute had been prepared for the Home Secretary who was to make an announcement in January 1987 about the Maguire Seven, Guildford Four and Birmingham Six cases. On 7 January, 1987 the Home Secretary, Douglas Hurd, held a meeting at which he wished to consider:

[54]Second Report – page 68. [55]Second Report – page 71.

> Was there a body of reputable scientific opinion which would now in the light of scientific developments since the trial, argue that there were doubts about the accuracy of the TLC test employed, or at least grounds for qualification which had not existed at the time?[56]

The May Inquiry stated there was discussion at the meeting about the idea of setting up a group of scientists to advise whether the TLC test was so discredited as a technique that it could no longer carry the weight which it did in this case. A note of the meeting was prepared. Sir John May went on to say that, when Douglas Hurd gave evidence to his Inquiry, he indicated the paragraph in the note of the meeting which he found the most compelling and which was the basis of his decision a few days later not to set up a scientific committee. It read:

> If the Home Secretary was doubtful about the weight which could be carried by the TLC test (and Mr Mellor indicated that he was satisfied this was not a basis for reference) then the case should be referred.

There clearly was no doubt about the TLC test. It was decided not to set up a scientific committee. However, it is questionable whether the proposed point for such a committee to examine was too narrow. Sir John May records that, at a second meeting of Ministers and officials on 12 January, 1987, the Home Secretary noted that the Maguire convictions were found on a narrow point, namely the forensic evidence that they had handled explosives. One point noted at that meeting was that if the Maguire Seven case was referred it could 'open the floodgates' for the large numbers of people convicted on the basis of forensic tests which had now been superseded by more modern techniques.[57] No reference was made to possible numbers in this regard. It may not have been nearly as many as was apparently thought and some of those cases might have been calling out for justice. Judith Ward, whose convictions were finally quashed in June 1992, comes to mind.

In giving evidence to Sir John May, the Home Secretary said the conclusive argument to him was that a scientific committee would cast the problem back on his desk without settling anything. However, he accepted that a scientific committee with fairly wide terms of reference might have realised the innocent contamination point, which might have led to an earlier reference to the Court of Appeal. Earlier in his

[56]Second Report – page 79. [57]Second Report – page 83.

report, on page 71, Sir John May had said he thought it unfortunate that no officials envisaged that a scientific committee might come up with something fresh. With their combined experience they might have sought to look at the RARDE notebooks.

It is difficult not to be left with the impression that the general Home Office view was that, whatever interpretation they might place on the setting up of a scientific committee, the inference drawn would be that they had sufficient doubt about the scientific evidence to think that this course was necessary.

It will be recalled that at the meeting with some members of the Deputation on 22 January, 1990, which had been requested by Sir John May, there was a general discussion about how the Deputation could best help him in his work on the Inquiry.[58] In the course of the meeting Sir John indicated that in his report he would be stating the facts of the Maguire case as he saw them, and would also be considering relevant aspects relating to law reform.

At the end of the meeting[59], Cardinal Hume had said that he could see that 'there was both a law reform aspect and an historical aspect to the Inquiry' and he expressed the hope that 'the law reform aspects would not be pursued at the expense of attributing culpability where this was due'.

This might be an appropriate stage at which to review the extent to which the May Inquiry established culpability in relation to the Maguire case by considering briefly some of the actions, and indeed lack of action, by some individuals as reported in the Interim and Second Reports of the Inquiry. Taken together, these possible deficiencies resulted in the Maguire Seven having to serve out their lengthy prison sentences before the truth could be established, and the fact that their convictions were not quashed until some 15 years after the trial.

It will be seen from the following extracts from the two reports on the Maguire Seven that the Inquiry did not always highlight sufficiently those who were in authority during the relevant period, and no individuals are brought to account for failing in their duties. In the light of this many considered that some of the conclusions in the reports, whilst they may have been correct, lacked the respect they might have commanded.

[58]Chapter Eight – pages 209 to 210. [59]See page 213.

INTERIM REPORT

On Mr Elliott and Mr Higgs

> . . . the failure to report the confusion of NG with PETN was honest but mistaken. However, before long, an element of calculation crept into the continuing failure. When Mr Higgs prepared a list for the consultation on 13 January, 1976 which purported to exclude all substances which might mimic NG by reference to three criteria, he deliberately left out PETN which could not be so excluded.
>
> they knew that the [TLC] test was not specific for NG when advising the prosecution team and when giving evidence, but they failed to say so. They knew that a second system was available to resolve the two substances but they did not mention it. Whilst these failures were in my own view deliberate, I do not believe they were borne of a conspiracy to deny justice to the defendants.[60]

Later he says:

> The scientists wrongly believed that they could rationalise their exclusion of PETN. They imperfectly understood their duties as forensic scientists and as witnesses.

Demonstrated by:

> . . . the manifest inadequacies of the treatment of PETN, their failure to report the second tests for nitro-toluenes, their selective reporting of the results of tests conducted during the trial . . .

If the Inquiry considered all these deliberate failures did not constitute a conspiracy, they might have sought to establish for what other reasons they took place, and whether anyone else was involved.

On the prosecution:

> I think this attitude to the disclosure of the scientists' notebooks was both regrettable and significant . . . had the prosecution been more open minded to disclosure of the scientists' notebooks it is very possible that events would have taken a different turn'.[61]

[60]Interim Report – page 47. [61]Interim Report – page 48.

SECOND REPORT

On reassessment of scientific evidence:

> It was at least a matter for consideration why the inquiries which I have been able to make since my appointment and the conclusions to which as a result, I came, could not much earlier have been made and arrived at by the Home Office.[62]

On the decision to prosecute:

> It is clear that Mr Silkin was concerned about the adequacy of the evidence against the Maguire Seven. He recognised that this was limited to the NG traces under their fingernails and on the plastic gloves. He also recognised the evidential difficulty in seeking to prove that the seven proposed defendants were breaking up and disposing of NG when no trace was later found in the Maguire house.[63]
>
> Sir Michael Havers and Mr Michael Hill emphatically assured the AG that the Woolwich method of analysis provided conclusive proof of the presence of nitroglycerine. They said it was comparable to fingerprint identification.
>
> In passing I have been unable to come to any conclusion about the origin of the assertion that TLC is comparable to fingerprint identification (in the context of specificity).

Then after saying that Maitland had it coming from Counsel, Sir John May said that Sir Michael Havers certainly put it to the jury in opening the Maguire trial. However, in evidence to the Inquiry Hill, Higgs and Elliott all said they could not recall the origin, and Dr Marshall of RARDE said he did not believe Higgs or Elliott would have used such an analogy. Sir John May went on to say:

> . . . There I fear I must let it rest. I believe that it was an unhelpful analogy in that it overstated the specificity of the TLC test.

At this point Sir John might have concluded that the matter was probably a major factor in the AG's decision to grant the fiat, and it therefore called for more determined efforts to establish the source of the analogy.

> There never was a policy either in the DPP's office or in the LOD not to prosecute on forensic evidence alone, but it appears that the

[62]Second Report – page 11. [63]Second Report – page 20.

> Maguire case was the only one in which a prosecution for unlawful possession of NG was based solely on such evidence.[64]

The reason why this was done might have been further explored to establish who made the decision.

On the kneading hypothesis

> However the submission on behalf of Mr Higgs that the intention of the scientists was to advance an opinion in qualified terms to the effect that the presence of NG under the fingernails only 'tended to show' rather than 'showed' that the subject had knowingly handled explosive, is in my view wholly at variance with the evidence given at the Maguires' trial and elsewhere.[65]
>
> . . . I believe that the kneading hypothesis was left in unambiguous and unqualified terms at the close of Mr Higgs' evidence in the Maguire case.
>
> . . . There was never any justification for stating the hypothesis in these terms.[66]
>
> I think that the failure to appreciate the importance of the kneading hypothesis reveals a defect in the system operated by the Home Office as it affected this particular case.[67]

When writing of the Appeal Judgement on 4 June, 1992 in the Judith Ward case, in which the kneading hypothesis had arisen in preparation for her trial, Sir John May said:

> . . . in their Judgement the Court of Appeal were highly critical of Mr Higgs and the late Mr Elliott. The Court found that these scientists withheld important information which might have weakened the prosecution case or which might have encouraged investigation by the defence.[68]

Those who acted for the Maguire Seven at their trial and appeal, and those who supported them in the early '80s, had reason to suspect this. Hence their efforts to establish the truth about the scientific evidence.

[64]Second Report – page 25. [65]Second Report – pages 39 and 40.
[66]Second Report – pages 39 and 40. [67]Second Report – page 91.
[68]Second Report – page 41.

On the prosecution:

> Why despite the inherent improbability of the prosecution case which is now apparent to me, were the Maguire Seven prosecuted and convicted?[69]

After recalling that Anne Maguire had been implicated for bomb making in the course of confession statements by Paul Hill and Gerard Conlon he went on:

> When the decision was made to prosecute the Maguire Seven, this fact was known to those in making the decision, and was taken into account as part of the background for the decision even though it was recognised that the material would not be admissible evidence.[70]

On the Court of Appeal:

> In 1977 the Court of Appeal heard detailed arguments based on the Defendants' movements and timings, and nevertheless held that these arguments gave rise to no lurking doubt. The Court's conclusion on this point contrasts markedly with that of the Court of Appeal in 1991.[71]

The Court of Appeal in 1991 said:

> In our judgement the Crown's case that all the appellants must have been knowingly handling bulk explosive was highly improbable.

On the Home Office:

> I have no doubt that the criteria applied by the Home Office before a referral can be made are soundly based both in law and logic and that no criticism can be made of the Department in this regard.

After referring to that policy resulting in a reactive approach by officials –

> The evidence I have heard leads me to conclude that within these limits the relevant officials have investigated the representations and cases coming to them with care and thoroughness.[72]

[69]Second Report – page 46. [70]Second Report – page 46. [71]Second Report – page 47.
[72]Second Report – page 88.

Sir John May then went on to make some 'gentle' criticisms of officials and made the point later that the FSS were not supplied by C3 Division with full details of the issues at the trial. They were in no position to provide the Home Office with independent advice, but rather acted as a conduit for communicating with RARDE. After saying it was apparent to C3 Division officials that the main challenge to the verdicts in the Maguire Seven trial was scientific, and that the evidence at that trial which was being challenged had been given by RARDE, Sir John May went on:

> I do not think that the officials took these facts sufficiently into account and as time passed and the challenges continued to be made I think that it would have been wise if they had sought scrutiny of the evidence given by the RARDE scientists at trial by suitably qualified independent scientists.[73]

Representations in this case started with the case of Giuseppe Conlon in 1979, extended to all the Maguire Seven by 1984, and continued until 1988, by which time the Guildford Four case had also been included. It has to be borne in mind that, if the Guildford Four convictions had not been quashed on 19 October, 1989, and if the May Inquiry had not been set up as a result of that, the convictions of the Maguire Seven might never have been quashed. The Maguire Seven case was only included in the May Inquiry because of the connection with the Guildford Four case. The Deputation had maintained from the outset there was such a connection.

[73]Second Report – page 92.

9

THE MAY INQUIRY (2)
The Guildford Four

THE INTERIM REPORT on the Maguire Seven by the May Inquiry resulted in the immediate referral of the case to the Court of Appeal in July 1990. A year later all seven convictions were quashed, including that of Giuseppe Conlon. However, the appeals were allowed only on the limited ground conceded by the DPP, namely that at the trial the Crown had not disproved the possibility that the hands of the defendants had been innocently contaminated with traces of nitroglycerine.

In the Second Report on the Maguires the first half was devoted to additional scientific information emanating from the 'West Committee' which Sir John May had established, and to the inception of the prosecution. In both areas some serious failings were exposed but these were by individuals rather than in the system itself. However, no individual was held to account. The latter half of the Second Report covered all relevant aspects of the role of the Home Office. By and large the action, or inaction, by the Home Office was regarded as satisfactory in that Sir John May 'had no doubt that the criteria applied by the Home Office before a referral can be made are soundly based in both law and logic and that no criticism can properly be made of that Department in this regard.'[1] No officials were brought to account because they were operating within the system and the criteria adopted by Ministers and officials.

Yet, against this background it is significant that, in looking to the future, Sir John May said:[2]

> All the evidence which I have heard and all the material which I have received leads me to the conclusion that some alternative machinery is indeed required in place of the existing powers of the Home Secretary to refer such cases to the Court of Appeal under section 17 of the Criminal Appeal Act 1968.

[1]Second Report – page 88. [2]Second Report – page 93.

Many people, including the Deputation, had held this view for some time. It could have been argued by some that, in the light of the May Inquiry, all that would have been required was for the Home Office to review the nature of the criteria and the terms of reference of C3 Division. However, even in this event, account would then also need to be taken of the standing of those making representations. No doubt some of them, by their very background, could not only be described only as 'distinguished' people, as the Home Office was prone to do in the Guildford case.

Turning now to the Guildford Four case, there can be no doubt that the inordinate delays in mounting the trial of the three Surrey police officers, although they suited their counsel, had a profound and very unfortunate effect on both the progress and effectiveness of the May Inquiry into that case. This was a matter of serious concern to all members of the Deputation. A sequence of events underlines the point:

19 Oct 89	Guildford Four convictions quashed and May Inquiry set up
12 Jul 90	Interim Report on Maguires published
12 Nov 90	DPP institutes proceedings against three Surrey police officers
11 Jul 91	Mr Bartle, magistrate at Bow St, discharges Surrey police officers on grounds of abuse of process (adverse publicity and lapse of time since alleged offences)
24 Jan 92	High Court reverses decision and case against three Surrey police officers reinstated
27 Mar 92	Surrey police officers committed for trial but delay granted because leading counsel for one of them engaged in another major case
5 Jun 92	Court agrees to defence request for trial to be fixed not before April 93
31 Jul 92	Before completing his work on the Maguire case Sir John May decides to proceed privately with investigations into Guildford Four case
3 Dec 92	Second report on Maguires published
20 Apr/ 13 May 93	Trial and acquittal of Surrey police officers
Jul 93	Report of Royal Commission published
3 Sep 93	Special meeting with Sir John May as requested by the Deputation
2 Feb 94	Exceedingly powerful letter from Birnbergs to May Inquiry relating to Gerard Conlon, the 'Burke Alibi' and information about reports by Avon and Somerset Police which had come to light during Paul Hill's appeal in

	Northern Ireland on 21 April 1994 and was hitherto unknown to the defence.
30 Jun 94	Final Report on Guildford Four case published.

As can be seen, the convictions of the Guildford Four were quashed by the Court of Appeal (Lord Lane) on 19 October 1989, but the trial and acquittal of the three Surrey police officers did not take place until April/May 1993, some three and a half years later. Before examining the background to the delays it would be as well to recall the words of Lord Lane in his judgement. After dealing with the evidence by the Avon and Somerset Police regarding the alleged confession of Patrick Armstrong he went on to say:

> The officers, to use Mr Amlot's somewhat anodyne expression, seriously misled the Court. In fact they must have lied . . .
>
> It is some comfort to know that these matters are now in the hands of the DPP . . . We earnestly express the hope that nothing will be allowed to stand in the way of a speedy progress of these proceedings . . .
>
> We hope that the evidence [by Avon and Somerset Police] may have paved the way for expeditious criminal proceedings.

The Lord Chief Justice's hopes were not to be fulfilled. Some two and a half years later, as the police trial was not now to take place before April 1993, Sir John May announced on 31 July, 1992 he would proceed privately with investigations into the Guildford Four case. There were to be no public hearings, and he would prepare a report using principally the many papers available to him, together with private hearings. Part of his intention in adopting this course of action was, as he put it, 'to minimise the further delay before I could conclude the Inquiry in accordance with my terms of reference'.[3] But there was another reason. He said that 'wider questions affecting the Criminal Justice System as a whole, on which it was thought that some lessons would be learned from the events surrounding the convictions of the Guildford Four, had been submitted for consideration by the Royal Commission on Criminal Justice, of which I was a member and which was due to report in mid 1993'.[4] He concluded that it was 'in the public interest' that he 'should go ahead with a more limited form of inquiry on the Guildford Four case'.[5]

The impact on the May Inquiry of the delays in the police trial was of considerable concern to the whole Deputation. The new arrangements resulting from these delays had been discussed by Sir John May with

[3]Final Report – page 8. [4]Final Report – page 8. [5]Final Report – page 8.

the Home Secretary, Kenneth Clarke, and Sir Nicholas Lyell, the Attorney General. In their announcement on 31 July, 1992 the Home Office said that Sir John May had decided to end all public hearings in the Inquiry in order to meet a deadline for preparing his report to the Royal Commission on Criminal Justice. This was to be published in July 1993. They said it would be 'impractical' to hold public hearings while the prosecution of the three Surrey police officers was still outstanding. This development was in stark contrast to the public hearings Sir John had already conducted into the related case of the Maguire Seven. These led to the quashing of their convictions, and to much hitherto unknown information being brought to light, including the workings, and failings, of the scientists, and the handling of the case in the Home Office.

There was even a report in *The Independent* of 1 August, 1992 that one MP had suggested that Sir John May's Inquiry had 'been nobbled from the moment that it became clear that he was not prepared to participate in a whitewash'. Indeed, as already recorded, Sir John had told the press on 1 November, 1989 that he anticipated the report would be published and added – 'there is no sort of whitewash or anything like that. I don't think it would serve one of the purposes of the Inquiry, which is to allay public disquiet'.[6]

It will be recalled that at their meeting on 22 November, 1989[7] the Deputation considered the nature of the May Inquiry which had just been set up, on 19 October, following the quashing of the convictions of the Guildford Four. In discussion it was noted that it was not clear from the terms of reference what in fact the May Inquiry was designed to achieve. It was thought there were elements of what could become a whitewash.

So concerned were the Deputation at the abandonment of public hearings by the May Inquiry that Cardinal Hume decided to place the matter in the public domain. Accordingly on 6 August 1992 he wrote to *The Times* and amongst the points he made were:

> . . . My primary interest lies in the removal of procedural obstacles in the pursuit of truth and justice rather than the prosecution of individual police officers . . .
>
> . . . It is in the public interest that the Lord Chief Justice and the Director of Public Prosecutions should each make a full statement as to why there has been such an unparalleled delay in mounting this trial until April 1993 . . .
>
> . . . Is the Court in difficulty, is the prosecution in difficulty, or is the defence in difficulty, and what is the nature of such difficulties.

[6]Chapter Eight – page 209. [7]Chapter Eight – pages 209 to 210.

Mrs Barbara Mills, then Director of Public Prosecutions, responded to Cardinal Hume's letter, also in *The Times*, on 8 August. In doing so she set out the relevant parts of the table of events referred to earlier.[8]. She spoke of the 'difficulty' encountered on 5 June concerning availability of counsel, and said she was writing to the Cardinal in greater detail.

In her explanatory letter to Cardinal Hume of 6 August, Mrs Mills covered in more detail the same points as in her letter to *The Times*. She referred again to the 'difficulties' at the meeting on 5 June. These related to counsel's involvement 'in another major case'. Towards the end she said, 'I entirely agree that the recent cases of miscarriages of justice have affected public confidence in our criminal justice system'. This letter was to mark the beginning of a somewhat unsatisfactory exchange of correspondence up to October 1992 to which brief reference will be made later.

Meanwhile, a concise and direct letter from Lord Scarman, going to the very roots of the matter, was published in *The Times* on 18 August. While sympathising with Sir John May 'in difficulties not of his own making' the main points he made were:

> . . . But closing down his inquiry in this way will have the serious consequence that we shall be deprived of a full public investigation into 'the circumstances leading to and deriving from the trial' as promised by his terms of reference . . .
>
> Sir John's task is to enquire into and report upon the facts. The Royal Commission's task is to study and report upon general issues of law reform. One very important area of fact has not been fully investigated by Sir John, namely the extent to which police officers of far greater seniority than those presently accused of perverting the course may have contributed to the miscarriage of justice that ultimately ensued in the two cases . . .
>
> Unless Sir John has the opportunity to enquire into all the circumstances and to do so publicly, I cannot see that the whole truth will ever be known . . .
>
> . . . If the delays that have arisen in bringing the presently accused police officers to trial mean Sir John cannot complete his enquiry until they have been tried, so be it . . .
>
> It is very much in the public interest that the full facts relating to this serious miscarriage of justice should be made known, even if we have to wait for it.

Sir John May responded in *The Times* on 22 August to Lord Scarman's letter but did not dispel the doubts and concerns that had been raised.

[8]Chapter Nine – pages 248 to 249.

Sir John adhered to his view that it was desirable he should let his colleagues on the Royal Commission have a draft report early in 1993 before it reported in July 1993. This draft report would not be for publication. He would then write an account of the Guildford and Woolwich cases from the extensive documentation available to him. He would submit this full report on the Guildford and Woolwich cases to ministers and would expect it to be published. He said the full report would deal with all aspects of the cases, including the conduct of any senior police officers.

The question which arose at the time in the minds of some observers was how effectively all this could be done without public hearings. The last sentence of Sir John May's letter indicated that he was not wholly happy with the situation in which he now found himself:

> That I have ultimately had to adopt this course of action is due largely to the delay that has occurred in the prosecution of the Surrey police officers.

If we return again to the correspondence between the Cardinal and the DPP, which had got under way before Lord Scarman's letter of 18 August to *The Times*, the central nub of Cardinal Hume's response on 12 August to the letter of 6 August from Mrs Mills was:

> I still have grave misgivings about the way in which things have been developing. You say the provisional date of October 1992 for the trial was discussed at a hearing on 27 March, 1992 but that involvement in another major case of both your Leading Counsel, and Leading Counsel for one of your defendants, meant the date could not be fixed. By implication you concede that the trial of the police officers, particularly in the context of its relation to progress by the May Inquiry, was 'a major case'. I do not know the nature of the other major case to which you referred. As a layman in legal matters, I find it strange that any case could take priority over one so closely connected with the Guildford Four case which by March 1992, together with others, had shaken considerably, rather than just affected, public confidence in our criminal justice system.

He then went on to say that presumably the 'difficulty' which arose on 5 June referred to a decision on priorities. He added it would be helpful to know how this discussion on 'difficulties' developed and why the efforts were unsuccessful.

> I am sorry to have to tell you that some reactions to your letter in *The Times* coming to my ears are not particularly favourable. Some

> people have gone so far as to say to me that they feel uncomfortable about the way things have developed. They are having to ask themselves whether the net result of all these 'difficulties' is that people will conclude there is a hidden agenda whereby the May Inquiry has been thwarted from pursuing truth and justice in a public forum.

Cardinal Hume concluded by saying he would welcome reassurance that the whole truth on the Guildford Four would eventually emerge, even though it might affect others beyond the three police officers.

In her response on 9 September Mrs Mills was quick to say she was sorry the Cardinal still had misgivings over the matter 'particularly when reports to me of reactions to my letter to *The Times* have been positive and favourable'. After saying she now agreed 'that the Guildford Four case has shaken public confidence in the criminal justice system', she went on to say that, when a conflict occurs between the hearing of two important cases, the Crown Prosecution Service alone is not in a position to make the final decision. She added that she placed the highest importance on bringing all cases to trial without unnecessary delay, and confirmed she was entirely satisfied that the Crown Prosecution Service 'had acted properly in its handling of this particular matter'.

Towards the end of her letter she said:

> I can give you an absolute assurance that there is no question of any hidden agenda designed to thwart the May Inquiry and thus prevent the examination of the Guildford Four case. I head an independent prosecuting authority which is committed to working in the interests of justice. Our independence is fundamental, and I would never allow it to be jeopardised.

She concluded by saying that the role of the Crown Prosecution Service was to prosecute the Surrey police officers in accordance with the principles which they applied to every criminal case. A copy of the Code for Crown prosecutors listing those principles was enclosed.

Cardinal Hume was still not satisfied with the situation and in his letter of 21 September, 1992 said:

> I have to say I am still unhappy about the delays, and would ask you again if you can expand a little more on the 'difficulties' you first referred to in your letter to *The Times*. You will appreciate that those of us who had to press so hard for so long to secure justice for the Guildford Four, and indeed the Maguires, soon realised the need to get to the bottom of any 'difficulties'.

He went on to say that he understood that change of counsel was a frequent occurrence, and often done at short notice. He continued – 'it would be helpful to know why this was not possible in this very important case, having regard to the fact that further delay would result in serious diminution of the effectiveness of the May Inquiry in its pursuit of truth and justice. This delay is not having a good effect on public morale in matters of justice'.

In her reply on 6 October Mrs Mills explained that the hearing for fixing the date of the trial was before Mr Justice Alliott, Presiding Judge for the South Eastern Circuit.

> . . . the availability of Counsel instructed by the prosecution and defence is one of many factors which is taken into account when fixing a trial date. Its significance depends upon the circumstances of each particular case. Whilst it may in some cases prevail so that one or more of the parties may have to brief different Counsel in order to accommodate a fixed date, there are also occasions when the court considers that the interests of fairness and justice require that the availability of the Counsel of the party's choice be afforded high priority as a factor in selecting a trial date. After fully considering all the circumstances, Mr Justice Alliott concluded that the Surrey Police officers case fell into the latter category.

After saying that availability of leading counsel for the prosecution therefore became a secondary issue, she added that the judge had been informed that his brief could be returned and a different counsel could be instructed. She ended the letter – 'I can only repeat that the Crown Prosecution Service has no hidden agenda to thwart the May Inquiry'.

There was no further correspondence with Mrs Mills until after the trial of the Surrey police officers in May 1993. Meanwhile, it would be appropriate to recall Sir John May's views on the delays that had taken place. In his Final Report[9] he said:

> There are other instances of delay in the whole story, but I regard that comprised in the period October 1989 to May 1993 as particularly regrettable.

He identified three periods. The first was October 1989 to November 1990 which was occupied by the wide-ranging investigation by the Avon and Somerset Police. In the event the resulting prosecution of police officers was based on factual material which was already known by October 1989 and indeed formed part of the basis for the decision

[9]Final Report – page 3.

of the Court of Appeal to quash the convictions of the Guildford Four. He might have added that, even so, the final charges against the Surrey police officers were framed on a very narrow front.

The second period, November 1990 to January 1992, was largely attributable to the defence application to stay the proceedings for abuse of process and the further consequences thereof. His comment here was – '. . . the length of time taken to resolve this aspect caused me some dismay'. He went on to say that, the defendants having been committed for trial in March 1992, it might reasonably have been expected the trial to start in about October 1992. He added that delay beyond this was due principally to the defence application on the ground that their leading counsel would be unavailable until a date well into the New Year. 'Again, I find this regrettable', he said. His final thoughts on this matter were:

> If a particular counsel retained in a matter cannot be available on the date fixed for trial, or within a reasonable period (as the case may be), then he or she should be replaced. In appropriate circumstances defendants must be told that they cannot always have counsel of their choice, certainly not if to permit this would involve unnecessary delay.[10]

It will be recalled that, in giving judgement on 19 October, 1989, the Lord Chief Justice had said it was some comfort to know that the matters concerning the Surrey Police were now in the hands of the DPP. However, his subsequent exhortation – 'we earnestly express the hope that nothing will be allowed to stand in the way of a speedy progress of these proceedings' – appears to have fallen on deaf ears within some parts of the criminal justice system. This was all the more disappointing because Lord Lane had also observed – 'the evidence by the Avon and Somerset police may have paved the way for expeditious criminal proceedings'.

As already noted, the May Inquiry was set up, with all its limitations which were considerable, on the same day as the Lord Chief Justice gave his judgement. It is difficult, with hindsight, not to recall, and probably agree with, the editorial in the November 1989 issue of *The New Law Journal* which, after referring to the unhappy record of past inquiries with inadequate powers, went on to say:

> The public would be forgiven if it were to believe that inquiries are there to provide a whitewash of authority; of the police, of the prosecutors, of the trial judge . . .

[10]Final Report – page 3.

> It is not too late for Sir John May to demand that he is given *carte blanche* to inquire just how and where things went wrong and where the buck really does stop. It is in everyone's interests – not least senior police officers and the Director of Public Prosecutions – to ensure this is done. If it is not, there will be whispers and sniggers that justice has once again been conducted behind closed doors and has come out in favour of the establishment.

The trial of the three Surrey police officers – Detective Chief Inspector Style, Detective Sergeant Donaldson, Detective Constable Attwell– finally started on 20 April, 1993. They were all found not guilty on 19 May. The trial attracted wide criticism in the press. Much of this stemmed from the procedure adopted by the judge (Mr Justice Macpherson as he then was) in that he permitted the defence to make an opening statement to the jury immediately after the prosecution's. This was a recent procedural development which had so far been restricted to complicated fraud trials. However, such opening statements are normally permitted only if the defendants are willing to give evidence. The judge did not ask them if they wished to give evidence. They did not do so. This procedure enabled the defence to influence the way in which the case was conducted by giving the appearance of legitimacy to the statements and allegations they were to make on behalf of their clients.

The police generally tended to be critical of other defendants who chose to exercise this right. In fact, in the aftermath of the Police and Criminal Evidence Act (PACE) of 1984, considerable pressure was built up by the police threatening the future of the right to silence on the grounds that PACE had rendered it obsolete. In 1987, Sir Peter Imbert, Commissioner of the Metropolitan Police, said:

> The right to silence might have been designed by criminals for their special benefit and that of their professional advisers. It has done more to obscure the truth and facilitate crime than anything else this century.[11]

People outside the criminal justice system, and indeed many within it, experienced bewilderment at the conduct and outcome of the case. In the words of *The Independent* on 20 May 1993 – 'The key defence tactic was to turn the trial of the Surrey police into a retrial of the Guildford Four'. There was a creeping sense of unease amongst the public.

Such unease can best be understood by a brief review of some of

[11]Presumed Guilty – Michael Mansfield QC, page 121.

the observations made in the press. The criminal justice system was again subjected to a range of criticisms not dissimilar to, but maybe not so extensive as, those that followed the quashing of the Guildford Four convictions. Some of the main examples were:

> None of these inconsistencies [in the Guildford Four confessions] were aired in the trial which ended yesterday. Nor were other problems with the evidence from Surrey police which prompted the Court of Appeal to free the Four in 1989 after 15 years in prison.
>
> At the Appeal, Roy Amlot QC, representing the Crown, said that as well as prima-facie questions about evidence in relation to Mr Armstrong's' confession, there were similar problems involving the other officers [in their report the Avon and Somerset Police had named 12 suspect officers] in relation to confessions taken from Mr Hill. Further there were two sets of custody records for the Four, implying one was false.
>
> The Director of Public Prosecutions decided to charge the three officers in relation to the Armstrong confession.
>
> – *The Independent*, 20 May, 1993

> Nineteen years of investigations into the horrific bombings of two Guildford pubs have cost the taxpayer £19m – and still we are no closer to finding out the truth . . . The law, which freed the Guildford Four by deciding the police had concocted evidence, was now saying the police were not guilty either. Surely both verdicts could not be true?
>
> – *The Sunday Times*, 23 May, 1993

> The case centred simply on whether the three officers fabricated one confession . . . More than three years after the acquittals [of the Guildford Four] no official body has made public, [or even informed the Guildford Four of] all the evidence that led to the quashing of the Guildford Four convictions.
>
> – *The Independent*, 20 May, 1993

Despite warnings from the judge that the jury only concern itself with the activities of the police officers:

> But from the start of the trial the defence contended that Armstrong had been guilty and that his imprisonment had not been a miscarriage. Mr Edmund Lawson QC for DC Attwell told the jury 'In one word the allegation in this case is fabrication. The question you have to ask yourselves is; Why fabricate the truth?'
>
> – *The Daily Telegraph*, 20 May, 1993

Anthony Evans QC for DS Donaldson:

> The innocent Patrick Armstrong [one of the Four] does not exist. He is being created by the ill-informed, the mis-informed, and the not-want-to-be-informed.
> – *The Independent*, 20 May, 1993

Anthony Glass QC for DCI Style:

> 'The Horse and Groom was the worst peacetime outrage since 1945. That bombing was carried out by Patrick Armstrong.' He added that the jury that had convicted him in 1975 'had reached a just conclusion'.
> – *The Times*, 20 May, 1993

> Mr Alastair Logan, solicitor for Armstrong, said the defence had made allegations against his client which they had never had to back up because the policemen declined to give evidence.
> – *The Daily Telegraph*, 20 May, 1993

> [The] . . . trial was the first opportunity for any court to hear details of several long statements made by two of the Guildford Four outside the context of the criminal proceedings against them . . . The statements were given by Mr Conlon and Mr Armstrong to Sir Peter Imbert . . . [who] was collecting anti-terrorist intelligence, not evidence for use in court[12] . . . These statements were disallowed in the Court of Appeal in 1977.
> – *The Daily Telegraph*, 20 May, 1993

> It was suggested, wrongly, that Armstrong had refused to come to court to defend his reputation. In fact, there had been a dispute with police about how he should make a statement because of his medical condition; but he was willing to give evidence.
> – *Sunday Times*, 23 May, 1993

> But the police also declined to give evidence.
> – *The Guardian*, 20 May, 1993

> The unexpected quashing of the [Guildford Four] convictions pre-empted an appeal set for the following January in which other serious points would have been voiced; points which the legal establishment and the Government has yet to answer . . . But it is safe

[12]Chapter 8 Pages 215 to 217 – *The Imbert Tapes.*

to assume that if the Crown still believed in the guilt of the Guildford Four it would not have thrown in the 'towel'.
– *The Guardian*, 20 May, 1993

In a leader:

In a remarkable speech last October, Sir John Woodcock, the Chief Inspector of Police, conceded that police forces had indulged in a century of corner-cutting expediency and being 'economical with the truth' . . .

. . . malpractice happened because of poor supervision and an adversarial game that encouraged officers to bend the rules to secure convictions . . . No response from the other, more serious culprits that Sir John identified in his speech: judges, prosecutors and the Bar . . .

. . . He rightly asserted that, without judicial complicity, the malpractice could not have continued . . .

The leader then concluded:

. . . Now May should reopen public hearings on the more senior figures involved. Without that, as Lord Scarman has grimly noted, the full truth will never be known.
– *The Guardian*, 20 May, 1993

Yesterday's acquittal of the three former Surrey policemen, accused of fabricating evidence at the 1975 trial of the Guildford Four cannot be left as the last word. It is imperative that Sir John May should now reopen the official inquiry which he had to adjourn in the light of impending proceedings against the three.
– *The Daily Telegraph*, 20 May, 1993

In the absence of any member of the Guildford Four or any of the policemen accused of 'framing' them, the Court case was not so much *Hamlet* without the prince as *Hamlet* without the entire royal House of Denmark.
– *The Daily Telegraph*, 20 May, 1993

After recalling the Appeal Court accepted the confessions which convicted the Guildford Four may have been concocted:

What a mess! But at least there is one clear lesson to be learned from the muddle of this most unsatisfactory judicial marathon: confessions uncorroborated by other evidence, are about as safe as unexploded bombs.
– *The Daily Mail*, 20 May, 1993

It was reported in many papers that, after the verdicts, Mr Justice Macpherson said – 'It seems to me that maybe the public and certainly those involved on the legal side would not wish to gaze at the entrails of this case further'. Kenneth Clarke, the Home Secretary, said – 'I hope we can put this whole unhappy episode behind us'. On 21 May 1993 *The Guardian* reported that Sir John May had indicated the previous day his determination to complete his report on the Guildford Four convictions. 'He is shrugging off what are being interpreted as veiled warnings from the judge who presided over the Old Bailey trial of three police officers.'

On 20 May Cardinal Hume wrote to Mrs Mills after the three police officers had been found 'not guilty' saying he was happy for them on that account. However there were some aspects of the whole situation which remained disturbing. The two central points on which he suggested there needed to be further investigation were:

> At no point during the trial was evidence offered that the notes in question were contemporaneous. The assumption must be, therefore, that they were not contemporaneous.
>
> The Lord Chief Justice said the evidence procured by the Avon and Somerset Police showed quite clearly that the so-called contemporaneous records of interviews with Armstrong, relied upon by the officers in giving evidence, were not contemporaneous records at all.

In her reply on 15 June Mrs Mills said that at the trial the three defendants accepted that they were responsible for creating the documents. The issue was not *who* created them but *when* they were created and for what purpose. She then devoted a whole paragraph to explaining the different standards of proof acceptable in the Court of Appeal and a criminal trial. She concluded – 'The acquittal of the Surrey police officers demonstrated that the Crown failed to satisfy the jury to the required standard'. She hoped this would explain why a further investigation would not assist matters.

Her letter was considered at a meeting of the Deputation. Concern was expressed at the presentation of the prosecution case at the trial. In particular, accepting that the prosecution had failed to convince the jury of the timing and purpose of the creation of the documents, the question remained whether there was some other explanation of their creation. A photocopy of the actual response to the DPP, signed by the four remaining members of the Deputation, Lord Devlin having died in 1992, is on the following pages.

ARCHBISHOP'S HOUSE, WESTMINSTER, LONDON, SW1P 1QJ

27 July 1993

Dear Mrs Mills,

At a recent meeting of the Deputation we considered your letter of 15 June 1993, which was in response to Cardinal Hume's letter of 20 May.

Perhaps we should say at the outset that we are aware of the different approaches and procedures adopted by the Court of Appeal and by courts hearing criminal trials, and we do understand that the findings by the Court of Appeal in their judgements do not constitute admissible evidence in a criminal trial.

In common with many people we found the press reports on the conduct of the Surrey police officers' trial somewhat confusing and even disconcerting. It was some time after the conclusion of the trial, in fact only a few weeks ago, that we had access to summaries of the official transcripts of parts of the proceedings and of the judge's summing up. From there it is clear that, as you say, the defendants accepted they were responsible for creating the documents. This left the issue of when they were created and for what purpose.

Turning to the transcripts of the proceedings and judgement of the Court of Appeal, there does not appear to have been any doubt whatsoever as to when they were created and for what purpose. Mr Amlot said:

> It is impossible to see why the draft notes take the form they do unless they were made before the manuscript notes. If they were, the manuscript notes cannot have been made during the interviews, nor can the officers offer a satisfactory explanation now. The inescapable conclusion is that no contemporaneous notes were made of each interview, as indeed was suggested by the defence at the trial, and that the officers seriously misled the court.

In the judgement the Lord Chief Justice said:

> It is accepted, and rightly accepted by the Crown, if I may say so, that the manuscript notes produced at the trial were not what the Surrey police officers said on oath they were. The officers, to use Mr Amlot's somewhat anodyne expression, seriously misled the court. In fact they must have lied.

We have no wish whatsoever to even appear to be vindictive towards the Surrey police officers. However, it came as nothing short of amazement to many people that the prosecution was unable to convince the jury in the same way that Mr Amlot, using all the same evidence by the Avon and Somerset police as was available to the prosecution, was able to convince the Court of Appeal.

We accept that an investigation into who prepared the manuscript notes is not now necessary since the three defendants admitted that they were responsible. But in the light of subsequent events and the repercussions emanating therefrom, you may well have already considered there could be merit in reviewing where things stand. Accepting that the police officers were found not guilty and that, as you say, the prosecution failed to convince the jury of the timing and purpose of the creation of the documents, is there some other explanation of their creation?

There is a further point here. We have heard it was common knowledge that the Crown knew for a considerable period of time that the defence case, in a nutshell, would be to try and convince the jury that Patrick Armstrong was guilty of the offences. It has now come to our hearing that some responsible press representatives present at the trial challenged Mr Bevan about the way he was allowing attacks to be made upon Patrick Armstrong, and about his refusal to intervene or protest at the way that defence were able to put their case. We understand that Mr Bevan's reply was that he was doing as he was instructed. Is this true, and if so what does it mean? This is a serious matter, particularly as Patrick Armstrong was not called to give evidence.

We raise these points not only because of their importance in relation to the Surrey officers' trial and the forthcoming report of the May Inquiry but also because they may be germane to future trials, and in particular the trial of West Midlands police officers involved in the Birmingham Six case.

We have heard reports that Mr Boal is to represent the Crown in the West Midlands police trial. In the Court of Appeal hearing of the Birmingham Six case, Mr Boal argued firmly that the Birmingham Six were guilty. Regardless of what instructions he might be given, the general public could be forgiven for questioning whether it is possible for counsel, no matter how able and honourable he might be, to perform the mental gymnastics required to ensure presentation of a forceful and effective case for the Crown in the police case. Such murmurings amongst the public could only damage even further the diminishing respect for the quality of British justice.

Yours sincerely,

Archbishop of Westminster

Lord Scarman

Lord Jenkins of Hillhead

Lord Merlyn-Rees

Mrs Barbara Mills QC
Director of Public Prosecutions
CPS Headquarters
4–12 Queen Anne's Gate
LONDON SW1H 9AZ

In her reply on 25 August the DPP regretted she could add very little to the explanation she had already provided. She spoke again about the different standards of proof between courts and added that, after a 'searching and thorough investigation into this matter' for four years, she did not believe 'that there is anything further to be reviewed'. She said the case was presented on the basis that the issue was whether the rough typed notes or the supposedly contemporaneous notes were created first. Mr Bevan denied making remarks, he was acting as instructed, and she was satisfied he 'presented the prosecution skilfully and professionally'. As to Mr Boal, she was confident he would handle the prosecution of the West Midlands police officers wisely and well.

After discussions with Lord Scarman, Cardinal Hume wrote again to Mrs Mills on 13 September. The key points made were:

> The issue at the trial was whether the claimed written record of confession by Armstrong was a true record or a fabrication. This is the one issue calling for a proper investigation.
>
> It is not understood why the mass of information and documents, elicited and reported on by the Avon and Somerset Police prior to the trial, and additional to what had been available to Mr Amlot at the Court of Appeal, was not brought to the attention of the court.
>
> The defence was allowed without protest to emphasise the contrast between the 'guilty' Armstrong who 'failed' to give evidence and the three respected policemen accused of fabricating his confession. The Crown neither objected nor even protested at this line of defence.

In her short reply on 22 September Mrs Mills said she had endeavoured to answer fully and carefully the points which had been raised about the prosecution. There was nothing further she could say. She added that Mr Graham Boal had unfortunately been taken ill and the prosecution of the West Midlands police would now be led by Victor Temple QC.

This exchange of letters marked the end of the correspondence between Cardinal Hume, on behalf of the Deputation, and the DPP. What remained to be seen now, at this time, was how all these matters would be handled by the May Inquiry, to which the Deputation, as a last resort, continued to attach the greatest importance.

Before finally leaving the police trial, Sir John May's comments on the outcome in his Final Report[13] are not without interest. He referred

[13]Final Report, page 6.

to 'the evidence about Armstrong's original confessions and about information on terrorist activities which he allegedly gave before his conviction . . . The evidence of senior Metropolitan and Surrey police officers was that he had confessed freely and that he gave extensive information'. Sir John May's observations on all this are reproduced below without comment:

> It is hardly surprising that Armstrong and others of the Guildford Four and their supporters should feel aggrieved at the admission of this evidence and the media attention which it attracted. It seems to me to be an example of the lengths to which trial judges go to achieve fairness for the defendants on trial before them. The rule against the admission of hearsay evidence is commonly waived out of fairness to a defendant whilst applied with full vigour to evidence against him. The fact is that in April and May 1993 the Guildford Four were not on trial and in jeopardy of conviction; the former police officers were.
>
> . . . It is in my view inevitable that the price of fairness to a defendant on trial (or an appellant before the Court of Appeal) is occasional apparent unfairness to others.

Over the period 1990 to 1993 there were two meetings between members of the Deputation and Sir John May. The first, an informal meeting, had been requested by Sir John shortly after his Inquiry had been set up and was held on 22 January, 1990[14]. The second meeting, on 3 September, 1993, was held at the request of the Deputation who were by then becoming anxious about developments within the Inquiry which had come to their knowledge. Reference will be made later to this second meeting.

At the first meeting various important aspects of both the Maguire Seven and Guildford Four cases were discussed at some length. It was at that meeting that Sir John May requested a brief on the Maguire Seven case on which he was about to start work. The brief[15] on the case was subsequently sent to the May Inquiry. A copy together with its Annex, is at APPENDIX XII.

In addition to the meetings, over the ensuing months copies of various documents were sent to the Inquiry. Amongst the most important were the Deputation's full submission, covering both cases, to the Home Secretary on 23 July, 1987 (pages 105 to 115 in Chapter Five); a register of some 19 letters on the Maguire Seven case from Cardinal Hume to various Home Secretaries and the Prime Minister over the

[14]Chapter Eight, page 211. [15]Chapter Eight, page 213.

period 1979 to 1987; a substantial Deputation letter to the Home Secretary on 22 September, 1988 (pages 148 to 153 in Chapter Six) disputing and refuting his reasons for not referring the Guildford Four case which he had given to Cardinal Hume on the visit to Archbishop's House on 8 September 1988; and, finally, on 16 November 1988 a letter[16] from Cardinal Hume to the Home Secretary in which the Deputation went public for the first time, in general terms on three considerations of compelling importance, while not departing from their self-imposed restriction of not revealing evidence not already in the public domain.

By May 1993, after the trial of the Surrey police officers, the assumption was that the Final Report of the May Inquiry would be published in the autumn as had been previously indicated. However, by June, word came to the Deputation that events were being protracted by discussions between the Inquiry, some members of the prosecution team for the Guildford Four case, and certain police officers. Rightly or wrongly, the assumption at Archbishop's House was that some people, who might be criticised in the Report, were, quite fairly, being given an opportunity to comment on the proposed text, and to explain their own version of events.

Confirmation of such possible discussions having taken place was indeed given on page 13 of the Final Report. Following the list of 14 issues to which the Inquiry had given special attention[17], Sir John May goes on to say – 'As part of my examination of these issues I heard oral evidence at a number of private hearings attended by witnesses and their legal representatives'. These hearings took place over the period 1 June 1993 to 22 February 1994. The witnesses listed included Michael Hill QC, Paul Purnell QC, and Philip Havers, all members of the prosecution team, and also Sir Peter Imbert (as he then was), together with Christopher Rowe and Ronald Underwood, former senior officers of the Surrey Constabulary. It is of interest that the 14 issues included, amongst others, the arrests of Frank Johnson, the evidence of Maura Kelly and Yvonne Fox, the 'Burke alibi', disclosure of forensic correlation statements, follow up of the Balcombe Street gang involvement and the handling by the Home Office of representations made on behalf of the Guildford Four.

The holding of these private hearings may well have contributed to the delay in publication of the Final Report from autumn 1993 to 30 June, 1994. But at least two other events also contributed. The first was a lengthy and forceful letter sent to the Home Secretary on 2 June, 1993 by Cardinal Hume. This letter included a list of 'eight questions' which the Deputation considered had to be answered fully by the May

[16]Chapter Six, pages 154 to 156. [17]Final Report, pages 12 and 13.

Inquiry if the 'whole truth' was to emerge. The second event was a letter from Birnbergs, representing Gerard Conlon, to the May Inquiry on 2 February, 1994. This letter dealt in great detail with, amongst other things, the possible nature of discussions going on within the Inquiry about the 'Burke alibi' which had come to their ears.

Against the background of these discussions, the Deputation letter together with the 'eight questions' was sent by Cardinal Hume to the new Home Secretary, Michael Howard, on 2 June, 1993. (A list of the 'eight questions' is at APPENDIX XIII.) A copy was also sent to Sir John May. At the time it was, of course, not known that Birnbergs would be writing to the May Inquiry on 2 February, 1994. It so happened that much of their letter impinged upon some of the 'eight questions', particularly in relation to the 'Burke alibi'. Consequently, by the time the Final Report of the Inquiry was published in June 1994, the Inquiry would have had an opportunity to study both the Deputation letter of 2 June, 1993, together with its 'eight questions', and also the Birnberg letter of 2 February, 1994.

In the light of this, it would be both appropriate and helpful to consider, first, the main points in the Deputation letter itself, but not the 'eight questions' at this stage, and then the main issues raised in the Birnberg letter. Consideration could then be given to the responses made by the Inquiry in their Final Report of 30 June, 1994 to the 'eight questions' which formed part of the Deputation letter of 2 June, 1993.

Essentially Cardinal Hume's letter of 2 June, 1993 to the new Home Secretary was by way of being a comprehensive brief on how the Deputation saw the present situation. The stage was set by the opening paragraph:

> I am writing to you to express my concern at the unsatisfactory state which has developed in the realm of criminal justice affairs. The appeal court hearing on the Guildford Four case in October 1989 was truncated because of the single but very grave matter raised by the DPP. The whole truth did not emerge, no more than it did in the recent trial of the Surrey police officers. Many share my view that action needs to be taken to rectify the general position which has now arisen, and later in this letter I make positive proposals.

The first few pages of the lengthy letter were given over to recalling, in some detail, the principal events relating to the Guildford Four and Maguire Seven cases which had taken place since 1986. The main events were:

1986/87 saw the coming together of the Deputation, each for their own reasons and of their own volition, and all convinced there had been a miscarriage of justice in the two cases.

On 23 July, 1987 a substantial submission[18] consisting of facts (new alibi evidence by Maura Kelly, Mr and Mrs Keenan, Yvonne Fox and Fathers Ryan and Carolan of the hostel) and a point of law presented to Home Secretary by whole Deputation.

Point of law was Joint Opinion by Lord Devlin and Lord Scarman who held that in 1977 the Court of Appeal erred so resulting in the whole of the evidence of Balcombe Street gang, part of which they had accepted, never being heard by a jury.

The Home Secretary received the Avon and Somerset Police report in April 1988. He said on a visit to Cardinal Hume on 8 September, 1988 that he would not be referring the case and gave his reasons.[19] These were refuted in a substantial letter[20] to the Home Secretary on 22 September, 1988. This led him to modify his view.

On 16 November, 1988,[21] because of delays on decision, Cardinal Hume drew attention in general terms, in a further letter, to three considerations of compelling importance without departing from the Deputation's self-imposed restriction of not revealing details of new evidence not in the public domain.

In January 1989 the Home Secretary referred the Guildford Four case but his decision not to refer the Maguire case came as a disappointment. Nevertheless, the Deputation was confident if the Guildford Four convictions were found not to be safe and satisfactory the Maguire convictions would immediately be brought into question. The two cases were inseparable.

The Appeal was heard by a hastily convened Court of Appeal on 19 October, 1989. In his masterly presentation[22] Mr Amlot concluded no contemporaneous notes were made of each interview with Patrick Armstrong and the trial court had been seriously misled.

In his judgement the Lord Chief Justice said the evidence showed that the so-called contemporaneous record of the principal interview

[18]Chapter Five, pages 105 to 115. [19]Chapter Six, page 114. [20]Chapter Six, pages 148 to 153. [21]Chapter Six, pages 154 to 156. [22]Chapter Seven, pages 180 to 188.

conducted by the Surrey Police with Patrick Armstrong which contained his 'confession', and on which the officers relied when giving evidence, was not a contemporaneous record at all.

After quashing the convictions, the Lord Chief Justice earnestly hoped that the DPP would allow nothing to stand in the way of speedy progress of proceedings following the matters reported by the Avon and Somerset Police.

It was indicative of the overriding significance the Crown attached to the report on statements and records by the Avon and Somerset Police that the three original grounds for reference by the Home Office (alibi statements by Maura Kelly and Yvonne Fox and medical reports on Carole Richardson)[23] were not presented to or considered by the Court.

Mr Amlot commented those grounds would have been resisted by the Crown. All defence counsel said there were compelling and powerful arguments as to why the convictions were unsafe and unsatisfactory included in, but also extending beyond, the original grounds for reference.

These additional matters included the decision by the prosecution not to reveal to the defence the fact that the method and idiosyncratic nature of the construction of the Balcombe Street gang bombs was a matter which would have been relevant at the trial.

Also the matter of the Burke alibi. He had made a statement to the police in January 1975, and a confirmatory statement to the Avon and Somerset Police in June 1988. None of this was known to the defence until May 1989.

Cardinal Hume went on to say:

The trial of the three Surrey police officers was finally concluded on 19 May, 1993. The three officers were found 'not guilty' and the Deputation is happy for them on that account. However, there are some aspects of the whole situation which the Deputation finds disturbing. To my knowledge, at no point during the trial was evidence offered that the notes in question were contemporaneous. The assumption must be, therefore, that they were not contemporaneous as was stated so clearly by Mr Amlot at the Court of Appeal and

[23]Chapter Seven, pages 189 to 191.

emphatically endorsed by the Lord Chief Justice. But the matter is very much more complex and serious than that.

There is a larger problem and it goes to the very roots of British justice. Justice is truth – and without truth there can be no justice. It has to be accepted that the whole truth when revealed can be harmful to individuals and to the institutions which they man. At all costs, even that of individual reputations, the integrity of and respect for institutions must be preserved. This can only be done in the eyes of the professionals who man the institutions, and in the eyes of the public, by taking steps to ensure the whole truth is revealed.

It must surely be that it is because the whole truth was not revealed at the Court of Appeal on 19 October, 1989, or during the recent police trial, that there is now a widespread uncomfortable feeling about at least some aspects of British justice. No official body has yet considered all the evidence relating to the Guildford Four that was available to the Court of Appeal both in the original grounds for reference by the Home Office and the additional grounds (e.g. the Burke statement) which Counsel would have presented if there had been a full hearing.

Regardless of what the Royal Commission on Criminal Justice might recommend, the only instrument left to clear up the past and so establish a firm platform on which to build the future is the May Inquiry. From the very outset our Deputation has strongly supported the May Inquiry and has had confidence in its courage and ability to establish the truth.

As you know, the May Inquiry was set up on 19 October, 1989 by the then Home Secretary, Mr Douglas Hurd MP, and its terms of reference were 'to inquire into the circumstances leading up to and deriving from the trials of the Guildford Four and the Maguire Seven'. Up until July 1992 it held public hearings as a result of which the Maguires case was referred to the Court of Appeal and the convictions were quashed.

After July 1992, because of the impending trial of the Surrey police officers, it was decided not to proceed with full public hearings in the Guildford and Woolwich cases. Provisional conclusions from an account of the cases based on documentary evidence were to be prepared, and those with an interest were to be invited to provide written, or possibly oral, observations on them. A draft report was then to be made available to the Royal Commission so that it can take account of any relevant conclusions before it completes its work.

I fully appreciate that the May Inquiry has extensive documentary evidence available to it and note that it has stated its investigations

> would go beyond matters dealt with at the recent trial, and further than the evidence before the Court of Appeal in 1989. It may well be that the draft report to be made available to the Royal Commission will focus on organisational and procedural matters, which are within their remit, rather than on incidents, actions or inactions which were special to these cases. In view of this, it is very unlikely that the whole truth about certain actions or inactions will emerge. This would be quite wrong.

Cardinal Hume said the Deputation would welcome specific answers to the 'eight Questions' (APPENDIX XIII) which were listed in the letter. He concluded the letter to the Home Secretary:

> I firmly believe that the confidence of the professionals engaged in the various parts of the criminal justice system, and most importantly that of the public, will not be restored until the whole truth about all eight of the above questions is made public however uncomfortable the consequences might be.

In his reply on 21 June, Michael Howard said, amongst other things, that the eight questions were not ones on which he was in a position to comment, but agreed they were very much a matter for the May Inquiry to consider. He confirmed he had sent a copy of the whole letter and the eight questions to Sir John May. It was, of course, a matter for him to decide how to conduct his Inquiry.

In the circumstances prevailing at the time, and bearing in mind discussions being held within the Inquiry, the importance of the 'eight questions' came very much to the fore. During August arrangements were therefore made for a meeting between Sir John May, and Cardinal Hume and Lord Scarman from the Deputation to take place on 3 September using as a basis full notes which had been prepared by the Deputation on each of the eight questions. The purpose of the meeting was to explain in some detail the concerns of the Deputation relating to each of the questions.

The meeting was followed on 16 September by a lengthy letter from Cardinal Hume to Sir John May expressing in forthright terms the need for full and clear answers to the eight questions. They were matters which all went to the very heart of the prosecution process and impinged on its integrity. The letter confirmed that all members of the Deputation were acutely aware that the stage had now been reached where the May Inquiry, and that alone, could expose the apparent procedural irregularities which appeared to have taken place.

It would be more fruitful to discuss the matters raised in the letter and the questions towards the end of the chapter when the responses to the questions by the Inquiry in their Final Report are examined. Meanwhile it would be appropriate to turn now to the Birnberg letter of 2 February, 1994 to the May Inquiry. The reason why, following several telephone conversations with the Inquiry, Gareth Peirce of Birnbergs had written the letter of 2 February, 1994 became apparent when the Final Report of the Inquiry was published. As already mentioned, on page 13 of the Report is the list of witnesses who attended private hearings during the period June 1993 to February 1994. No doubt these hearings were supplemented by correspondence both before and after the hearings. Clearly, word had got to Birnbergs that there had been much discussion in the Inquiry about alibis, particularly those for Gerard Conlon whom Gareth Peirce of Birnbergs was representing – hence her letter to the Inquiry of 2 February, 1994.

It is significant that, amongst the private hearings listed on page 13 of the Report, two of the witnesses heard at the last hearing on 22 February, 1994 were Gordon Ward, junior counsel for Gerard Conlon at trial and for the 1977 appeal, together with David Walsh of Conlon's solicitors in 1974/75. Also shown as 'present' at that hearing were Michael Hill QC and Gareth Peirce. Her presence was no doubt accounted for by the impact of her powerful letter of 2 February, 1994. The motivation for Birnbergs to write this letter is to be found near the end of the letter:

> We hope that having gone through some of the aspects that you will understand how and why it is that we feel excluded from the process that is and has been going on within the inquiry and yet party to it, and why it is that we are deeply concerned that this should not be the case . . .
>
> We wished, of course, to obtain Mr Conlon's consent before interviewing Mr Ward and Mr Walsh . . . we would wish to be reassured that we might now be present at any future relevant proceedings and able to raise questions with other parties where we have particular knowledge.

After referring at the beginning of the letter to the copies of correspondence between the Inquiry and Ward and Walsh, which had been sent to Gareth Peirce together with various transcripts, she continued that she did need to know 'what it is that the prosecution are now saying and what questions they want to ask'. She said she was left with the impression that the prosecution 'are now seeking to suggest that the defence knew Charles Burke was a witness who could potentially give evidence as to alibi, that they pursued this, that they found or could have found Charles Burke, and that they had become aware that his evidence was potentially valueless'.

Gareth Peirce went on to express concern at hearing of some of the assertions and assumptions now being made. She had been unaware of these until now and she set out to refute or correct them in the letter with substantial material. The main assumptions and assertions on which she commented were –

> The assumption that Sister Power [staff at the Conway House Hostel] necessarily had records in her possession which she provided to the police giving the current address of Charles Burke.
>
> The assumption that Mr Walsh [Conlon's solicitor in 1974/75] went to see Sister Power at the hostel for the purpose of obtaining Charles Burke's address.
>
> The expressed opinion that the defence knew that Burke's potential alibi was not effective.
>
> The prosecution assertion there was no contemporaneous evidence of Gerard Conlon being affected by drinks or drugs at the time, but only subsequently.
>
> The theme that now appears to be being put forward by the prosecution that Charles Burke was believed to have gone to Ireland.

The letter dealt with several other important points of detail relating to alibis and records. There was also the telling comment that the prosecution's 'assumptions as to any person's ability to recollect movements and activities in the disorganised context of a young man's life living in a hostel away from home are bereft of understanding of his social milieu'.

The letter ended with a startling revelation. Birnbergs had been told some considerable time before by David Clarke QC, Counsel to the Inquiry, that the Inquiry could not now go into the question of ill-treatment or otherwise in police stations as the matter was too old and it would not be profitable to explore differing opinions.

It so happened that Birnbergs were asked to act as agent for the solicitors representing Paul Hill in his appeal in the murder charge of an ex-soldier in Belfast. In the course of carrying out this function they were deeply concerned to find that 'since 1990 there have been in existence statements taken by the Avon and Somerset Police which disclose a number of critical factors affecting the entire case'. None of this was known to the defence until it was revealed at the Court of Appeal in Belfast in March 1994. Their letter listed eight factors as set out below:

1. A number of police officers serving in Surrey in 1974 state clearly that they either *saw* or *heard directly from* (or heard of) one police officer who pointed his gun into the cell where suspects to do with these bombings were being detained and that he subsequently boasted of having done this in such a way that numerous officers were aware. These are serious and sincere witnesses.
2. That two Metropolitan officers, one senior and one more junior, went in to the Godalming charge room (the cell complex) during the course of the detention of these bombing suspects and requested that the custody officer leave his post for 20 minutes while they went to the cells (to talk to one of the suspects).
3. Home office forensic examination suggests that records of Mr Underwood (one of the very senior Surrey officers in charge of this enquiry) were falsified in relation to interviews with Annie Maguire, and that this was done by officers ■■■ and ■■■.
4. ESDA test evidence suggests that interviews were falsified in relation to Frank Johnson by officers Longhurst, Wise and Mills. (These are the officers implicated in the altered notes of John McGuinness' interview sent to you by us now some time ago).
5. Forensic evidence suggests that interview notes were falsified in relation to Lisa Astin by officers Longhurst, Wise, Mills and Lewis.
6. Examination of documents suggest that notes of interviews made by officers Longhurst, Wise and Mills relating to Carole Richardson were falsified.
7. Further evidence suggests WPC Croxon further falsified notes relating to the above.
8. Evidence exists to suggest that Mr [Chief Superintendent] Simmons (another Surrey officer in charge of this enquiry) authorised improper and lengthy interviews with Paul Hill about which officers Blake and Lewis subsequently lied.

In connection with all this, the letter asserted that 'there is now evidence to suggest that 11 of the 12 Surrey officers can be implicated in malpractice, and 2 of the 3 (or 4) Metropolitan officers who interviewed the four defendants'.

In his Final Report[24] Sir John May made fleeting reference to only factor 1 above and did not investigate the rest. He was, however, quite specific on the implications of these revelations:

[24]Final Report, pages 8 and 9.

■■■ Names not already in public domain but known to May Inquiry.

> If the material which was before the Court of Appeal in Belfast had been before the judge and jury at the trial of the Guildford Four in 1975, there can be little doubt that the statements made by Hill and the other three defendants would have been ruled inadmissible and the jury directed to acquit all Four.

It was unfortunate that the May Inquiry did not pursue further the revelation that there were in existence statements held by the Avon and Somerset Police allegedly dealing with the treatment of the defendants and the falsification of interview notes relating to Anne Maguire, Frank Johnson, Lisa Astin and Carole Richardson.

It has to be noted that, at the Court of Appeal on 19 October, 1989, irregularities in relation to Patrick Armstrong's confession, the fifth statement by Paul Hill (in which he implicated Carole Richardson for the first time), and detention records (of which there were two sets) were brought to the attention of the Court. Sir John May does not appear to refer to the detention records but, as far as the irregularities concerning Paul Hill's statement are concerned, he states that[25] – 'after careful consideration of all the material the DPP decided not to institute proceedings'. Consequently only the three Surrey police officers involved in Patrick Armstrong's statements were brought to trial.

There was concern at the time of the Court of Appeal on 19 October, 1989 whether there had also been any irregularities found by the Avon and Somerset Police relating to statements by Gerard Conlon and Carole Richardson. Sir John May records[26] that the Attorney General and the DPP decided that the appeals of all four defendants should be unopposed on the advice of Counsel that 'because the truthfulness and reliability of police evidence was crucial to the convictions of all the four defendants, against whom there had been no evidence other than their respective confessions, the discovery of the suspect interview notes contaminated the case as a whole'. This related only to the confessions of Patrick Armstrong and Paul Hill.

Presumably the Avon and Somerset Police reports revealed above in the Birnberg letter of 2 February, 1994 were held by the DPP. They certainly were not made public, or even known to the defence before 1994 or thereafter. It would have been helpful if the May Inquiry had established who in the DPP had knowledge of these reports, what statements were recorded, what action, if any, was taken on them, and by whom, and why the Avon and Somerset Police had not found the evidence earlier in their searches before 1990.

It is, perhaps, significant that towards the end of his introductory chapter Sir John May recorded the Inquiry's gratitude to the many

[25]Final Report – page 36. [26]Final Report, page 5.

bodies and solicitors who had made material available. This included three of the Guildford Four. He then said:

> Pending the decision on his outstanding appeal in Northern Ireland against his conviction for Shaw's [ex-soldier] murder Hill felt unable to give me similar assistance. Since that appeal was allowed on the 21st April 1994 his solicitors have written saying that he has 'no confidence whatsoever' in my Inquiry, so there I regret that matter must rest.

Having referred to Cardinal Hume's letter of 2 June, 1993, which was sent to the Home Secretary and to Sir John May, and to the meeting with Sir John May on 3 September, 1993, we can now examine the responses in the Final Report of the May Inquiry to the 'eight questions' (APPENDIX XIII). The list of questions is not exhaustive but it does encapsulate some matters arising in the four areas which were of particular concern to the Deputation – namely the handling of alibis, alterations to scientific evidence, forensic links between offences, and non-disclosure of all three. As to alibis, in addition to those in the first question, the treatment of Frank Johnson who was an alibi witness for Carole Richardson was singled out by Sir John May and this was of concern to the Deputation. This will also be referred to later.

The Final Report is a very substantial document – some 300 pages of text, and 10 Appendices, most of which consist of statements by the Guildford Four and the Balcombe Street gang. Many notes of meetings, minutes between counsel, minutes from C3 Division to Ministers, and letters to and from the Home Office are reproduced – some only partially but many in full. As far as the task of focusing on the Inquiry responses to the Deputation's questions is concerned, there is what can fairly be described as an 'information overload' problem. It is, of course, out of the question to record fully all the material discussed, all the possibilities explored, and the sometimes conflicting statements. Every effort has therefore been made to identify and isolate only the key points which can stand alone without the need for possible qualifications or for setting in context.

But there are also some other difficulties in arriving at the true responses to the questions. Perusal of the whole of the Final Report does not reveal an apparent willingness by any part of the criminal justice system to explore positively the possibility of a miscarriage of justice. Refuge is sometimes taken in memory lapses by those giving evidence and being interviewed. Albeit subconsciously perhaps, these can lead to damage limitation. The objective observer could well deduce that a weakness of the prosecution was over-reliance on the validity of the confessions of the Guildford Four. It might be reasonable to conclude that some components of the criminal justice system did not want anything to shake the idea of guilt, and that they were driven by an anxiety not to undermine the validity of the confessions as they saw it.

Each of the eight questions will now be taken in turn. Answers will be sought, as well as can be, from the material in the Final Report.

Question 1
On the matters of fact in the original submission of 20 July 1987 what observations were made by the Avon and Somerset Police to the Home Office on the following parts of the submission, bearing in mind that the first inclination of the Home Office was not to refer the case: –

(a) The statement by Maura Kelly (Richardson alibi)

(b) The statement by Yvonne Fox (Hill alibi for Woolwich)

(c) The statement by Mr and Mrs Keenan (Hill alibi for Woolwich)

(d) The statements of Father Ryan and Father Carolan about Hill and Conlon at Quex Road hostel. (The hostel was the location of the Burke alibi which it was later discovered had been suppressed)

(e) The MacKeith-Gudjonsson medical report on Richardson.

It is not possible to answer this question directly from the Final Report. The Avon and Somerset Police submitted their report to the Home Secretary on 8 April, 1988.[27] The Report was never seen by the Deputation. As recorded in the May Inquiry the police report '. . . examined in detail three main issues. First, Paul Hill's alibi for the Woolwich bombing and the involvement of Mrs Fox; secondly, the alibi for Carole Richardson for the Guildford bombing and the evidence of Maura Kelly; and thirdly, the alibi for Gerard Conlon for the Guildford bombing and the evidence of Charles Burke'. As no direct comments by the police on the issues are recorded in the May Inquiry Report it can only be assumed that such comments as were made were reflected in notes and minutes prepared by C3 Division for Ministers. Some of these are quoted at length by Sir John May.

The introduction by the police of the Burke alibi is of considerable interest. There was no reference to it in the original submission in July 1987 and, even by April 1988, his existence was still unknown to both

[27]Final Report, page 262.

the defence and the Deputation. The Burke alibi is the subject of the second question.

On 25 May, 1988 Mr Baxter, who by then had become head of C3 Division, put a very lengthy and wide-ranging submission[28] to Ministers in which he covered many matters. As far as *Question 1* was concerned, he referred to the new evidence by Maura Kelly, Yvonne Fox and Mr and Mrs Keenan, and also to the MacKeith-Gudjonsson medical report on Carole Richardson. He made no reference to the statements by Father Ryan and Father Carolan.

On Mrs Fox, Baxter said her evidence was clear as was a television interview she gave[29] – 'consequently we cannot dismiss it lightly although we understand from the police that she is likely to be a poor witness and under cross-examination may appear more hesitant and confused than her statement and an edited television programme may suggest'. Later he said – 'we must be careful not to be guided unduly by the police assessments of the characters of the witnesses'. He added that, if Mrs Fox had been called at the trial and had given the evidence she now puts forward, then 'the jury might have been more inclined to believe the Keenan's evidence that Hill was with them at the material time and could not have gone to Woolwich'.

Baxter made no specific reference to the statement by Maura Kelly, but did make the general point that[30] 'Carole Richardson's alibi remains convincing, and timings given by witnesses show that she could not have had time to travel from Guildford to the concert in London where she was later seen'. On the medical evidence[31] in the MacKeith/Gudjonsson Report, Baxter referred to the observation that she is 'highly suggestible' but said this might have been more persuasive at the original trial. Nevertheless, he went on to say – '. . . as she claimed her confessions had been made under pressure from the police, the medical evidence now might weaken any reliance a court would be willing to place on them'.

Before moving on it would be of interest to recall here that the original medical report had been in the hands of the Home Office since April 1986. Sir John May records:[32]

> At a meeting on 6 January, 1987 the Home Secretary, Mr Douglas Hurd, considered with Mr Mellor and officials, including Dr Kilgour, . . . whether the report in itself gave grounds for intervention in her case . . . Mr Hurd concluded that it did not.

Baxter concluded his submission of 25 May, 1988 by saying – 'it is

[28]Final Report, pages 262 to 268. [29]Final Report, page 264. [30]Final Report, page 263. [31]Final Report, page 266. [32]Final Report, page 256.

suggested that the Guildford Four's case should be referred to the Court of Appeal'. However, much was to happen between May 1988 and 8 September, 1988 when the Home Secretary visited Cardinal Hume to inform him that the case would not be referred. He gave as his reasons the alleged discrepancy in statements made by Maura Kelly, the failure of Mr and Mrs Keenan and Paul Hill to mention a 'fourth person' (i.e. Yvonne Fox) in the flat, that the point of law had now been settled in the highest court in the land, and that in the medical evidence the timings were such that Carole Richardson could have been lucid at the time of her confession.

On 22 September, 1988, in response to the points made by the Home Secretary on his visit, Cardinal Hume wrote to him in forceful terms, and at considerable length, refuting his reasons for the non-referral.[33] The letter included as Annexes special reports by Alastair Logan on the police handling of interviews with Maura Kelly, Yvonne Fox and Mr and Mrs Keenan. The point was clearly made that full account would have to be taken of the report at Annex 1 to the letter before any public statement could be made advancing discrepancies in Maura Kelly's evidence as a reason for non-referral. Similarly it was assumed any public statement, based on the Avon and Somerset Police report that Mrs Fox was not present in the flat, would be accompanied by publication of the contents of the report at Annex 2. However, the need for this did not arise.

Following further letters from the Deputation, and the submission of much new additional material by Alastair Logan and Gareth Peirce, the case was referred in January 1989. The points of refutation of the Home Secretary's reasons for not referring the case in the letter of 22 September, 1988[34] were never responded to by the Home Office.

The Deputation regarded this substantial letter as being a turning point in their struggle to secure a referral. To them it marked 'the end of the beginning'. The Final Report made only a somewhat perfunctory reference to the letter – '. . . on 22 September 1988 Cardinal Hume wrote again to the Home Secretary reaffirming his Deputation's growing belief that the convictions were unsafe and unsatisfactory despite doubts raised by the Home Office . . .' There were no quotations from the letter, or indeed any other reference to the contents.

Referring back to *Question 1*, the Avon and Somerset Police were aware that by far the greater part of the new evidence submitted by the Deputation consisted of possible alibis for Carole Richardson, Paul Hill and Gerard Conlon. Any statements relating to alibis were, therefore, of prime importance and particularly as the whole basis of the case against the Guildford Four was their confessions.

[33]Chapter Six, pages 148 to 153. [34]Final Report, page 275.

Before leaving *Question 1*, it was noted earlier that Sir John May had investigated the situation regarding Frank Johnson. This should now be considered. Statements by him were not included in the submission by the Deputation to the Home Secretary in July 1987 because he had not made a new one. Frank Johnson was a key alibi witness for Carole Richardson. If charges against her had failed, there can be little doubt that the whole of the Guildford Four case would have collapsed. Sir John May readily recognised the importance of Frank Johnson and investigated aspects of his treatment in a very thorough fashion. The 'arrests' of Frank Johnson were, in fact, one of the 14 specific issues[35] to which he gave attention. Some of the key observations on Frank Johnson given in his main summary on page 301 of the Final Report were:

> Frank Johnson was arrested on two occasions, first on 19 December, 1974 and then again on 21 January, 1975. I do not think that Johnson's first arrest was justified' . . . the second arrest . . . 'I do not believe this was in fact a proper exercise by the police of their powers [under the PTA] . . .' 'The primary purpose of arresting Johnson . . . was not to elicit information about terrorism but to investigate the alibi.
>
> Believing as they did, that Richardson's confession was unassailable, Surrey's approach was to seek to destroy her alibi rather than investigate with a truly open mind.

Amongst his conclusions in this section of his Report, Sir John May stated:

> I have little doubt that once they had arrested Hill, had been led by him in succession to the other three members and had then obtained the confessions, the Surrey police were wholly satisfied that they had arrested and charged the right people. Any further material or evidence which suggested the contrary could not be credible and was, in effect, put out of mind.

In their notes to *Question 1*, which had been discussed with Sir John May at the meeting on 3 September, 1993, the Deputation had emphasised the need to establish who in the Surrey police was responsible for the adoption and pursuit of this policy. This was never answered.

[35]Final Report, pages 12 and 301.

Question 2
Why was the Burke alibi statement for Conlon of January 1975 placed in a bundle marked 'Not to be shown to the defence,' and by whom?

Why was the confirmatory alibi statement, taken by the Avon and Somerset Police early in 1988, not drawn to the attention of the Home Office or disclosed to the defence? Who was responsible?

Charles Burke made a statement to the police on 18 January, 1975 which constituted an alibi for Gerard Conlon in that it showed he could not have been at Guildford. In their report to the Home Office on 8 April, 1988 the Avon and Somerset Police referred to the evidence of Charles Burke, yet his name had not been mentioned in the Deputation's submission[36] to the Home Secretary in July 1987 because his existence was not known of at that time. The statement by Charles Burke was clearly found by the Avon and Somerset Police at some stage during the searches between August 1987 and the submission of their report to the Home Secretary in April 1988.

Sir John May stated[37] that in their report the Avon and Somerset Police assumed that what Charles Burke had had to say about events on 5 October, 1974 had been known to the defence. Their justification for this assumption was that from the bill of costs they knew the solicitors had written to Charles Burke and they '*believed*[38] that the statement had been among those made available to the defence before the trial'.

Sir John May says – 'This was expressly stated in the report to the Home Secretary'. It was a significant assertion to make. The police and the prosecution might well have asked the question why it was that Charles Burke was not called by the defence at the trial in view of the evidence he could have given. Earlier in his Report, Sir John May had said[39] '. . . it is most important to determine why defence solicitors were aware neither of Burke's address, nor that he had made a statement to the police, nor of the nature of the evidence he could give'.

Against this background, it is now appropriate to return to the specific issues raised in *Question 2*. Extensive notes on this and other questions had been prepared by the Deputation for the meeting with Sir John May on 3 September. The situation was that a copy of the statement by Charles Burke, together with many other documents, had been served in May 1989 on Gareth Peirce, by then representing Gerard Conlon, prior to the hearing in the Court of Appeal in October 1989. On a visit to Avon and Somerset Police, who were holding all the

[36]Chapter Five, page 11. [37]Final Report, page 262. [38]Author's italics.
[39]Final Report, page 81.

documentation from the Surrey police, she found the original statement. As the Deputation understood the situation, it was in a bundle marked 'Not to be shown to the defence'. The May Inquiry pointed out to the Deputation at the meeting on 3 September 1993 that the bundle was in fact marked 'Not shown to the defence'. In a subsequent letter to Sir John May on 13 September, 1993, Cardinal Hume made the point that the Inquiry version of how the bundle was marked made the suppression of the statement more serious in that their correct version confirmed a positive action had been taken whereas the Deputation version could be interpreted as being only one of intent.

Sir John May had researched in depth the confirmatory alibi statement by Charles Burke taken by the Avon and Somerset Police in June 1988. This revealed serious mishandling by the Avon and Somerset Police and within the Home Office. Apparently in July 1988 the Avon and Somerset Police told Mr Stanton of C3 Division that they had now learned that Burke's statement to the police of 18 January, 1975 had never been disclosed to the defence. (It was not revealed how they had learned this.) They also reported orally that they had themselves traced and interviewed Burke. Stanton put this in a minute to Ministers on 14 July, 1988, which included the phrase '. . . they have seen Burke and regard him as a hopeless witness. He is virtually an alcoholic and cannot now recall Conlon's name. He can only say that whatever he said to the police at the time must presumably be true'.

However, Sir John May established[40] that the Avon and Somerset Police had in fact traced Burke in June 1988 and had taken a statement from him dated 9 June, 1988. In that statement he confirmed that what he had said in January 1975 was true, though in 1988 he could only remember the name of Hill as one of his roommates. This statement was not sent to the Home Office and Sir John May added that the Home Office was not told that a statement had been taken, but only that Burke had been traced and interviewed.

Sir John went on to say that on 1 September, 1988 Baxter put a note[41] to Ministers about Gerard Conlon. The note stated that Burke had been interviewed by the police and did not have 'anything of consequence' to say; it made no reference to Stanton's submission of 14 July or to the fact that Burke's original statement to the police had never been disclosed to the defence. Later, in his conclusions,[42] Sir John May said – '. . . C3's approach to Burke had been based on their view of the value of his evidence rather than the significance of the non-disclosure of the statement'.

The whole issue of the Burke alibi was of such importance, that,

[40]Final Report, page 270. [41]Final Report, page 272. [42]Final Report, page 285.

in the interest of completeness, it would be appropriate now to record the main conclusions reached by Sir John May following evidence from, amongst others, Michael Hill QC of the prosecution team. Sir John investigated the issue of the Burke alibi at very great length.

The Guildford Four trial was in September/October 1975. In referring to an Opinion prepared on 16 May, 1975 Sir John recorded that counsel said only that it was 'probable' that the defence had discovered that Burke and Vine had made statements. He then went on to say:[43]

> Their evidence to me, however, was that what had been no more than only belief had hardened to 'actual knowledge' before the trial. Mr Hill told me in evidence that they received information later from which he came to know that the defence knew about Burke; but for this his name and address (though not his statement) would have been supplied.
>
> . . . Prosecuting counsel cannot now say how or from who they learned that the defence knew about Burke . . . I am satisfied that Conlon's defence team did not know about Burke . . . I find it difficult to see any good reason why anyone should pass such erroneous information to Mr Hill or any other member of prosecuting Counsel.

A conclusion reached on page 305 of the Final Report, where Sir John May was considering the handling of representations made on behalf of the Guildford Four, is repeated below without comment:

> The non-disclosure of Conlon's Burke alibi should have been one of the grounds on which the case was referred to the Court of Appeal. That it was not was the consequence of the policy and practice within the Home Department and no official deserves blame for it.

Sir John May's final observation[44] in the main section covering the Burke alibi issue was:

> . . . I reject any suggestion that counsel or the DPP or Surrey acted deliberately to suppress Conlon's alibi. On the other hand . . . I do not think that there was any sufficient reason for failing to disclose Burke's name and address under the then prevailing practice. This practice obscured the wider obligation of fairness which in my view should have led to the disclosure of the statement itself, or at least of such indication of the nature of the contents.

[43]Final Report, page 87. [44]Final Report, page 90.

The last paragraph under *Question 2* in the notes prepared by the Deputation for discussion with Sir John May at the meeting on 3 September, 1993 was –

> It has to be fundamentally wrong that those responsible for all these failures of disclosure have not been confronted with their actions.

In spite of his researches, Sir John did not establish who had decided to place the original statement by Charles Burke in a bundle marked 'Not shown to the defence', why this was done, why Burke's confirmatory statement in June 1988 was not drawn to the attention of the Home Office or the defence, and who was responsible for these various matters.

Question 3
At the Balcombe Street trial (1977) government forensic scientists testified that, before the Guildford trial they had prepared statements showing forensic links between the explosions at Guildford and Woolwich and other IRA explosions with which the accused could not be associated. Why was that report not disclosed to the defence at the Guildford trial and who was responsible?

It is important to note the chronology of events. The Guildford and Woolwich bombings took place on 5 October 1974 and 7 November 1974 respectively. The Guildford Four trial was held in September/ October 1975. The Balcombe Street Active Service Unit was arrested when the siege of Balcombe Street was concluded on 13 December 1975. Their trial was in February 1977. The appeal of the Guildford Four was heard by the Court of Appeal in October 1977.

It should also be recalled that the Balcombe Street ASU was engaged in two phases of operations – Phase 1, July 1974 to January 1975 (which included the Guildford and Woolwich bombings) and Phase 2, August 1975 (bombing of the Caterham Arms public house) to December 1975 when the ASU surrendered. The Caterham Arms bomb was in all respects, forensically speaking, a carbon copy of the Guildford bomb. Additionally, as Sir John May said in his Final Report,[45] –

[45]Final Report, page 165.

'... As at Guildford, the target was a busy public house used by soldiers, the bomb was placed under a bench seat and employed a Smith's pocket watch as its timing device'.

Sir John went into immense detail on the subject of scientific correlation with bombings in Phases 1 and 2. Specifically he covered some of the scientific statements prepared by Mr Higgs of RARDE. The first was a witness statement on 24 January, 1975. This linked the Woolwich bomb to other throw bombs of similar construction. The list included five throw bombs over the period 22 October, 1974 (Brooks Club) to 17 December, 1974 (17 Wilton Street, former home of Sir Edward Heath). The Woolwich bomb was on 7 November, 1974.[46] The second statement was on 13 August and was entitled 'Proposals for linked cases in Southern England'.[47] It linked the Guildford and Woolwich bombings to all the other Phase 1 bombings. Higgs said 'he intended to cover the same ground in a formal witness statement but that it would have to await his return from annual leave'.

It was produced on 10 October, 1975 after Higgs had given evidence at the Guildford Four trial. The trial started on 16 September, 1975 and was still in progress at that time. Neither of these statements was disclosed to the Guildford Four's defence team until long after the trial was over. They came to light during cross-examination at the trial of the Balcombe Street ASU. Moreover, the statement of 10 October, 1975 was clearly not prepared for purposes of the Guildford trial.

Towards the end of his main section on correlation Sir John May made this comment[48] which is not without interest in the angle it presents:

> In conclusion it is important to remember that Crown counsel's interest in the correlation work was in whether or not it linked the Guildford Four with other incidents. When the work in January 1975 failed to show such a link it is perhaps understandable that those representing the Crown in this case apparently lost sight of the possible correlation work in the context of the Guildford Four trial. At the Balcombe Street trial early in 1977 and thereafter the significance of the correlation work was argued the other way. It was contended that because Guildford and Woolwich could be forensically linked to the many Phase 1 and Phase 2 incidents in which the Balcombe Street gang and their associates were involved the Guildford Four were innocent.

Not surprisingly, Sir John made the question of disclosure of forensic correlation statements to the Guildford Four defence prior

[46]Final Report, page 158. [47]Final Report, page 164. [48]Final Report, page 169.

to, during, or after their trial in 1975 one of 14 specific issues to which he gave particular attention.[49] He summarised his findings on the wide investigation he had undertaken under the heading 'Disclosure of the scientific correlation evidence' on page 302 of the Final Report –

> On 24th January, 1975 Mr Douglas Higgs of RARDE made a witness statement linking the Woolwich bombing with other throw bomb incidents. That statement was not disclosed by the prosecution prior to the trial of the Guildford Four. It should have been. It was overlooked by all concerned. Counsel had it in their possession at the very beginning of the case but by the time questions of disclosure were being considered by them they had lost sight of its potential significance. The staff of the DPP's office should also have appreciated its continuing significance and sought Counsel's advice on disclosure. On 10th October, 1975 Mr Higgs made a statement linking the Guildford bombing with Woolwich and with many other bombings. This statement post dated the commencement of the trial and was not seen by Counsel until 1977. I have been unable to establish whether it was provided to the DPP before the trial ended. Had it been, it should have been disclosed. In any event, I have no doubt that these statements and the later amended versions of them should have been disclosed prior to the 1977 appeal irrespective of what had happened in the context of the trial.

Towards the end of the notes on *Question 3* which were discussed at the meeting with Sir John May on 3 September, 1993, the significant point was made that at the Guildford trial, the Guildford and Woolwich offences were presented by the prosecution as isolated acts of terrorism. Consequently, the evidence served related only to each offence separately. No details were given of any other similar offences where the modus operandi, material, or any other idiosyncratic factors were relevant.

The question posed by the Deputation at the end of the notes was why the correlation information was not disclosed to the defence, and who was responsible for this decision? Regrettably, even now, the question remains unanswered.

As will be seen from the list of questions at APPENDIX XIII *Questions 4 and 5* are very closely connected. It would therefore, be simpler, and more fruitful, to take them together.

[49]Final Report, page 12.

Question 4
At the same Balcombe Street trial they further testified that on orders from the DPP, communicated to them by the anti-terrorist squad, they had subsequently altered the statements to omit all reference to Guildford and Woolwich, for the purposes of the Guildford and Woolwich trial. Why was this done and who was responsible?

Question 5
They also testified that in this, the Balcombe Street trial, they had omitted all reference to the forensic links between the offences being tried there and the Guildford and Woolwich offences.

Why was this done and who was responsible?

Turning first to *Question 4*, the point has already been made that the scientific statements of 24 January, 1975 and 10 October, 1975 were not disclosed to the defence before the Guildford trial. However, the scientific evidence which was presented at the Guildford trial consisted of altered versions of the statements. This was done by making deletions expressly for purposes of the trial. The evidence served related only, and separately, to the Guildford and Woolwich offences. No details were given of any other similar offences. The question was, how had this arisen?

In the notes on *Question 4* sent to Sir John May for the meeting on 3 September, 1993, reference was made to the proceedings at the Balcombe Street trial. After a great deal of cross-examination Higgs admitted that he had made a statement in which he had made all the connections between the time-bomb devices which included Guildford. He had then been told by Detective Sergeant Lewis, attached to the anti-terrorist squad, to change his statement by deleting references to the Guildford and Woolwich offences. He believed, but did not know and had no communication to verify it, that the instructions had come from the DPP.

At this point Commander Nevill, of the Metropolitan Police, was put back into the witness box. He confirmed that on the instructions of the DPP he had instructed DS Lewis to tell Higgs to change his statement. (Mr Justice Cantley's remark was – 'I find this most extraordinary'). There can be little doubt that if the jury at the Guildford trial had known that the offences were part of a connected series of offences, with idiosyncratic forensic factors linking them with a series of offences which both preceded and succeeded the possible involvement of the Guildford Four, the outcome of the trial might well have been very different.

The question posed at the end of the notes on *Question 4* was 'Who in the DPP's office instructed Commander Nevill that the statements to be made at the Guildford trial by the expert witnesses were to be changed by deleting all reference to the Guildford and Woolwich offences, and why was this done?' The point was made that this was a very serious matter. It might possibly have been construed as a conspiracy to prevent, obstruct, pervert or defeat the course of justice. It is surprising that more was not said or done about it at the time.

The question remains unanswered.

Turning now to *Question 5,* Sir John May established[50] what alterations were made to the two witness statements of 24 January, 1975 and 10 October, 1975 by Higgs with a view to their use in the Balcombe Street trial in February 1977. The changes amounted to this.

On 19 February, 1976 Higgs produced a second version of his Phase 1 statement which still included Woolwich but excluded any reference to the Guildford bombings and the reference to the Guildford trial. It followed that the express reference to the links between Guildford and the remainder of the Phase 1 incidents was omitted. On 12 July, 1976 he produced a third and final version excluding not only Guildford but also Woolwich. On 17 June, 1976 he amended his throw bomb statement to exclude Woolwich. The question posed by Sir John May was why was this done and who was responsible?

It emerged that the Balcombe Street ASU, who had surrendered on 13 December, 1975, were initially charged with 6 offences all concerned with events on 6 December, 1975. Many more charges were to follow once the Crown had had an opportunity to consider their many admissions and other evidence found in safe houses such as Fairholme Road. The prosecution of the Balcombe Street ASU, and decisions on charges to be brought against them, were in the hands of the prosecution team – John Matthew QC, David Jeffreys and Graham Boal.[51]

It was apparent that during 1976, there was some conflict of views between Commander Habershon and D Supt Hucklesby of the Metropolitan Police on the one hand, and the DPP and the prosecuting team on the other, on the range of charges to be made against the Balcombe Street gang. The police had enough evidence to proceed against them for Woolwich, but not Guildford, and they also wanted them to be charged with as many, if not all, of the 66 incidents on the original list. It is to be noted that the transcripts of the interviews with the Balcombe Street ASU and Brendan Dowd conducted by Alastair Logan were served on the DPP and the Surrey Police in early January 1977.

[50]Final Report, page 168. [51]Final report, page 185.

They were therefore available before the trial which started on 25 January, 1977.

However, in the event, the original schedule of 66 incidents was finally whittled down to some 25 by the prosecution and the DPP, and Woolwich was excluded. Sir John May records[52] that John Matthew wrote to him on 18 May, 1993 confirming that the decision to exclude Woolwich was his. He said he felt 'very strongly that the original 66 offences had to be dramatically reduced to make the evidence comprehensible to the jury'. In the same letter when referring to the decision to reduce the original 66 offences to 45 [at that stage], Matthew said – 'It could well be that the conviction of Hill and Armstrong for that offence [Woolwich] was a factor in that decision, it almost certainly was. There was definitely no ulterior motive behind it . . . no pressure from anybody'.

At this point Sir John May recalled the alterations Higgs had made to his statements during 1976 for purposes of the Balcombe Street trial as given on page 288. At the Balcombe Street trial in January 1977, Higgs was cross-examined[53] as to why he had left Woolwich out of his 17 June 1976 statement. He said he was told to leave it out by DS Doyle of the Metropolitan Police, who he believed had been acting at the behest of Counsel, on the grounds that Woolwich had already been dealt with at trial. It was at this point that Mr Justice Cantley remarked – 'why you should leave it out because people tell you to I don't quite understand'. Higgs said his original throw bomb statement of 24 January, 1975 was still available. Mr MacDonald, counsel for Joseph O'Connell, pointed out that in effect the existence of the previous statement was of no use when it had not been disclosed, and that the later version on its own was misleading with Woolwich left out.

The Deputation's notes on *Question 5* for the meeting on 3 September said that during the trial the prosecution sought to withdraw other charges. These related to the Phase 1 operations, July 1974 to January 1975, and included incidents in which people had been killed. Furthermore, the forensic experts admitted at the Balcombe Street trial that, as well as changing prepared statements showing forensic links for purposes of the Guildford trial, they had also, for the Balcombe Street trial, omitted all reference to the forensic links between the offences being tried there and the Guildford and Woolwich offences.

The question posed in the notes discussed at the meeting on 3 September, 1993 was why all this had been done and who was responsible? Also, specifically, what action was taken by the DPP on Commander Nevill's report? This was not answered in the Final Report.

[52]Final Report, page 189. [53]Final Report, page 190.

Question 6
The Balcombe Street gang confessed to the anti-terrorist squad that they had carried out the Guildford and Woolwich bombings. This was not followed up. Why and who was responsible?

It was recalled in the notes on this question that, in November and December 1976, the Balcombe Street ASU and Brendan Dowd were interviewed in the presence of their solicitors by James Still (former Chief Superintendent of the Metropolitan Police) and Alastair Logan during which they made admissions concerning Guildford and Woolwich. These verbatim confessions were known to the DPP and the police well before the Balcombe Street trial (February 1977) and the Guildford Appeal (October 1977).

Sir John May records[54] that the Balcombe Street gang were interviewed at length after their surrender throughout the rest of December 1975, principally by the Metropolitan Police but also by other forces with an interest in their activities. The Inquiry account extends from pages 176 to 184 and concerns only those interviews which were relevant to the case of the Guildford Four. It would be simpler, and easier to assess them, if presented in a semi-tabular form:

> On 13 December, 1975 Edward Butler was interviewed by DCS Nevill and DCS Imbert. He admitted being at Woolwich but denied involvement in Guildford as he was not in England at that time.
>
> On 14 December DCS Nevill and DCS Imbert saw Joseph O'Connell. He was read a list of incidents which included Woolwich (but not Guildford) but would not confirm or deny involvement in any of them. Harry Duggan was also seen but took the same line.
>
> On 15 December Edward Butler 'and his associates' were seen by DCS Simmons and D Supt. Underwood of Surrey, and DCI Munday of the Metropolitan Police about the Caterham bombing. Neither Woolwich nor Guildford was discussed. [It is surprising the police did not question them on Guildford since they had the RARDE Reports and knew that, forensically speaking, the Caterham bomb was a carbon copy of Guildford.] Edward Butler was asked nothing further about Woolwich after this interview.
>
> On 18 December Joseph O'Connell and Hugh Doherty were interviewed by DCI Munday and DCI Chapman. In DCI Munday's statement of the interview of 19 January, 1976, Joseph O'Connell

[54]Final Report, page 176.

denied his ASU's involvement in Woolwich. At the Court of Appeal in 1977 Joseph O'Connell denied this interview had taken place.

On 24 December Joseph O'Connell was interviewed about the Caterham bombing on 27 August, 1975 by DCI Style and DCI Gladwell of Surrey in the presence of DCI Chapman of the Metropolitan Police. As with Edward Butler's interview on 15 December, Joseph O'Connell was not asked about Guildford for which Surrey Police had arrested the Guildford Four.

On 30 December Joseph O'Connell was seen by DCS Nevill, DCS Imbert, DS Hucklesby and DS Holbrook. He was taken through the list of incidents, including Guildford this time, about which he had nothing to say. He admitted to the police for the first and only time his ASU's involvement in Woolwich. He was not prepared to say any more until he had spoken to Brendan Dowd.

Hugh Doherty and Harry Duggan were also seen the same day but were not forthcoming about Woolwich.

Sir John May's summary of the situation was that, in Surrey's interviews about Caterham, both Joseph O'Connell and Edward Butler said their ASU was responsible but denied taking part themselves. He then said[55] that by the end of December 1975 –

> None of the Balcombe Street gang gave the slightest hint that they were responsible for or knew anything about Guildford – *though the questioning directed to them by the police about Guildford was very limited*[56] – and neither had Brendan Dowd.

Continuing Sir John May said it could have been expected to see evidence that the Balcombe Street gang were asked about Guildford, if not by the Metropolitan Police then certainly by Surrey whose case it was. In giving evidence to the Inquiry, Sir Peter Imbert said DCS Nevill had said at the Balcombe Street trial that it would have been for Surrey and not the Metropolitan Police to take up the matter of Guildford with the Balcombe Street gang if they so chose. When Mr Rowe and Mr Underwood, who were respectively ACC(O) and D Supt. in the Surrey Police in 1975, gave evidence, they said it had been left with the Metropolitan Police to do all the questioning.

At the end of this section Sir John May said that, in the face of what Edward Butler and Joseph O'Connell were saying, and their

[55]Final Report, page 182. [56]Author's Italics.

attitude, he was not minded to criticise either force for not pursuing Woolwich more closely with Edward Butler and for not making a concerted effort to interview any of the gang about Guildford. But he went on:

> . . . Nevertheless, I find it regrettable that in the overall history of this case, having regard in particular to the way in which the later admissions of the Balcombe Street gang and Dowd were open to accusations of collusion, that these matters were not pursued with vigour at the time.[57]

However, he then said in his main conclusions[58] about the admissions –

> Following their arrest in December 1975 two of the gang, O'Connell and Butler, did however make admissions to the Woolwich bombing. With the benefit of hindsight one might say that the Metropolitan Police should have pursued the precise involvement of these two in the Woolwich bombing further and then thought of the possible implications for the Guildford Four. It would no doubt have been better if they had done so.

Question 7
At their own trial in 1977 they refused to plead because they had not been charged with Guildford and Woolwich. Why was this not followed up and who was responsible? Why, after their Balcombe Street trial in 1977 were Dowd and O'Connell not put on trial for Woolwich and Guildford, and Butler and Duggan for Woolwich?

The Guildford Four's solicitors were not told about Joseph O'Connell and Edward Butler's admissions to Woolwich until 5 July, 1976.[59] At their trial in January 1977 the Balcombe Street ASU openly admitted membership of the IRA and did not attempt to defend themselves. Uniquely they refused to plead because they had not been charged with offences at Guildford which they had admitted.

Sir John May recorded[60] that on arraignment Joseph O'Connell refused to plead because the indictment did not contain the Guildford and Woolwich bombings, for which, he said, he and others were responsible and for which innocent people had been wrongly convicted. Edward Butler and Harry Duggan also refused to plead and on similar grounds, Edward Butler indicating involvement in Woolwich but Harry

[57]Final Report, page 184. [58]Final Report, page 303. [59]Final Report, page 200.
[60]Final Report, page 202.

Duggan in neither Guildford nor Woolwich. Hugh Doherty refused to plead on the ground that he could not expect justice from an English court. What Sir John May did not record, but was given in the Deputation's notes to this question, was that most newspapers, including *The Times,* reported that the defendants had refused to plead but their reason for not doing so was not given. Readers were left to assume that the conventional IRA procedure of not recognising the court had been followed, as indeed was done by Hugh Doherty. The embarrassing truth was disclosed only in *The Guardian* and *The Surrey Advertiser. The Guardian's* reporter, not being a holder of an accredited police press card, had not felt it necessary to respond to police lobbying to keep silent on the subject.

It was as a result of the refusal to plead that the prosecution reduced again the number of charges. The reductions related to Phase 1 operations which covered the period during which the Guildford and Woolwich offences took place. However, from the outset the Balcombe Street gang had not been charged with Guildford or Woolwich. Sir John May said[61] it emerged in evidence at the Balcombe Street trial that under cross-examination D Supt Hucklesby said he would have charged Edward Butler for Woolwich. Mr Harvey, junior counsel for Joseph O'Connell, then asked about the verbal admission by his client. When asked whether he had sufficient evidence for a prosecution on Woolwich, he responded – 'I submitted it to the Director of Prosecutions as such, yes'.

In giving evidence to the Inquiry Sir Peter Imbert confirmed he was in agreement at the time that the Woolwich offence should be included in the schedule. Later he indicated to Sir John May that 'whatever were the views of individual Metropolitan Police officers, however senior, counsel were determined to take a more robust and pragmatic line'. As already mentioned, counsel for the prosecution, John Matthew, decided not to include Woolwich.

In Chapter 16 (some 25 pages) of his Final Report Sir John May covered at some length 'The events which preceded the 1977 Appeal'. This included, amongst other things, the work undertaken by both the Metropolitan Police and Surrey in assessing the evidence given by Brendan Dowd and the Balcombe Street gang to Alastair Logan and James Still. Referring to a schedule[62] attached to the Metropolitan Police report of 7 March, 1977, Sir John May quoted:

> The schedule shows a remarkable similarity on many aspects of the admissions (Dowd and O'Connell re Guildford and Dowd, O'Connell, Butler, Duggan re Woolwich) to an extent of detail

[61]Final Report, pages 188 and 189. [62]Final Report, page 209.

which encompasses almost every pertinent point raised by witnesses . . .

. . . In the absence of a conspiracy between Still, Logan and the court shorthand writers[63] (which has been discounted) it is difficult to imagine how such detail could be retained without either first hand knowledge or access to committal bundles by at least one of them and the subsequent interchange of information while in custody. [It is to be noted that some of the information referred to, would, in fact, not have been in the bundles.]

In Chapter 17 (some 17 pages) of the Final Report Sir John May covered 'The 1977 Appeal'. Amongst the points he made were the following:

As a Metropolitan Police report of 14 November, 1977 reveals, the officers present were left with little if any doubt that he [O'Connell] had been at both Guildford and Woolwich and was one of the organisers of the attacks. O'Connell denied knowledge of any of the applicants [the Guildford Four] and stated that they were not involved in these offences in any way'.

About Joseph O'Connell when giving evidence at the 1977 Appeal by the Guildford Four:

Throughout his cross-examination O'Connell gave detailed answers in respect of locations, procedure and timing. However, when his various interviews with police were put to him he denied that the interview with DCI Munday on 18 December, 1975, in which he had said that 'Woolwich was not one of ours', had ever taken place.

In opening the case for the Crown Sir Michael Havers:

conceded that there was such a ring of truth about O'Connell's evidence that it was probable he was at both [Guildford and Woolwich].

In the judgement the Court of Appeal were:

content to assume that O'Connell's story of his presence and participation [Guildford] may indeed be true and that Dowd may also

[63]Alastair Logan had taken a short-hand writer to record the interviews he and James Still conducted with the Balcombe Street ASU.

have taken part, notwithstanding the doubts we have on the latter point.

Question 7 was framed on the basis of information available to the Deputation at the time of Cardinal Hume's letter to the Home Secretary on 2 June 1993. The subsequent revelations in the Final Report listed above serve only to reinforce the justification for posing the question.

For understandable reasons, Sir John May could not, and did not attempt to, answer *Question 7* above. This could only have been done if the office of the DPP had volunteered the answers or they had been asked to provide them. Neither of these happened.

Question 8
The question at (7) above was posed in Cardinal Hume's letter to the Home Secretary of 22 September, 1988. Why, even at this late hour, was it not followed up?

To some extent this question has been overtaken by events in the light of observations made on *Question 7* above. It is, however, important to recall the chronology of events, and so bear in mind the information available to the Deputation at any given time.

It will be recalled that Cardinal Hume's letter of 22 September, 1988 to the Home Secretary was written shortly after he had informed the Cardinal on a visit, on 8 September, 1988, that he would not be referring the case. It was, in fact, a fully comprehensive letter of some eight pages with two Annexes, and was designed to refute all the reasons the Home Secretary had given for not referring the case. The Deputation attached great importance to this letter and considered it marked 'the end of the beginning' in their quest to secure a referral.

As already mentioned, it was dismissed somewhat perfunctorily in one sentence by the Inquiry. No response was ever received from the Home Office to the many points which were raised. The Deputation's notes to Question 8 were prepared for the meeting with Sir John May on 3 September, 1993. Both the question and the notes reflected a reaction of frustration to the doubts and obstacles being raised by the Home Office.

In the interests of completion the point of the question is best made by quoting the relevant paragraphs from the letter of 22 September, 1988 which were repeated in the Notes:

> You referred to, but rejected, the possibility of a Tribunal under the 1921 Act. On reflection, I am becoming convinced that the cases themselves, as cases, are now matters of public importance.

In view of this, and your doubts about the merits of a reference to the Court of Appeal, it has to be recognised that if there is no referral pressure will continue for further investigation of a matter which has caused, and continues to cause, public misgiving. Inevitably, in this event, consideration would have to be given to a Tribunal being set up under the 1921 Act. This would ensure that at least all the facts are brought to light, and are fully considered and assessed. Such a step would have the merit of satisfying all the many interests in England and Ireland, and indeed North America, who are concerned about these cases.

An alternative, and perhaps even better, solution might be to put Dowd and O'Connell on trial for Woolwich and Guildford, and Butler and Duggan for Woolwich. They all refused to plead at the Balcombe Street trial because they were not also being charged with Guildford and/or Woolwich. Such a step would also bring to light the very worrying suppression of evidence that there was a forensic link between the Guildford and Woolwich bombings and other bombings which had taken place after the arrest of the Guildford Four.

Amongst the main conclusions[64] reached by Sir John May at the end of the Final Report were:

Nevertheless the miscarriages of justice which occurred in this case were not due to any specific weakness or inherent fault in the criminal justice system itself, nor in the trial procedures which are part of that system. They were the result of individual failings on the part of those who had a role to play in that system and against whose personal failings no rules could provide complete protection.

. . . If the various failings in the operation of the system had not occurred, then the verdicts of the jury at the trial or the outcome of the appeal in 1977 might have been different. Thus nothing should now derogate from the acquittals of each member of the Guildford Four.'

The Guildford Four spent 15 years in prison for crimes they did not commit. At the press conference to launch the Final Report of the May Inquiry the first question, by a journalist, was – 'Who was to blame?' The question was not properly answered.

Press coverage of the Final Report was not so extensive or so vociferous as that for the quashing of the Guildford Four convictions or the trial of the Surrey Police officers. The general air was one of

[64]Final Report, pages 308 and 309.

disappointment, but also dismay in some areas. A great part of the coverage was given to quotations from the Report about such important matters as the revelations about the Burke alibi and the disclosure of scientific evidence. These, and other similar matters, have already been covered in this account.

Consequently only a few selected observations by the press on the Report as a whole, rather than those covering details, are given below:

The Independent, 1 July, 1994
In a leader –

> Sir John May's inquiry has finally dashed hopes that the authorities will be shamed into penitence over one of this country's worst miscarriages of justice
>
> ... In the light of such injustice, the Guildford Four deserved something stronger than the weak brew served up yesterday ... A judiciary that proved itself to be so gullible in this case is vindicated, even praised.
>
> ... For years the police, the Court of Appeal and the Home Office could not countenance the thought that the wrong people were languishing in prison.
>
> The checks and balances of justice failed the Guildford Four not merely because the system, from the outset and for the years to follow, worked to confirm rather than question the original assumption that the Four were guilty'.

In a feature:

> ... He acknowledges that the Royal Commission on Criminal Justice, of which he was a member, recommended last year that the Court of Appeal change its procedures on admitting new evidence.

The Times, 1 July, 1994
In a feature:

> Sir John's disclosure that he had seen intelligence material linking the two men [Hill and Conlon] with the IRA provoked an accusation last night that he had smeared them and was trying to divert attention from the failings of the criminal justice system ... None of these came out at public hearings where their lawyers could have challenged it.

The Guardian, 1 July, 1994
In a leader:

> If Scott has scaled the heights, May plumbed the depths yesterday ... The criminal justice system, which serious researchers have found failing at every level – police, prosecution and judicial – was given a clean bill of health
>
> ... but even he notes the changes that have been made to the system: new rights for defendants, new independent review body to study miscarriages of justice. The system is being changed because the system needed to change

In a feature –

> The conduct of the first part of the Inquiry was impeccable. It was held in public. Witnesses were rigorously cross-examined. No one, not even the lawyers, were spared.
>
> The Interim Report was a solid piece of work, which led speedily to the quashing of the Maguire convictions. Then things started to go wrong – a lengthy fiasco followed during which the case against the officers [Surrey Police] was strung out for more than three years.

The Guardian, 4 July, 1994
In a feature:

> The Guildford case broke the dam. Month after month wrongful convictions were set aside: the Birmingham Six, the Broadwater Three, The Cardiff Three, The Swansea Two, The East Ham Two, Judith Ward, Stefan Kiszko and the Taylor sisters. All had been convicted of murder, and all were, in the proper sense, victims of miscarriages of justice – they didn't do it.

The Daily Telegraph, 1 July, 1994
In a feature:

> The May Inquiry into the Guildford Four case has failed to identify anyone responsible for the wrongful convictions that led to Paul Hill, Gerard Conlon, Patrick Armstrong and Carole Richardson spending 15 years in jail.

The Daily Mail, 1 July, 1994
In a feature:

> The most important lesson to be drawn from the case, he [Sir John

> May] said, was that the Four were convicted solely on the evidence of their own confessions

Perhaps it would be appropriate for the last word to be left to the Deputation. From the outset they were all convinced there had been a miscarriage of justice in both the Guildford Four and Maguire Seven cases – indeed it was that individual belief which brought them all together in the first place. They all believed that the defendants were innocent.

From the time it was set up on 19 October, 1989, the Deputation recognised the importance of the May Inquiry as being the only remaining body which could establish the truth – the whole truth – in an impartial fashion. They fully supported its work, and gave it all the assistance they could. It came as something of a disappointment to them that the final outcome fell short of what it had hoped would be achieved.

The Deputation did not make any press releases on publication of the Final Report on 30 June, 1994. They decided, instead, to express their views in public by way of a letter to *The Times* on 6 July, 1994. A photocopy of the letter is on the next page.

The Times 6 July 1994

From the Archbishop of Westminster and others

Sir. For many years we have, with others, regarded the Guildford Four case as a grave miscarriage of justice. Our initial reaction to Sir John May's final report is one of disappointment.

We are glad that he has confirmed that there was a miscarriage of justice and that serious mistakes were made in the handling of the case at various stages. Some of these, as he indicates, could have resulted from over-reliance by police and prosecution on the validity of the confessions of the Guildford Four.

Following on from that there is the likelihood that some components of the criminal justice system were being driven at the time by an anxiety not to undermine the validity of the confessions as they saw it.

A penetrating and more robust examination of these possibilities was, we believe, required. The weakness of the report is that it does not go far enough in exploring and attributing the extent of responsibility and blame for the miscarriage of justice which Sir John recognises did occur.

The whole truth has not yet been revealed.

Yours faithfully,
BASIL HUME,
ROY JENKINS,
SCARMAN,
MERLYN-REES,
Archbishop's House,
Westminster, SW1.
July 4.

10

THE EPILOGUE

AS WILL have been seen from the two previous chapters, there were some important features and failings in the Guildford Four and Maguire Seven cases which the Deputation found singularly disturbing. This was the more so as no satisfactory explanation appeared to be forthcoming from the May Inquiry, or any other source, about some of these failings. The more serious of these failings merit recapitulation in general terms before we review some of the weighty issues to which these two cases gave rise.

To recall but three in the Guildford Four case, there was particular concern about the general handling of the Burke alibi by the police, the prosecution and the Home Office. There was also the question of the alterations, for trial purposes, of statements prepared by the expert scientific witnesses. Some of these were done on instructions from Commander Nevill who testified that they, in turn, originated in the office of the DPP. Additionally there was the matter of the failure to disclose forensic correlation statements.

Turning to the case of the Maguire Seven, the one central fact was that they were convicted solely on scientific evidence as given by the expert witnesses from RARDE. It needs to be borne in mind that it was the reassessment of the scientific evidence presented at trial by the May Inquiry's scientific committee that enabled the Home Secretary to refer the case to the Court of Appeal. The Court quashed the convictions.

In both his Interim and Second Reports on the Maguire case, Sir John May examined many aspects of the scientific evidence. Specifically he also commented on the 'kneading' process. The forensic scientists called for the Crown had concluded that swabs taken from hands and from Mrs Maguire's gloves revealed that the Maguires must have been handling ('kneading') explosives sufficiently to warrant the inference they were making bombs. It is now known that this conclusion was unwarranted by the evidence. The Court of Appeal exposed a fatal flaw in this conclusion. Had there been full and timely disclosure of the relevant scientific information, the scientists for the defence would have been able to mount a successful challenge to the prosecution case.

Many people, including those who were in prison for so long and their solicitors, would assert that the Deputation played a pivotal role in securing justice for the Guildford Four, from which so much else flowed, and also for the Maguire Seven. They would also hold the view that had it not been for the new evidence which had been assembled, the sheer determination of the Deputation, and also the constant pressure they exerted to obtain a reference back to the Court of Appeal, the Guildford Four might still be in prison. In that event, the May Inquiry, which led to the quashing of the convictions of the Maguire Seven, would not have been set up on 19 October, 1989 when the convictions of the Guildford Four were quashed.

Moreover, there was more to come in relation to the so-called 'terrorist' cases. The Deputation had concentrated its efforts on securing justice for the Guildford Four, whilst others were acting in a similar fashion on behalf of the Birmingham Six. That case was first referred to the Court of Appeal by the Home Secretary on 20 January, 1987, but the appeal was dismissed on 28 January, 1988. By 1989, with fresh information becoming available, there was growing unease and renewed pressure for the case to be referred again. In the *Wolverhampton Express* and *Star* in October 1989, in referring to his 'appalling vista' judgement, Lord Denning said 'with the benefit of hindsight my comments can be justly criticised'. He went on to say – 'The situation has been greatly altered by the release of the Guildford Four. In view of that, the case of the Birmingham Six may have to be reconsidered.'

There was some similarity between the two cases. Both involved 'confessions' which were later retracted and the arrest, interrogation and trial phases took place over the same period during which there was an element of hysteria in the country, and revulsion against anyone thought to be involved in bombing incidents. As new information became available, the Home Secretary was able to refer the Birmingham Six case to the Court of Appeal for the second time, on 29 August, 1990. The Court quashed the convictions on 14 March, 1991. On the same day the Home Secretary, by then Kenneth Baker QC PC, announced he would be setting up a Royal Commission on the Criminal Justice System. This was done on 21 June 1991.

Shortly, after that, on 17 September, 1991, a third 'terrorist' case, that of Judith Ward, who had been convicted of the M62 coach bombing and who had spent 19 years in prison, was referred to the Court of Appeal. Her conviction was quashed on 4 June, 1992. Sir John May had referred to her case when discussing scientific evidence in the Maguire Seven case. It is to be noted that the judgement in this case was a damning indictment of the police officers, forensic scientists and prosecution lawyers responsible for her conviction.

Some people argued that the quashing of the Guildford Four convictions not only resulted in the setting up of the May Inquiry, but also paved the way, albeit indirectly, for the second referral of the Birmingham Six case, for the consequential appointment of a Royal Commission on the Criminal Justice System, and finally for the referral of the Judith Ward case to the Court of Appeal. A valid question suggests itself at this point – What would have happened if the Deputation had not come together to pursue the aim of securing a referral of the Guildford Four case to the Court of Appeal?

In his overall assessment of the Guildford Four case in the Final Report, Sir John May states, without any qualifications or reservations, that the miscarriages of justice which occurred were not due to any weakness or inherent fault in the criminal justice system or the trial procedures which are part of that system. He went on – 'They were the result of individual failings on the part of those who had a role to play in that system, and against whose personal failings no rules could provide complete protection'.

This statement exonerates the 'system' and, presumably, would also apply to the Birmingham Six and Judith Ward cases. But in both of these cases there were also some very serious individual failings. There are those who would say it could be argued that it is an essential function of any given 'system', and that could include the criminal justice system, to be able to detect and possibly rectify serious failings by any practitioners in any constituent part of the 'system' before it is too late.

The last sentence of the Final Report of the May Inquiry is – 'The truth, where I have not been able to establish it, must now and hereafter remain a matter for the consciences of all concerned'. Apart from three comparatively junior Surrey Police officers who stood trial, no policemen, particularly senior officers, forensic scientists or members of the legal profession were disciplined, even to the extent of a public rebuke let alone other punishment, in connection with malpractice in these, and the many other, proven cases of miscarriage of justice which followed them.

Many people thought this could not be right – but as Sir John May said, people do still have to live with their consciences. This would apply not only to those guilty of malpractice but also those above them who condoned such practices. It is a salutary thought to reflect on the heartbreaking trail of despair, unhappiness and, indeed, devastation in their personal lives which the victims of these miscarriages are having to live with now, and almost certainly to the end of their days. In seeking to minimise the burden of their memories of such long wrongful imprisonment, and their continuing problems of post-traumatic stress disorder, some are even finding themselves resorting to such solace as alcohol might appear to offer but never does.

A view put forward by many is that it can only be a mistaken belief for the custodians of the various parts of the criminal justice system to assume that, as it was thought there was no need to discipline anybody, public confidence in the system would thereby be maintained. The reverse is the more likely outcome, and with diminishing respect for the practitioners in the various parts of the criminal justice system.

Following the release of the Guildford Four some talk, damaging to them, about their supposed guilt began to gain ground. From some reports in the press it appears to have been started by some of those in the criminal justice system who had most to lose because of what had come to light. Regrettably, it is common knowledge that such talk, mainly but not solely in some police and legal circles, continues to this day. Some would say that is, perhaps, an indication of the possible guilt being felt by those who might have had a part in the malpractice which it is now clear contributed to miscarriages of justice in the cases of the Guildford Four and the Maguire Seven. It is also remarkable that those who indulge in such talk do not seem to appreciate the adverse thoughts about themselves that it could engender in others. In any event, the Guildford Four might reasonably wish to be spared any continuation of such talk.

It would be appropriate here to recall Sir John May's concluding words on page 309 of his Final Report:

> . . . If the various failings in the operation of the system had not occurred, then the verdicts of the jury at the trial or the outcome of the appeal in 1977 might have been different. Thus nothing should now derogate from the acquittals of each member of the Guildford Four.

Reverting to mid-1992, the Deputation was still at that time engaged in providing information and submissions for the May Inquiry, but it also then received an invitation to make a submission to the Royal Commission on Criminal Justice. Some details of this are given briefly in Chapter Eleven – THE AFTERMATH.

Throughout the period that it was active, 1986 to 1994, the Deputation had always borne in mind that it was miscarriage of justice (in the Guildford Four and Maguire Seven cases) that had brought them all together and so into the arena. They were conscious that they never were a legal or law-revising body and, as Lord Scarman remarked, with the loss of Lord Devlin in July 1992 they were even less so. Their contributions to the May Inquiry dealt essentially with 'facts' and how they had been handled during the period between the trials in 1975/76 and the quashing of the Guildford Four convictions on 19 October, 1989. By contrast, as will be seen in Chapter Eleven, as far as the Royal Commission was concerned, the Deputation argued for the principles (not facts) which were in their written submission.

It is the purpose of this book to present only the handling of the 'facts', and also the failings, that came to light in the Guildford Four and Maguire Seven cases, both as seen by the Deputation. This is done in the hope that the deficiencies which are revealed will help to safeguard against possible future miscarriages of justice. It is not the purpose of this book to record or take account of the changes in criminal law and practice which have taken place since the trials in 1975/76.

It so happened that in July 1992 Lord Devlin dictated a letter about evidence to the Royal Commission for consideration by the Deputation, but he died before he could sign it. His secretary sent a copy of the letter to Archbishop's House after his funeral.

In the letter, as well as making contributions to the submission to the Royal Commission being prepared at the time, at the end of it he referred to the question of an apology for those who had suffered a miscarriage of justice. The point he made, which is of considerable interest, can best be expressed in his own dictated words –

> There is a widespread feeling that when there has been a failure of justice of the magnitude of the Guildford Four case there ought to be someone in a position to offer an apology. The girl [Carole Richardson] in the Guildford Four, when she was told that she would be released and compensated, asked as in these cases the press always asks, what she 'felt' about it, said only 'I wish someone would say that they were sorry'.
>
> There are obvious difficulties about deciding whether and on what occasions a judge should say that he is sorry. Perhaps as Gibbon says of some events in his history, the sorrow should be veiled in the obscurity of a learned language, whereafter he proceeds in Latin. There have been cases in which Counsel has asked for judgement *ex debito justitiae.* To pronounce a judgement in a higher court as *ex debito* might be taken as an acknowledgement that justice has failed and might suffice.
>
> I think that the government would gain much credit from the British and other nations if it made a straightforward apology. The Lord Chancellor is the formal head of the judiciary; the Lord Chief Justice is the active head. I think that the Lord Chancellor would be the right person since it would be quite clear that in his case the formal could only be the legal system'.

Looking to the future, it would be a fitting end to this *Epilogue* to suggest that all practitioners, in all parts of the criminal justice system, would wish to dwell on the five matters referred to by Lord Justice Rose in March 1998 when the Court of Appeal quashed the conviction of Mr Mathan, a Somali seaman, who was hanged 45 years ago for the murder of a woman shopkeeper. He said it was 'a matter for very profound regret' that Mr Mathan was hanged and that it took 46 years to show that his conviction had been unsafe, – 'the Court can only hope that its decision today will provide some crumb of comfort for his surviving relatives'.

Lord Justice Rose then said that despite changes in criminal inquiries and trials, the case demonstrated five matters:

1 That capital punishment was 'not perhaps a prudent culmination for a criminal justice system which is human and therefore fallible.' [If capital punishment had not been abolished 10 years before the Guildford Four trial, only Carole Richardson, who was 17 at the time, would have survived].

2 That criminal law and practice had undergone changes for the better since Mr Mathan's trial.

3 That the Criminal Cases Review Commission was a necessary body without whose work the injustice in this case might never have been identified.

4 That no one associated with the criminal justice system 'can afford to be complacent'.

5 That injustices 'can only be avoided if all concerned in the investigation of crime and the presentation of criminal prosecutions observe the very highest standards of integrity, conscientiousness and professional skill'.

11

THE AFTERMATH

PUBLICATION of the Final Report of the May Inquiry brought to a climax the lessons to be learnt by the constituent parts of the criminal justice system from the cases of the Guildford Four and the Maguire Seven. Some aspects of these have been reflected upon and highlighted in Chapter Ten.

The two main events which could be said to constitute the aftermath were the Report of the Royal Commission on Criminal Justice, and the setting up of a new body to deal with miscarriages of justice. Contributions by the Deputation to these two matters will be briefly surveyed in this chapter, but sufficiently only for historical purposes.

The terms of reference of the Royal Commission on Criminal Justice were very wide-ranging. It was clear that it would have much detailed work to do: it would have detailed discussions, no doubt, with the practising professions, the judges, the Home Office, scientists, police and academics who were specialist in many fields. Consequently, as far as the Deputation was concerned, it was decided that their submission should concentrate only on those aspects of the criminal justice system which had come to the fore in the cases of the Guildford Four and the Maguire Seven.

The submission was drafted by Lord Scarman, in conjunction with Lord Devlin, and was considered and fully discussed at the meetings of the Deputation on 14 July and 14 October, 1991. Cardinal Hume then sent it to Lord Runciman of Doxford, CBE, FBA, Chairman of the Royal Commission on 7 November, 1991. For historical reasons, and for completeness, a copy of the whole submission as sent to the Royal Commission is at APPENDIX XIV.

As will be seen from paragraph 44 of APPENDIX XIV the principal specific recommendations were as below. (Paragraph numbers in brackets, refer to paragraphs in the submission at APPENDIX XIV)

Amendment of the law to disallow convictions on the strength of uncorroborated confession evidence. (para 8)

Judicial supervision, alternatively supervision by an officer of a judicial division of the Crown Prosecution Service, of the pre-trial phase of serious criminal cases. (paras 11 and 12)

The establishment of an independent service of forensic science available to the Court, the defence and the prosecution. (para 16)

A statutory re-statement of the duty of the Court of Appeal in criminal appeals. (para 26)

The repeal of section 17 of the Criminal Appeals Act 1968 and the establishment of a new Court of Review (para 27 et seq)

Just under a year later, on 30 September, 1992, the whole Deputation was invited to give oral evidence to all members of the Royal Commission. Regrettably Lord Devlin, who had made such a great contribution to the thinking and deliberations by the Deputation, had died a few months earlier.

The Royal Commission had referred in notes for the meeting to the main headings in the Deputation's submission (APPENDIX XIV) and posed a series of questions under each for discussion. As the Report of the Royal Commission on Criminal Justice was published in July 1993, a full account will not be given of the meeting. However, to indicate the breadth of the discussion, and again for historical interest, some of the questions discussed under the various headings as in the notes prepared by the Royal Commission are given below:

Supervision of police investigations

Choices are, build on codes of practice in Police and Criminal Evidence Act (PACE 1984), OR introduce extra dimension of judicial supervision, OR supervision by prosecution service

Confessions

Choices are, remain possible for confession alone to go before jury but only with strongly worded warning from the judge, OR have rule (enforced by judges' direction rather than exclusion or inadmissibility) that there must be some other evidence supporting confession.

Scientific Evidence

Should the pre-trial process be used to establish the areas of agreement and to clarify the areas of dispute so as to aid their clear presentation to the jury?

Inferences to be permitted from a defendant's silence

Should no adverse inference continue to be drawn from the suspect's silence under police questioning? Should defendant be required to disclose defence at pre-trial stage under judicial supervision, with adverse inference being drawn if departed from at the trial? Should jury be entitled to draw inferences if defendant stays silent?

Court of Appeal and miscarriages of justice

In fresh evidence cases should there be more retrials, and if not feasible because of many years delay, what should be done? After all court processes exhausted, should responsibility for reference be transferred from Home Secretary to a new body? Should new body be investigative or a court? Should it investigate cases itself (like SFO and DTI) or, in addition, supervise investigations by police forces commissioned direct or through Home Secretary?

In their background notes for discussion at the oral evidence session, the Commission had said that they had received a great deal of evidence to the effect that responsibility for considering allegations of miscarriage of justice after all court processes have been gone through should be removed from the Home Secretary and given to a new body. This had been the view of all members of the Deputation from the time they first started to come together in late 1986. It was well fortified after publication of the Final Report of the May Inquiry.

All this led to the Deputation proposing that consideration should be given to the need for a Court of Review. This was discussed briefly at the oral evidence session by way of reference to the appropriate part of the submission[1]. The basis of the Deputation's thinking was – 'What is needed is a court of inquiry into a matter of grave public importance. This is not appellate work: it is a search for the truth'.

In the event, in their Report the Royal Commission devoted a whole chapter (Chapter Eleven – pages 180 to 187) to 'Correction of Miscarriages of Justice' in which there were several recommendations. The

[1]APPENDIX XIV paras 27 to 43.

Commission concluded, 'it is neither necessary nor desirable that the Home Secretary should be directly responsible for the consideration and investigation of alleged miscarriages of justice as well as being responsible for law and order and for the police'. Amongst many others, the four key recommendations were:

> We recommend therefore that the Home Secretary's power to refer cases to the Court of Appeal under section 17 of the Criminal Appeals Act 1968 should be removed and that a new body should be set up to consider alleged miscarriages of justice, to supervise their investigation if further inquiries are needed, and to refer appropriate cases to the Court of Appeal. We suggest this body might be known as the Criminal Cases Review Authority.
>
> In cases which seemed to the Authority to call for further investigation, it would ensure that that investigation was launched.
>
> Where the Authority instructed the police to conduct investigations, it would be responsible for supervising the investigation and would have the power to require the police to follow up those lines of inquiry that seemed to it necessary for the thorough examination of the case.
>
> Where the result of the investigation indicated that there were reasons for supposing that a miscarriage of justice might have occurred, the Authority would refer the case to the Court of Appeal.

In due course, in 1994, the Home Office prepared a Discussion Paper on 'Criminal Appeals and the establishment of a Criminal Cases Review Authority'. Cardinal Hume attached very great importance to this document and it was carefully considered both by a group of members and by the whole Deputation.

On 24 May, 1994, Cardinal Hume sent to the Home Secretary the Deputation's response to the consultation paper. A copy of the response is at APPENDIX XV. Cardinal Hume said in his covering letter there was much in the Discussion Paper with which the Deputation would agree, but there were some fundamental points about the proposed Authority which caused great concern. Amongst the points he made were:

> The setting up of the new Authority needs to be clearly seen as the beginning of a new era in the handling of representations on miscarriages of justice.

> It is essential that the new Authority should emerge as, and is seen and acknowledged to be, a strong and independent body capable of fulfilling effectively, and with a sense of urgency, its tasks relating to allegations of miscarriages of justice.
>
> The Authority should be empowered to investigate a case, to refer a case, and to make recommendations, 'if it thinks fit'.
>
> Neither the investigation nor the reference should be encumbered by statutory requirements other than possibly a few which might be essential and unavoidable. However, such minimum limitations or restrictions should in no way be capable of being interpreted as inhibiting the pursuit of justice.

The Response to the consultation paper, at APPENDIX XV, sets out fully and clearly how the Deputation considered the new Authority should operate. Particular attention is drawn to 'Investigations' and 'Other Powers' which are dealt with in paragraphs 36 to 42. It will be seen that a recommendation under 'Investigations' was that 'there should be a *core* central unit within the Authority of civilians trained and experienced in conducting investigations and/or similarly qualified *retired* police officers'.

This *core* central unit would be used by the Authority to conduct smaller investigations and to oversee, on its behalf, larger and more complex types of investigation undertaken by selected police forces. The Deputation saw this arrangement as signalling that the Authority was credible, effective and truly independent.

Following this Response to the consultation paper, there was to be one final meeting between the Home Secretary, then Michael Howard, and the whole Deputation. It was after the publication of the Final Report of the May Inquiry in June 1994 that Cardinal Hume had first sought such a meeting. The main purpose of it was to express concern over various aspects of miscarriages of justice in the light of the revelations of the May Inquiry.

The meeting finally took place on 18 January, 1995. The opportunity was also taken to discuss those parts of the consultation paper entitled 'Criminal Appeals and the establishment of a Criminal Cases Review Authority', which were of particular interest to the Deputation.

One of the main points discussed was the organisation and conduct of 'Investigations'[2]. Each member of the Deputation spoke in support of the need for a *core* unit for investigating within the new Authority to operate as shown in APPENDIX XV. They were unanimously of

[2]APPENDIX XV para 36 to 42.

the view that this would be a clear indication of the independence of the Authority.

Their views were not wholly reflected in the final organisation of the new body. It came into being on 1 January, 1997. It was given the new title of 'Criminal Cases Review Commission' and was to be based in Birmingham.

The new Commission is now succeeding in gaining the respect of practitioners in various parts of the criminal justice system, and in attracting their increasing confidence. Its final establishment marked the end of a very long road in the history of miscarriages of justice.

APPENDIXES

Appendix I	Annex to Memorandum attached to Joint Opinion by Lord Devlin and Lord Scarman
Appendix II	Statement of Maura Kelly
Appendix III	Statement of Yvonne Dorothy Fox
Appendix IV	Statement of Francis Keenan
Appendix V	Statement of Anne Keenan
Appendix VI	Statement by Father F Ryan of Conway House
Appendix VII	Statement of Father P Carolan
Appendix VIII	Report dated 9 September, 1988 from Alastair Logan concerning evidence by Maura Kelly relating to Carole Richardson.
Appendix IX	Report dated 13 September, 1988 from Alastair Logan concerning witnesses for Paul Hill.
Appendix X	'Justice and the Guildford Four.' Typed text of the article by Lord Devlin and Lord Scarman as in *The Times* on 30 November, 1988
Appendix XI	A copy of the statement made by Charles Burke to the police 18 January, 1975
Appendix XII	The May Inquiry – A Submission on the Maguire case by the Deputation led by Cardinal Hume 22 March, 1990 with an Annex by Robert Kee.
Appendix XIII	The eight questions sent by Cardinal Hume to the Home Secretary and Sir John May on 2 June, 1993

APPENDIX I

ANNEX TO MEMORANDUM ATTACHED TO JOINT OPINION BY LORD DEVLIN AND LORD SCARMAN

1 The Court of Criminal Appeal, as it used to be called, was created in 1907 by statute. Its main power was expressed negatively. By section 9 of the Act of 1907 the Court was enjoined to dismiss the appeal unless it could be brought within one of the three following grounds:

A that the verdict 'is unreasonable or cannot be supported having regard to the evidence';
B that there had been at the trial a wrong decision on any question of law; and
C that there had been on any ground a miscarriage of justice.

2 These three grounds were all subject to the 'proviso' that the Court might dismiss the appeal if they considered that no substantial miscarriage of justice had actually occurred. The way in which the courts applied this proviso is known as the Stirland formula after the case in 1944 in which the House of Lords decided that, once one of the three grounds of appeal had been established, the conviction *must* be quashed unless the Court considered that a reasonable jury, properly directed, could not have failed to convict.

3 The Act gave power to the Court to receive new evidence which had not been given at the trial, but said nothing about how it should be treated. In the treatment of evidence a court has first to decide whether it is true or false: if true, it proves the facts to which the witness has deposed. This is proof by direct evidence. The court has next to decide what further facts may be inferred from the facts proved: this is proof by indirect evidence. In a criminal trial both decisions are to be made by the jury at the trial. In considering whether the verdict could not be supported by the evidence an

appellate court has always been less reluctant to interfere where the evidence is indirect than where it is direct. In direct evidence the conclusion of a jury which has seen and heard the evidence is rarely questioned.

4 But the Act gave no power to the Court of Appeal to sit with a jury or to order a new trial by jury. The judges dealt with this situation by treating the new evidence, once they had decided to admit it, as if it had been tendered at the trial and wrongly excluded, i.e. as though there had been an error of law or miscarriage of justice. So once the new evidence was admitted the appeal had to succeed unless it could be defeated by the proviso. Under the Stirland formula this meant that the conviction must be quashed unless the prosecution could show that the new evidence could not have made any difference to the verdict. This application of the formula remained unquestioned until 1974.

5 Before that year there were two legislative changes. First, a statute of 1964 empowered the Court, when it quashed a conviction on the ground that the new evidence might have made a difference, to order a new trial by jury. The second change was made incidentally by the statute of 1966 which reformed the Court of Criminal Appeal: it ceased to be a court on its own and became a division (the Criminal Division) of the Court of Appeal. At the same time the Act made some minor changes in the wording of the grounds of appeal. They were recommended by the Committee, whose report was the source of the new Act, as intended to increase the safeguards for an innocent person wrongly convicted. The definition of a verdict which the Court was empowered to quash (see para. 3 above) was changed from 'unreasonable or cannot be supported' to one that was under all the circumstances of the case 'unsafe or unsatisfactory'. The change was incorporated in section 2 of the 1968 Act and this was the text interpreted and applied by the House of Lords in 1974 in Stafford v D.P.P.

6 Before we consider that case we shall amplify what we have said in paragraph 4 above about direct and indirect evidence. In the former the question is whether the evidence is true or false. In the latter the question is as to what inferences of fact should be drawn from the direct evidence. These two questions are topped by a third, which is as to the weight of the totality of the evidence, direct and indirect. The answers to all three questions are ultimately to be determined by the jury. But in each of them there is a preliminary question for the judge to decide. This is whether under

each of the heads there is a sufficiency of material to go to the jury. Since we are concerned in this case with only the first of the three ultimate questions, we shall consider the preliminary question only in relation to that.

7 The preliminary question for the judge when new evidence is tendered is to decide whether or not it is credible, i.e. capable of belief. It is the fact that the evidence is new that gives rise to this preliminary question. At the trial the only question the Judge has to decide is whether the evidence tendered is admissible. If it is, it goes straight to the jury to decide whether it is true or false. The intermediate question of credibility arises only in the case of evidence not tendered at the trial. Since only a jury can decide whether it is true or false, its reception means that a new jury must be summoned for a new trial. Justice does not require that this should be done for a cock and bull story. Before a new trial is ordered the court must be satisfied that the new evidence is not incredible.

8 An excellent statement of the law on this point was made by Roskill L.J. We quote the passage abbreviated only by the omission of flourishes that are a natural part of speech but need not be included in the writing:

> Constitutionally the tribunal to whom falls the duty of determining issues of fact upon which verdicts of guilty or not guilty depend, is the jury . . . Where fresh evidence is adduced, this Court is not concerned to cast upon appellants the burden of proving that what the new evidence asserts is true. It is concerned that that new evidence is credible as opposed to incredible, that is, that it is capable of belief and if placed before a jury might be believed by them as opposed to something which it is impossible to believe. Once that evidence is shown to be credible, a conviction arrived at in the absence of that evidence is likely to be unsafe or unsatisfactory unless and until the truth or untruth of the facts which that new evidence asserts is determined one way or the other. The constitutional tribunal for the determination of that issue is a jury. Hence the power to order the new trial where credible new evidence is adduced. But the ordering of a new trial is not always possible, especially after a long lapse of time. In such a case it is the plain duty of the Court to quash the conviction, not because it is necessarily accepting the truth of what the new evidence has asserted, but because until that truth has been tested, any conviction reached

in the absence of that testing is likely to be unsafe or unsatisfactory.'

9 Eight years passed (since the Act of 1968 was on this point only a repetition of the Act of 1966) before the House of Lords announced a radical change in the law as stated above. In the interval the Courts continued to apply the well established test. In a case in 1971 Lord Chief Justice Parker said in relation to the new witnesses whose evidence was introduced into the Court of Appeal: 'The Court is quite unable to say that their evidence is incapable of belief; the sole question is what weight should be given to it. For that purpose one has to imagine a jury who heard their evidence together with all the other evidence in the case, and ask oneself whether nevertheless the jury must have come to the same conclusion'. The Court ordered a new trial.

10 Stafford v D.P.P. (1974), the case in which the House of Lords enunciated the new doctrine, was a case of murder in which the question was whether the accused were the culprits. The prosecution relied on a mass of circumstantial evidence which depended considerably on the observations of witnesses who were on the spot before and after the crime was committed. The jury convicted. On appeal the defence called a number of new witnesses who added to the circumstantial evidence. No question arose about the credibility of the new witnesses; they were not before the Court; their testimony was taken before an examiner and the Court had the written record. The question was simply as to its weight: was it enough to turn the scale? In saying that it was not, the Court of Appeal used a new formula. Instead of saying that no reasonable jury could think that it made any difference, they said that they themselves, the appeal judges, did not think that it made any difference.

11 The case went to the Lords who unanimously upheld the Court of Appeal. They said that the case depended entirely on the language of the 1968 Act Section 2 which in its material parts reads as follows: 'The Court of Appeal shall allow an appeal against conviction if they think that the verdict of the jury should be set aside on the ground that in all the circumstances of the case it is unsafe or unsatisfactory . . . and in any other case shall dismiss the appeal'. The House said that the Court of Appeal, having examined the old and the new evidence taken together and having concluded (quite rightly in the opinion of the House) that it proved guilt, could not say that the conviction was unsafe or unsatisfac-

tory and so were obliged by the words of the Act to dismiss the appeal. The Act said 'if they think'. It was what they, the appeal judges, thought that mattered, not what a hypothetical jury might think.

12 This was the main ruling in the case and in our opinion it is a misconstruction of the section. Certainly it is what they think that matters. The question is what under the Act have they to think about. They have to think about whether the verdict of a jury is satisfactory, not about how they themselves would decide the case. The verdict of a jury which has not heard all the relevant evidence must of its nature be unsatisfactory.

13 This ruling appears to upset numerous decisions of the Court of Appeal. But the House did not overrule them. They said that it was optional for a court in the future to follow the old practice if it wanted to. This seems to be inconsistent with the construction they adopted of the Act which obliges the court to dismiss the appeal if they think the verdict to be satisfactory. The inconsistency may be removed or at least concealed if the House's opinion that judges and juries always think alike is sound: 'if the court has no reasonable doubt about the verdict, it follows that the court does not think that the jury could have one'. But this dictum is as far removed from reality as it is from all the previous dicta on the subject going back to 1670. (Lord Devlin has expressed in full his opinion of the House of Lords decision in 'The Judge' O.U.P. (1979) p.156.)

14 Since 1974 there have been two cases in the Court of Appeal, both presided over by Roskill L.J., in which the court has chosen the option of determining for itself the effect of the new evidence. The Guildford case was the second. The first was the Luton Post Office Murder; see Lukovic Kennedy 'Wicked Beyond Belief', Granada 1980, in which at pp 15 and 140 Lord Devlin made contributions on the legal aspect of the case.

15 The Luton Murder was the murder of a postmaster by a gang of four. Matthews, a man with many previous convictions, was the only one of this gang whom the police were able to identify. He confessed to a minor part in the crime and alleged that Cooper, McMahon and Murphy were the other three. He turned Queen's Evidence to obtain immunity. His evidence was virtually the only evidence against the three. They were all convicted.

16 The next step in a case that dragged on from 1969 to 1980 was that Murphy produced strong evidence of an alibi. The Home Secretary referred the evidence to the Court of Appeal who quashed his conviction. This threw doubt on the identification of the other two and eventually their cases were referred back to the Court of Appeal. The appellants were given leave to have Matthews recalled to explain how, if he was wrong about Murphy, he could be sure that he was right about Cooper and McMahon. His evidence was that he was still sure about all three. After vicissitudes, not very creditable to the Court of Appeal, a further reference was heard in April 1976 by the court in which Roskill L. J. presided.

17 By this time the decision of the House of Lords in Stafford v D.P.P. had been published. The Court took it as their authority to conduct a partial re-trial of the case, presumably so as to decide whether or not on the whole of the evidence they thought the conviction satisfactory. So Matthews was allowed to tell the whole story over again. The Court said that they each of them watched him closely and that, while he told a number of lies in the course of his evidence, on the vital part of his story he was clearly telling the truth. So they held that the conviction was not unsafe or unsatisfactory. Four years later 'Wicked Beyond Belief' was published and in a very short time the Home Secretary released the accused.

18 In the Guildford case the evidence of the Woolwich Bombers tendered to the Court of Appeal obviously required the most careful scrutiny. It could be false evidence given by witnesses who had nothing more to lose in an attempt to exonerate those whom they would regard as their companions in arms. The defence accepted this; they did not ask for an acquittal but for a new trial by jury. The Court adopted the Stafford approach to the new evidence in preference to the old.

19 The Court did not therefore adjudge the new evidence to be 'incapable of belief'. Roskill L. 3., who delivered the judgment, referred to various pieces of the evidence as incredible, but the test applied to the whole was that propounded by Lord Dilhorne in Stafford v D.P.P. They quoted the following sentence from his speech: 'The proper approach to the question they have to decide may vary from case to case and it should be left to the Court and the Act leaves it to the Court to decide what approach to make'. They decided, not expressly but by implication, to make the new approach and not the old. For Roskill L.J. went on: 'We have to

ask ourselves whether our appraisal and evaluation of the new evidence . . . leads us to think that any of the four convictions is unsafe or unsatisfactory'. They accepted it as possible, if not true, that Butler and O'Connell had themselves taken part in the Guildford bombings but disbelieved their denial that the Guildford convicts had also taken part. They concluded that all the Woolwich witnesses were lying, saying that Dowd was a deplorable witness and Butler almost as bad. Sitting presumably as a court of appeal on their own conclusions of fact, they rejected the submission that they ought to be left with 'lurking doubt'.

20 This judgment of the Court of Appeal is wholly dependent on the law as stated in Stafford v D.P.P. which the Court applied as 'final and authoritative'. The House of Lords does not refuse to review its pronouncements and in our opinion should be asked to do so in this case. But it is also our opinion that, even if the House was right, the Court of Appeal in this case was wrong. The Lords decision should not be pressed beyond its facts. It was a case of indirect evidence. Granted that its observations were wide enough to cover all cases, they must nevertheless in relation to direct evidence be treated as obiter, i.e. entitled to great respect but not binding. The House left it to future appellate courts to make the choice between the old approach and the new. Surely the choice should not be the arbitrary and unreasoned one which the Roskill court made. It should be a choice which avoids or at least minimises the violations enumerated in para. 2 of the Note. Surely the dividing line should be drawn between cases of direct and cases of indirect evidence. It is one thing to dispense with a jury when what is in issue is the correctness of inferences and perhaps even when it is a question of weight; and quite another when the issue is whether or not witnesses are lying.

21 All that we have written above represents our opinion given on material last considered in or about 1978. Research is needed to see what has happened since then. We should not be surprised if nothing has happened. Radical innovations in the law are not usually welcomed. Since appellate courts were offered an option to follow the old and established law, we suspect that they may unostentatiously have taken it. A negative result should not be unhelpful to the Guildford convicts since they would then be left as the only persons who had suffered under a dubious decision.

(Signed): DEVLIN
16 July 1987 SCARMAN'

APPENDIXES II to VII

STATEMENTS BY WITNESSES

Appendix II	Statement of Maura Kelly
Appendix III	Statement of Yvonne Dorothy Fox
Appendix IV	Statement of Francis Keenan
Appendix V	Statement of Anne Keenan
Appendix VI	Statement by Father F Ryan of Conway House
Appendix VII	Statement of Father P Carolan

APPENDIX II

STATEMENT OF MAURA KELLY

IN 1974 I was aged 15 and I lived in Primrose Hill. I was at school with Lisa Astin at a school called St George's. Lisa left school. When she left I still remained in contact with her. She used to visit the school occasionally and on some of these occasions she brought with her a girl called Carole Richardson. I got to know Carole over a period of two or three months in the summer of 1974. We all referred to each other as sisters. They would come and visit me at school. I felt sorry for Carole. She seemed a bit below on intelligence and had no family to speak up for her and was living in a squat.

As far as I could see the squat was nothing out of the ordinary. I only went into the room that was occupied by Carole and Lisa and Paddy Armstrong. It was the downstairs front room and it was dark. I didn't ask who else lived there and I didn't know any of them. I remember there were two beds in the room. I wouldn't have wanted to live in a place like that. I never have lived in squats and I didn't need to because I could live at home.

Although I was attending school regularly I had a job as a sale assistant in the ABC Bakery at Englands Lane NW3 which I had for about a year before the summer of 1974. I used to work there on Saturdays and in school holidays and I used to finish between 5.15 and 5.30 although very occasionally, if I was there on my own, I could go earlier than that at about 5.00 after all fresh cakes and bread were sold. I think I was left on my own twice. The Manageress was very fussy.

I recall an occasion, which I am certain was 5th October 1974, when Carole and Lisa came to visit me at the Bakery Shop. Their visit was not planned ahead and I did not know they were coming to visit me. I remember it because my attention was drawn to it quite shortly afterwards when Carole was arrested and Lisa came to see me.

That day I was working at the ABC Bakery. Carole and Lisa came to visit me during the afternoon quite early I think at about 2.30pm or so. I told them that I had to work and that my Manageress was in the shop but she was going off leaving me in charge and so I suggested to them that they went off to look at shops in Englands Lane. I had no prior warning before that day that the Manageress was going off early. They went away and came back sometime later. They gave me a present of a wooden doll dressed as a nurse. It had a nurse's uniform on and wooden legs, a red cross on the front of the nurse's uniform and it had a hat. I kept it until about two years ago when I threw it out because its leg had got broken by then.

I would describe them on that day as being happy-go-lucky, as they usually were. I remember that they were wearing long dresses and certainly one of them, I think Lisa, had no shoes on. They came up to borrow some money from me. They told me that they were going to a Pop Concert at the Elephant and Castle and they wanted some money. I knew I would get paid before the Manageress left and I therefore agreed to lend them £2, when I was paid.

I also remember that day because it was the day I went to see the film 'The Exorcist'. I knew I was going to see that film when they came up to visit me at the shop in Englands Lane.

As far as I remember there was no one else with them. As far as I was concerned the money was a loan and not a gift.

We agreed that when they came back to the shop, that if I could get away early we would walk off down the road together. I did in fact lock up the shop early and we walked down together to the bus stop in Adelaide Road. As far as I can recall this was the first occasion on which Carole had visited me in the shop although Lisa had done so before.

I remember them telling me that they were going to get a shower at Swiss Cottage Swimming Baths but I cannot remember whether they told me the name of the group that they were going to see at the Pop Concert.

Later on after Carole's arrest and before Christmas 1974, Lisa came to see me. She told me that she and Carole were at the Pop Concert on the 5th October and that's what triggered off my memory that that was the day they had come to see me and the day I had gone to see 'The Exorcist'. Lisa hadn't remembered when we discussed it that she and Carole had come up to see me at Englands Lane on that day. I told her that she had. I then went to see Carole's solicitor with Lisa and made a statement.

I went to Ireland originally for a holiday in the summer of 1975. I was staying with an Uncle. I decided to stay on because I was enjoying it and also I had met a boyfriend and I did not want to leave. I was terrified about appearing in Court and my mum didn't want me to have anymore connection with it which is one of the reasons why I agreed to go off to Ireland.

Whilst I was in Ireland I kept in contact with Carole by letter and she wrote to me. Neither she nor her solicitors mentioned that I was expected to go to Court. Then a summons came for me when I was in Ireland to attend Court to give evidence on behalf of Carole Richardson but I ignored it. I ignored it because I honestly thought that the case was going to be over quickly and that it would prove Carole's innocence. I felt that my statement was not needed to help Carole as I believed the Police had no evidence against her and the case against her would be thrown out. I was told I could stay in Ireland, by my mother, whom I telephoned when I got the summons.

24 March 1987 (Signed): M. KELLY

APPENDIX III

STATEMENT OF YVONNE DOROTHY FOX

I HAVE KNOWN Anne and Frank Keenan for many years. I had known them for about 18 months before November 1974.

I remember that time very clearly. At that time I had two children. My eldest daughter Amanda was at school and my youngest daughter was still in a pram and I used to take her to work with me. Anne Keenan and myself both worked at the Easi-Phit shoe shop. However, we had to look after our small children, in my case, Deborah all the time I worked, and in Mrs Keenan's case Francis Jnr, during the lunch-hour. It meant that Anne had to collect her child from the school and bring him back to the shop. The management had no objection but ultimately some sort of directive came down from above to the effect that we could not have the children in the shop. It appeared to be change in policy on behalf of the management but it meant that we could not work there any longer so both Anne and I decided to leave.

At this time my mother had had a slight stroke. That was another reason why I could not leave the child with anyone else. Anne and I discussed the matter and then we decided to leave Easi-Phit to find another job. We were interviewed for canteen assistants in the local Polytechnic. I recall that we were interviewed in the week commencing 4th November 1974.

We got on well together and that is why we decided to try and find a job together. My eldest daughter's birthday is on 11th November. We got the job as canteen assistants and were due to start on the same day as my eldest daughter's birthday.

I decided to go round and pay a social call on Anne as I did from time to time on Thursday 7th November 1974. I had dinner with my husband at approximately 5.45pm, as we normally did, and after supper I washed up. I then told my husband I was popping up to see Anne Keenan about the new job.

It took about 10 to 15 minutes for me to walk from my house to Anne and Frank's flat.

I think I arrived at Anne and Frank's flat about 7.00 in the evening. My husband was looking after our two daughters. I sat in the sitting room and discussed with Anne the attitude of Easi-Phit to us which had caused us to give up our jobs and the new job we had been interviewed for. By my recollection we had been interviewed early in the morning on the day before, namely Wednesday 6th.

As we sat and chatted we also watched TV. In the room with Anne and myself was Anne's husband, Frank, and Anne's nephew, Paul Hill. Paul was in the room for most of the time that I was there. However, he left the house saying that he was going to ring his girlfriend. As far as I can recollect he was gone for about 20 minutes. I remember that he just got up and walked out saying that he was going to make the telephone call to his girlfriend.

He came back about 20 minutes later as I have said and sat in the room watching television with us until I got up to leave.

By my recollection I saw the beginning of the News at Ten that night and I left about the end of Part One. I did not see any part of the Part Two of the News nor did I see any News Flash.

Shortly afterwards, and I cannot remember precisely when, I was told by Anne that Paul was charged with having done a bombing that night in Woolwich. Both Anne and I knew perfectly well that he had been in the house at the time and that he could not have done any bombing in Woolwich because he was only out of the house for about 20 minutes.

My husband told me about the Woolwich Bombing when I returned home because he had seen the News Flash and I had not. Later Anne told me about Paul being charged with this offence.

I was never interviewed by anyone from Paul Hill's solicitors. However I received a letter from a Mr Melton from Paul Hill's solicitors referring to the evening of 7th November 1974, to which I replied. In my reply I set out everything that I could recall about that evening and sent it off to him. The next letter I received from Mr Melton was a Summons to attend Court. It had a date in it being the day on which I had to attend. I attended Court in accordance with the Summons. I had to wait at Court a few days. It was the week commencing 9th October 1975. On the first day that I attended Court, Mr Melton called out my name and I identified myself to him. He asked me what I could remember of the 7th November 1974, and I went over the events again with him. I remember asking him whether or not my address would have to be read out in Court and he told me that he could not guarantee that my address would not be given out in Court.

I had in fact attended Court with Anne and Frank Keenan because they had to give evidence on behalf of Paul Hill as well. We all sat together for those days before the evidence was called.

I was told by Mr Melton, I believe, at Court, that I would no longer be needed. No explanation was given to me as to why my evidence was not needed. I, in fact, did not remain at the Court but left before Anne and Frank gave their evidence. I believe I attended Court for two or three days.

I did not make it a condition of giving evidence that my address should not be read out, although I was concerned about it bearing in mind the nature of the case and the amount of public attention that it attracted. I saw Mr Melton on each of the days that I attended Court.

No explanation was ever offered to me as to why I did not give evidence and I was at all times willing to do so even if my address was going to be mentioned because I understood that the same thing had been said to Mr & Mrs Keenan about their address.

There is absolutely no doubt in my mind that Paul Hill was in the house all that evening that I was there apart from the short trip that he took out to make a telephone call. I cannot be precise about the time he spent outside the house but it was about 20 minutes and not longer than half an hour. During the time that Paul was in the house he sat in the same room with us. I found him a pleasant boy, polite and courteous. I knew he was working with Frank Keenan on a building site.

When Anne Keenan told me that Paul Hill had been charged with carrying out a bombing on that night, I knew perfectly well he could not have done so bearing in mind that we were in North London and the bombing was carried out in Woolwich in South East London.

I have not kept any of the letters that Mr Melton sent to me nor the Summons and I did not make any copy of the letter that I wrote to Mr Melton in response to his letter to me setting out my recollections of the evening of the 7th November 1974.

15 July 1987 (Signed): Y.D. FOX

APPENDIX IV

STATEMENT OF FRANCIS KEENAN

PAUL MICHAEL HILL is my nephew. I have known him for some time. He used to come regularly to England from Belfast to work in England and on the occasions when he did so he would call at our house regularly. He formed a strong attachment to our son and was always very gentle and kind with him and used to take him out and buy him sweets and toys and take him to football matches.

During the latter part of 1974 he stayed with us having no where else to stay. He shared a room with my son. The last time he came back to England we were unaware that he was back until he met my wife in the Easi-Phit Shop where she worked in Kentish Town Road. He came in with another boy who I did not see and do not know but I understand to be Gerard Conlon.

He told my wife that they were staying in the hostel for Catholic young men in Quex Road, Kilburn. He asked my wife to lend him some money which she did. He told my wife that he was staying weekends with the sister of his girlfriend with whom his girlfriend was living. We did not then know his girlfriend.

As a result of him losing his accommodation he came and moved in with us on the 18th October 1974. Before that I remember he had come to the flat one night. He said he had a couple of tickets for a dance in Camden, possibly at the Carousel Club but I don't remember. I went with him. The Maguires were at that dance being Anne Maguire and her husband but I did not know them at the time and only realised who they were and that I had seen them after they had been arrested.

Paul was working for Harts a firm that carried out civil engineering work. I worked for them as well. I worked for them as a labourer. Paul had worked for them before when he had been in the country. He started working for them two weeks before he moved into our house. He had previously worked for Harts in the summer before (1973) and he had returned back to Belfast in December 1973. He worked under a Ganger-man called Tucker Clarke, in 1974, who gave him the job.

Every Thursday night he stayed with us he would go out and ring the girlfriend Eugenia Clarke in Southampton. He did it as regular as clockwork to make the arrangements as to where they would meet for that weekend. He went to a number of phone boxes either outside the Sorting Office at the end of Leighton Road or there were two other phone boxes outside Kentish Town Station and 4 inside the Tube Station as well as a number of others in the area. He was never away very long. On the weekend before the 7th November 1974 his girlfriend came to the house and stayed with us and that was the first time that we met her.

I recall vividly the night of 7th November 1974. I recall it partially because it was unusual and partially because I had good reason to recall it later on when I knew that Paul had been charged with an offence alleged to have been committed on that night.

On that night Paul was in our house. It was a Thursday. It was the night he always went to ring his girlfriend. I remember that our friend, Yvonne Fox, was in the house at that time. Paul could not have left the house for more than 20 minutes that night. We sat and watched television. We had both worked together at Harts and both had left for work together and came home together. I can say that apart from the time that Paul was out phoning his girlfriend which was no more than 20 minutes he did not leave the house at all that night and he was in the room with me. My wife and Mrs Fox talked about a new job they were going to start together. I remember the night also because there was the News Flash coming up on the television screen about the bombing at Woolwich. Paul, I am certain, was in the room at the time when this came up but I believe that Mrs Fox had left to go home to her husband by that time.

I remember that Gina was staying with us at around the Guy Fawkes time because we had fireworks on the steps at the front door which Paul let off for us for our young son. Gina was with him at the time.

There is no possibility that I have in any way forgotten any of the aspects of this matter. Neither is there any possibility that Paul Hill could have left our house on the 7th November and gone to do a bombing at Woolwich. When I heard that Paul Hill had been charged with the Woolwich bombing I couldn't believe it. On 7th November 1974 Paul and I left for work at 7.30 am as usual. At no time did he leave the site that day. We finished work at 5.00 pm and went straight home, as we did every day, getting home at about 6.00 pm. I believe that Paul went out approximately 8.00 pm to ring his girlfriend Gina. I gave all this information to the solicitor who acted for Paul during the course of his trial, a Mr Melton. I was also called as a witness for the defence at the Old Bailey on Friday 13th October 1975. I recall on 7th November that we watched Top of the Pops, Monty Python's Flying Circus, Mastermind and then the News at Ten, after which we saw the News Flash about the bombing.

15 July 1987 (Signed) : FRANK KEENAN

APPENDIX V

STATEMENT OF ANNE KEENAN

I AM the wife of Francis Keenan, the mother of Francis Keenan Junior and the Aunt of Paul Michael Hill. I have read my husband's statement and insofar as it relates to the periods of time when we are together it is absolutely accurate.

On the 7th November 1974, Paul had been in work with my husband all day and they had both gone to work together and returned from work together as usual. Paul was sitting on the settee and Frankie was getting washed in the bathroom when a friend of mine, Yvonne Fox, called. I had known Yvonne Fox for a long time. To put it properly into context Paul had been in this country during the summer of 1973 but returned home to Belfast at Christmas 1973. My husband got Paul the job with Harts in the summer of '73 where he worked until Xmas '73 when he returned to Belfast. I did not know he had come back from Belfast until some time during late September or early October 1974 when he called at the shoe shop at which I worked called Easi-Phit in Kentish Town Road. He was with another boy whom he introduced to me as Gerry Conlon. I had never met Gerry Conlon before. He told me that they were both living in a hostel for Catholic young men in Quex Road, Kilburn which I knew well, because this is the road that The Sacred Heart Church is in where my husband and I had married. He said he was short of money and asked me if I would lend him some which I did, just a few pounds. He told me that he had been looking for work in this country and that he had a girlfriend who was living with her sister in Southampton and that he went down and stayed weekends with her. I did not know before that conversation that he had a girlfriend.

Later on he came to the house to see us and my young son. He had a couple of tickets for a dance in Camden Town. I do not remember the details of the dance but I think that it was at the Carousel Club. I did not want to go but I encouraged my husband Frankie to do so. I said it would be a change for him as he never went out without me. Shortly after that on the 18th October 1974, Paul moved in to live with us. Paul had got a job with Harts, where my husband worked, by seeing the Gangerman, Tucker Clarke.

Every Thursday Paul would ring his girlfriend from a pay call box in the vicinity of our flat to make arrangements to meet at the weekend. Most weekends he went down and stayed in Southampton but the first occasion when his girlfriend came up and we met her was close to Guy Fawkes night and Paul let fireworks off for my young son. He always got on well with our son, buying him sweets and presents, taking him out and also taking him to football matches along with my husband.

As far as I know he used to go to the phone box outside the Sorting Office or there were two phone boxes at the end of Leighton Road or there were 4 inside Kentish Town Tube Station. He went every weekend except for one that I remember, to Southampton that he was staying with us.

Yvonne Fox and I met when we had been working together and we had known each other for about 18 months by then. We worked together at Easi-Phit. However, we had small children who had to be coped with. I had to collect my son from play school and kept him during the lunch-hour at the shop. Yvonne's youngest child was a baby and that meant she had her with her at work at the shop. The management had no objection but ultimately some sort of directive came down from above to the effect that we could not keep the children in the shop whilst we worked. We, therefore, both decided to leave Easi-Phit.

We got on so well together we decided to try and find another job together. In the end we went for an interview in the week of 7th November 1974. I remember this because it was Yvonne's eldest daughter's birthday on 11th November and we were due to start work on 11th November in the canteen at the Polytechnic.

Yvonne came round on the evening of the 7th November. She frequently came round to see me. She would normally leave her children with her husband. We would sit and chat and watch television. My husband would always be there as well. My husband did not go out of an evening. On this particular night I remember it firstly, because we were discussing the new job and we were not a little displeased at the attitude of Easi-Phit, and, secondly, Yvonne's mother had had a slight stroke and she was talking about that. Thirdly, we had to make arrangements for the children to be looked after and, fourthly, there was the News Flash about the bombing at Woolwich.

Yvonne came to my house I suppose about 7.00 pm but she had left by the time that the News Flash came on to the television. She wasn't in the house when the News Flash came on. I remember that we had gone for our job interviews at the Polytechnic early in the morning on the day before and this was the first opportunity that we had had a chance to discuss the whole matter.

Paul could not have left the house on 7th November for more than 20 minutes. I remember that evening we watched Top of the Pops, Monty Python's Flying Circus and Mastermind. I had every reason to recall this soon after the event because Paul was charged with the bombing at Woolwich and because I had checked my recollections with Yvonne. I gave all this information to Mr Melton.

I have absolutely no doubt whatsoever that Paul was in the house, apart from that 20 minutes when he went to ring Gina, for the whole evening of 7th November, after he returned from work.

I would describe Paul as a happy-go-lucky kind of character. He got on well with my son and I would trust my son with him at any time.

We lived at 91c Brecknock Road, London N7 in November 1974.

15 July 1987 (Signed): ANNE KEENAN

APPENDIX VI

STATEMENT BY FATHER F. RYAN OF CONWAY HOUSE

DURING my summer holidays of 1974, I was contacted by our Provincial, Fr John Dore, and informed that I was being changed from Parish work, and was being sent to the Irish Centre, 52 Camden Square, London NW1. This appointment was effective immediately, and I was told to go to the Irish Centre without any delay. Within a short time, I had taken up the new post at the Irish Centre. Work at the Centre involved mainly working with the homeless. It also meant giving support to our girl's hostel at Hornsey Lane Gardens, NW7, and some support to the men's hostel, known as Hope House, in Kilburn. In late September 1974 the manager of the hostel, Fr P. Carolan went on holidays, and I was assigned to his duties while he was away. This meant living in the hostel.

The idea of the hostel was to assist new arrivals in becoming integrated into the host society. This meant giving them accommodation, and helping them to find jobs. Most of the clients were from a marginalised background. In spite of this, the hostel, which held 100 men, did a good job in helping young people to get started in London.

Before taking up temporary duties in the hostel, I was given a very good briefing as to how the hostel was run, and the problems which were to the fore at that time. Taking charge of the hostel was a very anxious time for me, even though there was good supportive staff. I decided it would be a good time to assert authority at an early stage. The opportunity for this came when a number of thefts occurred which required investigation. Some shoes, clothes, money, and a radio were stolen from different parts of the house. I decided to search everywhere in order to recover the goods which were stolen. I spent the whole day, searching every room, every locker, every suitcase, every nook and cranny within the building for clues on the goods which were stolen. This search occurred on or about the 3rd of October. In this search, bath panels were taken out, and even manholes lifted. I was not just looking for stolen goods, but also informing myself of the state of the building itself.

Hill and Conlon were allocated a room on the ground floor and shared this room with two other people. It was called St. Louis then, and is now numbered 220. This room was situated approximately four feet from the manager's bedroom. The room was also close to the administration area. It would have been very easy to detect any unusual activity in this room. There was no disturbance in this room during my stay at the hostel.

The position of the room made it extremely dangerous for Hill and Conlon to use as a jumping-off ground for any serious illegal activities. The search of the room on the 3rd October revealed nothing suspicious. One of the occupants of the room at that time, stayed in the hostel for some months afterwards. His character was such that he would have reported anything suspicious going on at the time.

I have no recollection of Hill at all. Conlon left a clear impression on me. On a Friday evening, about 5.30 pm Gerard came to the office, appeared distressed, and asked for money to go home. He said his father was unwell. Residents usually said something like this when they needed to go home urgently. I did not believe him. A discussion followed which lasted at least a half hour. Gerard was a young, skinny, curly-haired youth and at this time he wore a sheepskin coat, which came down to his knees. The edges of the coat were lined very conspicuously with white wool. His coat was totally unsuitable and made him look very conspicuous. He appeared very agitated, and under a great deal of stress. I formed the conclusion that he had a mental breakdown of some kind, and was not in a fit state to travel. I tried to persuade him to remain in the hostel, and I would arrange for him to see a doctor in the morning. I refused to give him any money. He went off and returned in about an hour. He had succeeded in getting almost all the money he needed to go home. He required another £5.00 to get him home. Seeing that he was going to go anyway, I thought I had no option but to give him the remainder of the money he wanted. I understood that he was going to travel from Stranraer to Larne, and as it was now very late wondered whether this would be possible. I was concerned for him as he left, because the weather conditions in the north-west of England at that time were very inclement. I had visions of him trying to hitch a lift over the M6 around the Shap, and having problems of exposure, I was concerned for some time after he had left, and hoped he made it home alright.

After Gerard Conlon was picked up by the police, they came to interview Fr Carolan who was in charge of the hostel at that time. He was taken to Guildford for questioning and released that evening. In due course they came to interview me at the Irish Centre, and I made a statement incorporating the information already supplied here. During the interview, the police gave me to understand that they had no doubts that Conlon and Hill had committed the bombing at Guildford. I recall saying vulgar things about the IRA for not even paying their bombers for doing their work, and I resented having to subsidise Conlon's exit from London. It seemed strange that he did not have sufficient money to leave London. Conlon was formally charged, and found guilty.

At no stage during the three pre-trial investigations were we contacted by his defence counsel. No efforts were made to seek alibis for Conlon and Hill. No efforts were made by his defence to piece together his activity in the hostel during his stay here. We thought this was rather surprising as surveillance of the residents can be quite detailed.

This story has been given to the press and others on numerous occasions. It has not been taken up, presumably because it has not been regarded as a news item.

(In retrospect, this condition would be consistent with abuse of drugs.)

14 November 1986 (Signed): F. RYAN

APPENDIX VII

STATEMENT BY FATHER P. CAROLAN (FORMERLY OF CONWAY HOUSE)

I VIVIDLY remember the night Gerry Conlon and Paul Hill came to the Hostel. It was raining. They were wet and looked miserable. They had no money. They arrived from Northern Ireland some time ago, could no longer stay where they were staying and they had a job on a building site in the Camden Town area. I did not want to take them, but they were so miserable looking, I had pity on them, and took them in. They filled in cards. I gave them beds in one of the four-bed rooms, just next to my own room. There were two men occupying the other two beds, one of these men was very reliable and stayed in the hostel for some time.

I was always very conscious of the I.R.A. and the danger that they might use the hostel. My church authorities asked me to be very vigilant. We obtained as much information as we could about each person that we took in, even if that meant ringing their priest at home. I felt at that time Conlon and Hill had told me the truth. They certainly did not look like young men who had come over to do an I.R.A. job.

At this time I was the Irish representative on the Camden Race Relations Board. There was a senior policeman from Hampstead on the Board. I asked him to send uniformed policemen to the hostel from time to time. He told me they were getting all the information they needed. We always suspected the police had a man planted in the hostel. When I suspected a young man, he left. Another one I asked was he a police informant, he too left without telling us. The police were regularly in and out of the hostel. One day two officers came in without their jackets and obviously armed, I asked them to leave.

In early October, I went to Ireland to visit my mother. Fr Frank Ryan took over from me. While I was at home the Guildford bombs went off.

On my return Gerry Conlon had left. Paul Hill stayed from some weeks. He always needed money to get to work – which I gave him. I got to know him very well. On the morning he left the hostel, he came to thank me for being so good to him. I can still see him going out the door with his case. That evening when the men returned from work their lockers had been raided and there were items missing. We knew Paul Hill had done it.

Two detectives from Guildford came to see me about the bombings. They wanted information on Conlon and Hill. They told me they would take me to Guildford the following morning, for questioning. I was worried and informed my superiors. I was worried that the police might plant or try to pin something on me.

I was taken to Guildford by car by the same two detectives. On the way down, we chatted away. I was taken to a room with a table and some chairs in it. Another detective joined us. I was told that Hill implicated me in his statement and that my name was running all through it. I was read long passages from Hill's statement. I totally denied everything. One of the detectives was very rough with me. I was taken out to a pub for lunch and on the way shown the pubs that were bombed and then taken back for more questioning. When the questioning was over I told one of the detectives that he was the greatest bastard I had ever met. One of the others said he was the only Catholic among them. He was so rude. They took me back to the hostel that evening.

Myself or the staff could not believe that Conlon and Hill did the bombings. They were not the type. The I.R.A. would not use the hostel, as the police visited it and knew it so well. I was very vigilant.

I had a good relationship with the men. I knew what was happening in the hostel, and was informed by the men what was going on. Hill never had any money during the week. He was always borrowing money from me. I knew him well. He was incapable of organising or planning such raids. I think too the police knew this and thought I was the organiser.

We were dismayed by their defence lawyers that they never asked to see us or visit us. It was our assumption that they thought they were guilty. Mr Logan has done a good deal of talking since the trial but at the time it was our impression he did not do his homework. How could Hill be defended if his defence did not speak to those who were with him before and after the 'bombings'? Surely the picture should have been built up. I knew Paul Hill very well. I was very annoyed that he tried to drag me in, however I was surprised he did not ask me to go as a witness for him.

14 November 1986 (Signed): P. CAROLAN

APPENDIX VIII

REPORT DATED 9 SEPTEMBER 1988 FROM ALASTAIR LOGAN CONCERNING EVIDENCE BY MAURA KELLY RELATING TO CAROLE RICHARDSON

I WRITE to confirm the conversation that I had with you on the afternoon of 8th September concerning certain allegations which have been raised by the Police and which the Home Office are anxious to investigate.

You told me that it was being alleged that Maura Kelly had said in 1974/5 that she had only worked in the shop during the morning of the Saturday in question, and that in 1987 she was saying that she had worked in the shop in the afternoon.

Neither of these statements is true. In the first place, Maura Kelly was never interviewed by the Police in 1974. She was interviewed by the Police in 1975 but she did not make a statement. The Avon Constabulary had in their possession notes which were made by the officers after the event of an interview which they allege took place between themselves and Miss Kelly. Such parts of those interview notes as the officers chose to read out to Miss Kelly, Miss Kelly told them were inaccurate. Indeed the whole of the interview was not read out to her but it was evident that the interview was cast in an entirely different light from what was vividly recalled by Miss Kelly. Significantly missing from the Police record of the interview and confirmed by both Miss Kelly and her mother was the fact that during the course of the interview, the female Police Officer present struck Miss Kelly on the face.

The Police Officers have without the slightest shadow of a doubt re-jigged the interview so far as their notes are concerned in order to present it as a totally innocent exercise by two worthy Police Officers intent on carrying out their normal and lawful duty. In reality the interview was carried out of a juvenile in the presence of her mother at a time when the juvenile had been arrested for no offence whatsoever. No enquiry was made by West Hampstead Police Station as to the nature of the offence which it was alleged had been committed by Miss Kelly and which justified her arrest by the Surrey officers. No doubt the Surrey officers will say she came voluntarily to the Police Station.

Miss Kelly has never resiled from her statement. It is recorded in a statement that she made to the solicitors acting for Miss Richardson in late December 1974. That statement was offered to the Avon and Somerset Police but they declined to take it. They also declined to take a copy of the fuller statement made by Miss Kelly concerning the circumstances of her interview by the Surrey Constabulary. Indeed, the Superintendent in charge of the interview of Miss Kelly stated quite categorically that he was not in any way concerned with any allegations that were being made of conduct by the Surrey Police Officers.

In the circumstances I find it difficult to understand how on the one hand the Avon and Somerset Constabulary can purport to investigate a matter pursuant to the instructions given to them by the Home Secretary, and yet at the same time refuse to investigate aspects of that matter and then later on accuse Miss Kelly of having said that she was in the shop for half a day on Saturday morning in 1975 and for half a day on Saturday afternoon in 1987, and yet never once during the course of the interview of Miss Kelly, at which I was personally present, was that allegation ever put to her.

I had severe reservations about the way that the officer in the Avon and Somerset Constabulary carried out the interview of Maura Kelly's mother, and I was forced to write to them recording my reservations about the way in which that interview was carried out, and the selectivity employed by the Police officers about what they told Mrs Kelly about the content of the Police officers statements concerning that interview.

It however must be apparent to the Avon and Somerset Constabulary that Maura Kelly told them in the clearest possible terms that she did not accept what little she was told about the alleged record of the interview by the Surrey officers in February 1975.

Moreover it is known and was stated by Miss Kelly that the Manageress of the ABC shop where she worked was seen by Surrey officers and her presence during the whole of the day on 5th October 1974 was confirmed by the Manageress until the time that the Manageress left the shop, which was approximately 4pm on that day.

I consider it to be deeply disturbing that trivial matters of this nature should be raised now as some sort of explanation for unreliability on the part of Miss Kelly when such matters were not canvassed to her directly and have not been raised with me.

I would be obliged if you would confirm to me that this report will be forwarded to the Home Secretary. If you feel unable to do so then I shall, on behalf of my client Miss Richardson, feel obligated to send a copy of this letter to the Home Secretary, because I must ensure that nothing stands in the way of the reference back of this case to the Court of Appeal.

Addendum

Since our subsequent conversation in which you said that on clarification it appeared that the allegation that was being made by the Avon and Somerset Constabulary is that Maura Kelly said that Carole visited her in the morning, when she was interviewed in 1975, and is now saying that she visited her in the afternoon, I would refute that on three grounds. Firstly, record of interview by the officers is, for the reasons given in this report, completely erroneous and in my view a lying attempt by the officers to cover up for conduct which should have resulted in one of the officers being prosecuted for assault. Any statement that failed to record the striking of a person under interrogation (and there can be no doubt that it happened since no one has sought to contravert either Miss Kelly or her mother) must be suspect from the outset. The officers very clearly felt they had to justify themselves against what they must have realised at the time that they were making that record of interview would very probably be an allegation of assault and improper conduct. It must also be remembered that Miss Kelly was a juvenile and therefore one might say that the assault was even more reprehensible.

Secondly, she made a statement which pre-dates her interview with the Surrey officers to the solicitors acting for Carole Richardson, in which she confirmed the details as she did now, and that statement was offered to the Avon and Somerset Constabulary and they refused to take it.

Thirdly, she made a very full statement to me at a time when she did not know about the existence of the record of this interview. That statement was also offered to the Avon and Somerset Constabulary and they refused to take it. I would comment that the Avon and Somerset Constabulary appear to be a little selective about the material that they are willing to receive.

Finally, I would say that I have no record of the point being put to Miss Kelly at the interview that she told the officers that she only saw Carole in the morning of 5th October, in February 1975. I would have expected that point to have been put to her if any credence was placed on the Surrey officers' record by the Avon and Somerset Constabulary.

APPENDIX IX

REPORT DATED 13 SEPTEMBER 1988 FROM ALASTAIR LOGAN CONCERNING WITNESSES FOR PAUL HILL

I WRITE pursuant to my discussion with you when you asked me to set down my understanding of the situation so far as Paul Hill's witnesses are concerned. As you know I do not act for Paul Hill any longer.

The factual sequence of events as I understand it is this: –

A. (i) The Woolwich Bombing occurred on the 7 November, 1974.

(ii) Mr and Mrs Keenan were arrested by the Surrey Constabulary on or about 28th November, 1974 by Surrey Officers and taken to Guildford Police Station. Mrs Keenan was then removed to Godalming Police Station.

(iii) The Surrey Constabulary were advised by Mrs Smalley [a relative] that both Mr and Mrs Keenan suffered from chronic heart conditions. Notwithstanding this advice no attempt was made by Surrey Constabulary to have either Mr or Mrs Keenan medically examined as to their fitness to be detained.

(iv) Neither Mr or Mrs Keenan were interviewed in circumstances where any notes were made of the interview concerned. Mrs Keenan was subjected to a particularly unpleasant form of humiliation where a police officer insisted that she look up Mrs Keenan's skirt although Mr and Mrs Keenan had been in bed at the time that they were arrested by the police officers who burst open the door of their flat in the early hours of the morning.

(v) Mr Keenan separated from Mrs Keenan, was subjected to a frightening experience when an officer who was escorting him to Guildford Police Station produced a gun. Mr Keenan genuinely thought that he was going to be killed. Subsequently he was told that if he was thought to be a member of the IRA he would go up a certain flight of stairs and given to understand that the consequences of going up that flight of stairs would be extremely unpleasant. He was taken into the cell complex at Guildford Police Station but later on after a conversation with Mr Walter Simmonds, the Head of Surrey CID, during which Mr Simmonds accused him of being a 'sleeper' and providing accommodation for known members of the IRA and thus a member of the IRA himself, he was then taken up the very flight of stairs that he had been told would have dire consequences for him. He collapsed trying to negotiate the stairs and was eventually taken upstairs where he was brought into a room containing Mr Ronald Underwood, the Deputy Head of Surrey CID and Mrs Keenan. Mr Keenan collapsed crying in her arms in the presence of Mr Underwood, which may give you some indication of the stress under which he was labouring at the time.

(vi) The traumatic experience that Mr Keenan suffered from was so great that on one occasion he attempted to take his own life. He was standing in front of the wash basin and cut his wrists without realising that he had done so.

(viii) Mr and Mrs Keenan were returned to their flat to find that the place had been devastated by Surrey officers who had carried out a thoroughly messy and dirty search during the course of which they had extensively used fingerprint powder including that on the interior of the fridge. Bundles of papers had been left very close to the pilot light on the gas stove and it was only by the grace of God that their entire flat and its contents were not subject to a severe fire. The door of the flat was left open and there was a general air of vindictiveness and brutality about the way the flat had been searched and the premises had been left.

B. When Mr and Mrs Keenan appreciated that Paul Hill had been charged with an offence alleged to have been committed at Woolwich on 7th November, 1974 they volunteered to Mr Hill's solicitors the fact that he had been with them on that night. Paul Hill himself remembered being there. Mr and Mrs Keenan also knew that Mrs Yvonne Fox had been in the house that night. They were interviewed by solicitors acting for Paul Hill who we understand used an enquiry agent. The solicitors themselves did not apparently carry out any interview of Mr and Mrs Keenan themselves. Mr and Mrs Keenan were then interviewed by the Surrey Constabulary as alibi witnesses for Paul Hill. They did not mention the existence of Mrs Fox during the course of that interview.

C. The reason given by Mr and Mrs Keenan, although perhaps not clearly expressed as it might have been, was that they had not spoken to Paul Hill's solicitor about it before being interviewed by the police with the consequence that they had not had an opportunity of discussing the matter with Paul Hill's solicitor. It may perhaps be readily appreciated in the climate of opinion that exists today, although perhaps not in 1974/5, that in view of the experiences which Mr and Mrs Keenan had gone through themselves, they were not going to put their good friend Yvonne Fox, perhaps the only solid friend that they had in London at that time, through the same experience that they themselves had gone through at the hands of the Surrey Constabulary by volunteering her name to the Surrey Constabulary.

D. After the interview with the Surrey Constabulary at which they were interviewed as alibi witnesses, they told Mr Bennett, the enquiry agent appointed by Paul Hill's solicitors to attend upon that interview, that Mrs Fox was present. Mr and Mrs Keenan are quite positive that at no stage did they indicate to anyone that Mrs Fox had left any earlier than the time which they have always maintained was some time after the commencement of the News at Ten on Channel 3 on the evening of 7th November.

E. Mr and Mrs Keenan do not know what contact there was between Mrs Fox and Paul Hill's solicitors save for what they have heard from Mrs Fox herself, but they are quite satisfied that they told the true story to Mr Bennett. They are also satisfied that at no stage was there any doubt, either in their minds, or the mind of Mrs Fox, that she was present on that night.

F. Mrs Fox is quite convinced that at no stage did she telephone the solicitors and indicate anything other than the fact that she was concerned about her forthcoming appearance at the trial. If they chose to interpret unwillingness on her part to testify or uncertainty as to dates and times, it may have been the product of considerable anxiety and nerves prior to what was being billed at the time as the show trial of the decade. There was no doubt whatsoever from the way in which the press approached the trial of the Guildford Four that it merited massive publicity and the feelings of nervousness that might be expected to accompany an innocent witness caught up in a trial involving allegations of terrorism in a Court surrounded by armed officers and accompanied by massive publicity. It would, in my contention, have been surprising if Mrs Fox had not quailed at the thought of appearing on such a public stage in such circumstances. However she stuck to her guns and told Mr Melton outside Court that she was prepared to give evidence but did not want her address revealed. Again, I ask, what more natural thing for an innocent witness with young children and a husband to protect, willing nonetheless to give evidence, but asking only for that facility which had been made universally available to the prosecution witnesses that she should not have to reveal her own private address? Mr Melton told her that he could not guarantee that. That was a truthful answer on the part of Mr Melton because of course the only person who could give such authority was the Judge. It may be said, and the Home Office are probably unaware of this, that the Judge did refuse in the case of certain witnesses attached to the defence of Patrick Armstrong the facility of not revealing their address simply because they came from Ireland, but he did not refuse any such request that was made by or on behalf of the prosecution or their witnesses.

G. The decision not to call Mrs Fox to give evidence was one which must have been taken by Mr Melton and/or Counsel instructed on behalf of Mr Hill. As I understand it Mr Hill was not consulted about that decision. In my view the fact that Mrs Fox had not been made part of the alibi notice which had been served upon the prosecution in relation to the events of 7th November, 1974 must have weighed quite heavily in the minds of those who had to take the decision as to whether or not Mrs Fox would give evidence because undoubtedly some explanation was going to be demanded of them as to why she was not included. I have not had the benefit of seeing the file of Woodford and Ackroyd, Mr Hill's solicitors at the time, so I cannot comment on whether or not there is any evidence on that file as to how that decision came to be taken. Nonetheless it is clear that the solicitors were in possession of the information that Mrs Fox was present on the night of 7th November on the date upon which that information was conveyed to Mr Bennett.

H. I cannot give any information to you concerning Paul Hill's recollection concerning these matters. It may be that he did not initially remember Mrs Fox being present. My records of the evidence given at the trial by Mr and Mrs Keenan and Paul Hill is that none of them mentioned the existence of Mrs Fox. Mr and Mrs Keenan say that was because they were never asked any questions about Mrs Fox and simply answered the questions that they were asked. I have not spoken to Paul Hill as to his explanation for that.

APPENDIX X

JUSTICE AND THE GUILDFORD FOUR

Two Lords of Appeal argue that the convictions of four alleged IRA bombers 14 years ago rest upon a fundamental error of law which threatens Britain's system of trial by jury.

By Lord Devlin and Lord Scarman

TRIAL

THE WHOLE of the evidence against the four accused consists of confessions, obtained by the police within a few days of the arrests, in which each implicated himself and betrayed the others. The accused said that they were obtained by violence. The jury did not believe that.

Nevertheless, the verdict leaves a question mark. No doubt the prisoners were roughly treated. But is it likely that the fanatical murderers whom the IRA sends out would succumb so quickly to blows and harsh words?

The Guildford Four were by their own account a pitiable lot. Certainly Paul Hill and probably Gerard Conlon were IRA members, but not among the elite. Conlon was a petty criminal who thrived on drink, gambling and girls, getting the money he needed by stealing everything that he could sell.

Patrick Armstrong came to England in 1972, he says, to escape the troubles. It was then that he progressed from drink and betting shops to drugs. In 1974 he was unemployed and living in a squat in Kilburn with his girlfriend, Carole Richardson, who was English. She had been on drugs since she was 11. There is no indication that any of them were, as in the case of its regular units, financed by the IRA.

They were all of the sort that lives from hand to mouth, that does not look beyond the hour and that tells a lie as easily as the truth. Their answers under interrogation were contradictory and confused.

An English court is at its best when it is dealing with the 'reasonable man.' Passengers on the Clapham omnibus do not willingly confess to crimes which they have not committed. So what stronger evidence can there be than a voluntary confession?

The criminal courts are only now just beginning to relax their grip on the touchstone of the Clapham Man and to allow expert evidence about the factors which may without brutality produce false confessions. A letter about Armstrong from a person whom the judge described as 'a distinguished consultant psychiatrist of a London hospital' was given to the judge, but only after conviction. It described Armstrong as a timid man, frightened in particular of physical violence and of authoritarian figures.

It is the task of the police first to find suspects and then to find the evidence that will convict them. When they arrested the four they had been searching for seven weeks during which the murders multiplied, the most shocking being at Birmingham on November 21, 1974, when 21 persons were killed and 150 injured. The police were under the pressure of events to get results and, when they arrested the Guildford Four, they still had nothing.

The accused also were under pressure – the pressures of fear, confinement and helplessness – to give what was wanted. What happens when the pressures meet no one really knows. The police have made pretty secure the secrecy of the interrogation. They do not choose times convenient to lawyers nor when their suspects are likely to be at their best.

After the interrogations, the police charged eight persons with the Guildford murders. Four confessed and were convicted. The cases against the other four were abandoned.

Is this trial by ordeal? Is the court trial only a ceremonial? This is what we used to say of the state trials in the dictatorships when prisoners were led into court to confess their sins.

That would not be a fair description of the English procedure. An issue *is* left for the jury to try. But it is not the real issue. Whatever the theory, the prosecution, where there are confessions, does not have to start by removing the presumption of innocence. The prisoners go into the dock with the halters of their confessions about their necks and unless they can slip free of them they are doomed. The trial is about slipping free.

It was a fair and correct trial according to English ideas. Other jurisdictions may think differently. Some think it unsafe to act on a confession that is not corroborated. Others draw a line between 'helping the police with their inquiries', which is the duty of the good citizen, and self-incrimination. Before the 'help' can be turned into evidence, it must be given to a judicial authority.

Any ponderings about what other nations might think would have been put aside when an event occurred that seemed to make them irrelevant. While the Four were awaiting the hearing of their appeal, an IRA gang with whom the Four had no known connection claimed what they regarded as the credit for the Guildford killings.

APPEAL

The gang – or active service unit as it would prefer to be called – which on January 24, 1977, formally claimed to have planted the bombs in Guildford – began its campaign in England with the Guildford explosions and followed them with about twenty other crimes until it was caught and defeated at the Balcombe Street siege in 1975.

The case for the defence on the new evidence is that the bomb in the Horse and Groom was planted by Brendan Dowd, a young man who came from a committed Sinn Fein family. He arrived in England in August 1974 with Joseph O'Connell, a bomb-maker in the IRA. They established a 'safe house' in Fulham.

The task of the unit was to bomb pubs frequented by the military. Late in February they reconnoitred Guildford and decided on their targets there. On October 4 they made the bombs in their safe house. On the 5th they drove to Guildford with another man and two women unnamed. Dowd and one of the women planted the bomb in the Horse and Groom; O'Connell and the other man and woman planted another in the Seven Stars.

Not long after this initial achievement they were joined by Eddie Butler and Harry Duggan. All four were on the expedition which bombed the King's Arms at Woolwich on November 7; O'Connell was the one who threw the bomb. This was the second crime. Only Hill and Armstrong 'confessed' to it.

On July 10, 1975, Dowd surrendered after an incident in Liverpool. On December 13 O'Connell and Butler were among those captured in the Balcombe Street siege. In the interrogations which followed they hinted that the wrong people had been sentenced for the Guildford murders.

These *pourparlers* began what the Court of Appeal was to call 'a cunning and skilful attempt to deceive the court.' They were right of course to treat it as suspect. The chieftains had been caught red-handed and had no hope; they had nothing to lose by looking after henchmen.

It looked at first as if the *pourparlers* would lead to nothing. All they did indeed was to start some loose talk which in May 1976 reached the ears of Alastair Logan. He was and is a Guildford solicitor working on his own. Offered the case by the Legal Aid Panel he refused it as too heavy. When no one else would take it, he did. He is one of those pilgrims of the law who, when Justice beckons, pick up the staff and the scrip and walk. Legal aid has long since dried up. He is walking still.

He is also a prudent man. He took with him to the interviews he obtained with O'Connell and the others a retired police superintendent to conduct them and a stenographer to record them.

The Balcombe Street men were put on trial on January 24, 1977, and condemned. They refused to plead, adding to the customary denial of the jurisdiction the reason that the indictment did not include two charges on which they were guilty and on which innocent people had been convicted.

In October of the same year the appeal of the Guildford Four was heard. The four men who had done the bombings at Guildford and Woolwich went into the witness box. They were all fanatics for whom the truth was a servant of the cause. But their testimony did not have to stand alone. Their command of details which they could have known only by participation compelled a reluctant measure of belief.

So the court accepted that O'Connell's story (he said that he had planted the bomb at the Seven Stars) might be true and that Dowd (who said that it was he who planted the bomb at the Horse and Groom) might also have taken part. But they refused to believe that the Guildford Four were not involved.

They did not discuss the probability of involvement. There was no circumstantial evidence from which the presence of the Four could be inferred, nothing indeed to connect any of them in any way with the Balcombe Street gang. Neither operation needed more than the five members of the gang itself. The other four were certainly not key operators; after their arrests operations continued as before. Is it probable that this professional gang took along with them four extras, three identifiably Irish, to hang about and maybe leave clues behind them?

There is another facet of the judgment to be considered. What did it do to the proof of guilt?

The court described the confessions as 'the partially true intermingled with the deliberately false.' They did not seem to appreciate that this damaging criticism was being made of the only evidence of guilt that the Crown had produced.

The court did not re-examine the confessions to determine how far their reliability was affected by such parts of the new evidence as had been accepted. The only evidence now left against Hill and Armstrong that they were present at the scene of the crimes was their confessions that they had actually committed them.

These are criticisms that could have been made on appeal. But the Court of Appeal had spent itself on finding the facts. It can be very difficult, if not impossible in a complicated case, for the advocate to frame an effective argument on the facts when he does not know what evidence is going to be believed. This is the importance of a court of review. The amalgamation of trial and appeal was the first and not the least serious of the deprivations that flowed from the decision not to order a new trial.

Another deprivation was the loss of the defendant's right to have the case against him presented as a whole. The split made the process unreal from the start. If the verdict was right, the new evidence must be false: if it was wrong, there was no need for more evidence. There was no way in which justice could be done except by beginning again.

Beginning again was what the statute said was to be done. The fresh evidence would be received only if it was 'likely to be credible'. Only a jury had the power to say whether it was actually false or true. Why were the judges usurping that power?

ERROR OF THE LAW

What should the legal system do with evidence that turns up after the trial is over? The sleep of the final verdict is disturbed by the nightmare of miscarriage. For centuries English law stood robustly on finality: no appeal from the verdict and no indulgence for a party who did not bring all his evidence with him. The Act of 1907, which created the Court of Criminal Appeal, permitted also fresh evidence, but did not say what was to be done with it. In 1908 the new Court decided that it had no power to order a re-trial.

So all that could be done, if the new evidence was credible and substantial, i.e. might have affected the result, was to quash the verdict. Many accused who were more than probably guilty escaped in this way. This was the situation until a statute of 1966 permitted a court which had quashed a verdict in this way to order a re-trial.

In *DPP v Stafford*, which came before the Lords in 1974, the House had in front of it what was virtually a dossier, i.e. a written record. The prosecution was based entirely on circumstantial evidence. Proof of guilt was to be inferred from data observed by credit worthy witnesses. After the verdict more witnesses were found with more data; their evidence was recorded in writing.

Whether the new evidence was weighty enough to destroy the verdict of guilty was doubtful. If it was not, the case would be over. If it was, there must be a new trial in which all the old witnesses would repeat orally their recorded evidence: this to be followed by the new witnesses with their evidence; then maybe a second appeal.

An unconscientious judge might have been tempted to give the facts a nudge to the more convenient side of the margin. The five Law Lords did not do that. *Fiat justitia ruait caelun.* They had conceived a novel way of keeping the heavens in their place.

They took a new look at section 2 of the Criminal Appeal Act 1968 which contains the directions for allowing and dismissing appeals. They found in it an explosive substance, capable of blowing a large hole in trial by jury, which had for six years lain undetected by the lower courts. This section provided that the Court of Appeal should 'allow an appeal against conviction if they think that the verdict of the jury should be set aside on the ground that under all the circumstances of the case it is unsafe or unsatisfactory.'

The House said that it was what *they* thought that mattered, not what a new jury might think. True. But what *they* had to think about was not whether in their view the accused were guilty on the dossier, but about the verdict of guilty given by the jury at the trial.

A verdict does not stand by itself and cannot be thought about without reference to what it is upon. In a trial it is upon evidence: the jury is charged to give 'a true verdict according to the evidence.' It is not suggested that in this case it did not do so. If thereafter new evidence is discovered that proves innocence, the verdict is not thereby made untrue.

So up to this point the verdict is 'safe and satisfactory'. But the statute requires it to be safe 'under all the circumstances of the case.' If the court has received new evidence which might destroy the verdict, that is a circumstance which alters the case. It makes it unsafe to proceed. So under the statute the verdict must be set aside as unsafe. If the Crown wants to proceed further, it must ask for a retrial.

This is the procedure that has been followed since 1966. In the Stafford case the House did not follow it; but did not say what was wrong with it.

The House did not quash the verdict of guilty. It – so to speak – suspended the verdict while it was itself examining the old and the new evidence. When it decided that the new evidence made no difference, it treated the verdict as if it had simply dropped back into place. But it was in truth a new 'verdict' made upon a combination of old and new evidence; and it was not made by a jury.

There is nothing in the statute to authorise this process which is contrary to two fundamental principles: the first is that only a jury can make a verdict and the second that only a jury can find the facts. With respect it seems to us that it can be explained only as a misconstruction of the word 'verdict.' It interprets the word, not as the actual verdict of a jury, but as a label which can be attached to any conclusion of guilt or innocence.

There are two general considerations which support the limited construction we are putting on section 2.

First, the effect of the section as interpreted in the Stafford case is to authorise the judges to displace the jury as triers of fresh evidence. Parliament would not have done this without using express words and after a full debate. There was no debate at all in the Commons. In the Lords it was assumed that the object of the section was only to replace with the words 'unsafe and unsatisfactory' the narrower words in the 1907 Act.

Second, the Stafford interpretation of section 2 is in conflict with section 7, the one that empowers the court which received the new evidence to order a new trial. It shows the court is not expected to adjudicate upon it itself.

JURY THREAT

From time immemorial all indictable crime has been tried by jury. When in 1968 Parliament permitted a re-trial in cases in which fresh evidence, credible and substantial, had come to light, the re-trial was naturally by jury.

Then in 1974 the House of Lords in the Stafford case put a new construction on section 2 of the Criminal Appeal Act 1968 and asserted its power to hear and determine the new evidence itself. The House staged what was in substance, if not in form, a re-trial. The evidence was mainly circumstantial; except for the accused themselves nothing depended on the demeanour of the witnesses. The House combined the new evidence with the old, tried the case on paper and found the accused guilty.

The House said that this new approach was not compulsory. Each court must decide its own approach. But any hope that there might still be a role for the jury in re-trials was speedily quelled.

All approaches, it was made clear, would lead only to the new destination of the judge-made verdict. 'If the court has no reasonable doubt about the verdict,' the Lords said, 'it follows that the court does not think that the jury could have one.'

So far as we know, the only occasion on which such an astounding proposition has been put to a court of law was when it was rebuffed by Chief Justice Vaughan in 1670 in Bushell's Case. If it were so, he said, *'every man sees that the jury is but a troublesome delay, great charge, and of no use in determining right and wrong, and therefore the tryals by them may be better abolish'd than continued; which were a strange new-found conclusion. How then comes it to pass that two persons may not apprehend with reason and honesty what a witness, or many, say, to prove in the understanding of one plainly one thing, but in the apprehension of the other, clearly the contrary thing . . . And this often is the case of the Judge and jury.'*

The doctrine which Vaughan ridiculed and which was revived in the Stafford case, when the House of Lords declared that if the judge had no reasonable doubt then the jury could not have one either, has been sharpened by the Court of Appeal in the case of the Guildford Four so as to pierce the heart of trial by jury. The court refused to order a new trial of the new evidence. There could be no need for it, it implied, since, if a judge disbelieves a witness, so must a jury – 'a strange new-found conclusion' indeed.

There is a passage in Blackstone in which he gives warning against a precedent that 'though begun in trifles . . . may gradually increase and spread, to the utter disuse of juries in questions of the most momentous concern.' It was in a marginal dispute that the Stafford case set the precedent. If pursued to the end it must logically lead to the utter disuse. But the pursuit may be halted by the forces of tradition and common sense.

The life imprisonment of the Four may not be momentous enough. But a concern most momentous to the State has now arisen. Britain is fighting off attacks by ruthless fanatics who live outside the law. The Crown will not fight them by depriving suspects of the rights they enjoy within the law. But it does hope for the support of the world in a fight against terrorism and has pledged itself to justice for all.

But there can be a fair trial by judges as well as by juries, can there not? True. But trial by jury is what we offer to all. It happens also to be what the two nations whose support we most need, the Irish Republic and the United States, offer to all. We cannot discriminate and still be fair.

The original trial of the Guildford Four was by jury. It was directed by a judge who was scrupulous in ensuring that all the protections of English law were given to the accused. The only issue – whether the confessions were voluntary and the truth – was a simple one. The jury was as scrupulous as the judge in considering it. The members debated for an afternoon, slept on it and talked again till midday before they delivered their verdict of guilty. Would the new evidence have made no difference?

Four new witnesses appeared who had committed twenty massacres of the same type. They said that they did this one and knew nothing of the Guildford Four. Were they lying when they said that? That was a question for a jury as it certainly would have been if the evidence had been given at the trial.

The Court of Appeal judges accepted that vital parts of what the new witnesses said might well be true. If a jury thought the same, it would be for it and not for judges to put a value on the fragments that were left of the confessions and the Crown's case.

Justice for the Guildford Four is now in the forefront of a larger issue. Their fate has shattered our belief that there is no one in any English prison serving a sentence of more than a year who has not been found guilty by a jury which has heard substantially all the relevant evidence. Our constitutional law on which our freedoms depend has been disordered.

It is being said that the Home Secretary plans to extend the law providing for criminal re-trials. Unless he first restores the foundations, he will be building on rubble.

This article first appeared in The Times *of 30 November 1988 and is reproduced by kind permission of the Editor.*

APPENDIX XI

AVON and SOMERSET CONSTABULARY

ENQUIRY INTO STATEMENTS RELATING TO THE GUILDFORD AND WOOLWICH BOMBINGS 1974

DOCUMENTS

VOLUME SIX
Pages 501–600

MARCH 1983

CONFIDENTIAL

SURREY CONSTABULARY

Station or Section: Guildford Division: 'G'
Date: 18th January, 1975

Statement of: Charles Joseph BURKE.
Age of witness: Born: 31.7.45. Newcastle West.
Occupation of witness: Greengrocers Assistant Manager.
Address: 131, Harvest Road, Kilburn, London.

This statement (consisting of 4 pages each signed by me) is true to the best of my knowledge and belief and I make it knowing that, if it is tendered in evidence, I shall be liable to prosecution if I have wilfully stated in it anything which I know to be false or do not believe to be true.
Dated the 18th. day of January, 1975.
Signature:- Charles Burke.

States:-
"I am a native of Southern Ireland, and first came to this Country sometime in 1960. Since I've been here I admit I've not had a very good record, but when I'm not in prison I'm always in work. I've always been living in the Willesdon or Kilburn area. I am not, and have never been a member of any political party either Irish or British. I do not support the I.R.A. in any shape or form. In May, 1974, I went home to Newcastle West, Limerick, to see my uncle, Edward BURKE, of 7 Connelley Terrace, Newcastle West, (Tel. 347). He brought me and my sister up when my parents died. He wasn't too pleased to see me, he doesn't like it when I'm not working. I was employed while I was there by Maurice HARTNETT, a builder, of Ballingarry, Co. Limerick. I stayed for about 4 months I think, and when I got enough saved up, I came back to England, on the 5th. September. I stayed in a bed and breakfast place in Cricklewood for three days, and then moved into Father CARYLYN's place in Quex Road, on the 8th. of September. I was put in St. Louis Room, which has four beds in it. I

have shown you on my sketch where the beds were (Exhibit C.J.B.1.). When I first moved in the beds I show Paul and Gerry in were as follows:- Paul's bed was occupied by a solicitor's clerk, and the bed I show Gerry in was empty. The bed I show Pat in was occupied by a baker from Dublin. After I had been in St. Louis room about one week, the solicitor's clerk moved out and the baker fellow went home to Ireland. That's when Paul and Gerry moved in, and Pat the labourer from Northern Ireland. While Paul and Gerry were there I went out with them on one evening only, to the Memphis Belle. They met two girls there, I don't know their names. I will describe them. (1). About 5′–7″, 17–18 years, blonde, fairly plump, well built, English. Gerry was attracted it seemed to her, she knew his name. She was dressed in hippy gear, a long coat, with a big shoulder bag. (No. 2), was more attracted to Paul. She was 17 years old, built smaller, fairish hair, shoulder length. I can't remember her clothing. I never spoke to her nor she to me. Paul and Gerry, apart from this once, kept very much to themselves at Quex Road. In fact I never asked to go out with them, I met them by accident in the Memphis. They never discussed work, but I knew they worked on the buildings. I was in work all the time, seven days a week at B. & M. Fruiterers, 308, Neasden Lane. Paul was the quiet one of the two, but Gerry was mouthy. I knew he didn't like the English, for when it said on T.V. a soldier had been shot, he laughed and said something like ''Bloody good job''. On the Friday before I left Quex Road, the 4th. of October, I remember Paul said he was going to Southampton for the weekend, to see some friends. When I left work on Saturday, 5th. October, 1974, I had found a new place to live, this address, as I was fed up sharing a room. I got back to Quex Road about 7.00 p.m., because we take stock Saturday night. I packed my gear, and Gerry was in his bed. He was the only other person in St. Louis Room. He said he was broke and asked to borrow a quid, but I never let him have it. About 7.30 p.m. I caught a taxi and left Quex Road for the last time. When I left he was still in bed. I came straight to this address, and I haven't seen Gerry or Paul since. As far as I knew Father CARYLYN wasn't there the night I left. I never said goodbye to anybody except Gerry. I don't owe no money at Quex Road and they don't owe me any either''.

Signed:- Charles Burke.

Statement taken at 121, Harvest Road, Kilburn, by
D/C. 673. STANDEN on 19.1.75.

APPENDIX XII

THE MAY INQUIRY

A Submission on the MAGUIRE Case by the Deputation led by Cardinal Hume

1 THE DEPUTATION submits that in the interest of justice the Maguire case should be referred to the Court of Appeal. We welcome the inclusion of the Maguire case in the terms of reference of your Inquiry: for, as we shall argue, there has as yet been no thorough or penetrating examination of all the aspects of that case. In particular, the possibility of police misconduct in relation to certain samples sent for scientific analysis has never yet been investigated. Notwithstanding the inevitable delay we accept that a Court of Appeal review should wait upon publication by you, Sir, of your findings related to the case. So much time has already elapsed since the convictions of the Maguire Seven in 1976 that a further delay can be accepted in order to ensure that justice be done, and be seen to be done.

2 The Maguire case is closely related to that of the Guildford Four. We attach to this submission by way of an ANNEX some notes prepared by our consultant, Robert Kee, with which we agree, and which demonstrates the closeness of the relationship. In a historical sense, though not of course in a technical and legal sense, the two cases are 'one case': the link is certainly very close in that the police investigation of the Maguire case arose from their inquiries into the Guildford Four case: the 'bombers' of Guildford by the 'confession' of one of them, the young Conlon, led the police to suspect a 'bomb factory' at the Maguires' house. As long as the Guildford Four remained convicted murderers, so long would the case against the Maguires be at risk of appearing stronger than in truth it was. But when in October 1989 the convictions of the Guildford Four were quashed on the ground of police misconduct in relation to the 'confessions' which were the only evidence of guilt, the supposed link of the Maguires with bombers disappeared. The supposed bombers had been cleared of the crime of bombing and there was and never has been any evidence of a link between the Maguires and any other bomber. It follows that

the Maguires if guilty must have been running a bomb factory in a family home for a market that was purely imaginary. At last the Maguire case can be examined strictly on its own strengths and weaknesses: and at once the flimsy nature of that case stands out like a sore thumb.

THE MAGUIRE TRIAL

3 We know that we need not burden this submission with what you, Sir, are already very familiar, the detail of the proceedings at trial. We will simply put the points which we believe to be of critical importance. The Maguire Seven were charged with unlawful possession of an explosive substance, nitro-glycerine. Led to the Maguire home by the young Conlon's 'confession' the police searched for explosives. They found none: but they took some swabs from the hands of those in the house and from a pair of Annie Maguire's kitchen gloves. They took them away and in due course transmitted them to RARDE for scientific examination and analysis.

4 The scientists, using the TLC test, identified on the swabs and gloves traces of nitro-glycerine. The safety of the identification by this test was strongly challenged at the trial by the defence who called as an expert witness Mr Yallop, who, notwithstanding the unflattering comments later made of him by the Court of Appeal when leave to appeal was refused, was very experienced in this class of work. Mr Yallop's evidence was to the effect that the TLC test could not be relied on as excluding with certainty the possibility of the traces being of some other substance than nitro-glycerine: in other words, it was possible that another substance could give on the test the same reading as nitro-glycerine. The Chief Scientific Officer called by the Crown, however, expressed his confidence in the 'uniqueness' of the test, i.e. that the traces were of nitro-glycerine as indicated. The jury clearly accepted his view. But there remains a lurking doubt. For since the trial the Home Office has introduced a requirement that in criminal proceedings the TLC test must be supported by independent evidence confirming its results.

5 So far from there being any supporting evidence in this case, the indications were negative. None of the Maguires confessed: they protested their innocence. Despite intensive search of house and neighbourhood no other traces of nitro-glycerine were found. The Crown were aware of the weakness in their case created by the feature that no nitro-glycerine or traces of it was found other than on the swabs and gloves. (A point which the judge mentioned at the beginning of his summing up but failed to follow up.) If the place was a bomb

factory, where had the raw material for bombs gone? Save on the swabs and gloves it had vanished without trace.

6 The Crown's answer to this awkward question was to suggest that the Maguires or their friends had disposed of it. There was an inherent improbability about the suggestion. The Maguires had no prior warning of the police raid on their house. And they would have had great difficulty in removing explosives under the eyes of the police. The Crown did have a suggestion to counter the difficulty. Mr Maguire and another had departed to a nearby public house for a drink: they could have taken, it was said, the factory's store of explosive with them and disposed of it in the bar, or elsewhere, in the public house (or presumably on the way there). If they did so, they succeeded in leaving no trace – other than the swabs. Their visit to the public house was not all that long: and there were plenty of people around. The whole suggestion carried with it the feel of a desperate after-thought to rescue some degree of possibility to buttress what on the face of it was becoming increasingly unlikely, namely that there was any nitro-glycerine anywhere other than that which was found, if the TLC test can be accepted, on the swabs and gloves.

7 At the end of the day the TLC test result was the only direct evidence of the possession by any of the accused of nitro-glycerine. The rest of the Crown case was inference. Perhaps, given the state of public opinion in 1976 and the lead to the Maguires from a Guildford Four 'bomber' (a lead scrupulously excluded from consideration at trial by the jury, but already public knowledge and very well known to the Crown and the judge), it is not surprising that the jury felt confident that the case of unlawful possession had been proved. But unease was expressed by some: and the Maguire Seven have never ceased to protest their innocence. One of the Seven died in prison still protesting his innocence. The other six, all of whom have now completed their sentences, have continued both before and after their release from prison to assert their innocence.

8 The link between the Guildford and Maguire cases was too close for comfort even before 1989: it is certainly, we submit, too close for comfort now.

9 It is not surprising that no issue of police misconduct in the handling of the swabs and gloves really arose at the trial. The police had emerged unscathed from the defence challenge in the Guildford four trial, the jury being satisfied that their confessions were voluntary and true confessions. The defence, had, therefore, no material on which to base a thorough or penetrating cross-examination of the police. Their one opportunity was the absence of any direct evidence of the existence of any nitro-glycerine other then that said to have been found on the swabs and the gloves. The issue was never developed. Three questions

remain unanswered. Did the police, or anyone else, falsify the critically important evidence of the swabs and gloves so as to make sure of a case against the accused? Did they contaminate the samples as some officers fabricated the confessions in the Guildford Four case? Did anyone else, even perhaps in RARDE, from amongst those who handled the samples contaminate them? This line of challenge and inquiry could not have been taken with any prospect of success so long as the Guildford Four convictions stood. Naturally enough, therefore, the defence devoted its attention to Mr Yallop's doubts about the efficacy of the TLC test.

10 A second line of challenge and inquiry referred to in paragraph 2 above, comes into view now that the Guildford convictions have been quashed; namely the fact there was no evidence of a link between the Maguires and any other bombers. There is certainly no evidence that the Balcombe Street gang needed anybody to make their bombs for them. It might be that Scotland Yard or RARDE could give you, Sir, an indication of whether there were any bombers operating at the time who could have been supplied by the Maguires.

THE CURRENT SITUATION

11 As we understand the situation, you, Sir, will be investigating police conduct not only in the Guildford case but in the Maguire case as well. We respectfully suggest that the possibility of contamination of the swabs and gloves should be investigated and that particular attention be given to the possibility of police misconduct in causing the contamination. We ourselves, of course, do not have access to documents or other information which may reveal where the truth lies. But we are certain that a thorough investigation is called for.

CONCLUSION

12 Whatever be the results of your investigation of police conduct in the handling and transmission of the swabs and gloves, we believe that the risk of a miscarriage of justice in the Maguire case can be eliminated only by a review of the whole case by the Court of Appeal. The Crown case at trial was so thin that there must be a genuine doubt as to whether, had the truth be known at the date of the trial as to police procurement of false evidence in the Guildford case, the jury could have been satisfied beyond reasonable doubt that the Maguire Seven were guilty.

13 For these reason we submit that the change of circumstances

brought about by the acquittal of the accused in the closely related Guilford Four case makes it necessary in the interest of justice that the Home Secretary do refer the case for review by the Court of Appeal. If it be necessary that there should be 'new evidence or matter of substance' to justify a reference under s.17 of the Act of 1968 (a proposition current in the Home Office but not to be found in the section), the radical change in the circumstances of the Maguire case arising from the acquittal of the Guildford Four by the quashing of their convictions in 1989 is certainly new matter of substance which calls for a reference to the Court of Appeal. We would put the case for review thus. Upon a consideration of the history of these two related cases it is in the interest of justice that the Home Secretary does refer the Maguire case to the Court of Appeal for review. There was a case for doing so before 1989: the case for doing so now is even stronger, granted the innocence established by law of the Guildford Four.

22 March 1990

Annex to APPENDIX XII

THE GUILDFORD AND MAGUIRE EXPLOSIVE CASES

Some notes by Robert Kee

ONE CASE

THE two cases started as one. Police had obtained from four people (Paul Hill, Gerard Conlon, Patrick Armstrong and Carole Richardson) confessions to the Guildford bombings which also implicated four others: Anne Maguire, Brian Anderson, Paul Coleman and John MacGuinness. These last four were also charged with the murders. But since they would not confess and continued to deny all knowledge of the bombings (as the first four had originally done) the murder charges against these last four had to be dropped after many weeks. Anderson, Colman and MacGuinness were released. However when the police, acting on the confessions, had gone to arrest Anne Maguire they had also arrested all the adults found in her house and her teenage sons. Since she had been named in the confessions as a bomb-maker as well as a bomb-planter, swabs were taken of the hands of all arrested. Some of these swabs together with some plastic household gloves of Anne Maguire's were soon afterwards alleged to reveal traces of nitroglycerine. All those thus apparently incriminated were charged with the unlawful possession of nitroglycerine and it was on this charge that Anne Maguire and others of her household were indicted after the murder charge against her had to be dropped. (The charge against two of her sons which was not brought for three months was eventually brought on the day on which the murder charge had to be dropped against her.)

TWO TRIALS

Two trials thus took place, one of the Guildford Four for murder, and the other of the Maguire household for unlawfully possessing nitro-glycerine.

EVIDENCE

In both trials there was only one substantive piece of evidence against the accused: in the Guildford trial each individual's confession; in the

Maguire trial the result of the scientific tests on the hand-swabs and gloves which allegedly revealed nitroglycerine. Other evidence, such as identification parades in the first trial and searches of the Maguire house and its neighbourhood in the second, failed in support. But a jury believed in the first trial that the confessions though retracted were genuine in relation to each individual, and, in the second, that the results of the scientific tests accurately denoted what had been on the accused's hands.

MAGUIRE CASE

Since in this case the only evidence for conviction was the result, as announced, of the scientific test on the hand swabs and gloves which no longer materially existed even at the time of the trial in 1976, a new version of this is, by definition, impossible. But in any new argument of matter not properly developed at the trial, as provided for in Lord Diplock's judgement of 1983 (see below), it would be most strongly argued to a jury that, given other attendant circumstances, the fact that nitroglycerine may have been on the swabs as analysed was no proof that it had been on the hands of the accused.

There is, in this case, one peripheral piece of evidence which was never put to a jury. The prosecution suggestion that a 'piece of chalk' handled by one of the Maguire sons, as described by him, could have been 'a stick of gelignite' may have had some effect on the jury. The fact that this son, on being returned to the family house, showed the police officers who returned him the piece of chalk in question never came out in the trial.

To any contemporary jury in a re-trial the letters from prison over a long period of the Maguire household would, like those of the Guildford convicted Four, inevitably carry weight, as would their demeanour in continuing to assert their innocence, a factor by definition not observable twelve years ago.

LEGAL PRECEDENT OVER-RIDES THE REQUIREMENT FOR NEW EVIDENCE

New evidence is not in itself, according to legal precedent, an imperative consideration where a miscarriage of justice may have taken place. Walton J. laid down as long ago as 1909 that 'further' evidence could be called in the Court of Appeal when the fact that it had not hitherto been called was due to 'the mistaken conduct of the case'. Lord Scarman concurred with this judgement when citing it in a case in 1975. Lord Diplock in a judgement (Regina v Chard) in 1983 made clear with reference to cases sent back to the Court of Appeal under the Criminal Appeal Act of 1968 that: '. . . since it is the whole case that is referred this must include all questions of fact and law involved in it' and that what would concern the Court of Appeal would be '. . . some cogent argument that had not been advanced at the previous hearing would, if it had been properly developed at such hearing, have resulted in the appeal against conviction being allowed. . .'

Lord Scarman, speaking in the House of Lords on 4th November 1986, reminded the Government of this.

'The whole case' involving 'all questions of fact and law involved in it' and new 'cogent argument' – not new evidence – are laid down as the necessary criteria for pursuit of justice where a miscarriage of justice may have taken place.

APPENDIX XIII

THE 'EIGHT QUESTIONS' SENT BY CARDINAL HUME TO THE HOME SECRETARY AND SIR JOHN MAY ON 2 JUNE 1993

1 *On the matters of fact in the original submission of 20 July 1987 what observations were made by the Avon and Somerset police to the Home Office on the following parts of the submission, bearing in mind that the first inclination of the Home Office was not to refer the case:–*

- (*a*) *statement by Maura Kelly (Richardson alibi)*
- (*b*) *statement by Yvonne Fox (Hill alibi for Woolwich)*
- (*c*) *statement by Mr and Mrs Keenan (Hill alibi for Woolwich)*
- (*d*) *statements of Father Ryan and Father Carolan about Hill and Conlon at Quex Road hostel. (The hostel was the location of the Burke alibi which it was later discovered had been suppressed)*
- (*e*) *the MacKeith-Gudjonsson medical report on Richardson.*

2 *Why was the Burke alibi statement for Conlon of January 1975 placed in a bundle marked 'not to be shown to the defence,' and by whom?*

Why was the confirmatory alibi statement taken by the Avon and Somerset police early in 1988 not drawn to the attention of the Home Office or disclosed to the defence?

Who was responsible?

3 *At the Balcombe Street trial (1977) government forensic scientists testified that, before the Guildford trial they had prepared statements showing forensic links between the explosions at Guildford and Woolwich and other IRA explosions with which the accused could not be associated. Why was that report not disclosed to the defence at the Guildford trial and who was responsible?*

4 At the same Balcombe Street trial they further testified that on orders from the DPP, communicated to them by the anti-terrorist squad, they had subsequently altered the statements to omit all reference to Guildford and Woolwich, for the purposes of the Guildford and Woolwich trial.

Why was this done and who was responsible?

5 They also testified that in this, the Balcombe Street trial, they had omitted all reference to the forensic links between the offence being tried there and the Guildford and Woolwich offences.

Why was this done and who was responsible?

6 The Balcombe Street gang confessed to the anti-terrorist squad that they had carried out the Guildford and Woolwich bombings. This was not followed up. Why and who was responsible?

7 At their own trial in 1977 they refused to plead because they had not been charged with Guildford and Woolwich. Why was this not followed up and who was responsible? Why, after their Balcombe Street trial in 1977 were Dowd and O'Connell not put on trial for Woolwich and Guildford, and Butler and Duggan for Woolwich?

8 The question at (7) above was posed in Cardinal Hume's letter to the Home Secretary of 22 September 1988. Why, even at this late hour, was it not followed up?

APPENDIX XIV

SUBMISSION BY CARDINAL HUME'S DEPUTATION TO THE ROYAL COMMISION ON CRIMINAL JUSTICE

DEPUTATION

Cardinal Basil Hume

The Right Honourable The Lord Devlin

The Right Honourable The Lord Scarman

The Right Honourable The Lord Jenkins of Hillhead

The Right Honourable Merlyn Rees, MP

IN ATTENDANCE
Robert Kee, Esq

Patrick M. Victory, Esq

SUBMISSION BY CARDINAL HUME'S DEPUTATION TO THE ROYAL COMMISSION ON CRIMINAL JUSTICE

CONTENTS

SUBMISSION BY CARDINAL HUME'S DEPUTATION TO THE ROYAL COMMISSION ON CRIMINAL JUSTICE

INTRODUCTION

1 THE DEPUTATION takes its name from the fact that we were members with Cardinal Hume of a Deputation which under his leadership made representations to the Home Secretary on the miscarriages of justice that had occurred in the Guildford Four and Maguire cases. We pressed for a reference of the two cases to the Court of Appeal for review of the convictions.

2 In the course of our deliberations we considered also, but not in the same detail, other recent cases of miscarriage of justice arising within the criminal justice system. They are disturbingly numerous. A fundamental question now troubles public opinion: is our criminal justice system safe and satisfactory? The Commission's terms of reference are of sufficient width and detail to enable the Commission to study and answer this question as well as to propose reform where reform is needed.

3 We can now see that a major casualty of the IRA 'mainland' bombing campaign of 1974–5 was the English criminal justice system. The process of the criminal justice system begins with arrest and interrogation of a suspect by the police. In the Guildford Four case convictions of murder were obtained by false police evidence of confessions said to have been the genuine and voluntary confessions of the accused: there was no other evidence of guilt. We now know that there was evidence available which, if true, made it improbable, and, in the case of one accused, impossible, that the accused could have been in Guildford when the bombs were planted. When in 1977 the case reached the Court of Appeal two IRA men gave evidence in which they admitted to the bombing, and asserted that the Guildford Four were not there or played any part. The appeals were dismissed,

the Court finding that part of the new evidence was incredible. Twelve years later on a reference by the Home Secretary to the Court of Appeal quashed the convictions, the Lord Chief Justice commenting that the police must have lied.

4 In the Maguire case the seven accused were convicted of being in unlawful possession of an explosive substance. A more unlikely group of bombers or a more unlikely place for a bomb factory it would be difficult to imagine than the Maguires, their sons, and friends in their family home. There was no evidence of guilt other than some scientific evidence which we now know was misleading. The Maguires applied for leave to appeal: their application was rejected on the strength of the scientific evidence. In 1991 the Court of Appeal on a review of the case required by the Home Secretary quashed the convictions as unsafe and unsatisfactory because of the flaws in the scientific evidence.

5 What went wrong? Was it merely police dishonesty and scientific error going undetected? Or was it perhaps a weakness in the criminal process itself? Is it too adversarial, not sufficiently inquiring? Does the system leave truth to emerge as a spin off from the conflict of adversaries? Should not the court in a criminal case be under a duty to initiate, if need be, a full investigation of the facts and the issues before trial as well as at trial, during appeal if there be an appeal, and even after appeal, if there be grounds for fearing there may have been a miscarriage of justice? In any event we shall submit that injustice could be greatly reduced by greater judicial supervision of the pre-trial stages of the criminal process. And we shall also submit that, if after trial and appeal there remain or arise grounds for thinking that there may have been a miscarriage of justice, the investigation should be entrusted not to the Court of Appeal but to a court of inquiry. For, when the process of trial and appeal has run its course and miscarriage of justice either remains or comes to be seen as a real possibility, the time for adversarial conflict is past. There must be a public inquiry not restrained by the rules of evidence but as wide-ranging as is necessary to establish whether it has occurred, and where the responsibility lies. Miscarriage of justice is a public wrong which it is the duty of the State to investigate and correct.

OUR SUBMISSIONS AND RECOMMENDATIONS – THEIR GENERAL SCOPE

6 There are four phases in the process of English criminal justice. They are the pre-trial phase from arrest to trial, the trial, appeal, and, where appeal rights have been exhausted, review by the Court of Appeal on a reference by the Home Secretary. All four phases (not

all, of course, are reached in every case: and very few cases are referred for review) are covered by the Commission's terms of reference. We wish to place before the Commission a submission of basic principle, that some relaxation be made of the strictly adversarial character of the criminal process. We also wish to put forward a submission as to the admissibility of confession evidence: a recommendation for the establishment of an independent forensic science service available to the courts and parties: a proposal for amending the law which lays down the duty of the Court of Appeal in criminal cases: a proposal for substituting a court of inquiry for the Court of Appeal where an inquiry is required into the possibility of miscarriage of justice in cases in which the right of appeal no longer exists or is inappropriate: and a number of submissions for improving the supervision of the police in the pre-trial phase of arrest, interrogation, and assembly of evidence.

PRE-TRIAL SUPERVISION

7 A measure of judicial supervision of the preparation of a serious criminal case for trial has existed in English law for many years. Supervision can be exercised by local magistrates in proceedings for committal to trial. If magistrates are not satisfied that there is a case to go to trial, they can throw it out. The procedure has, however, proved an inadequate safeguard and is now little more than a formality which the parties can avoid. The truth is that the early and critical period of the pre-trial phase, that is to say, arrest, detention and interrogation before charge, is in the hands of the police and is un-supervised save by the police themselves.

8 The danger period for confessions is between arrest and charge. During this period the suspect is in police custody and interrogations do take place with no lawyer or independent person present. The temptation this period offers to police eager to secure evidence from a suspect whom we must assume they believe to be guilty has proved too great for some of them to resist (notably in the Guildford Four and Birmingham Six cases). And no wonder. For under our law a man can be convicted of serious crime, including murder, on the evidence alone of his uncorroborated confession. Of course, the confession must be voluntary and not obtained by oppression, inducement, or violence: but when an 'honourable' policeman rejects at trial such horrible imputations, what chance has the 'scallywag' in the dock of establishing them? The Guildford Four know the answer. Police misconduct in obtaining, and even in fabricating, confessions from suspects in their custody before charge was in 1974/5 well protected by the law. Even today the opportunity remains. Undoubtedly the Police and Criminal Evidence Act 1984 has done much to restrict the opportunity. But the

period between arrest and charge still remains unsupervised save by the police themselves: and some of the safeguards required by the Act, notably the right to have a solicitor present when under interrogation, can be and in many cases are without difficulty circumvented. Under the existing system there will be no real safeguard against miscarriage of justice by false confession until the law is reformed so as to exclude convictions on the basis of confession evidence alone. We, therefore, recommend legislation to give effect to this reform.

9 If, however, an effective judicial supervision of the pre-trial phase should be introduced, a judicial officer could supervise and direct police preparation for trial and the assembling of evidence, including confession evidence. It could be provided that no confession obtained by police should be admitted in evidence unless the judicial officer had satisfied himself at a hearing where the accused was present that it was a voluntary confession without pressure or inducement.

10 There could be other advantages in an effective judicial supervision. The judicial officer should be made responsible for expedition and the prevention of delay in the preparation for trial, could give directions as to expert evidence and require the disclosure of documents. Indeed, he could exercise many of the functions of a Master in civil proceedings in the High Court – but he must have the power to refuse to allow a case to go to trial – a power comparable to that of magistrates in committal proceedings.

11 We ask the Commission to look carefully at the proposal for judicial supervision of the pre-trial phase. It could solve many problems.

12 If, however, it should be rejected on the grounds of lack of resources, we suggest that the Crown Prosecution Service be expanded to take over the function of pre-trial supervision. The service already exercises a beneficial influence, but it really needs to be able to exercise judicial powers of control and supervision comparable to those we have outlined in paragraphs 9 and 10. Perhaps, there is a lesson to be learnt from the role of the procurator-fiscal in Scotland. We would stress that the work would be difficult and would require the service of experienced criminal lawyers. It should be seen to be a judicial function and the officer should have the power of dismissing a prosecution, where the evidence, or lack of evidence, justified such a course.

EXPERT EVIDENCE

13 Expert evidence presents serious problems for the defence in criminal cases. Few defendants have the resources to afford it: and if they are on legal aid, the funding is never generous, sometimes insuf-

ficient, and frequently delayed. The Crown, as prosecuting authority, has no such problems, and it is not always the case that the defence can get full disclosure of all relevant scientific documents and reports in the possession of the prosecution and its expert advisers.

14 In his Interim Report on the Maguire case Sir John May has made some disturbing findings on the scientific evidence given in the case. And the Court of Appeal in its review of the case has exposed a fatal flaw in the conclusion drawn by the forensic scientist called for the Crown. He had concluded that what was found on the hands of six accused and on the kitchen gloves of the seventh, Mrs Maguire, revealed that the accused must have been handling ('kneading' was the word used) explosive in such quantities as to warrant the inference that they were making bombs. We now know that this conclusion was unwarranted by the evidence. Had there been full disclosure of the relevant scientific information in time to enable scientists engaged by the defence to examine the data thoroughly, there would inevitably have been a successful challenge to the scientific reasoning and conclusion which provided the critically important support for the Crown case.

15 The defence must have the same opportunities as the Crown has for instructing scientists and undertaking scientific research. And both the Crown and defence must exchange scientific reports and proofs of evidence. Further, the Court must be able to initiate scientific inquiry and call for reports. Justice and truth require that scientific investigation, report, and opinion must not be a pawn (or piece of higher denomination) in a game played out by adversaries in a court battle. In present practice it is the Crown as prosecutor who usually commissions the preparation and defines the scope of the scientific evidence to be given at trial. The defence is too often restricted to a critical appraisement of the evidence against it: independent original research is too often beyond its resources and capabilities. And the defence is too often at the mercy of the prosecution's discretion as to what scientific material will be disclosed and what not. This will not do: an unsupervised adversarial system denies the defence a fair opportunity of meeting the prosecution case or developing its own.

16 We recommend that a genuinely independent Service of Forensic Science should be established, sufficient in numbers and expertise to provide the defence as well as the prosecution with the evidence needed to assist the parties and the court to get at the truth. There should be a full exchange of scientific reports before trial: and the parties should be encouraged to agree, if they can, the scientific reports. The 'adversarial' model of an English criminal trial is ill suited to eliciting the truth discoverable by science. The role of the scientist in a criminal court's search for truth should be that of a witness called by the court,

both prosecution and defence retaining the right of cross-examination. And the principle underlying the presentation of such evidence must be full and timely disclosure of all the relevant research, findings, and reports. Had this been the practice, the Maguire case would never have been brought to trial.

17 There is a problem, however, with regard to scientific assistance for police in their work of crime detection. This work, of course, precedes arrest, and is often of crucial importance in leading the police to the identification of a suspect and to an arrest. Care will have to be taken to ensure the right of the police to engage or employ scientists or other experts on the work of detection and, in appropriate cases, to claim public interest immunity for the protection of the information obtained. If, of course, at a later stage this work becomes the foundation of scientific evidence to be given at trial, then it should be treated like any other scientific inquiry and report for the purposes of trial.

THE RIGHT OF SILENCE

18 The terms of reference specifically raise the question whether the accused's right of silence in criminal proceedings, as presently understood, should be modified: they require the Commission to consider whether changes are needed in:–

> opportunities available for an accused person to state his position on the matters charged and the extent to which the courts may draw proper inferences from primary facts, the conduct of the accused, and any failure on his part to take advantage of an opportunity to state his position.

Existing law allows the accused to remain silent under interrogation, to say nothing prior to trial, and to refuse to give evidence at his trial: and he has a right to make an unsworn statement from the dock. If he holds his tongue and does not avail himself of these opportunities of stating his position, no adverse inference may be drawn from the mere fact of his silence. Under the strict adversarial system the defendant is entitled to require the prosecution to prove its case against him without his assistance.

19 We believe this right of silence is a necessary protection in a system which permits conviction for serious crime on the strength of uncorroborated confession evidence. Police interrogation being unsupervised save by the police themselves, the suspect needs the protection of his right to say nothing. There is, however, force in the comment that in very many cases the suspect knows more about the case against himself than anyone else: and it would be appear to

be unjust that he should be able to conceal what he could say about the charge against him.

20 Relax the adversary character of the pre-trial proceedings, and it should be possible to protect the accused by independent judicial supervision from improper pressure to confess. The accused could be given a fair opportunity of stating his position to the judge or judicial officer in charge of the pre-trial proceedings. If he did not avail himself of this opportunity, the court should be allowed to draw such inference from his silence as the circumstances of the case justified: likewise, we would add, in the event of the accused deciding not to give evidence at his trial. But unless further measures than those which now exist are taken to protect accused persons and unless there is effective enforcement of those which already exist under the Police and Criminal Evidence Act 1984 we would not advocate any diminishing of the present right of silence. Effective judicial, (or, conceivably CPS) supervision of the pre-trial phase is necessary if the right of silence is to be diminished.

THE ROLE OF THE COURT OF APPEAL IN CONSIDERING NEW EVIDENCE ON APPEAL

21 In the Guildford Four appeal, heard in 1977, the Court of Appeal had an outstanding opportunity to correct a very serious miscarriage of justice. They did not take it. The injustice of the wrongful convictions persisted for another twelve years.

22 The opportunity arose when new evidence was received by the Court. The history of how this evidence came to be heard is well known, and we need not repeat it. The 'Balcombe Street' men had protested at their own trial for terrorist crimes that they would not plead until the injustice done to the Guildford Four was remedied. One of them, O'Connell, with another IRA man, Dowd, but not the Guildford Four, had, they said, bombed the pubs in Guildford. When the Guildford appeal reached the Court, the evidence of these men was received. They told the Court the Guildford Four had no part in the bombings: they were responsible: the police had accused the wrong people.

23 The Court of Appeal, while willing to assume that they participated in the bombings, found their evidence that the Guildford Four did not participate to be incredible. Reaching that view, the Court could not think that such evidence could warrant a finding that the verdict of the trial jury was unsafe or satisfactory; and they noted that the statute (Criminal Appeals Act 1968 s.2) required them to make up their own minds and to make the decision as to the safety of the convictions.

24 They were supported in this view by the decision of the House of Lords in the case of *Stafford V. Luvaglio* (1974 A.C. 789) in which Lord Diplock ruled that it was the duty of the Court of Appeal to ask *themselves* (emphasis added) this question:

> under all the circumstances of the case as it now stands in the light of the additional evidence, am I myself (i.e. each member of the Court) satisfied that the verdict of the jury was safe and satisfactory? (p.906)

25 Two of our members (Lord Devlin and Lord Scarman) are on record as arguing that, if this be the state of the law (as it is unless and until either the House of Lords in its judicial capacity rules otherwise or Parliament legislates for reform), it is a departure of the principle of trial by jury, which is the right of those committed for trial in the Crown Court. Certainly years of injustice would almost certainly have been avoided had the Court of Appeal ordered a new trial: but how could it do so, given their view of the law and their finding that the additional evidence, which exculpated the accused, was incredible?

26 We recommend, therefore, a review of the statutory duty of the Court of Appeal in appeals against conviction. The principle to be found in s.2 of the Criminal Appeals Act that it is for the Court to decide whether the verdict is safe and satisfactory appears, with respect, to be sound, but it must not be allowed to lead the Court into usurping the jury's function of finding the facts. We recommend that s.2 be amended so as to ensure that when the Court of Appeal is presented with new evidence which is admissible and which, if true, would exculpate the appellant(s) the Court cannot dismiss the appeal but, if it is not disposed to quash the conviction (s), must order a new trial. It is for a jury, not the appeal court, to decide whether new evidence which, if true, would exculpate the appellants is not to be believed. An accused is not to be convicted save upon the verdict of a jury which has heard all the evidence.

A NEW COURT OF REVIEW

27 Our proposal is the repeal of s.17 of the Criminal Appeals Act 1968 ('s.17') and the establishment of a Court of Review. The Court must be a court of inquiry. The Court's duty would be to receive applications for review of a conviction on the ground of miscarriage of justice, to inquire into, and to determine all cases within its jurisdiction which it accepted for hearing. If after a full inquiry into all relevant circumstances and a full hearing it should conclude that the conviction (s) is (are) unsafe and unsatisfactory its duty would be to quash the

conviction (s). It would be able, but only if in its opinion justice so required, to order a new trial.

28 Access to the Court would not be restricted to the Home Secretary. It would be for the Court to determine what cases it would hear. It would, of course, still be possible for a Home Secretary, or, if one should ever be appointed, a Minister of Justice, to apply for a review: but applications for a hearing could be made by others direct to the Court. We recognise that this proposal would involve a major piece of law reform calling for detailed consideration before it could be implemented by statute.

29 The existing law and practice under s.17 are unsatisfactory, delaying and even on occasion obstructing the correction of injustice occurring within the criminal justice system. There is no way open under existing law for a convicted person to get a miscarriage of justice corrected after appeal rights have been exhausted other than by persuading the Home Secretary either to recommend a pardon, or to set up an informal inquiry with no judicial powers, or to refer the case to the Court of Appeal for review. The making of such 'arrangements' is a matter for him: the citizen has no right to pardon or to an inquiry or to a judicial remedy. If the Home Secretary sets up an inquiry (as he did when he appointed Sir John May to inquire into the Guildford and Maguire cases), the inquiry is dependent upon the co-operation of police and others for its information: it lacks the power of a court to summon witnesses or to procure documents and it cannot go beyond a report. And its findings are not binding, as, indeed, has become evident since Sir John's Interim Report on the Maguire case was published.

30 If the Home Secretary thinks fit to exercise his power under s.17 to refer for review a case to the Court of Appeal, the review takes the form of an appeal by the convicted person, who becomes an appellant with the burden of arguing the appeal. He is likely to have neither the resources nor the authority to put together the case or to commission the investigation needed to establish the miscarriage of justice of which he complains. It is, we submit, wrong in principle that the burden should be thrown upon the convicted person. What is being undertaken is, or should be, a public inquiry into the possibility of a grave wrong done by the state to an individual.

31 Sometimes, as has happened in the Guildford Four and Maguires cases, there is a prolonged delay before any steps are taken: and when ultimately something is done we can be faced with the confusion of both an informal public inquiry and a review by way of 'appeal' in the Court of Appeal.

32 For these reasons we believe that a Court of Review such as we propose is needed.

33 The constitution and staffing of the Court will require detailed consideration. We propose a Court of five members which would include two judges and three lay members served by a secretariat headed by an experienced criminal lawyer who would be the Secretary to the Court. As we shall later explain, we see the Secretary as an important figure, one who by delegation from the Court will exercise some important judicial and preparatory functions as well as performing the normal duties of a court's registrar.

34 MEMBERSHIP. We suggest for consideration:-

A President who would be a senior judge (a law lord or senior appellate judge) and could well be appointed by the Lord Chancellor for a period of years;

A second senior judge to be appointed by the Lord Chancellor on a case by case basis, and

A panel of distinguished lay members (men and women), three of whom the Lord Chancellor would select for appointment to the Court on a case by case basis.

The Court should sit as a court of five for a full hearing of a case: but a court of three could deal with preliminary questions which would include appeals from any judicial decisions made by the Secretary on the Court's behalf: the most important judicial decision appealable to the Court would be a refusal by the Secretary of an application for a Court hearing of a complaint of miscarriage of justice.

35 THE SECRETARIAT. In addition to the normal administrative duties of a court's registrar the Secretary and staff would have important duties in the preparation of cases for full hearing by the Court, some of which we will discuss in dealing with what we see to be two important matters, namely access to the Court and the facilities to be available to the Court for ensuring that it obtains the fullest possible information needed for the effective discharge of its statutory functions.

36 There are two problems which have to be solved:-

(1) how to 'filter' applications so that groundless applications do not overload the Court, and
(2) how to ensure that the Court can obtain all the information and advice it needs in order to discharge its duty of full inquiry.

These problems can, we believe, be solved without having to retain the present restriction under which only a minister, the Home Secretary, can refer a case for review.

37 The danger of restricting access to a Court of Review has been demonstrated in the Guildford and Maguire cases. Under existing s.17 practice, the Home Secretary, understandably, relies to a great extent on his departmental advisers. They are civil servants: few, if any, of

the Home Office team (the 'C.3 Division') are lawyers: certainly none of them has, for example, the expertise in the criminal law to be found in the Crown Prosecution Service. Their practice, which they would seem to have elevated into a principle, is: – no reference to the Court of Appeal unless some new evidence or matter of substance has arisen since the conclusion of the criminal law process. The Home Secretary's consideration ordinarily, if not invariably, follows the practice. References to the Court of Appeal are thereby obstructed by departmental principle and practice not prescribed by law: for, of course, the Home Secretary's discretion under s.17 is unfettered by any specific restriction. The injustice that this approach can bring about is devastatingly illustrated by the difficulties and delay in persuading the Home Secretary to refer the Guildford and Maguire cases.

38 But it would be wrong to disregard certain genuine advantages which the Home Secretary has to offer under the existing law and practice. He is enabled to act as a filter eliminating groundless claims for review: and he can, and does in many cases, call for factual investigation by a police force other than the one involved in the case and for such other factual reports, scientific or other expert advice as he deems necessary. And in practice, if he refers the case, he does make available the reports, or if not the reports, at least the findings of the police, scientific, and other investigations to the Court so that the appropriate evidence can be called.

39 These preliminary investigations and reports are of great importance. As an example we would draw attention to the inquiry and report of the Avon and Somerset Police requested by the DPP in the Guildford Four case. This report proved to be of critical importance. But it does not follow that such investigations and reports can be made available to the Court only if reference or access to the Court is restricted to the Home Secretary. The true conclusion is, we suggest, that the Home Secretary's co-operation can be had without restricting to him the sole duty of activating the Court of Review. The link between Minister and Court should be the Secretary to the Court, upon whose role we would like now to add a few more comments.

40 Put briefly, the Secretary's duty should be not only to act as Registrar of the Court but also to act as a judicial officer of the Court in charge of processing applications from their reception by the Court to hearing. Acting on behalf of the Court, he should have power, after hearing the applicant, to refuse an application as disclosing no sufficient ground for a hearing. The applicant should, however, have the right to challenge the Secretary's refusal by appeal to the Court itself.

41 The Secretary on behalf of the Court should have the right to require the assistance of the Home Secretary in obtaining the police and other investigations and reports which the Home Secretary has

the power to require or obtain. Co-operation in this way would not only enable the Court to discharge to the full its duty to inquire but would ensure that the Minister, and through him Parliament, would be fully informed of progress and any reasons for any delay in the work of the Court. This could be an important feature of our proposal. Parliament is the body to listen to, and attempt to secure a remedy for citizens' grievances. Members will be able to put questions to the Home Secretary as at present: and he will be in a position to answer them – but without in any way either weakening the independence of the Court or preventing access to it.

42 The two problems, 'filter' and 'information', are, therefore capable of an excellent solution. The assistance of the Home Secretary to the work of the Court can be secured without putting upon him the responsibility of determining whether a case should go to the Court. It is significant that Mr Douglas Hurd, the Home Secretary who referred the Guildford Four case to the Court of Appeal and who for a long time declined to refer the Magurie case, has concluded that leaving to the Home Secretary the responsibility for determining whether or not there is to be a reference is not appropriate or satisfactory.

43 Should our proposal for an independent Court of Review served by its own Secretary at the head of an experienced and adequately staffed secretariat be accepted, clearly it would be necessary to embark upon a more detailed consideration of ways and means than we have undertaken. But the principle we submit is clear. What is needed is a court of inquiry into a matter of grave public importance. This is not appellate work: it is a search for the truth to be conducted by a court having power to correct major injustice if it finds that it exists.

SUMMARY OF RECOMMENDATIONS

44 For an overall view of our basic approach and conclusions of principle, see paras.5 and 6.

Our principal specific recommendations are: -

(a) amendment of the law to disallow convictions on the strength of uncorroborated confession evidence, para.8;
(b) judicial supervision, alternatively supervision by an officer of a judicial division of the Crown Prosecution Service of the pre-trial phase of serious criminal cases, paras. 11 and 12;
(c) the establishment of an independent service of forensic science available to the Court, the defence, and the prosecution, para 16;
(d) a statutory re-statement of the duty of the Court of Appeal in criminal appeals, para.26;

(e) the repeal of s.17 of the Criminal Appeals Act 1968 and the establishment of a new Court of Review, para.27 et seq.

45 There is no doubt that public opinion has become greatly disturbed by the sequence of miscarriages of justice and the difficulties and delays in getting complaints of injustice inquired into or corrected. We believe that this situation has arisen as a direct result of the weaknesses in the existing law and practice which govern the legal process in serious criminal cases and the reference procedure available under s.17 after conviction and the exhaustion of the right of appeal. We would end our submission with a quotation from Robert Kee. In his book 'Trial and Error' 1986 pp.266–7 he made this comment:-

> One of the ironical aspects of both the Guildford and the Maguire cases is that pointers to the innocence of the accused still lie in that very field of everyday common-sense judgement which does not take too much notice of legal niceties and which in the end it is the jury's right to assert. After two trials and two Appeal Court hearings the areas of unresolved doubt in both cases are today enormous.

The 'areas of unresolved doubt' persisted from 1974 until October 1989 for the Guildford Four and until June 1991 for the Maguires. The Birmingham Six suffered similarly. A legal system which has allowed failure of justice to endure for so long needs thorough examination. The call for reform cannot be denied.

7 November 1991

APPENDIX XV

RESPONSE BY CARDINAL HUME'S DEPUTATION TO THE HOME OFFICE DISCUSSION PAPER (1994) ON 'CRIMINAL APPEALS AND THE ESTABLISHMENT OF A CRIMINAL CASES REVIEW AUTHORITY'

INTRODUCTION

1 THE DEPUTATION takes its name from the fact that we came together in late 1986, each for our own reasons and of our own volition, as members with Cardinal Hume of a Deputation which, under his leadership, made representations to the Home Secretary on the miscarriages of justice that had taken place in the Guildford Four and Maguire Seven cases. Since then the Deputation has continued to meet on an on-going basis.

2 By the time we made our submission to the Royal Commission on Criminal Justice on 7 November 1991, when the late Lord Devlin was still with us, there had been disturbingly numerous cases of miscarriages of justice. These included the Birmingham Six and other cases, with none of which we had been directly involved but which we had followed with close interest.

3 Early in our discussions during the preparation of the submission to the Royal Commission it became clear to us that a major casualty of the IRA 'mainland' bombing campaign of 1974–75 was the English criminal justice system. In the first place we did not consider that the current system for handling possible referrals to the Court of Appeal – C3 and the Home Secretary – was working satisfactorily. We also sought other reasons. Was it merely police dishonesty and scientific error going undetected? Or was it perhaps a weakness in the criminal process itself? Is it too adversarial, not sufficiently inquiring? Does the system leave truth to emerge as a spin off from the conflict of

adversaries? Should not the Court in a criminal case be under a duty to initiate, if need be, a full investigation of the facts and the issues before trial as well as at trial, during appeal if there be an appeal, and even after appeal, if there be grounds for fearing there may have been a miscarriage of justice?

4 We concluded that, if after trial and appeal there remain or arise grounds for thinking there may have been a miscarriage of justice, the investigation should be entrusted not to the Court of Appeal but to a Court of Inquiry. We considered that by that stage the time for adversarial conflict was past and the need now was for proceedings of an inquisitorial nature. We did not see C3 playing any part in a new structure, but we also foresaw that the setting up of a new investigative body could raise problems about the relationship between the Court of Appeal, the new body, and the parties to the appeal.

5 It was partly for these but also for other reasons we proposed the repeal of s.17 of the Criminal Appeals Act 1968 ('s.17') and the establishment of a Court of Review. This would have been a Court of Inquiry not concerned with appellate work but with a search for the truth. It would have inquired into all applications for a review of conviction on the grounds of miscarriage of justice, and would have determined all cases within its jurisdiction which it accepted for hearing. We saw it ranking, for purposes of legal precedent, as if it were a division of the Court of Appeal.

6 We note, and accept, that the Royal Commission made, and the Government has now adopted, a recommendation that the Home Secretary's power to refer cases to the Court of Appeal under section 17 of the Criminal Appeal Act 1968 should be removed, and that a 'Criminal Cases Review Authority' should be set up to consider alleged miscarriages of justice, to supervise any necessary investigation, and to refer appropriate cases to the Court of Appeal.

7 It is against this background that we now respond to the Home Office Discussion Paper and, specifically, to the proposal to establish a 'Criminal Cases Review Authority' (the Authority) which is not seen as coming within the Court structure.

GENERAL PRINCIPLES

8 We wish to emphasise at the outset that it is essential to ensure, in the structures now envisaged, that the new Authority emerges as, and is seen and acknowledged to be, a strong and independent body capable of fulfilling effectively, and with a sense of urgency, the task of considering and investigating allegations of miscarriages of justice when appeal rights have been exhausted.

9 The Authority should investigate cases, and make recommendations thereon, as it thinks fit. The criteria and procedures it adopts

should be limited by statute only to an essential and unavoidable extent, and in no way should such minimum limitations or restrictions be capable of being interpreted as inhibiting the pursuit of justice.

10 We turn now to selected proposals in the Discussion Paper under the main headings as in that paper.

REFORM OF THE COURT OF APPEAL

11 We agree with:-

(a) Royal Commission recommendation (323) that 'in fresh evidence cases where a retrial was desirable but not practicable' the Court should decide the appeal itself.

(b) Royal Commission recommendation (324) – the majority view – that in cases *other than* fresh evidence cases, where a retrial is desirable but not practicable, the Court should automatically allow the appeal. There is no evidence to examine and the Court should therefore apply the 'lurking doubt' test.

UNCONTESTED APPEALS

12 Where the Crown does not contest an appeal, the Court of Appeal is nevertheless left with the responsibility of deciding whether the conviction should be quashed, and, if so, whether to order a retrial. It has been suggested the Court might have power to appoint counsel to examine witnesses on its behalf.

13 We do not agree with this suggestion. The Court of Appeal should not desert its true role of being the ultimate arbiter by what would virtually amount to becoming part of the prosecution.

POWER OF THE COURT OF APPEAL TO COMMISSION INVESTIGATIONS

14 The Royal Commission recommended that the Court of Appeal should have power to refer matters which require investigation to the new Authority. We would see the need to request information, additional to that which it can obtain from one of the parties, only rarely arising.

15 If such an occasion should arise, and the Court is considering whether to make a request to the Authority, we consider the Authority should be empowered to accept or decline such a request, as it thinks fit. Furthermore, if the Authority accepts such a request it should be empowered to make a recommendation, if it considers it appropriate and in the interests of justice to do so, whether or not it comes across other relevant matters during its investigation.

CRIMINAL CASES REVIEW AUTHORITY – SCOPE OF AUTHORITY'S POWERS

16 The Government has accepted the Royal Commission's recom-

mendation that the Authority should take over the present functions of the Home Secretary in considering representations alleging miscarriages of justice in criminal cases.

17 Before considering the rest of this section we wish to register emphatically at this stage of our response that we would not agree with any possible concept that the deficiencies of the criminal justice system could be even partially eliminated merely by the transfer to the Authority of the functions of C3.

18 The setting up of the Authority needs to be clearly seen as the beginning of a new era in the handling of representations on miscarriages of justice. We outlined our general principles in paragraphs 8 and 9 above and we expand on these later in this response.

19 There remains under this section the need to consider arrangements for representations about sentence and about cases tried summarily.

Representations as to sentence

20 We agree that the Authority should have power to refer a case to the courts in relation to sentence but only where there is reason to doubt the validity of the sentence in law, or where new information suggests that the factual basis on which a sentence was calculated was substantially wrong and no other remedy exists.

21 We also agree the Authority's power should be limited to referring sentences which might be too great.

Summary cases

22 We note there is currently no power to refer summary cases to the courts for appeal, and the only recourse lies in the exercise of the Royal Prerogative of Mercy.

23 We also note that cases range from those requiring significant investigation to others (the majority) in which the convictions stand entirely on information later shown to be erroneous, or where relevant evidence is subsequently produced by the defendant.

24 We agree that :–

(a) the Authority should have power to consider summary cases requiring significant investigation and to refer them to the appropriate court – usually the Crown Court.

(b) There should be a 'simplified' route for summary cases (the majority) involving late evidence (para 20 above) which do not need to be investigated by the Authority.

(c) The clerk to the justices in the convicting magistrates court should carry out a preliminary sift of cases as between categories in (a) and (b) above.

25 We consider that the Authority should be empowered to decide

whether or not to investigate a case passed to it by the clerk, and to make a recommendation if it considers it appropriate and in the interests of justice to do so.

Exclusion of sub judice cases

26 We agree that:-

(a) the Authority should be precluded from *referring* a case to the courts where a direct avenue of appeal remains open.

(b) The Authority should not be precluded from *investigating* a case which was outside the ordinary 28 day limit for lodging an appeal.

(c) If the Authority finds material touching on the safety of the conviction it should notify the convicted person leaving it to him to decide whether or not to lodge an appeal.

GROUNDS FOR REFERRING CASES TO THE COURTS

27 We accept that in considering whether to refer a case to the courts the Authority will have regard (but will not 'be bound' to do so as in para 42 of the Discussion Paper) to the courts' statutory powers, policy and practice, and to the likely practical value of further appeal proceedings.

28 We consider that, while having such regard, the overriding consideration by the Authority in referring a case should be whether or not it is convinced there is a grave danger of there having been a miscarriage of justice.

29 Additionally, we consider that if the Authority thinks that a case should be referred to the Court of Appeal it should be empowered to make a recommendation if it considers it is appropriate and in the interests of justice to do so.

30 We consider it would be quite wrong for the Authority to be encumbered by statutory tests in making references to the Court; and it would be equally wrong if the Authority was bound by statute to have regard to certain factors in deciding whether to investigate a case.

31 We are firmly of the view that the Authority should be empowered to investigate a case, and to refer a case, 'if it thinks fit'. Neither the investigation nor the reference should be encumbered by statutory requirements other than possibly a few which might be essential and unavoidable. However, such minimum limitations or restrictions must in no way be capable of being interpreted as inhibiting the pursuit of justice.

32 Unless the Authority has, and is seen to have, such stature and powers it will quickly come to be regarded as little more than a slightly improved C3. This will not be sufficient to recapture for the criminal justice system the confidence and respect of practitioners and the

public. Moreover, it would not attract a chairman, members and staff of the calibre required for such an important task.

PROCEDURE FOR CONSIDERATION BY THE AUTHORITY

General

33 We agree that, as a non-adversarial body, the Authority would proceed by means of investigation rather than by conducting hearings with the parties as would be the case if it were a tribunal.

34 We see the Authority fulfilling the three functions of enquiry, investigating and, in cases where it thinks it would be appropriate, making recommendations. We consider it would be for the Authority to determine the character of its proceedings in these three areas.

35 We consider that investigations conducted by the Authority would normally be in private but that it should be empowered, if it thinks fit, to conduct part of its investigations in public. Apart from the petitioner there may be other interested parties who wish to be heard or whom the Authority wishes to hear. This should be for the Authority to decide. As its affairs are to be conducted on an inquisitorial rather than adversarial basis, there will be no danger of it in effect beginning itself to hear an appeal.

Investigations

36.We agree that it will be essential for the Authority to be able to make use of the skills and expertise of the police in criminal investigations if its enquiries into possible miscarriages of justice are to be effective.

37 We have carefully considered the issues raised in paras 55 to 64 of the Discussion Paper. Our central concern is that if the Authority is to be fully effective it must be seen to be truly independent. We therefore consider that the way forward should be on the following lines which obviate many of the difficulties raised in the Paper : –

(a) The Authority must have powers to require police forces, if necessary in consultation with the Home Secretary, to conduct enquiries on its behalf and to decide whether the original or a fresh police force should be commissioned.

(b) The Authority must be empowered to oversee investigations by whichever force or police officers are undertaking them on its behalf.

(c) There should be a *core* central unit within the Authority of civilians trained and experienced in conducting investigations and/or similarly qualified retired police officers (who might have taken early retirement to be selected for the post).

(d) This *core* central unit would be used by the Authority to conduct smaller investigations and to oversee, on its behalf, larger and more complex types of investigation.

(e) In parallel with police enquiries it must be open to the Authority to seek relevant reports from forensic laboratories and individual scientists, and the medical profession together with information or documents from Government Departments and other public authorities.

Other powers to facilitate the authority's enquiries

38 We consider provision should be made in legislation to establish the Authority's right of access to certain documents and information. We would see these powers being used by the Authority only in situations where it is convinced of the need if it is to fulfil its task effectively and justice will be seen to have been done.

39 We would certainly see such documents as case papers held by counsel, transcripts of evidence adduced at trial together with transcripts of judgements being included.

Investigations in cases where there is also a complaint against the police subject to investigation under the supervision of the police complaints authority.

40 This section raises a point of principle. We would not agree that one solution would be to seek to establish at the outset what enquiries will be necessary to fulfil the separate purposes of miscarriage of justice and complaints investigations.

41 The Authority will be concerned with a possible miscarriage of justice. This is a very serious matter. Moreover, the convicted person may have been in prison for some years.

42 We therefore consider that, as a matter of principle, the requirements and affairs of the Authority must take priority.

INFORMING APPLICANTS OF THE PROGRESS AND OUTCOME OF CASES

43 We agree that the Authority itself should determine what information it is appropriate to provide to applicants about the progress of enquiries and the decisions taken at their conclusion, with a view to being open and fair while preserving necessary confidentiality.

APPEALS AND JUDICIAL REVIEW

44 We agree that there should be no avenue of appeal on the substance of the Authority's decisions.

45 Judicial review of the decisions of the Authority cannot, and ought not, to be eliminated. The Authority is a public body which will make decisions affecting the individual. For instance: the Authority may refuse to 'consider' an application by a convict for review of his

conviction; it may refuse an 'investigation'; conceivably, though most improbably, it may refuse to report on a case; and it certainly may refuse to refer a case to the Court of Appeal. If any such decision was in the circumstances so unreasonable as to constitute an abuse of the power vested in the Authority, judicial review would lie. And so it should.

46 We, therefore, accept that in such cases judicial review should lie against the Authority.

THE ROYAL PREROGATIVE OF MERCY

47 If there is to be legislation amending the exercise of the Royal Prerogative, it should be separate from the Act of Parliament establishing the Authority. The Authority is concerned with legal right i.e. redress for the wrong of miscarriage of justice; the Royal Prerogative is concerned with the exercise of mercy. Both are needed, but they are separate.

MEMBERSHIP AND STAFF OF THE AUTHORITY

48 We consider that the Chairman, who should be full-time, has to be a person of distinction, widely experienced and greatly respected. A legal qualification, or past membership of the judiciary, could be helpful though not essential, but should not mean exclusion from consideration. The overall qualities, ability, and suitability for the post of the person concerned are the primary considerations.

49 Members of the Authority could be up to seven in number but need not all be fulltime. Some should be experienced lawyers, particularly if the Chairman is not legally qualified; there should be a retired policeman of suitable standing and experience; and there must be some lay persons selected for their ability to bring an open-minded and fresh approach to the work of the Authority. All the members must be persons of high-standing in the community and readily recognised as such.

50 The staff should have similar general qualities to those of the members. They need to be people of ability, with analytical minds and high pressure thresholds, so that the work of the Authority is conducted with despatch and thoroughness.

RESPONSIBILITY FOR DECISION MAKING

51 We note the points made and the variations considered in the Discussion Paper.

52 Given a statutory structure, we do not think that the lines of responsibility for decision making are an area in which it would be appropriate for the Government to become involved. These are matters solely for the Authority itself.

APPOINTMENT AND ACCOUNTABILITY

53 We agree that:–

(a) The Chairman and members of the Authority should be appointed by Her Majesty the Queen on the advice of the Prime Minister.

(b) The Home Secretary should receive and lay before Parliament an annual report made by the Authority.

COMPENSATION IN CASES OF WRONGFUL CONVICTION

54 We agree there should be no change to the present arrangements for deciding whether compensation should be awarded and for determining the amount of such awards.

24 May 1994

TABLE OF STATUTES

INDEX

INDEX

INDEX